Taste of Home
QUICK
COOKING

ANNUAL RECIPES

Taste of Home

RDA ENTHUSIAST BRANDS, LLC • MILWAUKEE, WI

QUICK COOKING
ANNUAL RECIPES 2021

MINT WATERMELON SALAD
(p. 45)

International Standard Book Number:
D 978-1-62145-715-2
U 978-1-62145-716-9
Component Number:
D 117800100H
U 117800102H
International Standard Serial Number: 1552-6603

Executive Editor: Mark Hagen
Senior Art Director: Raeann Thompson
Editor: Hazel Wheaton
Art Director: Maggie Conners
Senior Designer: Courtney Lovetere
Designer: Arielle Jardin
Deputy Editor, Copy Desk: Dulcie Shoener
Cover Photography: *Taste of Home* Photo Studio

Pictured on front cover:
Pasta with Asparagus, p. 36; Basil Grilled Corn on
the Cob, p. 237; Garden Tomato Salad, p. 38; Fruity
Waffle Parfaits, p. 183; Black Bean Rice Burgers, p. 60;
Vegetable & Cheese Focaccia, p. 198

Pictured on back cover:
Quinoa Arancini, p. 306; Lamb Pitas with Yogurt
Sauce, p. 317; Steak Fajitas p. 314; Sticky Maple
Pepper Glazed Chicken Wings, p. 249; Classic
Carrot Cake, p. 288

Printed in USA
1 3 5 7 9 10 8 6 4 2

BRANDY SLUSH (p. 14)

GLAZED SPATCHCOCKED CHICKEN
(p. 91)

AVOCADO CRAB BOATS
(p. 116)

CAULIFLOWER AU GRATIN
(p. 33)

BERRY PUFF PANCAKE
(p. 182)

CREATE A HOME-COOKED MEAL YOUR FAMILY WILL LOVE TONIGHT!

CHICKEN PESTO
ROLL-UPS
(p. 82)

HALIBUT SOFT TACOS
(p. 107)

SALMON
CROQUETTE
BREAKFAST
SANDWICH
(p. 187)

CUPPA JOE
CARAMEL CAKE
(p. 294)

For dedicated home cooks, a winning recipe is one that hits all the right notes—not just convenient and easy to prepare, but so delicious that the whole family raves!

NOW MORE THAN EVER... MAKE IT QUICK!

Today's families are eating in like never before, but that doesn't mean you want to spend more time in the kitchen. With *Quick Cooking Annual Recipes*, you don't have to. We give you all you need to create scrumptious meals that your family will love, all made with an eye on the clock.

Smart cooks know a treasured recipe doesn't have to take hours of work to create lasting memories. The recipes in this volume are ones you'll turn to again and again for mealtime solutions. And since they've all been tested by the experts in the *Taste of Home* Test Kitchen, you know that whichever dish you choose will work every time.

This edition includes over 475 delicious recipes, from tasty appetizers to dazzling desserts and everything in between. There are chapters dedicated to recipes that require no more than five ingredients, recipes that take just 30 minutes (or less!), and kid-friendly dishes. Every recipe includes full nutrition information, making it a snap to plan the healthiest meals. And step-by-step photos, a meal-planning section and helpful hints throughout the book give you the techniques and strategies you need to save time without cutting corners on flavor. You'll love adding these easy dishes to your home-cooking repertoire!

ICONS IN THIS BOOK

These **fast-fix recipes** are table-ready in just 30 minutes or less.

Dishes that use **five or fewer ingredients** (they may also call for water, salt, pepper, canola or olive oil, and optional items).

Our **healthiest recipes**, these dietitian-approved dishes are lower in calories, fat and sodium.

Freezer-friendly items that include directions for freezing and reheating.

Recipes that use a **slow cooker**—one of the most convenient kitchen tools.

Recipes made using a handy **Instant Pot**™ electric pressure cooker.

SOUVLAKI PITA POCKETS (p. 226)

PESTO VEGETABLE PIZZA (p. 115)

GET DINNER ON THE TABLE IN A FLASH WITH
500+ RECIPES & TIPS

IN THIS EDITION
Give Me 5 or Fewer
Each recipe in this chapter calls for just a handful of ingredients (not counting water, oil, and salt and pepper), so you save time both in the kitchen and in the store! These budget-friendly recipes are a breeze to pull together on short notice.

30-Minute Dinners
These main courses go from pantry to table in just half an hour or less. You'll find tons of recipes perfect for the most hectic weeknights. Check out the Quick Shrimp Curry (p. 105), Blue Cheese-Stuffed Steaks (p. 109), or Thai Chicken Pasta (p. 108).

Slow-Cooker Sensations
This chapter is filled with recipes that make the most of long, slow cooking. Soups, mains, sides and desserts—they're all in here! Use the slow cooker to make Slow-Cooked Mac & Cheese (p. 214) or Indulgent Coconut Rice Pudding (p. 221).

Delectable Desserts
There's always time for dessert, even on the busiest nights—and you'll find the proof in this chapter! Whether it's your Favorite Banana Cream Pie (p. 295) or a Pear & Pecan Crisp with Lemon Sauce (p. 289), you and your family can indulge anytime.

Lightened-Up Delights
Every recipe in the book includes complete nutrition facts, but this chapter makes it even easier to choose the healthiest meal options for your family. Stovetop Tarragon Chicken (p. 141) and Greek-Style Stuffed Peppers (p. 149) are just two recipes that prove that healthy is delicious!

Easy Odds & Ends
This special chapter highlights the most popular new kitchen gadgets, with recipes for the air fryer and the Instant Pot™, plus a section of recipes that use the tried-and-true cast-iron skillet to make scrumptious desserts.

30 DAYS OF QUICK COOKING

To get you started, here are a full month's worth of meals you can make using recipes from this book. Keep an eye out for how to use leftovers. For example, the roasted turkey on Day 22 provides the basis for meals through the week, including the turkey a la king on the next day and the turkey soup on Day 25!

DAY 1
Buttery Herb-Roasted Chicken (p. 128)
MENU ADD-ONS
• Balsamic Zucchini Saute (p. 40)
• Indian Ginger Potatoes (p. 52)

DAY 2
Angel Hair Pasta with Sausage & Spinach (p. 98)
MENU ADD-ONS
• Bacon-Parmesan Popovers (p. 196)

DAY 3
Simple Chicken Enchiladas (p. 147)
MENU ADD-ONS
• Eddie's Favorite Fiesta Corn (p. 43)

DAY 4
Grilled Cheese Steakhouse Burger (p. 69)
MENU ADD-ONS
• Grilled Sweet Potato Wedges (p. 234)
• Hearty Baked Beans (p. 37)

DAY 5
Classic French Onion Soup (p. 64)
MENU ADD-ONS
• Harissa Sweet Potato Fritters (p. 34)

DAY 11
Ultimate Pastrami Sandwiches (p. 57)
MENU ADD-ONS
• Upstate Minestrone Soup (p. 63)

DAY 12
Quick & Easy Vegetable Potpie (p. 135)
MENU ADD-ONS
• Applesauce

DAY 13
Lemon Herbed Salmon (p. 100)
MENU ADD-ONS
• Shaved Brussels Sprout Salad (p. 51)

DAY 14
Carnitas Huevos Rancheros (p. 180)
MENU ADD-ONS
• Seasoned Oven Fries (p. 51)

DAY 15
Pepper-Crusted Sirloin Roast (p. 88)
MENU ADD-ONS
• Cauliflower au Gratin (p. 33)

DAY 21
Pesto Vegetable Pizza (p. 115)
MENU ADD-ONS
• Green salad

DAY 22
Apple & Herb Roasted Turkey (p. 271)
MENU ADD-ONS
• Green Beans with Creamy Pistachio Sauce (p. 278)

DAY 23
Turkey a la King (p. 100)
MENU ADD-ONS
• Cheese & Garlic Biscuits (p. 202)

DAY 24
Halibut Soft Tacos (p. 107)
MENU ADD-ONS
• Eddie's Favorite Fiesta Corn (p. 43)

DAY 25
Greens & Beans Turkey Soup (p. 77)
MENU ADD-ONS
• Weeknight Skillet Spinach Pie (p. 124)

DAY 6
Cilantro Shrimp & Rice (p. 101)

MENU ADD-ONS
• Crunchy Asian Coleslaw (p. 39)

DAY 7
Healthy Chipotle Chicken Pumpkin Pizza (p. 137)

MENU ADD-ONS
• Hot buttered noodles

DAY 8
Spicy Pork Roast with Apricots (p. 311)

MENU ADD-ONS
• Seasoned Brown Rice Pilaf (p. 46)
• Easy Green Beans with Mushrooms (p. 32)

DAY 9
Pork Spanish Rice (p. 125)

MENU ADD-ONS
• Garden Tomato Salad (p. 38)

DAY 10
Tacos in a Bowl (p. 121)

MENU ADD-ONS
• Green salad

DAY 16
Sausage & Asparagus Pasta with Cajun Cream Sauce (p. 105)

MENU ADD-ONS
• Garden Tomato Salad (p. 38)

DAY 17
Lime Chipotle Carnitas Tostadas (p. 146)

MENU ADD-ONS
• Sour Cream Cucumbers (p. 47)

DAY 18
Steak Sandwiches with Quick-Pickled Vegetables (p. 67)

MENU ADD-ONS
• Cream of Cauliflower Soup (p. 57)

DAY 19
Chili Mac Casserole (p. 134)

MENU ADD-ONS
• Vegetable & Cheese Focaccia (p. 198)

DAY 20
Lobster Rolls (p. 76)

MENU ADD-ONS
• Warm Apple & Pistachio Spinach Salad (p. 37)

DAY 26
Matthew's Best Ever Meat Loaf (p. 133)

MENU ADD-ONS
• Mom's Macaroni & Cheese (p. 34)

DAY 27
Fish & Fries (p. 144)

MENU ADD-ONS
• Old Bay Cauliflower (p. 45)

DAY 28
Sausage & 'Shroom Dutch Oven Pizza (p. 127)

MENU ADD-ONS
• Fruit cocktail

DAY 29
Rosemary Pork Medallions with Peas (p. 99)

MENU ADD-ONS
• Cranberry-Apple Red Cabbage (p. 40)

DAY 30
Perfect Four-Cheese Lasagna (p. 131)

MENU ADD-ONS
• Garlic Bread (p. 194) & green salad

Quick Tips for Quick Cooking

Even the quickest of quick recipes requires some prep work—and when you're counting the minutes on a busy weeknight, some of that prep work can make you want to reach for a takeout menu. But there are some steps that can be done days in advance so that you have key ingredients ready and waiting.

Bacon

Cook bacon in bulk on a baking sheet in the oven. Store it in a freezer bag for up to 6 months for a ready supply of cooked bacon. Microwave it for a ready-to-eat breakfast, or crumble it into dishes and salads.

Shredded Meat

A staple for Tex-Mex classics and a host of other recipes, shredded meat—pork, chicken or beef—is smart to have on hand. It takes a step out of the recipe process and provides a home-cooked alternative to prepackaged meats. For example, cooking a pork shoulder to shreddable consistency takes 6 to 8 hours in a slow cooker and about 2 hours in the Instant Pot—all hands-off time.

Cooked Rice

Prepare a batch of rice in advance and keep it in the fridge to provide a base for stews and stir-fries. Cook it on the stove or in a rice cooker or Instant Pot—whatever your preferred method—then refrigerate for 3 to 4 days. Cold rice can get a little crunchy, but it softens up nicely in the microwave; leftover rice is actually better for making fried rice.

Garlic

Peeled garlic cloves or minced garlic keep in the fridge—just be sure to use an airtight container, like a Mason jar. To quickly peel a head of garlic, use two stainless steel bowls: Use the base of one to break up the head, then place one bowl over the other and shake vigorously to remove the skins.

Lemon Zest & Juice

The zest of any citrus fruit can be frozen in an airtight container—then simply break off a piece when you need it. For the juice, freeze it in ice cube trays and store the cubes in a freezer container. An ice cube cup holds about ¼ cup of liquid.

Fresh Herbs

Freeze herbs several ways: minced in bags; by the tablespoonful in ice cube trays and covered with water; pureed with oil and frozen flat; or as whole sprigs, rolled up in a freezer bag. Frozen herbs won't have the texture to be a garnish but will be fine in recipes.

Yes, You Can Freeze That

If you thought some foods were off-limits for freezing, think again!

• **Applesauce:** Freeze in an airtight container for up to a year.

• **Avocados:** Wash and halve before peeling. Freeze as halves, or puree with lime or lemon juice. Frozen avocados become mushy, so they shouldn't be eaten by the slice, but are great for sauces and dips.

• **Bananas:** Freeze with or without the peel. Like avocados, bananas will get mushy when frozen, so use these for banana bread, pancakes and smoothies—anything that calls for mashed or pureed bananas.

• **Butter:** Freeze it in its wrapper in a freezer bag or foil. If your recipe calls for softened butter, you can soften frozen butter by grating it.

• **Cheese:** Place grated cheese in an airtight bag (in 1- or 2-cup portions for convenience). If desired, add a tablespoon of cornstarch and shake— it'll help avoid clumping. Hard and semisoft cheeses like Parmesan, cheddar and mozzarella freeze better than soft cheeses.

• **Cream Cheese, Sour Cream, Heavy Cream:** You can freeze dairy products for use in baking and cooking, but the texture won't be suitable for using straight. Frozen heavy cream can be used in recipes and sauces but will not whip. Thaw it in the fridge overnight, then reheat slowly and stir constantly so it doesn't separate, become crumbly or curdle.

Get the Most Out of Your Gadgets

Follow these tips for making your convenient gadgets work even faster.

Instant Pot
• A hot Instant Pot comes to pressure faster than a cold one, so turn it to the saute setting to let it warm up while you're doing prep work (even if the recipe doesn't call for sauteing).
• Use your Instant Pot to hard-boil eggs by the dozen to have them ready for use. This gadget makes perfect hard-cooked eggs in under 10 minutes.

Air Fryer
• Check the size of your air fryer against the recipe. Many models are sized to cook for one or two people, so you may have to cook food in batches. Avoid surprises by accounting for that in your planning.

Slow Cooker
• One hour on high is roughly equal to 2 hours on low, so you usually can adjust the recipe if you want your food finished faster.
• In most cases you can prepare and load ingredients into your slow cooker insert ahead of time and keep it in the refrigerator overnight. But remember that a ceramic insert can crack if exposed to rapid temperature changes, so let it sit out for 20 to 30 minutes to come to room temperature before placing it in the slow cooker.
• Don't peek! Each time you lift the lid, you'll need to add at least 15 minutes to the cooking time. Open the lid only when the recipe specifically calls for it.

Immersion Blender
• Also known as a stick blender, this device is especially useful for pureeing soups, as you can lower it right into the pot and not have to fuss with transferring soup to a blender and back again in batches.
• Use an immersion blender when whipping small batches of whipped cream; it saves breaking out the bowl and beaters.

APPETIZERS
& BEVERAGES

For a get-together with friends or an afternoon snack for the family, these delicious bites are just the thing! And to go along with the food, summer sippers and winter warmers are just what you need to make any snack special!

VANILLA CITRUS CIDER

My mom used to make cider for the holidays, so I based my citrus-vanilla variation on her recipe. I think it hits the spot! The longer the cider simmers, the stronger the flavors will be.
—Kristin Weglarz, Bremerton, WA

Prep: 10 min. • **Cook:** 70 min.
Makes: 10 servings

- 8 cups apple cider or juice
- ¼ cup packed brown sugar
- ¼ cup thawed orange juice concentrate
- ⅛ tsp. salt
- 3 cinnamon sticks (3 in.)
- 1 tsp. whole cloves
- ¼ tsp. vanilla extract
    Orange slices, optional

1. In a large saucepan, combine the apple cider, brown sugar, orange juice concentrate and salt. Place cinnamon sticks and cloves on a double thickness of cheesecloth. Gather corners of cloth to enclose seasonings; tie securely with string. Add to pan.
2. Bring to a boil. Reduce heat; simmer, covered, 1 hour to allow flavors to blend. Discard spice bag. Stir in vanilla. If desired, serve with orange slices.

¾ cup: 127 cal., 0 fat (0 sat. fat), 0 chol., 52mg sod., 32g carb. (28g sugars, 0 fiber), 0 pro.

SPICY-GOOD CHICKEN WINGS

SPICY-GOOD CHICKEN WINGS

These chicken wings make a great dish to pass for any occasion—my family loves it when I make a platter to enjoy while watching football on TV. The hot pepper sauce gives just the right amount of spice.
—Della Clutts, New Tazewell, TN

Prep: 30 min. • **Bake:** 20 min.
Makes: about 1½ dozen

- 1 cup self-rising flour
- 1 tsp. celery salt
- 1 tsp. garlic powder
- 1 tsp. onion salt
- 1 tsp. barbecue seasoning
- ½ tsp. salt
- 2 lbs. chicken wingettes
    Oil for frying
- ½ cup butter, melted
- 1 bottle (2 oz.) hot pepper sauce
    Blue cheese salad dressing

1. In a large shallow dish, mix the first 6 ingredients. Add chicken, a few pieces at a time, and toss to coat.
2. In an electric skillet, heat 1 in. of oil to 375°. Fry wingettes, a few at a time, until browned, 4-5 minutes on each side. Drain on paper towels. Preheat oven to 350°.
3. In a 13x9-in. baking dish, mix melted butter and pepper sauce. Add wings and turn to coat. Bake, uncovered, 10 minutes. Turn; bake until chicken juices run clear, 10-15 minutes longer. Serve with dressing.

Note: To make a substitute for 1 cup of self-rising flour, place 1½ tsp. baking powder and ½ tsp. salt in a measuring cup. Add all-purpose flour to measure 1 cup.

1 wing: 225 cal., 18g fat (6g sat. fat), 51mg chol., 473mg sod., 5g carb. (0 sugars, 0 fiber), 10g pro.

ONION TART

Onion lovers are sure to be asking for second helpings of this appetizing tart—it uses two kinds of onions! Parmesan and feta cheese, nutmeg and hot pepper sauce enhance the flavor nicely. With its quichelike filling, the dish is ideal for a brunch or buffet.
—Christine Andreas, Huntingdon, PA

Prep: 20 min. • **Bake:** 45 min.
Makes: 6 servings

- 1 unbaked pastry shell (9 in.)
- 2 medium sweet onions, thinly sliced
- 2 Tbsp. olive oil
- 3 large eggs
- ½ cup crumbled feta cheese
- ½ tsp. salt
- ¼ tsp. coarsely ground pepper
- ⅛ tsp. ground nutmeg
- ⅛ tsp. hot pepper sauce
- ¾ cup half-and-half cream
- ½ cup whole milk
- 1 Tbsp. Dijon mustard
- 6 green onions, thinly sliced
- 2 Tbsp. minced chives
- ⅓ cup grated Parmesan cheese

1. Preheat oven to 450°. Line unpricked pastry shell with a double thickness of heavy-duty foil. Bake for 8 minutes. Remove foil; bake 5 minutes longer. Cool on a wire rack. Set oven to 375°.
2. In a small skillet, saute the onions in oil until tender; cool. In a food processor, combine the eggs, feta cheese, salt, pepper, nutmeg and hot pepper sauce; cover and process until smooth. Gradually add cream and milk; process until blended.
3. Brush the inside of crust with mustard. Sprinkle the green onions, chives and sauteed onions over the crust. Carefully pour egg mixture over onions. Top with Parmesan cheese.
4. Bake at 375° for 30-40 minutes or until a knife inserted in the center comes out clean.

1 slice: 361 cal., 23g fat (10g sat. fat), 139mg chol., 627mg sod., 26g carb. (7g sugars, 2g fiber), 11g pro.

ONION TART

CILANTRO & LIME CHICKEN WITH SCOOPS
PICTURED ON P. 7

I came up with this recipe when I was preparing for a large party and wanted a healthy Tex-Mex chicken to serve in tortilla cups. You can make this dish ahead of time to free yourself for time-sensitive dishes. Serve it in tortilla chip cups or any other savory crispy cup you like. Enjoy leftovers over salad greens or wrapped up in tender tortillas for burritos.
—Lori Terry, Chicago, IL

Prep: 15 min. • **Cook:** 3½ hours
Makes: 16 servings (4 cups)

- 1 lb. boneless skinless chicken breasts
- 2 tsp. chili powder
- 2 Tbsp. lime juice
- 1½ cups frozen petite corn (about 5 oz.), thawed
- 1½ cups chunky salsa
- 1½ cups (6 oz.) finely shredded cheddar cheese
- 1 medium sweet red pepper, finely chopped
- 4 green onions, thinly sliced
  Minced fresh cilantro
  Baked tortilla chip scoops

1. Place chicken in a 1½-qt. slow cooker; sprinkle with chili powder and lime juice. Cook, covered, on low for 3-4 hours or until tender.
2. Remove chicken; discard cooking juices. Shred chicken with 2 forks; return to slow cooker. Add corn and salsa; cook, covered, on low about 30 minutes or until heated through, stirring occasionally.
3. Transfer to a large bowl; stir in cheese, pepper and green onions. Sprinkle with cilantro; serve with tortilla scoops.

¼ cup chicken mixture: 97 cal., 4g fat (2g sat. fat), 26mg chol., 183mg sod., 5g carb. (2g sugars, 1g fiber), 9g pro.
Diabetic exchanges: 1 medium-fat meat.

5i
BRANDY SLUSH

This citrussy slush is a Midwestern party go-to. If you like, swap in other spirits, like a berry vodka or blackberry brandy for the regular brandy.
—Taste of Home *Test Kitchen*

Prep: 15 min. + freezing
Makes: 21 servings (about 4 qt. slush mix)

- 4   **green or black tea bags**
- 9   **cups water, divided**
- 2   **cups brandy**
- 1   **can (12 oz.) frozen lemonade concentrate, thawed**
- 1   **can (12 oz.) frozen orange juice concentrate, thawed**

EACH SERVING
- ¼   **cup lemon-lime soda, chilled**

GARNISH
- **Lime wedge, optional**

1. Place tea bags in a small bowl. Bring 2 cups water to a boil; pour over tea bags. Cover and steep for 5 minutes. Discard tea bags. Transfer tea to a large pitcher; stir in the brandy, lemonade concentrate, juice concentrate and remaining water. Pour into a 4-qt. freezer container. Freeze overnight or until set.

2. For each serving, scoop ¾ cup slush into a rocks glass. Pour lemon-lime soda into the glass; if desired, serve with a lime wedge.

¾ cup: 129 cal., 0 fat (0 sat. fat), 0 chol., 8mg sod., 20g carb. (19g sugars, 0 fiber), 0 pro.

Old Fashioned Slush: Combine 9 cups water, 2 cups bourbon, 2 cans orange juice concentrate and and 2 Tbsp. bitters. Pour into a 4-qt. freezer container. Freeze overnight or until set. For each serving, scoop ¾ cup slush into a rocks glass; top with lemon-lime soda.

Cranberry Bog Slush: Combine 9 cups water, 2 cups vodka, 1 can cranberry juice and 1 can limeade concentrate. Pour into a 4-qt. freezer container. Freeze overnight or until set. For each serving, scoop ¾ cup slush into a rocks glass; top with ginger ale.

Southern Sweet Tea Slush: Combine 9 cups water, 2 cups sweet tea vodka and 2 cans lemonade concentrate. Pour into a 4-qt. freezer container. Freeze overnight or until set. For each serving, scoop ¾ cup slush into a rocks glass and top with lemon-lime soda.

Negroni Slush: Combine 9 cups water, 1½ cups gin, ½ cup Campari, 1 can of limeade concentrate, 1 can cranberry juice concentrate and 2 Tbsp. sweet vermouth. Pour into a 4-qt. freezer container. Freeze overnight or until set. For each serving, scoop ¾ cup slush into a rocks glass; top with lemon-lime soda.

MAMMA'S CAPONATA

Great as an appetizer, but you can easily turn this into a meal. Instead of topping bread, serve over warm pasta.
—Georgette Stubin, Canton, MI

Prep: 30 min. • **Cook:** 40 min.
Makes: 6 cups

- 1 large eggplant, peeled and chopped
- ¼ cup plus 2 Tbsp. olive oil, divided
- 2 medium onions, chopped
- 2 celery ribs, chopped
- 2 cans (14½ oz. each) diced tomatoes, undrained
- ⅓ cup chopped ripe olives
- ¼ cup red wine vinegar
- 2 Tbsp. sugar
- 2 Tbsp. capers, drained
- ½ tsp. salt
- ½ tsp. pepper
  French bread baguettes, sliced and toasted

1. In a Dutch oven, saute eggplant in ¼ cup oil until tender. Remove from pot and set aside. Saute onion and celery in remaining oil until tender. Stir in tomatoes and eggplant. Bring to a boil. Reduce heat; simmer, uncovered, for 15 minutes.
2. Add the olives, vinegar, sugar, capers, salt and pepper. Return to a boil. Reduce heat; simmer, uncovered, for 20 minutes or until thickened. Serve warm or at room temperature with baguettes.
¼ cup: 57 cal., 4g fat (1g sat. fat), 0 chol., 134mg sod., 6g carb. (4g sugars, 2g fiber), 1g pro. **Diabetic exchanges:** 1 vegetable, ½ fat.

MAMMA'S CAPONATA

HERBED LEEK TARTS
PICTURED ON P. 7

This savory tart is a favorite among our family and friends! It's delicious and different—and surprisingly easy to make.
—Jean Ecos, Hartland, WI

Prep: 25 min. • **Bake:** 20 min. + cooling
Makes: 2 tarts (8 servings each)

- 3 cups thinly sliced leeks (about 4 medium)
- ½ cup chopped sweet red pepper
- 4 garlic cloves, minced
- 2 Tbsp. olive oil
- 1½ cups shredded Swiss cheese
- 2 Tbsp. Dijon mustard
- 1 tsp. herbes de Provence
- 2 sheets refrigerated pie crust
- 1 tsp. 2% milk
- 2 Tbsp. chopped almonds or walnuts, optional

1. Preheat oven to 375°. In a large skillet, saute the leeks, red pepper and garlic in oil until tender. Remove from the heat; cool for 5 minutes. Stir in the cheese, mustard and herbs; set aside.
2. On a lightly floured surface, roll each sheet of crust into a 12-in. circle. Transfer to parchment-lined baking sheets. Spoon the leek mixture over crusts to within 2 in. of edges. Fold edges of crust over filling, leaving center uncovered. Brush folded crust with milk; sprinkle with nuts if desired.
3. Bake for 20-25 minutes or until the crust is golden and filling is bubbly. Using parchment, slide tarts onto wire racks. Cool for 10 minutes before cutting. Serve warm. Refrigerate leftovers.
1 slice: 194 cal., 12g fat (5g sat. fat), 14mg chol., 177mg sod., 17g carb. (2g sugars, 1g fiber), 5g pro.

**GUAVA COCONUT
RUM COCKTAIL**

COWBOY BEEF DIP

In a foods class, a group of us developed this recipe for the North Dakota's annual Beef Bash. We won the contest, and now my family requests this dip for all our special gatherings!
—Jessica Klym, Dunn Center, ND

Prep: 20 min. • **Cook:** 25 min.
Makes: 3 cups

- 1 lb. ground beef
- 4 Tbsp. chopped onion, divided
- 3 Tbsp. chopped sweet red pepper, divided
- 2 Tbsp. chopped green pepper, divided
- 1 can (10¾ oz.) condensed nacho cheese soup, undiluted
- ½ cup salsa
- 4 Tbsp. sliced ripe olives, divided
- 4 Tbsp. sliced pimiento-stuffed olives, divided
- 2 Tbsp. chopped green chiles
- 1 tsp. chopped seeded jalapeno pepper
- ¼ tsp. dried oregano
- ¼ tsp. pepper
- ¼ cup shredded cheddar cheese
- 2 Tbsp. sour cream
- 2 to 3 tsp. minced fresh parsley
  Tortilla chips

1. In a large skillet, cook the beef, 3 Tbsp. onion, 2 Tbsp. red pepper and 1 Tbsp. green pepper over medium heat until the meat is no longer pink; drain. Stir in the soup, salsa, 3 Tbsp. ripe olives, 3 Tbsp. pimiento-stuffed olives, chiles, jalapeno, oregano and pepper. Bring to a boil. Reduce heat; simmer, uncovered, for 5 minutes.
2. Transfer to a serving dish. Top with cheese, sour cream and parsley; sprinkle with the remaining onion, peppers and olives. Serve with tortilla chips.
¼ cup: 116 cal., 7g fat (3g sat. fat), 26mg chol., 336mg sod., 4g carb. (1g sugars, 1g fiber), 8g pro.

GUAVA COCONUT RUM COCKTAIL

My beverage is so sensational it's like a taste of the tropics in a glass. The guava adds a touch of sweetness to this coconut drink.
—Melanie Milhorat, New York, NY

Takes: 5 min. • **Makes:** 1 serving

  Ice cubes
- 2 oz. coconut rum
- 2 oz. guava nectar
- 2 tsp. lemon juice
- 3 to 4 dashes bitters
- 1 tsp. simple syrup
- 2 oz. coconut water

GARNISH
  Fresh pineapple wedge

Fill a mixing glass or tumbler three-fourths full with ice. Add rum, guava nectar, lemon juice, bitters and simple syrup; stir until condensation forms on the outside of glass. Strain into a chilled cocktail glass. Add ice and top with coconut water. Garnish as desired.
1 serving: 197 cal., 0 fat (0 sat. fat), 0 chol., 77mg sod., 16g carb. (13g sugars, 2g fiber), 1g pro.
For nonalcoholic version: Increase coconut water and guava nectar to 3 oz. each. Eliminate bitters and add ⅛ tsp. coconut extract.

COWBOY BEEF DIP

CRANBERRY JALAPENO CHEESE SPREAD

My easy spread is based on several different relishes and spreads I've tasted or made before. I love the unexpected combination of sweet and spicy flavors!
—Diane Nemitz, Ludington, MI

Prep: 25 min. + cooling • **Makes:** 2 cups

- 1 cup dried cranberries
- ½ cup packed brown sugar
- ½ cup orange juice
- 4 tsp. chopped seeded jalapeno pepper
- 1 Tbsp. lemon juice
- 1 tsp. grated orange zest
- ¼ tsp. Chinese five-spice powder
- 1 pkg. (8 oz.) reduced-fat cream cheese
  Assorted crackers or sliced sweet yellow and orange peppers

1. In a small saucepan, combine the first 7 ingredients. Bring to a boil. Reduce heat; simmer, uncovered, for 10 minutes or until thickened. Remove from the heat; cool completely.

2. In a large bowl, beat the cream cheese until fluffy. Beat in cranberry mixture until blended. Serve with crackers or sliced sweet peppers.

2 Tbsp.: 88 cal., 3g fat (2g sat. fat), 10mg chol., 63mg sod., 14g carb. (13g sugars, 0 fiber), 2g pro.

PEPPERONI FOCACCIA BREAD

PEPPERONI FOCACCIA BREAD

This focaccia bread recipe is perfect to serve with a pasta dinner, either as an appetizer or sliced for sandwiches. You will love the smell of it baking—it's hard to wait for it to be done! I like to add some thinly sliced plum tomatoes and a bit of fresh basil on top.
—Trisha Kruse, Eagle, ID

Prep: 25 min. • **Bake:** 20 min. + cooling
Makes: 8 servings

- 1 pkg. (3½ oz.) sliced pepperoni, chopped
- ½ medium onion, thinly sliced
- 1 large egg, room temperature
- 1 cup 2% milk
- ½ cup plain Greek yogurt
- ¼ cup olive oil
- 2½ cups all-purpose flour
- 2½ tsp. baking powder
- ½ tsp. garlic powder
- ¼ tsp. salt
- ¾ cup shredded Parmesan cheese, divided
  Optional: Marinara sauce and fresh basil leaves

1. Preheat oven to 425°. Heat a 10-in. cast-iron or ovenproof skillet over medium-high heat. Add pepperoni and onion; cook and stir until pepperoni is crisp and onion is tender, 6-8 minutes. Remove and keep warm. In a large bowl, beat egg, milk, yogurt and oil until well blended. In another bowl, whisk flour, baking powder, garlic powder and salt; gradually beat into egg mixture. Stir in ½ cup cheese and pepperoni mixture (batter will be thick).

2. Transfer to same skillet; sprinkle with remaining ¼ cup cheese. Bake until bread is golden brown and a toothpick inserted in center comes out clean, 20-25 minutes. Cool for 10 minutes in skillet on a wire rack. Serve warm. If desired, serve bread with marinara sauce and top with fresh basil leaves.

1 slice: 339 cal., 18g fat (6g sat. fat), 47mg chol., 580mg sod., 33g carb. (3g sugars, 1g fiber), 12g pro.

PINEAPPLE-COCONUT SMOOTHIE

Use fresh or frozen fruits in this coconutty recipe. It's like a pina colada, but better for you and more versatile.
—Gunjan Dudani, Bellevue, WA

Takes: 10 min. • **Makes:** 4 servings

- 1 pkg. (16 oz.) frozen pineapple chunks
- 1 cup (8 oz.) frozen mango chunks
- ½ cup unsweetened finely shredded coconut
- 3 pitted dates
- 3 cups coconut milk

Pulse all ingredients in a blender until smooth. Serve immediately.

1¼ cups: 460 cal., 33g fat (33g sat. fat), 0 chol., 69mg sod., 35g carb. (24g sugars, 3g fiber), 4g pro.

READER REVIEW

"Wow! I like to experiment with different fruits and this recipe is a really fresh idea for these ingredients."

NELLIE, TASTEOFHOME.COM

TZATZIKI SHRIMP CUCUMBER ROUNDS
PICTURED ON P. 7

I created this recipe with what I had on hand one night, and now it's one of my husband's favorites! The bacon-wrapped shrimp, garlicky sauce and burst of cool cuke flavor make these irresistible.
—Shannon Trelease, East Hampton, NY

Prep: 25 min. • **Cook:** 10 min./batch
Makes: 2 dozen

- ¼ cup reduced-fat plain yogurt
- 2 Tbsp. finely chopped peeled cucumber
- ⅛ tsp. garlic salt
- ⅛ tsp. dill weed
- 6 bacon strips
- 24 uncooked shrimp (31-40 per lb.), peeled and deveined
- 1 to 2 Tbsp. canola oil
- 2 medium cucumbers, cut into ¼-in. slices

1. In a small bowl, combine the yogurt, chopped cucumber, garlic salt and dill; set aside.
2. Cut each strip of bacon in half widthwise and then lengthwise. Wrap a piece of bacon around each shrimp. Secure with toothpicks.
3. In a large nonstick skillet, heat oil over medium heat; cook shrimp in batches for 3-4 minutes on each side or until the bacon is crisp.
4. Spoon a rounded ½ tsp. of yogurt sauce onto each cucumber slice; top with shrimp.

1 appetizer: 30 cal., 2g fat (0 sat. fat), 18mg chol., 64mg sod., 1g carb. (0 sugars, 0 fiber), 3g pro.

PINEAPPLE-COCONUT SMOOTHIE

ORANGE SPICED CIDER

Every time I serve this wonderful hot beverage, someone asks for the recipe. Orange juice adds a bit of sweetness and Red Hot candies are a fun substitute for traditional cinnamon sticks.

—Erika Reinhard, Colorado Springs, CO

Prep: 5 min. • **Cook:** 2 hours
Makes: 8 servings

- 4 cups unsweetened apple juice
- 1 can (12 oz.) orange juice concentrate, thawed
- ½ cup water
- 1 Tbsp. Red Hots
- ½ tsp. ground nutmeg
- 1 tsp. whole cloves
   Optional: Orange slices, apple slices and cinnamon sticks

1. In a 3-qt. slow cooker, combine the first 5 ingredients. Place cloves in a double thickness of cheesecloth; bring up corners of cloth and tie with kitchen string to form a bag. Add bag to slow cooker. Cover and cook on low for 2-3 hours or until mixture is heated through.

2. Before serving, discard spice bag and stir cider. If desired, serve with orange slices, apple slices and cinnamon sticks.
¾ cup: 128 cal., 0 fat (0 sat. fat), 0 chol., 6mg sod., 31g carb. (0 sugars, 1g fiber), 1g pro. **Diabetic exchanges:** 2 fruit.

CHEESY PIZZA ROLLS

CHEESY PIZZA ROLLS

The cast-iron skillet browns these delicious rolls to perfection. My family can't get enough. Use whatever pizza toppings your family likes best.

—Dorothy Smith, El Dorado, AR

Prep: 15 min. • **Bake:** 25 min.
Makes: 8 appetizers

- 1 loaf (1 lb.) frozen pizza dough, thawed
- ½ cup pasta sauce
- 1 cup shredded part-skim mozzarella cheese, divided
- 1 cup coarsely chopped pepperoni (about 64 slices)
- ½ lb. bulk Italian sausage, cooked and crumbled
- ¼ cup grated Parmesan cheese
   Minced fresh basil, optional
   Crushed red pepper flakes, optional

1. Preheat oven to 400°. On a lightly floured surface, roll dough into a 16x10-in. rectangle. Brush with pasta sauce to within ½ in. of edges.

2. Sprinkle with ½ cup mozzarella cheese, pepperoni, sausage and Parmesan. Roll up jelly-roll style, starting with a long side; pinch seam to seal. Cut into 8 slices. Place the slices in a greased 9-in. cast-iron skillet or a greased 9-in. round baking pan, cut side down.

3. Bake 20 minutes; sprinkle with the remaining mozzarella cheese. Bake until golden brown, 5-10 minutes longer. If desired, serve with minced fresh basil and crushed red pepper flakes.
1 roll: 355 cal., 19g fat (7g sat. fat), 42mg chol., 978mg sod., 29g carb. (3g sugars, 0 fiber), 14g pro.

TEST KITCHEN TIPS
- If you have a favorite homemade or store-bought fresh dough, swap it for the frozen dough.
- Give rolls a little room in the pan to stretch; they will expand once they're in the oven.
- Prefer a crispier pizza crust? Bake an additional 5-10 minutes.

PUMPKIN SEED CHEESE BALL

The next time you carve a pumpkin, roast the seeds with a couple of teaspoons of butter and some salt and pepper—it takes only 15-20 minutes at 350°. If you don't have roasted seeds on hand, you can use pepitas, sold in stores, to coat this creamy cheese ball.
—Taste of Home *Test Kitchen*

Prep: 15 min. + chilling
Makes: 1 cheese ball (1¾ cups)

- 1 pkg. (8 oz.) cream cheese, softened
- 1 cup shredded mozzarella cheese
- ½ cup chopped green onions
- 1 tsp. Italian seasoning
- ½ tsp. dried parsley flakes
- ⅛ tsp. cayenne pepper
- ¼ cup roasted fresh pumpkin seeds
- ¼ cup unsalted sunflower kernels
  Assorted crackers or fresh
  vegetables

1. In a small bowl, combine the first 6 ingredients. Cover and refrigerate for 30 minutes or until easy to handle. Meanwhile, on a plate, combine pumpkin seeds and sunflower kernels; set aside.
2. Shape the cream cheese mixture into a ball; gently roll in pumpkin seed mixture (lightly press seeds into cream cheese ball if necessary). Wrap and refrigerate for at least 2 hours or until firm. Serve with crackers or vegetables.
2 Tbsp.: 99 cal., 9g fat (5g sat. fat), 24mg chol., 79mg sod., 2g carb. (1g sugars, 0 fiber), 4g pro.

PUMPKIN SEED
CHEESE BALL

⑤j
SWISS POTATO PUFFS

Encourage guests to mingle by serving these cute little morsels. They're transportable, mess-free and easy to eat in a few bites.
—Myra Innes, Auburn, KS

Prep: 20 min. • **Bake:** 20 min.
Makes: about 3 dozen

- 1⅓ cups water
- ¼ cup butter, cubed
- ½ tsp. salt
- ¾ cup all-purpose flour
- ¼ cup mashed potato flakes
- 3 large eggs
- 1 cup shredded Gruyere or
  Swiss cheese

1. Preheat oven to 375°. In a large saucepan, bring the water, butter and salt to a boil. Remove from the heat.
2. Combine the flour and potato flakes; slowly stir into pan. Cook and stir over medium heat until a smooth ball forms. Remove from the heat. Add eggs, 1 at a time, beating well after each addition. Continue beating until mixture is smooth and shiny. Stir in cheese.
3. Drop by tablespoonfuls 2 in. apart onto greased baking sheets. Bake for 18-22 minutes or until golden brown.
1 potato puff: 37 cal., 2g fat (1g sat. fat), 22mg chol., 53mg sod., 2g carb. (0 sugars, 0 fiber), 2g pro.

PUMPKIN MILK SHAKES

My son loved this festive milk shake when he was growing up—it's nicely spiced and tastes like pumpkin pie! I like cutting off both ends of a licorice twist and serving it as a straw.
—Joan Hallford, North Richland Hills, TX

Takes: 10 min. • **Makes:** 6 servings

- 1 cup orange juice
- 4 cups vanilla ice cream
- 1 cup canned pumpkin
- ½ cup packed brown sugar
- 1 tsp. ground cinnamon
- ½ tsp. ground ginger
- ½ tsp. ground nutmeg
- Black licorice twists, optional

In batches, place the first 7 ingredients in a blender. Cover and process until smooth, 20-30 seconds. Serve immediately, with licorice stirrers if desired.

1 cup: 287 cal., 10g fat (6g sat. fat), 39mg chol., 78mg sod., 47g carb. (42g sugars, 2g fiber), 4g pro.

MUFFULETTA WELLINGTONS

MUFFULETTA WELLINGTONS

Inspired by the muffuletta, a deli sandwich originating in New Orleans, I created these snack-sized sandwiches baked in pizza dough. You can substitute your own favorite meats, like turkey or roast beef.
—Chelsea Madren, Fullerton, CA

Prep: 25 min. • **Bake:** 20 min. + standing
Makes: 6 servings

- 3 Tbsp. melted butter, divided
- 1 Tbsp. cornmeal
- 1 tube (13.8 oz.) refrigerated pizza dough
- 6 Tbsp. olive bruschetta
- 18 slices thinly sliced hard salami
- 12 slices thinly sliced Black Forest deli ham
- 6 slices part-skim mozzarella cheese
- 6 slices provolone cheese
- 1 Tbsp. sesame seeds

1. Preheat oven to 425°. Grease a 12-in. cast-iron or other ovenproof skillet with 1 Tbsp. butter. Sprinkle with cornmeal; set aside.

2. Unroll pizza dough; cut into 6 portions. On a floured surface, roll each portion into a 6-in. square. Place 1 Tbsp. bruschetta in center of each square; top with salami, ham, mozzarella cheese and provolone cheese. Bring 4 corners of each portion of dough together above the filling; pinch edges to seal.

3. Place in prepared skillet, seam side down. Brush with the remaining 2 Tbsp. butter; sprinkle with sesame seeds.

4. Bake until sandwiches are golden brown, 20-25 minutes. Let stand for 10 minutes before serving.

1 sandwich: 562 cal., 33g fat (14g sat. fat), 93mg chol., 1815mg sod., 37g carb. (6g sugars, 1g fiber), 32g pro.

1. Make the syrup
In a large saucepan, combine sugar, 1 cup of the water, and lemon zest.

2. Keep stirring!
Cook and stir over medium heat until the sugar is dissolved, about 4 minutes.

3. Add more liquid
Remove from heat. Stir in the lemon juice and the remaining 4 cups water. Refrigerate until cold, and serve over ice. Garnish with lemon slices, if desired.

Luscious Lemonade
This delicious, classic lemonade is the perfect summer sipper—just like Grandma used to make!

5i
OLD-FASHIONED LEMONADE
This sweet-tart lemonade is a traditional part of my Memorial Day and Fourth of July menus. Folks can't get enough of the fresh-squeezed flavor. The key to making this treat is to start by making a lemon-flavored simple syrup.
—Tammi Simpson, Greensburg, KY

Prep: 10 min. • **Cook:** 5 min. + chilling
Makes: 7 servings

1⅓ cups sugar
5 cups water, divided
1 Tbsp. grated lemon zest
1¾ cups lemon juice (about 10 large lemons)
Additional lemon slices, optional

1 cup: 142 cal., 0 fat (0 sat. fat), 0 chol., 1mg sod., 37g carb. (35g sugars, 0 fiber), 0 pro.

SO VERY BERRY BRIE

SO VERY BERRY BRIE

I needed a quick dish for a party and had some berries on hand. Combining them with warm Brie cheese made for an impressive appetizer.
—Kristin Larson, Newton, KS

Prep: 15 min. + standing • **Bake:** 10 min.
Makes: 8 servings

- ½ cup sugar
- 2 Tbsp. water
- ½ cup fresh or frozen raspberries, thawed
- ½ cup fresh or frozen blueberries, thawed
- ½ cup fresh or frozen blackberries, thawed
- 1 Tbsp. cornstarch
- 2 Tbsp. cold water
- 1 round (8 oz.) Brie cheese, halved horizontally
  Bagel and/or baked pita chips

1. Preheat oven to 400°. In a small saucepan, heat sugar and water until sugar is dissolved. Add berries. Bring to a boil. Reduce heat; simmer, uncovered, for 3 minutes.
2. Combine cornstarch and cold water until smooth; gradually stir into the pan. Bring to a boil. Cook and stir for 2 minutes or until thickened. Remove from the heat; let stand for 10 minutes.
3. Place the bottom half of the cheese in a small ungreased cast-iron or ovenproof skillet; pour ½ cup of the berry mixture over the cheese. Top with the remaining cheese and berry mixture.
4. Bake, uncovered, until the cheese is softened, 8-10 minutes. Serve with chips.
1 serving: 160 cal., 8g fat (5g sat. fat), 28mg chol., 179mg sod., 17g carb. (14g sugars, 1g fiber), 6g pro.

LOBSTER & ARTICHOKE QUESADILLAS

LOBSTER & ARTICHOKE QUESADILLAS

Lobster, artichokes, cheese and spices—my favorite things! Put them together in a quesadilla and it is simply fantastic fare. I like to serve the quesadillas with fresh avocados seasoned with fresh lemon juice and lemon pepper.
—Allene Bary-Cooper, Wichita Falls, TX

Takes: 30 min. • **Makes:** 6 servings

- ½ cup grated Parmesan cheese
- ½ cup fat-free mayonnaise
- 1 can (14 oz.) water-packed artichoke hearts, rinsed, drained and chopped
- 4½ tsp. chopped roasted sweet red pepper
- 1 garlic clove, minced
- 6 flour tortillas (10 in.)
- 1 cup cooked lobster meat or canned flaked lobster meat
- ½ cup shredded part-skim mozzarella cheese

1. In a small bowl, combine Parmesan cheese, mayonnaise, artichokes, red pepper and garlic. Spread over three tortillas. Top with lobster, mozzarella cheese and the remaining tortillas; press down lightly.
2. In a greased cast-iron skillet or griddle, cook quesadillas over medium heat until cheese is melted, 2 minutes on each side. Cut each into 6 wedges.
1 wedge: 113 cal., 3g fat (1g sat. fat), 16mg chol., 390mg sod., 15g carb. (1g sugars, 1g fiber), 5g pro.

CREAMY ARTICHOKE DIP

This creamy dip is a family favorite. My sister Teresa got this recipe from a friend and passed it along to me. It's loaded with four types of cheese, artichoke hearts and just the right amount of spice.
—Mary Spencer, Greendale, WI

Prep: 20 min. • **Cook:** 1 hour
Makes: 5 cups

- 2 cans (14 oz. each) water-packed artichoke hearts, rinsed, drained and coarsely chopped
- 2 cups shredded part-skim mozzarella cheese
- 1 pkg. (8 oz.) cream cheese, cubed
- 1 cup shredded Parmesan cheese
- ½ cup mayonnaise
- ½ cup shredded Swiss cheese
- 2 Tbsp. lemon juice
- 2 Tbsp. plain yogurt
- 1 Tbsp. seasoned salt
- 1 Tbsp. chopped seeded jalapeno pepper
- 1 tsp. garlic powder
  Tortilla chips

In a 3-qt. slow cooker, combine the first 11 ingredients. Cover and cook on low for 1 hour or until heated through. Serve with tortilla chips.

¼ cup: 152 cal., 12g fat (5g sat. fat), 27mg chol., 519mg sod., 4g carb. (1g sugars, 0 fiber), 7g pro.

MARMALADE MEATBALLS

MARMALADE MEATBALLS

We had a potluck at work, so I started cooking these meatballs in the morning. By lunchtime they were ready. They were a big hit!
—Jeanne Kiss, Greensburg, PA

Prep: 10 min. • **Cook:** 4 hours
Makes: about 5 dozen

- 1 bottle (16 oz.) Catalina salad dressing
- 1 cup orange marmalade
- 3 Tbsp. Worcestershire sauce
- ½ tsp. crushed red pepper flakes
- 1 pkg. (32 oz.) frozen fully cooked home-style meatballs, thawed

In a 3-qt. slow cooker, combine the salad dressing, marmalade, Worcestershire sauce and pepper flakes. Stir in meatballs. Cover and cook on low for 4-5 hours or until heated through.

Freeze option: Freeze cooled meatball mixture in freezer containers. To use, partially thaw in refrigerator overnight. Microwave, covered, on high in a microwave-safe dish until heated through, gently stirring; add water if necessary.

1 meatball: 73 cal., 4g fat (1g sat. fat), 12mg chol., 126mg sod., 6g carb. (5g sugars, 0 fiber), 2g pro.

Easy Party Meatballs: Omit the first 4 ingredients. Combine 1 bottle (14 oz.) ketchup, ¼ cup A.1. steak sauce, 1 Tbsp. minced garlic and 1 tsp. Dijon mustard in slow cooker; stir in the meatballs. Cook as directed.

MARINATED SHRIMP

My husband's aunt shared this recipe with me ages ago. Not only is it now a Christmas Eve tradition in my home, but in the homes of our grown children as well!
—Delores Hill, Helena, MT

Prep: 10 min. + marinating • **Cook:** 10 min.
Makes: about 3 dozen

- 2 lbs. uncooked jumbo shrimp, peeled and deveined
- 1 cup olive oil
- 2 garlic cloves, minced
- 4 tsp. dried rosemary, crushed
- 2 tsp. dried oregano
- 2 bay leaves
- 1 cup dry white wine or chicken broth
- ¾ tsp. salt
- ⅛ tsp. pepper

1. In a bowl, combine the shrimp, oil, garlic, rosemary, oregano and bay leaves. Cover and refrigerate for 2-4 hours.

2. Pour shrimp and marinade into a large deep skillet. Add wine or broth, salt and pepper. Cover and cook over medium-low heat for 10-15 minutes or until shrimp turn pink, stirring occasionally. Discard bay leaves. Transfer with a slotted spoon to a serving dish.

1 shrimp: 40 cal., 2g fat (0 sat. fat), 31 mg chol., 42mg sod., 0 carb. (0 sugars, 0 fiber), 4g pro.

SIMPLE ICED COFFEE

My husband came up with this recipe to replace the soda he was drinking every morning. It's a simple and delicious alternative to expensive iced coffees from the local cafe.
—Sarah Lange, Watertown, WI

Takes: 5 min. • **Makes:** 8 servings

- 2 cups water
- ¼ cup instant coffee granules
- ¼ to ½ cup sugar
- 4 cups 2% milk
- 2 cups half-and-half cream
- 2 tsp. vanilla extract or hazelnut flavoring syrup, optional

Microwave water 90 seconds. Stir in instant coffee. Add sugar. Stir in milk, cream and, if desired, extract or flavoring until combined. Serve over ice.

1 cup: 174 cal., 8g fat (6g sat. fat), 40mg chol., 88mg sod., 15g carb. (14g sugars, 0 fiber), 6g pro.

MARINATED SHRIMP

SPEEDY SIDES & SALADS

The main dish may take center stage, but a great side makes the meal! When you're looking for something to accompany your enticing entree, check out these sides and salads. It doesn't take a lot of time to create a tasty dish that might just steal the show.

Roasted Tater Rounds with Green Onions & Tarragon (p. 31) **Broccoli with Garlic, Bacon & Parmesan** (p. 46)
Fast Macaroni Salad (p. 53) **Spanakopita Mashed Potatoes** (p. 47) **Hearty Baked Beans** (p. 37)

SICILIAN BRUSSELS SPROUTS

I love to make this dish because the flavors jumping around in your mouth keep you coming back bite after bite. Other nuts can be used in place of the pine nuts.
—Marsha Gillett, Yukon, OK

Prep: 30 min. • **Bake:** 20 min.
Makes: 12 servings

- 12 oz. pancetta, diced
- 2 lbs. fresh Brussels sprouts, halved
- 3 Tbsp. capers, drained
- ¼ cup olive oil
- 3 Tbsp. champagne vinegar
- 1 tsp. lemon juice
- ¼ tsp. salt
- ¼ tsp. pepper
- ¾ cup golden raisins
- ½ cup pine nuts, toasted
- 1 tsp. grated lemon zest

1. In a large cast-iron or other ovenproof skillet, cook the pancetta over medium heat until browned. Remove to paper towels with a slotted spoon.
2. Add Brussels sprouts to pan; cook and stir until lightly browned. Remove from the heat. Stir in the capers, oil, vinegar, lemon juice, salt and pepper.
3. Bake, uncovered, at 350° until caramelized, 15-20 minutes, stirring occasionally. Add the raisins, pine nuts, lemon zest and pancetta; toss to coat.

¾ cup: 235 cal., 17g fat (4g sat. fat), 23mg chol., 723mg sod., 15g carb. (8g sugars, 4g fiber), 9g pro.

YOU'RE-BACON-ME-CRAZY POTATO SALAD

YOU'RE-BACON-ME-CRAZY POTATO SALAD

My kids and I always want potato salad when we grill or barbecue, but we don't like the store-bought versions. I toyed with many combinations until I developed this one. Now if I mention grilling to the family, this is their top side-dish request.
—Paul Cogswell, League City, TX

Prep: 10 min. • **Cook:** 25 min. + chilling
Makes: 12 servings

- 2½ lbs. small red potatoes, cut into 1-in. pieces
- 3 tsp. salt
- 1 lb. bacon strips, finely chopped
- 1 large onion, chopped
- 3 celery ribs, finely chopped
- 2 cups mayonnaise
- 2 Tbsp. Dijon or yellow mustard
- ¾ tsp. dill weed
- ½ tsp. celery salt
- ¼ tsp. celery seed

1. Place potatoes in a 6-qt. stockpot; add water to cover. Add salt; bring to a boil. Reduce heat; cook, uncovered, until the potatoes are tender, 12-15 minutes.
2. Meanwhile, in a large skillet, cook bacon over medium heat until crisp, stirring occasionally. Remove with a slotted spoon and drain on paper towels; reserve 4 Tbsp. bacon drippings. Cook and stir onion in the reserved drippings until browned, 6-8 minutes.
3. Reserve ¼ cup cooked bacon for topping. Add onion, drippings, celery and the remaining bacon to potatoes.
4. In a small bowl, mix mayonnaise, mustard and seasonings. Pour over the potato mixture; toss to coat. Refrigerate, covered, until chilled, about 1 hour. Just before serving, sprinkle salad with the reserved bacon.

¾ cup: 424 cal., 36g fat (7g sat. fat), 20mg chol., 1147mg sod., 17g carb. (2g sugars, 2g fiber), 7g pro.

CURRIED CARROTS WITH CRUNCHY PEANUT TOPPING

My homegrown carrots are sweet and tender. When I have a bumper crop, I use this recipe to make the most of them.
Warm curry spice and crunchy peanutty topping make this a no-leftovers dish. If you want to add a burst of green, use half carrots and half broccoli florets.
—Trisha Kruse, Eagle, ID

Prep: 20 min. • **Bake:** 20 min.
Makes: 6 servings

- 2 lbs. fresh carrots, cut into ½-in. slices
- 2 medium onions, halved and sliced ¼ in. thick
- ¾ cup mayonnaise
- ⅓ cup half-and-half cream
- 1 to 2 Tbsp. curry powder
- 1 tsp. salt
- ¼ tsp. pepper
- 20 Ritz crackers, crushed (about 1 cup)
- ½ cup chopped salted peanuts
- 2 Tbsp. butter, melted

1. Preheat oven to 350°. In a large saucepan, bring 2 in. of water to a boil. Add carrots; return to a boil. Reduce heat; simmer 4 minutes. Add onions; return to a boil. Reduce heat; simmer until carrots are tender, 4-5 minutes. Drain vegetables; return to pan.
2. Whisk together mayonnaise, cream, curry powder, salt and pepper. Pour over vegetables; toss to coat. Transfer to a greased 11x7-in. or 8-in. square baking dish. Combine crushed crackers and peanuts; sprinkle over carrots. Drizzle melted butter over top. Bake, uncovered, until bubbly, 20-25 minutes.
⅔ cup: 438 cal., 35g fat (8g sat. fat), 19mg chol., 820mg sod., 28g carb. (10g sugars, 6g fiber), 6g pro.

CURRIED CARROTS WITH CRUNCHY PEANUT TOPPING

ROASTED TATER ROUNDS WITH GREEN ONIONS & TARRAGON
PICTURED ON P. 25

I am crazy for potatoes, especially when they're roasted and toasted. Toss them with fresh herbs and green onions for a bold finish.
—Ally Phillips, Murrells Inlet, SC

Prep: 25 min. • **Broil:** 10 min.
Makes: 8 servings

- 4 lbs. potatoes (about 8 medium), sliced ¼ in. thick
  Cooking spray
- 2 tsp. sea salt
- 1 tsp. coarsely ground pepper
- 6 green onions, thinly sliced (about ¾ cup)
- 3 Tbsp. minced fresh parsley
- 2 Tbsp. minced fresh tarragon
  Olive oil, optional

1. Preheat broiler. Place potatoes in a large microwave-safe bowl; spritz with cooking spray and toss to coat. Microwave, covered, on high for 10-12 minutes or until almost tender, stirring halfway through cooking.
2. Spread potatoes into greased 15x10x1-in. baking pans. Spritz with additional cooking spray; sprinkle with salt and pepper. Broil 4-6 in. from heat 10-12 minutes or until golden brown, stirring halfway through cooking.
3. In a small bowl, mix green onions, parsley and tarragon. Sprinkle over potatoes; toss to coat. If desired, drizzle with olive oil.
¾ cup: 185 cal., 1g fat (0 sat. fat), 0 chol., 497mg sod., 41g carb. (2g sugars, 5g fiber), 5g pro.

READER REVIEW

"I halved the recipe and now wish I hadn't! I did use a little olive oil and it gave the dish a nice finish."
ANNRMS, TASTEOFHOME.COM

GRANNY'S APPLE SCALLOPED POTATOES

I created this dish because I love scalloped potatoes and apples. It is delicious with breaded baked pork chops, which you could cook at the same time in another cast-iron pan. We are retired and it's just the two of us, but you could easily double the recipe for a crowd.
—Shirley Rickis, The Villages, FL

Prep: 25 min. • **Bake:** 55 min. + standing
Makes: 4 servings

- 1 medium Granny Smith apple, peeled and thinly sliced
- 1 tsp. sugar
- 1 tsp. lemon juice
- 2 Tbsp. butter
- ½ cup sliced sweet onion
- 4 medium red potatoes, thinly sliced (about 1 lb.)
- ¾ cup plus 2 Tbsp. shredded Parmesan cheese, divided
- ½ cup heavy whipping cream
- ½ tsp. minced fresh thyme or ¼ tsp. dried thyme
- ¼ tsp. salt
- ¼ tsp. pepper
- 4 bacon strips, cooked and crumbled Chopped fresh parsley, optional

1. Preheat oven to 350°. In a small bowl, combine apple slices, sugar and lemon juice; toss to coat. Set aside.
2. In an 8- or 9-in. cast-iron or other ovenproof skillet, heat the butter over medium heat. Add onion; cook and stir until crisp-tender, about 3 minutes. Remove from the heat.
3. Alternately arrange potato and apple slices in a single layer in the same skillet. Combine ¾ cup Parmesan cheese, the cream, thyme, salt and pepper; pour over top. Bake, uncovered, 50 minutes.
4. Top with bacon and the remaining 2 Tbsp. Parmesan cheese. Bake until potatoes are tender and top is lightly browned, 5-10 minutes longer. Let stand 10 minutes before serving. If desired, sprinkle with parsley.

1 serving: 376 cal., 25g fat (15g sat. fat), 70mg chol., 651mg sod., 27g carb. (7g sugars, 3g fiber), 13g pro.

EASY GREEN BEANS WITH MUSHROOMS

My family looks forward to this side dish every holiday. I add sliced almonds for crunch and garlic for a little kick.
—Cheryl Wittman, Bergen, NY

Prep: 10 min. • **Cook:** 5 hours
Makes: 10 servings

- 2 lbs. fresh green beans, trimmed
- 1 lb. sliced fresh mushrooms
- 1 large onion, finely chopped
- 2 Tbsp. butter, melted
- 2 Tbsp. olive oil
- 3 garlic cloves, minced
- ½ tsp. salt
- ¼ tsp. pepper
- ½ cup sliced almonds, toasted

In a 6-qt. slow cooker, combine all of the ingredients except the almonds. Cook, covered, on low 5-6 hours or until beans are tender. Remove with a slotted spoon. Top with almonds.

1 serving: 116 cal., 8g fat (2g sat. fat), 6mg chol., 145mg sod., 11g carb. (4g sugars, 4g fiber), 4g pro. **Diabetic exchanges:** 1½ fat, 1 vegetable.

GRANNY'S APPLE SCALLOPED POTATOES

CAULIFLOWER
AU GRATIN

CAULIFLOWER AU GRATIN

This lower-carb side dish pairs well with pork, ham or beef. It's so creamy and delicious that even the kids will ask for seconds! If you like a little crunch, sprinkle buttered bread crumbs over the top after 30 minutes of baking.
—Mary Zinchiak, Boardman, OH

Prep: 25 min. • **Bake:** 45 min.
Makes: 8 servings

- 1 large head cauliflower, cut into florets
- 2 Tbsp. olive oil
- 1 tsp. salt, divided
- 1 tsp. pepper, divided
- 4 Tbsp. butter, cubed
- 3 Tbsp. all-purpose flour
- 2 cups 2% milk
- 1 cup shredded Swiss cheese
- ½ cup grated Parmesan cheese
- ½ tsp. onion powder
- ½ tsp. ground mustard
- ½ tsp. Worcestershire sauce
- ⅛ tsp. cayenne pepper
  Chopped fresh thyme, optional

1. Preheat oven to 375°. Place cauliflower on a rimmed baking sheet. Drizzle with oil; sprinkle with ½ tsp. salt and ½ tsp. pepper. Toss to coat. Bake 8 minutes. Stir; bake until crisp-tender and lightly browned, 7-8 minutes longer.

2. In a large saucepan, melt butter over medium heat. Stir in flour until smooth; gradually whisk in milk. Bring to a simmer, stirring constantly; cook and stir until thickened, 2-3 minutes. Remove from heat. Stir in the next 6 ingredients and the remaining ½ tsp. salt and ½ tsp. pepper until smooth.

3. Pour ¾ cup cheese sauce into a greased 2-qt. baking dish. Top with cauliflower and the remaining cheese sauce. Bake, uncovered, until bubbly and lightly browned, 30-35 minutes. If desired, top with chopped fresh thyme.

¾ cup: 196 cal., 14g fat (7g sat. fat), 34mg chol., 291mg sod., 11g carb. (5g sugars, 2g fiber), 9g pro.

TEST KITCHEN TIP
To add additional texture, top this dish with buttered panko bread crumbs before baking. Add more flavor and color by topping with minced fresh thyme.

HARISSA SWEET POTATO FRITTERS

MOM'S MACARONI & CHEESE

The wonderful homemade goodness of this creamy macaroni and cheese makes it a staple side dish in my mother's kitchen and now in mine as well! It has tender noodles and a crowd-pleasing golden crumb topping.
—Maria Costello, Monroe, NC

Prep: 30 min. • **Bake:** 30 min.
Makes: 6 servings

- 1½ cups uncooked elbow macaroni
- 5 Tbsp. butter, divided
- 3 Tbsp. all-purpose flour
- ½ tsp. salt
- ¼ tsp. pepper
- 1½ cups whole milk
- 1 cup shredded cheddar cheese
- 2 oz. cubed Velveeta
- 2 Tbsp. dry bread crumbs

1. Cook macaroni according to package directions. Meanwhile, in a saucepan, melt 4 Tbsp. butter over medium heat. Stir in the flour, salt and pepper until smooth. Gradually add milk. Bring to a boil; cook and stir for 2 minutes or until thickened. Reduce heat. Add the cheeses, stirring until melted. Drain macaroni.
2. Transfer macaroni to a greased 1½-qt. baking dish. Pour cheese sauce over the macaroni; mix well. Melt the remaining butter; add the bread crumbs. Sprinkle over top. Bake, uncovered, at 375° for 30 minutes or until heated through and topping is golden brown.

1 serving: 309 cal., 20g fat (13g sat. fat), 60mg chol., 569mg sod., 22g carb. (4g sugars, 1g fiber), 11g pro.

TEST KITCHEN TIP
It's usually cheaper to buy cheese in blocks rather than pre-shredded. So purchase large quantities of cheddar, Monterey Jack and mozzarella, then use a food processor to shred it. Store the shredded cheese in the freezer so you have it when you need it.

HARISSA SWEET POTATO FRITTERS

I had a couple of sweet potatoes left over after making a big meal and had to think up a new way to use them. We love spice, so I flavored these fun fritters with harissa, just enough for flavor but not too spicy. You can add more or less spice to please your taste buds!
—Teri Rasey, Cadillac, MI

Prep: 20 min. + standing
Cook: 5 min./batch • **Makes:** 6 servings

- 6 cups boiling water
- 3 cups peeled and shredded sweet potatoes, slightly packed (about 2 medium)
- 2 large eggs
- ¼ cup all-purpose flour
- 1 tsp. baking powder
- 1 tsp. cornstarch
- 1 tsp. seasoned salt
- 2 to 3 tsp. harissa
- 1 small onion, grated
- ¼ cup coconut oil
- ½ cup crumbled queso fresco
  Optional: Sliced avocado, sliced tomato and minced fresh cilantro

1. Pour boiling water over sweet potatoes in a large bowl; let stand 20 minutes. Drain, squeezing to remove excess liquid. Pat dry.
2. In a large bowl, whisk the eggs, flour, baking powder, cornstarch, seasoned salt and harissa. Add the sweet potatoes and onion; toss to coat.
3. In a large nonstick skillet, heat 2 Tbsp. coconut oil over medium heat. Working in batches, drop sweet potato mixture by ¼ cupfuls into oil; press slightly to flatten. Fry 1-2 minutes on each side until golden brown; use remaining oil as needed. Drain on paper towels. Serve with queso fresco, and optional ingredients as desired.

2 fritters: 217 cal., 13g fat (10g sat. fat), 69mg chol., 421mg sod., 20g carb. (3g sugars, 2g fiber), 6g pro.

HARISSA SWEET POTATO FRITTERS

MOM'S MACARONI & CHEESE

QUICK PICKLED RADISHES

These pickled radishes are the perfect addition to tacos, barbecue or just about any sandwich you can dream of. Each sliced radish is just a little bit sweet, slightly crunchy and has an amazing amount of zing. You're probably going to want to have a batch in your fridge at all times!
—Colleen Delawder, Herndon, VA

Prep: 25 min. + chilling • **Makes:** 3 cups

- 1 lb. radishes
- ½ cup water
- ½ cup cider vinegar
- ¼ cup sugar
- ¼ cup packed light brown sugar
- 1 Tbsp. mustard seed
- 1 tsp. kosher salt
- 1 tsp. whole peppercorns
- 1 to 2 bay leaves

With a mandoline or vegetable peeler, cut radishes into very thin slices. Place in a 1-qt. jar. In a large saucepan, bring the remaining ingredients to a boil. Carefully ladle the hot liquid over radishes. Cover and refrigerate overnight.

¼ cup: 11 cal., 0 fat (0 sat. fat), 0 chol., 296mg sod., 2g carb. (1g sugars, 1g fiber), 0 pro.

PASTA WITH ASPARAGUS

PASTA WITH ASPARAGUS

Many terrific recipes change hands at the monthly get-togethers of my ladies' bridge group. That's where I discovered this zippy, tempting dish. The garlic, asparagus, Parmesan cheese and red pepper flakes create quite an irresistible taste combination.
—Jean Fisher, Redlands, CA

Takes: 20 min. • **Makes:** 6 servings

- 5 garlic cloves, minced
- ¼ to ½ tsp. crushed red pepper flakes
- 2 to 3 dashes hot pepper sauce
- ¼ cup olive oil
- 1 Tbsp. butter
- 1 lb. fresh asparagus, cut into 1½-in. pieces
  Salt to taste
- ¼ tsp. pepper
- ¼ cup shredded Parmesan cheese
- ½ lb. mostaccioli or elbow macaroni, cooked and drained

In a large cast-iron or other heavy skillet, cook garlic, red pepper flakes and hot pepper sauce in olive oil and butter for 1 minute. Add asparagus, salt and pepper; saute until the asparagus is crisp-tender, 8-10 minutes. Stir in cheese. Pour over hot pasta and toss to coat. Serve immediately.

1 cup: 259 cal., 13g fat (3g sat. fat), 8mg chol., 83mg sod., 30g carb. (2g sugars, 2g fiber), 7g pro.

WARM APPLE & PISTACHIO SPINACH SALAD

The salad started as part of a recipe from a cookbook by Barton Seaver, who was one of the first to push for cooking with sustainable seafood. My tweaks to the original recipe, including adding ricotta, ginger and Dijon, resulted in something amazing. This is a salad worthy of bringing to a dinner party or eating by itself, and it's super quick and easy to make. You could make this into a main course salad by simply adding grilled fish—salmon makes a great pairing.
—Justine Kmiecik, Crestview, FL

Takes: 25 min. • **Makes:** 6 servings

- 3 Tbsp. butter
- 2 cups chopped crisp apples, unpeeled (about 2 medium apples)
- 1 tsp. grated fresh gingerroot
- 1 cup shelled roasted pistachios
- 2 tsp. Dijon mustard
- 1 pkg. (5 oz.) fresh baby spinach
- 1 cup whole-milk ricotta cheese
- 2 Tbsp. honey
  Coarsely ground pepper

1. In a large skillet, melt the butter over medium-high heat. Add apples and ginger; cook and stir until the apples soften and begin to caramelize, 3-5 minutes. Stir in shelled pistachios and Dijon mustard. Reduce heat; simmer for 5 minutes, stirring occasionally.
2. Pour two-thirds of the apple mixture over the spinach. Add spoonfuls of ricotta cheese; top with the remaining apple mixture. Drizzle with honey. Add fresh pepper to taste.

1 serving: 278 cal., 19g fat (8g sat. fat), 32mg chol., 243mg sod., 20g carb. (14g sugars, 4g fiber), 10g pro.

WARM APPLE & PISTACHIO SPINACH SALAD

HEARTY BAKED BEANS
PICTURED ON P. 25

This saucy dish is flavorful and satisfying, loaded with ground beef, bacon and four varieties of beans. I've had this recipe for years, and I make it often to satisfy big appetites at home and for potlucks at work and church.
—Cathy Swancutt, Junction City, OR

Prep: 15 min. • **Bake:** 1 hour
Makes: 18 servings

- 1 lb. ground beef
- 2 large onions, chopped
- ¾ lb. sliced bacon, cooked and crumbled
- 4 cans (15 oz. each) pork and beans
- 1 bottle (18 oz.) honey barbecue sauce
- 1 can (16 oz.) kidney beans, rinsed and drained
- 1 can (15¼ oz.) lima beans, rinsed and drained
- 1 can (15 oz.) black beans, rinsed and drained
- ½ cup packed brown sugar
- 3 Tbsp. cider vinegar
- 1 Tbsp. liquid smoke, optional
- 1 tsp. salt
- ½ tsp. pepper

In a large skillet, cook beef and onions over medium heat until the meat is no longer pink; drain. Transfer to a 5-qt. Dutch oven. Stir in the remaining ingredients. Cover and bake at 350° for 1 hour or until heated through.

¾ cup: 228 cal., 6g fat (2g sat. fat), 18mg chol., 770mg sod., 32g carb. (18g sugars, 4g fiber), 11g pro.

READER REVIEW
"I make this all the time and everyone loves it. Don't be afraid of the amount it makes—it freezes beautifully."
PMEDEMA, TASTEOFHOME.COM

BROCCOLI & APPLE SALAD

Even my picky daughter loves this one! My yogurt dressing on crunchy veggie salad makes a cool and creamy side dish.
—Lynn Cluff, Littlefield, AZ

Takes: 15 min. • **Makes:** 6 servings

- 3 cups small fresh broccoli florets
- 3 medium apples, chopped
- ½ cup chopped mixed dried fruit
- 1 Tbsp. chopped red onion
- ½ cup reduced-fat plain yogurt
- 4 bacon strips, cooked and crumbled

In a large bowl, combine the broccoli, apples, dried fruit and onion. Add yogurt; toss to coat. Sprinkle with the crumbled bacon. Refrigerate until serving.

1 cup: 124 cal., 3g fat (1g sat. fat), 7mg chol., 134mg sod., 22g carb. (17g sugars, 3g fiber), 4g pro. **Diabetic exchanges:** 1½ starch, ½ fat.

GARDEN TOMATO SALAD

For as long as I can remember, my mom made a salad of tomatoes and cucumbers. Now I make it myself whenever tomatoes are within reach.
—Shannon Copley, Upper Arlington, OH

Takes: 15 min. • **Makes:** 8 servings

- 3 large tomatoes, cut into wedges
- 1 large sweet onion, cut into thin wedges
- 1 large cucumber, sliced

DRESSING
- ¼ cup olive oil
- 2 Tbsp. cider vinegar
- 1 garlic clove, minced
- 1 tsp. minced fresh basil
- 1 tsp. minced chives
- ½ tsp. salt

In a large bowl, combine tomatoes, onion and cucumber. In a small bowl, whisk the dressing ingredients until blended. Drizzle over the salad; gently toss to coat. Serve immediately.

1 cup: 92 cal., 7g fat (1g sat. fat), 0 chol., 155mg sod., 7g carb. (5g sugars, 1g fiber), 1g pro. **Diabetic exchanges:** 1½ fat, 1 vegetable.

BROCCOLI & APPLE SALAD

CANNELLINI BAKED BEANS

CRUNCHY ASIAN COLESLAW

This flavor-packed twist on traditional creamy coleslaw is a perfect complement to any Asian-themed meal.
The light, tangy vinaigrette enhances the fresh vegetables.
—Erin Chilcoat, Central Islip, NY

Prep: 15 min. + chilling
Makes: 2 servings

- 1 cup shredded Chinese or napa cabbage
- ½ cup sliced water chestnuts, chopped
- ½ small zucchini, julienned
- 2 Tbsp. chopped green pepper
- 4½ tsp. rice vinegar
- 1 tsp. sugar
- 1 tsp. sesame seeds, toasted
- 1 tsp. reduced-sodium soy sauce
- ½ tsp. sesame oil
  Dash crushed red pepper flakes

In a small bowl, combine the cabbage, water chestnuts, zucchini and green pepper. In another small bowl, whisk the remaining ingredients. Drizzle over salad; toss to coat. Refrigerate for at least 1 hour.
1 cup: 65 cal., 2g fat (0 sat. fat), 0 chol., 120mg sod., 11g carb. (5g sugars, 2g fiber), 2g pro. **Diabetic exchanges:** 2 vegetable.

CANNELLINI BAKED BEANS

My sister developed this recipe after a Christmas holiday. We were still all together but nobody wanted to go to the store, so we made do with what we could find in the pantry and fridge, and it turned out great! This recipe would be good with a combination of beans, too, like half black beans and half white.
—Debra Keil, Owasso, OK

Prep: 25 min. • **Bake:** 20 min.
Makes: 6 servings

- 3 bacon strips, chopped
- 1 medium onion, chopped
- 3 garlic cloves, minced
- 2 cans (15 oz. each) white kidney or cannellini beans, rinsed and drained
- ⅔ cup beer or chicken broth
- ¼ cup packed brown sugar
- 2 Tbsp. balsamic vinegar
- 2 Tbsp. tomato paste
- 1 Tbsp. Dijon mustard
- 1 tsp. Worcestershire sauce
- ¼ tsp. salt
- ¼ tsp. minced fresh thyme or ⅛ tsp. dried thyme
- ⅛ tsp. pepper

1. Preheat oven to 400°. In a 10-in. cast-iron or other ovenproof skillet, cook the bacon over medium heat until crisp, stirring occasionally. Remove with a slotted spoon; drain on paper towels.
2. Cook and stir onion in bacon drippings until tender, 5-6 minutes. Add garlic; cook 1 minute longer. Stir in the remaining ingredients and the reserved bacon; bring to a boil.
3. Place skillet in oven. Bake until mixture is bubbly and sauce is slightly thickened, 20-25 minutes.
⅔ cup: 228 cal., 6g fat (2g sat. fat), 9mg chol., 444mg sod., 34g carb. (12g sugars, 6g fiber), 8g pro.

CRANBERRY-APPLE RED CABBAGE

When I was looking for something new, I started playing with flavors and came up with this tasty and colorful side dish. It's just right served with pork. My German grandmother would be impressed, I think!
—Ann Sheehy, Lawrence, MA

Prep: 15 min. • **Cook:** 3 hours
Makes: 8 servings

- 1 medium head red cabbage, coarsely chopped (8 cups)
- 1 can (14 oz.) whole-berry cranberry sauce
- 2 medium Granny Smith apples, peeled and coarsely chopped
- 1 large white onion, chopped
- ½ cup cider vinegar
- ¼ cup sweet vermouth or white wine, optional
- 1 tsp. kosher salt
- ¾ tsp. caraway seeds
- ½ tsp. coarsely ground pepper

Combine all ingredients; transfer to a 5-qt. slow cooker. Cook, covered, on low for 3-4 hours or until cabbage is tender. Serve with a slotted spoon.
¾ cup: 131 cal., 0 fat (0 sat. fat), 0 chol., 295mg sod., 32g carb. (20g sugars, 4g fiber), 2g pro.

BALSAMIC ZUCCHINI SAUTE

BALSAMIC ZUCCHINI SAUTE

This super fast vegetarian dish is flavorful and only uses a few ingredients, so it's easy to whip up as your entree is cooking.
—Elizabeth Bramkamp, Gig Harbor, WA

Takes: 20 min. • **Makes:** 4 servings

- 1 Tbsp. olive oil
- 3 medium zucchini, cut into thin slices
- ½ cup chopped sweet onion
- ½ tsp. salt
- ½ tsp. dried rosemary, crushed
- ¼ tsp. pepper
- 2 Tbsp. balsamic vinegar
- ⅓ cup crumbled feta cheese

In a large skillet, heat oil over medium-high heat; saute the zucchini and onion until crisp-tender, 6-8 minutes. Stir in the salt, rosemary and pepper. Add vinegar; cook and stir 2 minutes. Top with cheese.
½ cup: 94 cal., 5g fat (2g sat. fat), 5mg chol., 398mg sod., 9g carb. (6g sugars, 2g fiber), 4g pro. **Diabetic exchanges:** 1 vegetable, 1 fat.

CLASSIC RED BEANS & RICE

After 25 years in a place where Cajun cooking is common, we've come to rely on this staple menu item. If you've never tried red beans and rice before, I assure you you'll like this recipe!
—*Jackie Turnage, New Iberia, LA*

Prep: 10 min.
Cook: 2¼ hours + standing
Makes: 8 servings

1   lb. dried kidney beans
8   cups water
1   ham hock
2   bay leaves
1   tsp. onion powder
1   lb. ground beef
1   large onion, chopped
1   tsp. salt
½   tsp. pepper
1   garlic clove, minced
    Hot cooked rice
    Chopped fresh parsley, optional

1. Sort beans and rinse with cold water. Place beans in a Dutch oven; add water to cover by 2 in. Bring to a boil; boil for 2 minutes. Remove from the heat; cover and let stand until beans are softened, 1-4 hours.

2. Drain and rinse beans, discarding liquid. Return to Dutch oven. Add 8 cups water, ham hock, bay leaves and onion powder. Bring to a boil. Reduce heat; cover and simmer for 1 hour.

3. In a large cast-iron or other heavy skillet, cook the beef, onion, salt and pepper over medium heat until meat is no longer pink. Add garlic; cook 1 minute longer. Drain. Add to the bean mixture. Simmer, uncovered, for 1 hour. Discard bay leaves.

4. Remove ham hock; allow to cool. Remove meat from bone; discard bone. Cut meat into bite-sized pieces and return to the broth. Heat through. Serve with rice and, if desired, top with chopped fresh parsley.

1 serving: 309 cal., 7g fat (3g sat. fat), 35mg chol., 346mg sod., 37g carb. (4g sugars, 9g fiber), 25g pro.

TEST KITCHEN TIP
Smoked or cured ham hocks are usually available in your grocer's meat department. If you can't find them, ask your butcher for some leftover ham bones.

CLASSIC RED BEANS & RICE

**GREEN BEAN
PASTA SALAD**

GREEN BEAN PASTA SALAD

I like to prepare this special pasta salad with fresh green beans and homegrown dill. Serve chilled or at room temperature.
—*Chris Snyder, Boulder, CO*

Takes: 30 min. • **Makes:** 10 servings

- 8 oz. uncooked spiral pasta
- 1 lb. fresh green beans, trimmed and cut into 1-in. pieces
- ¼ cup olive oil
- 2 Tbsp. white wine vinegar
- ⅛ tsp. cayenne pepper
- 1 cup cubed fully cooked ham
- 4 green onions, thinly sliced
- 2 Tbsp. minced fresh parsley
- 1 to 2 Tbsp. snipped fresh dill or 1 tsp. dill weed
  Salt to taste
- 1 cup chopped walnuts, toasted

1. Cook pasta according to package directions. Meanwhile, place beans in a large saucepan and cover with water. Bring to a boil; cook, uncovered, until crisp-tender, 8-10 minutes.
2. Drain pasta and beans; rinse in cold water. Place in a large bowl. In a small bowl, whisk the oil, vinegar and cayenne. Drizzle over the pasta mixture and toss to coat.
3. Add ham, onions, parsley, dill and salt; toss to coat. Refrigerate until serving. Stir in walnuts just before serving.
¾ cup: 246 cal., 14g fat (2g sat. fat), 7mg chol., 184mg sod., 22g carb. (2g sugars, 3g fiber), 9g pro.

> **TEST KITCHEN TIP**
> Instead of snapping off the ends of each green bean like Grandma did, trim a bunch in seconds. Gather beans in a small pile, lining up the tips on one side. Cut off tips with a single slice using a chef's knife. Flip the pile over and do the same on the other side.

EDDIE'S FAVORITE FIESTA CORN

EDDIE'S FAVORITE FIESTA CORN

Whenever sweet corn is available, I love making this splurge of a side dish. Frozen corn works, but taste as you go and add sugar if needed.
—*Anthony Bolton, Bellevue, NE*

Prep: 15 min. • **Cook:** 25 min.
Makes: 8 servings

- ½ lb. bacon strips, chopped
- 5 cups fresh or frozen super sweet corn
- 1 medium sweet red pepper, finely chopped
- 1 medium sweet yellow pepper, finely chopped
- 1 pkg. (8 oz.) reduced-fat cream cheese
- ½ cup half-and-half cream
- 1 can (4 oz.) chopped green chiles, optional
- 2 tsp. sugar
- 1 tsp. pepper
- ¼ tsp. salt

1. In a 6-qt. stockpot, cook the bacon over medium heat until crisp, stirring occasionally. Remove with a slotted spoon; drain on paper towels. Discard drippings, reserving 1 Tbsp. in pan.
2. Add the corn, red pepper and yellow pepper to drippings in pan; cook and stir over medium-high heat 5-6 minutes or until tender. Stir in remaining ingredients until blended; bring to a boil. Reduce heat; simmer, covered, 8-10 minutes or until thickened.
⅔ cup: 249 cal., 14g fat (7g sat. fat), 39mg chol., 399mg sod., 22g carb. (9g sugars, 2g fiber), 10g pro.

HERB-BUTTERED BABY CARROTS

The herb butter in this recipe can be used for everything from vegetables to roast chicken, turkey, game hens—let your imagination be your guide!
—Sandra Corey, Caldwell, ID

Prep: 10 min. • **Bake:** 50 min.
Makes: 4 servings

- 1 lb. fresh baby carrots, trimmed
- ¼ cup butter, cubed
- 1 garlic clove, minced
- 1½ tsp. minced fresh parsley or ½ tsp. dried parsley flakes
- ¼ tsp. dried basil
- ⅛ tsp. dried marjoram
- ⅛ tsp. dried oregano
- ⅛ tsp. dried rosemary, crushed
- ⅛ tsp. dried thyme

Preheat oven to 375°. Place carrots in a greased 1½-qt. baking dish. In a microwave, melt the butter; stir in garlic and herbs. Toss with carrots. Bake, covered, until the carrots are tender, 50-60 minutes, stirring once.

1 serving: 143 cal., 12g fat (7g sat. fat), 31mg chol., 180mg sod., 10g carb. (5g sugars, 2g fiber), 1g pro.

MANGO BARLEY SALAD

MANGO BARLEY SALAD

I made this fresh, colorful mango salad on the fly and it was a big hit! The bright flavor is perfect for a spring or summer picnic, served right away or chilled.
—Dan Wellberg, Elk River, MN

Takes: 25 min. • **Makes:** 6 servings

- 1¾ cups water
- 1 cup quick-cooking barley
- 2 medium limes
- ¼ cup olive oil
- 1 Tbsp. Dijon mustard
- 1 Tbsp. honey
- ½ tsp. salt
- ¼ tsp. ground cumin
- ¼ tsp. pepper
- ½ cup chopped sweet red pepper
- ½ cup chopped green pepper
- ¼ cup chopped red onion
- 1 medium mango, peeled and chopped
- ¼ cup minced fresh cilantro

1. In a small saucepan, bring water to a boil. Stir in barley. Reduce heat; simmer, covered, until the barley is tender, 10-12 minutes. Remove from heat; let stand 5 minutes.

2. Finely grate enough zest from limes to measure 1 tsp. Cut limes crosswise in half; squeeze juice from limes. In a small bowl, whisk the lime juice, lime zest, olive oil, mustard, honey, salt, cumin and pepper until blended.

3. In a large bowl, combine the barley, peppers, red onion, mango and cilantro. Add dressing; toss to coat. Refrigerate until serving.

¾ cup: 185 cal., 10g fat (1g sat. fat), 0 chol., 261mg sod., 25g carb. (9g sugars, 5g fiber), 2g pro. **Diabetic exchanges:** 2 fat, 1½ starch.

TEST KITCHEN TIP
You can add fresh pineapple or papaya to this salad, or use one or either of them to replace the mango. And we call for barley, but you can also try making this with quinoa, farro or other grains. It's all going to be delicious!

SPINACH SOUFFLE SIDE DISH

You just can't make an easier, more delicious side dish than this. It's great with beef, pork and lamb, and I especially like serving it for a festive occasion like New Year's Eve.
—Bette Duffy, Kenmore, WA

Prep: 20 min. • **Bake:** 35 min.
Makes: 6 servings

- 2 pkg. (10 oz. each) frozen chopped spinach, thawed and squeezed dry
- 1 pkg. (8 oz.) cream cheese, cubed
- 1½ cups shredded Monterey Jack cheese
- 4 large eggs, lightly beaten
- ¼ cup butter, melted
- 1 garlic clove, minced
- ½ tsp. salt

In a large bowl, combine all ingredients. Transfer to a greased 1½-qt. baking dish. Bake at 350° until edges are lightly browned, 35-40 minutes.

½ cup: 375 cal., 33g fat (20g sat. fat), 228mg chol., 630mg sod., 5g carb. (0 sugars, 3g fiber), 17g pro.

OLD BAY CAULIFLOWER

Ready in 10 minutes, this bowlful of veggies has just three ingredients and a whole lot of flavor. It's the perfect cauliflower side dish.
—Elizabeth Bramkamp, Gig Harbor, WA

Takes: 10 min. • **Makes:** 4 servings

- 1 pkg. (16 oz.) frozen cauliflower
- 1 to 2 Tbsp. butter, melted
- 1 to 2 tsp. seafood seasoning

Prepare cauliflower according to package directions; drain. Drizzle with butter; sprinkle with seafood seasoning.
1 cup: 53 cal., 3g fat (2g sat. fat), 8mg chol., 216mg sod., 5g carb. (3g sugars, 3g fiber), 2g pro. **Diabetic exchanges:** 1 vegetable, ½ fat.

**SPINACH SOUFFLE
SIDE DISH**

MINT WATERMELON SALAD

I invented this refreshing fruit salad one sultry afternoon while my friends were gathered around my pool. It was quick to prepare and disappeared from their plates even quicker. Even the kids loved it!
—Antoinette DuBeck, Huntingdon Valley, PA

Takes: 20 min. • **Makes:** 8 servings

- 6 cups cubed seedless watermelon
- 2 Tbsp. minced fresh mint
- 1 Tbsp. lemon juice
- 1 Tbsp. olive oil
- 2 tsp. sugar

Place watermelon and mint in a large bowl. In a small bowl, whisk lemon juice, oil and sugar until sugar is dissolved. Drizzle over salad; toss gently to combine.
¾ cup: 56 cal., 2g fat (0 sat. fat), 0 chol., 2mg sod., 9g carb. (9g sugars, 1g fiber), 1g pro. **Diabetic exchanges:** ½ fruit.

SEASONED BROWN RICE PILAF

SEASONED BROWN RICE PILAF

For those of us who are white rice lovers at heart, this recipe makes brown rice taste terrific! Everyone takes seconds— it's just that good. To convert it for vegetarians, substitute vegetable broth for the beef broth. And if there are any leftovers, they're ideal as a second meal the next day.
—Amy Berry, Poland, ME

Prep: 10 min. • **Cook:** 55 min.
Makes: 10 servings

- 1 Tbsp. olive oil
- 2 cups uncooked brown rice
- 1 small onion, finely chopped
- 5 cups reduced-sodium beef broth
- 1 Tbsp. dried parsley flakes
- 1 tsp. garlic powder
- 1 tsp. seasoned salt
- ½ tsp. onion powder
- ½ tsp. ground turmeric
- ½ tsp. pepper
- ½ cup uncooked whole wheat orzo pasta

In a Dutch oven, heat oil over medium heat. Add rice and onion; saute until the rice is lightly browned, 8-10 minutes. Add broth; stir in the next 6 ingredients. Bring to a boil. Reduce heat; simmer, covered, for 35 minutes. Add orzo. Cook, covered, until orzo is tender, 10-15 minutes longer.
⅔ cup: 190 cal., 3g fat (0 sat. fat), 3mg chol., 380mg sod., 36g carb. (1g sugars, 4g fiber), 5g pro. **Diabetic exchanges:** 2½ starch, ½ fat.

BROCCOLI WITH GARLIC, BACON & PARMESAN

PICTURED ON P. 25

My approach to broccoli is, cook it slowly in broth so the garlic blends with smoky bacon. A few simple ingredients make ordinary broccoli irresistible.
—Erin Chilcoat, Central Islip, NY

Takes: 30 min. • **Makes:** 8 servings

- 1 tsp. salt
- 2 bunches broccoli (about 3 lbs.), stems removed, cut into florets
- 6 thick-sliced bacon strips, chopped
- 2 Tbsp. olive oil
- 6 to 8 garlic cloves, thinly sliced
- ½ tsp. crushed red pepper flakes
- ¼ cup shredded Parmesan cheese

1. Fill a 6-qt. stockpot two-thirds full with water; add salt and bring to a boil over high heat. In batches, add broccoli and cook until broccoli turns bright green, 2-3 minutes; remove with a slotted spoon.
2. In a large skillet, cook the bacon over medium heat until crisp, stirring occasionally. Remove with a slotted spoon; drain on paper towels. Discard drippings, reserving 1 Tbsp. in pan.
3. Add oil to the drippings; heat over medium heat. Add garlic and pepper flakes; cook and stir until the garlic is fragrant, 2-3 minutes (do not allow to brown). Add broccoli; cook until tender, stirring occasionally. Stir in bacon; sprinkle with cheese.
¾ cup: 155 cal., 10g fat (3g sat. fat), 11mg chol., 371mg sod., 11g carb. (3g sugars, 4g fiber), 8g pro. **Diabetic exchanges:** 2 fat, 1 vegetable.

SOUR CREAM CUCUMBERS

We have a tradition at our house to serve this dish with the other Hungarian specialties my mom learned to make from the women at church. It's especially good during the summer when the cucumbers are freshly picked from the garden.
—Pamela Eaton, Monclova, OH

Prep: 15 min. + chilling
Makes: 8 servings

- ½ cup sour cream
- 3 Tbsp. white vinegar
- 1 Tbsp. sugar
  Pepper to taste
- 4 medium cucumbers, peeled if desired, thinly sliced
- 1 small sweet onion, thinly sliced and separated into rings

In a large bowl, whisk the sour cream, vinegar, sugar and pepper until blended. Add cucumbers and onion; toss to coat.

Refrigerate, covered, at least 4 hours. Serve with a slotted spoon.
¾ cup: 62 cal., 3g fat (2g sat. fat), 10mg chol., 5mg sod., 7g carb. (5g sugars, 2g fiber), 2g pro. **Diabetic exchanges:** 1 vegetable, ½ fat.

Cucumbers with Dill: Omit the first 4 ingredients. Mix ¾ cup white vinegar, ⅓ cup snipped fresh dill, ⅓ cup sugar and ¾ tsp. pepper. Stir in the cucumbers and onion.

TEST KITCHEN TIP
Many grocery store cucumbers are coated with protective wax to prolong freshness. They should be peeled before eating. However, there's no need to peel English cucumbers that are wrapped in plastic instead. Ditto for cukes from the farmers market or your own garden—whether or not to peel these is a simple taste preference.

SPANAKOPITA MASHED POTATOES
PICTURED ON P. 25

I learned to cook by watching my mom in the kitchen. I created this one after trying—and loving—a spinach-topped baked potato. Flecks of red from the potato skin and green from the spinach make these potatoes look festive. And when you leave the potatoes' skins on, you not only keep valuable nutrients, but also save on prep time.
—Ashley Laymon, Lititz, PA

Prep: 10 min. • **Cook:** 25 min.
Makes: 6 servings

- 6 medium red potatoes, quartered
- 1 pkg. (6 oz.) fresh baby spinach
- ¼ cup 2% milk
- 1 Tbsp. butter
- ½ tsp. salt
- ½ tsp. pepper
- ¾ cup crumbled feta cheese

1. Place potatoes in a large saucepan and cover with water. Bring to a boil. Reduce heat; cover and cook for 15-20 minutes or until tender.
2. Meanwhile, in another large saucepan, bring ½ in. of water to a boil. Add the spinach; cover and boil for 3-5 minutes or until wilted. Drain and coarsely chop; keep warm.
3. Drain the potatoes and return them to the saucepan. Add milk, butter, salt and pepper; mash until smooth. Fold in cheese and spinach.
¾ cup: 145 cal., 5g fat (3g sat. fat), 13mg chol., 379mg sod., 20g carb. (2g sugars, 3g fiber), 6g pro. **Diabetic exchanges:** 1 starch, 1 fat.

SOUR CREAM CUCUMBERS

SLOW-COOKER CITRUS CARROTS

STILTON, BACON & GARLIC SMASHED POTATOES

Bold, savory flavor from bacon, Stilton cheese and fresh garlic take mashed potatoes to a whole new level. This side dish is so rich and satisfying, it could almost be eaten as an entree!
—Jamie Brown-Miller, Napa, CA

Prep: 25 min. • **Bake:** 35 min. + cooling
Makes: 8 servings

- 6 garlic cloves
- 1 tsp. olive oil
- 2 lbs. small red potatoes
- ½ cup butter, softened
- 4 oz. cream cheese, softened
- ¼ to ⅓ cup 2% milk
- ½ cup Stilton cheese
- 6 bacon strips, cooked and crumbled
- 3 Tbsp. minced fresh parsley, divided
- 1 tsp. coarsely ground pepper
- ½ tsp. salt

1. Preheat oven to 400°. Cut stem ends off unpeeled garlic cloves. Place cloves on a piece of foil. Drizzle with oil; wrap in foil. Bake until cloves are soft, 35 minutes.
2. Meanwhile, place potatoes in a Dutch oven; add water to cover. Bring to a boil. Reduce the heat; cook, uncovered, until tender, 15-20 minutes.
3. Unwrap garlic cloves; cool 10 minutes. Squeeze the garlic from skins. Mash with a fork.
4. Drain potatoes; return to pan. Coarsely mash potatoes, gradually adding butter, cream cheese, garlic and enough milk to reach desired consistency. Stir in Stilton cheese, bacon, 2 Tbsp. parsley, pepper and salt. Sprinkle with remaining parsley.
⅔ cup: 292 cal., 21g fat (12g sat. fat), 56mg chol., 433mg sod., 20g carb. (2g sugars, 2g fiber), 7g pro.

SLOW-COOKER CITRUS CARROTS

These yummy carrots are so simple to prepare. The recipe is from my mom, who tweaked it a bit to suit her tastes. If you're serving this for a dinner party, you can make it a day in advance and refrigerate until needed. Then just reheat before serving.
—Julie Puderbaugh, Berwick, PA

Prep: 10 min. • **Cook:** 4¼ hours
Makes: 12 servings

- 12 cups frozen sliced carrots (about 48 oz.), thawed
- 1¾ cups orange juice
- ½ cup sugar
- 3 Tbsp. butter, cubed
- ½ tsp. salt
- 3 Tbsp. cornstarch
- ¼ cup cold water
  Minced fresh parsley, optional

1. In a 3- or 4-qt. slow cooker, combine the first 5 ingredients. Cook, covered, on low 4-5 hours or until carrots are tender.
2. In a small bowl, mix the cornstarch and water until smooth; gradually stir into slow cooker. Cook, covered, on high until sauce is thickened, 15-30 minutes. Garnish with fresh parsley, if desired.
¾ cup: 136 cal., 4g fat (2g sat. fat), 8mg chol., 208mg sod., 25g carb. (18g sugars, 5g fiber), 1g pro.

STILTON, BACON & GARLIC
SMASHED POTATOES

Garlic Croutons

Don't settle for bagged croutons to top your salads or soups—make your own!

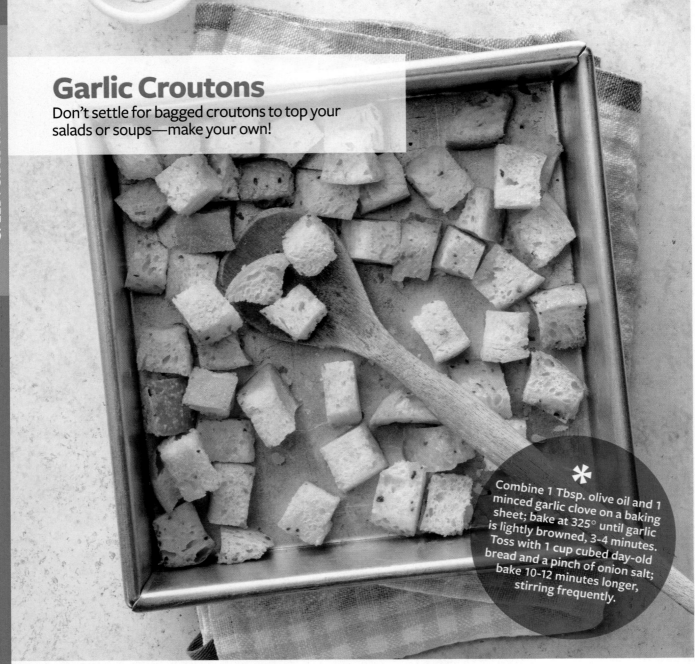

* Combine 1 Tbsp. olive oil and 1 minced garlic clove on a baking sheet; bake at 325° until garlic is lightly browned, 3-4 minutes. Toss with 1 cup cubed day-old bread and a pinch of onion salt; bake 10-12 minutes longer, stirring frequently.

BAKED PARMESAN BROCCOLI

I began making this creamy side dish years ago as a way to get my kids to eat their broccoli. They've since grown up but still request this satisfying casserole. It's truly a family favorite.

—Barbara Uhl, Wesley Chapel, FL

Prep: 30 min. • **Bake:** 15 min.
Makes: 12 servings

- 4 bunches broccoli, cut into florets
- 6 Tbsp. butter, divided
- 1 small onion, finely chopped
- 1 garlic clove, minced
- ¼ cup all-purpose flour
- 2 cups 2% milk
- 1 large egg yolk, beaten
- 1 cup grated Parmesan cheese
- ½ tsp. salt
- ⅛ tsp. pepper
- ½ cup seasoned bread crumbs

1. Preheat oven to 400°. Place half of the broccoli in a steamer basket; place basket in a large saucepan over 1 in. of water. Bring to a boil; cover and steam 3-4 minutes or until crisp-tender. Place broccoli in a greased 13x9-in. baking dish; repeat with the remaining broccoli.

2. Meanwhile, in a small saucepan over medium heat, melt 4 Tbsp. butter. Add onion; cook and stir until tender. Add garlic; cook 1 minute longer.

3. Stir in flour until blended; gradually add milk. Bring to a boil; cook and stir 2 minutes or until thickened. Stir a small amount of hot mixture into the egg yolk; return all to the pan, stirring constantly. Cook and stir 1 minute longer. Remove from heat; stir in the cheese, salt and pepper. Pour over broccoli.

4. In a small skillet, cook bread crumbs in remaining butter until golden brown; sprinkle over the top.

5. Bake, uncovered, 15-18 minutes or until heated through.

¾ cup: 191 cal., 10g fat (5g sat. fat), 41mg chol., 388mg sod., 19g carb. (7g sugars, 6g fiber), 11g pro.

SEASONED OVEN FRIES

For a speedy, health-conscious side dish, these fun wedges are just as tasty as the deep-fried version, but with less fat and much less mess!

—Pat Fredericks, Oak Creek, WI

....

Takes: 25 min. • **Makes:** 2 servings

- 2 medium baking potatoes
- 2 tsp. butter, melted
- 2 tsp. canola oil
- ¼ tsp. seasoned salt
  Minced fresh parsley, optional

1. Preheat oven to 450°. Cut each potato lengthwise in half; cut each piece into 4 wedges. In a large shallow dish, combine the butter, oil and seasoned salt. Add potatoes; turn to coat.

2. Place potatoes in a single layer on a baking sheet coated with cooking spray. Bake until tender, 20-25 minutes, turning once. If desired, sprinkle with parsley.
8 wedges: 263 cal., 9g fat (3g sat. fat), 10mg chol., 242mg sod., 44g carb. (3g sugars, 4g fiber), 4g pro.

READER REVIEW

"I serve this to a very picky group of kids I watch after school and they all love them with or without the potato skin on. From now on, I'll leave it on to save nutrients and time."

GALINTHEWOODS, TASTEOFHOME.COM

SHAVED BRUSSELS SPROUT SALAD

The first time my friends tasted my new side dish, they said it was phenomenal. The longer you let this salad chill in the refrigerator, the more tender the Brussels sprouts will become.

—Nick Iverson, Denver, CO

....

Prep: 20 min. + chilling
Makes: 6 servings

- 1 Tbsp. cider vinegar
- 1 Tbsp. Dijon mustard
- 2 tsp. honey
- 1 small garlic clove, minced
- 2 Tbsp. olive oil
- 1 lb. Brussels sprouts, halved and thinly sliced
- 1 small red onion, halved and thinly sliced
- ⅓ cup dried cherries, chopped
- ⅓ cup chopped pecans, toasted

1. Whisk together the first 4 ingredients; gradually whisk in oil until blended.
2. Place the Brussels sprouts, onion and cherries in a large bowl; toss with dressing. Refrigerate, covered, at least 1 hour. Stir in pecans just before serving.
¾ cup: 156 cal., 9g fat (1g sat. fat), 0 chol., 79mg sod., 18g carb. (10g sugars, 4g fiber), 3g pro. **Diabetic exchanges:** 2 fat, 1 vegetable, ½ starch.

SEASONED OVEN FRIES

INDIAN GINGER POTATOES

This easy potato dish is so flavorful! Make it even faster by cooking the potatoes ahead of time or using leftover potatoes.
—Erin Kelkar, Norcross, GA

Takes: 30 min. • **Makes:** 4 servings

- 4 medium potatoes (about 1½ lbs.), peeled and cut into 1-in. pieces
- 2 Tbsp. canola oil
- 1 medium onion, coarsely chopped
- 1 jalapeno pepper, seeded and finely chopped
- 1 Tbsp. minced fresh gingerroot
- ½ tsp. ground turmeric
- ¼ cup water
- ½ tsp. salt
- ¼ tsp. garlic powder
- ⅛ tsp. cayenne pepper
- 2 Tbsp. chopped fresh cilantro

1. Place the potatoes in a large saucepan; add water to cover. Bring to a boil. Reduce heat; cook, uncovered, until potatoes are tender, 8-12 minutes. Drain.
2. Meanwhile, in a large skillet, heat oil over medium-high heat. Add the onion, jalapeno and ginger; cook and stir until onion is lightly browned, 3-4 minutes. Add turmeric; cook 1 minute longer.
3. Reduce heat to low; add potatoes, water, salt, garlic powder and cayenne pepper. Cook, covered, until potatoes are heated through, 4-6 minutes, stirring occasionally. Sprinkle with chopped cilantro before serving.

¾ cup: 201 cal., 7g fat (1g sat. fat), 0 chol., 301mg sod., 32g carb. (4g sugars, 3g fiber), 3g pro. **Diabetic exchanges:** 2 starch, 1½ fat.

COCONUT LENTILS WITH RICE

COCONUT LENTILS WITH RICE

Years ago I made this recipe for my kids, and they loved it. One of my daughter's friends would always request this dish whenever she came over to visit us. I recommend using basmati rice.
—Diane Donato, Columbus, OH

Prep: 20 min. • **Cook:** 35 min.
Makes: 6 servings

- 1 Tbsp. canola oil
- 6 green onions, chopped
- 1 Tbsp. minced fresh gingerroot
- 2 garlic cloves, minced
- ¼ tsp. crushed red pepper flakes
- 1½ cups dried lentils, rinsed
- 1 tsp. ground turmeric
- ½ tsp. salt
- 5½ cups vegetable stock
- 2 large tomatoes, chopped
- ½ cup flaked coconut
- 2 Tbsp. minced fresh mint
- 3 cups hot cooked rice
- ⅓ cup plain Greek yogurt

1. In a large saucepan, heat canola oil over medium heat; saute green onions, ginger, garlic and pepper flakes until the onions are tender, 2-4 minutes. Stir in lentils, turmeric, salt and stock; bring to a boil. Reduce heat; simmer, covered, until the lentils are tender, 25-30 minutes, stirring occasionally.
2. Stir in tomatoes, coconut and mint. Serve with rice; top with yogurt.

1 serving: 374 cal., 7g fat (4g sat. fat), 3mg chol., 757mg sod., 63g carb. (7g sugars, 7g fiber), 16g pro.

QUICK HARVARD BEETS

We grow beets in our own garden, and they're so good in this recipe. They have such a nice flavor and are very pretty when served.
—*Stella Quade, Carthage, MO*

Takes: 30 min. • **Makes:** 6 servings

- 3 cups sliced raw beets or 2 cans (16 oz. each) sliced beets
- ½ cup sugar
- 1 Tbsp. all-purpose flour
- ½ cup white vinegar
- ½ tsp. salt
- 2 Tbsp. butter

1. In a saucepan, place raw beets and enough water to cover. Cook until tender, 15-20 minutes. Drain, reserving ¼ cup liquid. (If using canned beets, drain and reserve ¼ cup juice.)

2. In another saucepan, combine sugar, flour, white vinegar and reserved beet juice. Cook over low heat until thickened. Stir in beets, salt and butter. Simmer for 10 minutes.

½ cup: 133 cal., 4g fat (2g sat. fat), 10mg chol., 280mg sod., 24g carb. (21g sugars, 2g fiber), 1g pro.

FAST MACARONI SALAD

PICTURED ON P. 25
Chopped veggies give this salad crunch, and cherry tomatoes add vibrant color.
—*Frankiee Bush, Freedom, IN*

Prep: 20 min. + chilling
Makes: 2 servings

- ½ cup uncooked elbow macaroni
- ½ cup quartered cherry tomatoes
- 3 Tbsp. chopped celery
- 3 Tbsp. chopped carrot
- 3 Tbsp. chopped peeled cucumber
- 2 Tbsp. chopped radishes
- ¼ cup fat-free mayonnaise
- ⅛ tsp. salt
- ⅛ tsp. pepper

1. Cook macaroni according to package directions; drain and rinse in cold water. In a small bowl, combine the macaroni and vegetables.

2. In another bowl, combine the mayonnaise, salt and pepper. Pour over the salad and toss to coat. Cover and refrigerate until chilled. Stir before serving.

¾ cup: 107 cal., 2g fat (0 sat. fat), 3mg chol., 408mg sod., 22g carb. (5g sugars, 2g fiber), 3g pro. **Diabetic exchanges:** 1 starch, 1 vegetable.

QUICK HARVARD BEETS

QUICK SOUPS & SANDWICHES

For a weekend lunch or a light dinner, these recipes are quick, tasty and satisfying. Serve them with a salad on the side, or mix and match for a classic soup & sandwich combo—you'll have an amazing meal on the table in no time!

CHICKEN & SPINACH TORTELLINI SOUP

Here's a hearty soup that takes advantage of the convenience of cheese tortellini and rotisserie chicken.

—Charlene Chambers, Ormond Beach, FL

Takes: 25 min. • **Makes:** 8 servings (2 qt.)

- 1½ cups sliced fresh mushrooms
- 2 Tbsp. butter
- 2 garlic cloves, minced
- 4 cans (14½ oz. each) reduced-sodium chicken broth
- 1 pkg. (9 oz.) refrigerated cheese tortellini
- 4 cups shredded rotisserie chicken
- 1 pkg. (6 oz.) fresh baby spinach, coarsely chopped
- ½ tsp. pepper
- 8 tsp. grated Parmesan cheese

1. In a Dutch oven, saute mushrooms in butter until tender. Add garlic; cook 1 minute longer.
2. Add broth and bring to a boil. Stir in tortellini; return to a boil. Cook for 7-9 minutes or until tender, stirring occasionally. Add the chicken, spinach and pepper; cook until spinach is wilted. Sprinkle each serving with 1 tsp. cheese.

1 cup: 287 cal., 12g fat (5g sat. fat), 90mg chol., 1130mg sod., 17g carb. (2g sugars, 1g fiber), 27g pro.

BASIL CHICKEN SANDWICHES

BASIL CHICKEN SANDWICHES

I got the inspiration for this recipe when family members with food allergies were coming to see our new home. For our lunch, I created this chicken sandwich with fresh basil.

—Kerry Durgin Krebs, New Market, MD

Takes: 15 min. • **Makes:** 6 sandwiches

- ½ tsp. pepper
- ¼ tsp. salt
  Dash paprika
- 1 lb. boneless skinless chicken breasts, cut into ½-in. slices
- 6 Tbsp. prepared olive oil vinaigrette salad dressing, divided
- 6 ciabatta rolls, split
- 18 basil leaves
- 1 jar (7 oz.) roasted sweet red peppers, drained
- ¼ cup shredded Romano cheese

1. In a bowl, combine pepper, salt and paprika; sprinkle over the chicken slices. In a nonstick skillet over medium-high heat, cook the chicken in 2 Tbsp. salad dressing for 4-5 minutes on each side or until the chicken is no longer pink.
2. Brush the remaining salad dressing on rolls. Place basil leaves on rolls; top with chicken and red peppers. Sprinkle with Romano cheese.

1 sandwich: 308 cal., 8g fat (2g sat. fat), 45mg chol., 824mg sod., 33g carb. (3g sugars, 2g fiber), 22g pro. **Diabetic exchanges:** 2 starch, 2 lean meat, 1 fat.

CREAM OF CAULIFLOWER SOUP

This mildly cheesy cauliflower soup is a favorite of mine. I make it often in summer, although it's good anytime.
—Karen Brown, West Lafayette, OH

Takes: 20 min.
Makes: 6 servings (1½ qt.)

- ⅓ cup thinly sliced green onions (tops only)
- 2 Tbsp. butter
- 2 Tbsp. all-purpose flour
- ½ tsp. salt
- 2 cups chicken broth
- 2¼ cups frozen cauliflower, thawed and chopped
- 2 cups 1% milk
- 1½ cups shredded reduced-fat cheddar cheese
- 2 Tbsp. dry sherry, optional
- 1 Tbsp. minced chives

1. In a saucepan, saute onions in butter until tender. Stir in the flour and salt until blended. Gradually add broth. Bring to a boil; cook and stir for 2 minutes or until thickened. Reduce heat.
2. Add cauliflower; simmer for 2 minutes. Add milk and cheese; cook and stir until the cheese is melted. Stir in sherry if desired. Garnish with chives.
1 cup: 186 cal., 11g fat (6g sat. fat), 36mg chol., 792mg sod., 10g carb. (6g sugars, 1g fiber), 13g pro.

CREAM OF CAULIFLOWER SOUP

ULTIMATE PASTRAMI SANDWICHES

This peerless pastrami sandwich was adapted from a menu favorite at Primanti Bros. Restaurant in Pittsburgh. Its marketing office graciously shared the basic ingredients: grilled cold cuts, cheese, fried potatoes and tomatoes— all stacked between slices of chewy Italian bread. From there, we created this faithful copy, which includes our version of the secret coleslaw topping.
—Taste of Home *Test Kitchen*

Prep: 25 min. + standing • **Bake:** 5 min.
Makes: 4 servings

- ½ cup sugar, divided
- ½ cup cider vinegar, divided
- 4 cups shredded cabbage
- 3½ cups frozen waffle-cut fries
- ¼ tsp. salt
- ¼ tsp. celery seed
- ¼ tsp. pepper
- 1 lb. sliced deli pastrami
- 4 slices provolone cheese
- 8 slices Italian bread (¾ in. thick), toasted
- 2 medium tomatoes, thinly sliced

1. In a large bowl, combine ¼ cup sugar and ¼ cup vinegar; add the cabbage and toss to coat. Cover and let stand for 30 minutes. Meanwhile, bake the fries according to package directions.
2. Drain the cabbage. In a small bowl, combine the salt, celery seed, pepper and the remaining sugar and vinegar; pour over cabbage and toss to coat.
3. On an ungreased baking sheet, divide the pastrami into 4 stacks; top each with cheese. Bake at 450° for 2-3 minutes or until the cheese is melted. Place pastrami on 4 toast slices. Layer with fries, coleslaw, tomato slices and the remaining toast. Serve immediately.
1 sandwich: 586 cal., 17g fat (7g sat. fat), 80mg chol., 1655mg sod., 72g carb. (18g sugars, 6g fiber), 36g pro.

FIESTA SWEET POTATO SOUP
PICTURED ON P. 51

Here's a simple soup with plenty of taste and just a little heat. Loaded with sweet potatoes, black beans and sausage, it tastes even better the next day—if you have leftovers, that is!
—Gilda Lester, Millsboro, DE

Takes: 30 min.
Makes: 6 servings (2¼ qt.)

1   pkg. (9 oz.) fully cooked spicy chicken sausage links, chopped
2   medium sweet potatoes, peeled and cubed
1   large onion, chopped
1   small green pepper, diced
2   Tbsp. olive oil
2   tsp. ground cumin
2   cans (14½ oz. each) reduced-sodium chicken broth
1   can (14½ oz.) diced tomatoes with mild green chiles, undrained
1   can (15 oz.) black beans, rinsed and drained
2   Tbsp. minced fresh cilantro
    Sour cream
    Thinly sliced green onions

1.   In a large saucepan, saute sausage, sweet potatoes, onion and pepper in oil until the onion is tender. Add cumin; cook 1 minute longer. Stir in the broth, tomatoes and beans. Bring to a boil. Reduce heat; cover and simmer for 10 minutes or until potatoes are tender.
2.   Stir in the cilantro. Garnish individual servings with sour cream and green onions.
1½ cups: 247 cal., 8g fat (2g sat. fat), 33mg chol., 1036mg sod., 29g carb. (11g sugars, 6g fiber), 15g pro.

CRANBERRY SALSA TURKEY WRAPS

CRANBERRY SALSA TURKEY WRAPS

Once your family tastes these mouthwatering roll-ups, they'll never look at leftover turkey in the same way! The cranberry salsa combines both sweet and spicy flavors.
—Elke Rose, Waukesha, WI

Prep: 25 min. + chilling
Makes: 6 servings

2   cups fresh cranberries, coarsely chopped
¼   cup sugar
¼   cup sliced green onions
1   Tbsp. minced fresh cilantro
1   Tbsp. lime juice
1   jalapeno pepper, seeded and chopped
¼   tsp. grated fresh gingerroot
¾   cup spreadable cream cheese
6   flour tortillas (8 in.), room temperature
3   cups shredded cooked turkey
6   lettuce leaves

1.   In a small bowl, combine cranberries, sugar, onions, cilantro, lime juice, jalapeno pepper and ginger. Cover and refrigerate for 1 hour.
2.   Just before serving, spread 2 Tbsp. of cream cheese over each tortilla. Top with 3-4 Tbsp. cranberry salsa, ½ cup turkey and a lettuce leaf; roll up.
1 wrap: 418 cal., 17g fat (9g sat. fat), 83mg chol., 400mg sod., 40g carb. (12g sugars, 2g fiber), 27g pro.

LAUREN'S BOUILLABAISSE

This golden soup is brimming with an assortment of tender seafood and is paired with savory, colorful sourdough toast with spread.
—Lauren Covas, New Brunswick, NJ

Prep: 30 min. • **Cook:** 20 min.
Makes: 12 servings (5 qt.)

- ⅔ cup chopped roasted sweet red pepper, drained
- ¼ cup reduced-fat mayonnaise

TOASTS
- 6 slices sourdough bread
- 1 garlic clove, halved

BOUILLABAISSE
- 1 medium onion, chopped
- 1 Tbsp. olive oil
- 2 garlic cloves, minced
- 2 plum tomatoes, chopped
- ½ tsp. saffron threads or 2 tsp. ground turmeric
- 3½ cups cubed red potatoes
- 2½ cups thinly sliced fennel bulb
- 1 carton (32 oz.) reduced-sodium chicken broth
- 3 cups clam juice
- 2 tsp. dried tarragon
- 24 fresh littleneck clams
- 24 fresh mussels, scrubbed and beards removed
- 1 lb. red snapper fillet, cut into 2-in. pieces
- ¾ lb. uncooked large shrimp, peeled and deveined
- ¼ cup minced fresh parsley

1. Place red pepper and mayonnaise in a food processor; cover and process until smooth. Refrigerate until serving.

2. For toasts, rub 1 side of each bread slice with garlic; discard the garlic. Cut bread slices in half. Place on an ungreased baking sheet. Bake at 400° for 4-5 minutes on each side or until lightly browned.

3. In a stockpot, saute onion in oil until tender. Add garlic; cook 1 minute longer. Reduce heat; stir in tomatoes and saffron. Add the potatoes, fennel, broth, clam juice and tarragon. Bring to a boil. Reduce heat; simmer, uncovered, for 10-12 minutes or until the potatoes are almost tender.

4. Add the clams, mussels, snapper and shrimp. Cook, stirring occasionally, for 10-15 minutes or until the clams and mussels open and the fish flakes easily with a fork. Discard any unopened clams or mussels.

5. Spoon into bowls; sprinkle with parsley. Spread pepper mayo over toasts; serve with bouillabaisse.

1⅔ cups with 2 tsp. spread on ½ slice of bread: 239 cal., 5g fat (1g sat. fat), 70mg chol., 684mg sod., 23g carb. (3g sugars, 2g fiber), 24g pro. **Diabetic exchanges:** 3 lean meat, 1½ starch, ½ fat.

LAUREN'S BOUILLABAISSE

SANTA FE CHIPOTLE CHILI

BLACK BEAN RICE BURGERS

A salsa and sour cream sauce helps dress up these filling vegetarian burgers. My fiance, a confirmed meat-and-potatoes man, loves these sandwiches and asks for them often.
—Laura Wimbrow, Ocean City, MD

....

Takes: 20 min. • **Makes:** 4 burgers

- 1   small onion, very finely chopped
- 2   Tbsp. vegetable oil, divided
- 1   can (15 oz.) black beans, rinsed and drained
- 1   cup cooked brown rice
- ¼   cup dry bread crumbs
- 2   large egg yolks, lightly beaten
- 2   Tbsp. plus ¼ cup salsa, divided
- ½   tsp. salt
- ¼   tsp. pepper
- ¼   cup reduced-fat sour cream
- 4   lettuce leaves
- 4   slices reduced-fat cheddar cheese (1 oz. each)
- 4   hamburger buns, split
     Optional: Sliced tomato and sliced red onion

1. In a large nonstick skillet, cook the onion in 1 Tbsp. oil over medium heat until translucent but not browned, 2-4 minutes; remove from heat and set aside.
2. In bowl of food processor fitted with blade attachment, pulse half the beans and rice until mixture forms a thick paste.
3. In a large bowl, combine processed bean mixture, the remaining black beans and rice, onion, bread crumbs, egg yolks, 2 Tbsp. salsa, salt and pepper; mix well with hands, squeezing until the mixture holds together. Form bean mixture into 4 patties. Cook burgers over medium heat in the remaining 1 Tbsp. oil until firm and browned, 4-5 minutes on each side.
4. In a small bowl, combine sour cream and the remaining salsa. To assemble, place lettuce leaf, burger, cheese and sour cream mixture on bun. If desired, also add sliced tomato and red onion.
1 burger: 482 cal., 18g fat (6g sat. fat), 101mg chol., 1070mg sod., 55g carb. (7g sugars, 6g fiber), 21g pro.

SANTA FE CHIPOTLE CHILI

Sausage and ground beef make this spiced chili a meat lover's delight. Plus, I can freeze and reheat it later without sacrificing any of the flavor.
—Angela Spengler, Niceville, FL

....

Prep: 15 min. • **Cook:** 35 min.
Makes: 8 servings (3 qt.)

- 1   lb. ground beef
- 1   lb. bulk pork sausage
- 1   medium onion, chopped
- 2   cans (14½ oz. each) diced tomatoes, undrained
- 2   cans (15 oz. each) tomato sauce
- 2   cans (16 oz. each) kidney beans, rinsed and drained
- 1   cup frozen corn
- ¼   cup canned diced jalapeno peppers
- ¼   cup chili powder
- 1   chipotle pepper in adobo sauce, finely chopped
- 1   tsp. salt
     Optional toppings: Sour cream, shredded Monterey Jack cheese and crushed tortilla chips

1. In a 6-qt. stockpot, cook beef, sausage and onion over medium heat 8-10 minutes or until the beef and sausage are no longer pink and the onion is tender, breaking the beef and sausage into crumbles; drain.
2. Add the tomatoes, tomato sauce, beans, corn, jalapeno peppers, chili powder, chipotle pepper and salt. Bring to a boil. Reduce heat; simmer, covered, for 20-25 minutes or until heated through. Serve with toppings as desired.
1½ cups: 419 cal., 21g fat (6g sat. fat), 66mg chol., 1646mg sod., 36g carb. (8g sugars, 11g fiber), 27g pro.

SANTA FE CHIPOTLE CHILI

COBB SALAD SUB

When we need a quick meal to share, we turn Cobb salad into a sandwich masterpiece. Sometimes I substitute tortillas for the bread and make wraps instead.
—Kimberly Grusendorf, Medina, OH

Takes: 15 min. • **Makes:** 12 servings

- 1 loaf (1 lb.) unsliced Italian bread
- ½ cup balsamic vinaigrette or dressing of your choice
- 5 oz. fresh baby spinach (about 6 cups)
- 1½ lbs. sliced deli ham
- 4 hard-boiled large eggs, finely chopped
- 8 bacon strips, cooked and crumbled
- ½ cup crumbled Gorgonzola cheese
- 1 cup cherry tomatoes, chopped

Cut loaf of bread in half lengthwise; hollow out top and bottom, leaving a ¾-in. shell (discard the removed bread or save for another use). Brush vinaigrette over bread halves. Layer spinach, ham, eggs, bacon, cheese and tomatoes on bread bottom. Replace top. Cut loaf in half lengthwise from top to bottom; cut crosswise 5 times to make 12 pieces.

1 slice: 233 cal., 10g fat (3g sat. fat), 97mg chol., 982mg sod., 17g carb. (3g sugars, 1g fiber), 18g pro.

CHICKEN WILD RICE SOUP WITH SPINACH

I stir together this creamy chicken soup whenever we're craving something warm and comforting. Reduced-fat and reduced-sodium ingredients make it a healthier option.
—Deborah Williams, Peoria, AZ

Prep: 10 min. • **Cook:** 5¼ hours
Makes: 6 servings (about 2 qt.)

- 3 cups water
- 1 can (14½ oz.) reduced-sodium chicken broth
- 1 can (10¾ oz.) reduced-fat reduced-sodium condensed cream of chicken soup, undiluted
- ⅔ cup uncooked wild rice
- 1 garlic clove, minced
- ½ tsp. dried thyme
- ½ tsp. pepper
- ¼ tsp. salt
- 3 cups cubed cooked chicken breast
- 2 cups fresh baby spinach

1. In a 3-qt. slow cooker, mix the first 8 ingredients until blended. Cook, covered, on low 5-7 hours or until rice is tender.
2. Stir in chicken and spinach. Cook, covered, on low until heated through, about 15 minutes longer.

1¼ cups: 212 cal., 3g fat (1g sat. fat), 56mg chol., 523mg sod., 19g carb. (4g sugars, 2g fiber), 25g pro. **Diabetic exchanges:** 3 lean meat, 1 starch.

COBB SALAD SUB

BANH MI BURGER

PICTURED ON P. 51

I love burgers cooked in a cast-iron pan, and banh mi sandwiches are delicious, so why not combine the two? You can make your own banh mi burger sauce with Sriracha, mayonnaise, lime juice, fish sauce and sugar.
—Jessica Thompson, Manor, TX

Prep: 15 min. • **Cook:** 20 min.
Makes: 4 servings

- ½ cup water
- ½ cup white vinegar
- ¼ cup sugar
- 1 tsp. salt, divided
- 1 large carrot, julienned
- ½ medium daikon radish, julienned
- 1 lb. ground beef
- ⅛ tsp. pepper
- 4 kaiser rolls, split
- ½ cup Sriracha mayonnaise
- ½ medium cucumber, thinly sliced
- 8 sprigs fresh cilantro

1. In a small saucepan, combine water, vinegar, sugar and ½ tsp. salt. Bring to a boil; whisk until sugar is dissolved. Remove from heat. Add carrots and radish; let stand until serving.
2. Shape beef into four ¾-in.-thick patties. Sprinkle with pepper and the remaining ½ tsp. salt.
3. In a 12-in. cast-iron or another heavy skillet, cook the burgers over medium heat until a thermometer reads 160°, 8-10 minutes on each side. Remove and keep warm. Wipe pan clean.
4. In same pan, toast rolls over medium heat, cut side down, 30-60 seconds. Spread rolls with mayonnaise. Drain pickled vegetables. Serve the burgers on rolls with the pickled vegetables, cucumber and cilantro.
1 burger: 576 cal., 36g fat (8g sat. fat), 72mg chol., 858mg sod., 36g carb. (5g sugars, 3g fiber), 27g pro.

UPSTATE MINESTRONE SOUP

If you love vegetables, you'll find this minestrone especially satisfying. Keep the recipe in mind when you have a bounty of fresh garden produce.
—Yvonne Krantz, Mount Upton, NY

Prep: 25 min. • **Cook:** 1½ hours
Makes: 8 servings

- 1 lb. Italian sausage links, cut into ½-in. slices
- 1 Tbsp. olive oil
- 1 cup finely chopped onion
- 1 cup sliced fresh carrots
- 1 garlic clove, finely minced
- 1 tsp. dried basil
- 2 cups shredded cabbage
- 2 small zucchini, sliced
- 2 cans (10½ oz. each) condensed beef broth, undiluted or 3 beef bouillon cubes plus 1½ cups water
- 1 can (14½ oz.) diced tomatoes, undrained
- ¼ tsp. salt
- ¼ tsp. pepper
- 1 can (15½ oz.) great northern beans, rinsed and drained
  Minced fresh parsley

1. In a Dutch oven, brown the sausage in oil. Add onion, carrots, garlic and basil; cook for 5 minutes. Stir in the cabbage, zucchini, broth, tomatoes, salt and pepper. Bring to a boil. Reduce heat; cover and simmer for 1 hour.
2. Add beans; cook 20 minutes longer. Garnish with parsley.
Freeze option: Freeze cooled soup in freezer containers. To use, partially thaw in refrigerator overnight. Heat through in a saucepan, stirring occasionally; add a little broth or water if necessary.
1 serving: 236 cal., 14g fat (4g sat. fat), 31mg chol., 1329mg sod., 16g carb. (4g sugars, 5g fiber), 12g pro.

Tres Magnifique!

This elegant soup actually requires little prep work; the magic is in delicious ingredients, simply cooked!

Tips for Making Perfect French Onion Soup

CLASSIC FRENCH ONION SOUP

Enjoy my signature soup the way my granddaughter Becky does: I make it for her in a French onion soup bowl complete with garlic croutons and gobs of melted Swiss cheese on top.
—Lou Sansevero, Ferron, UT

Prep: 20 min. • **Cook:** 2 hours
Makes: 12 servings (2¼ qt.)

- 5 Tbsp. olive oil, divided
- 1 Tbsp. butter
- 8 cups thinly sliced onions (about 3 lbs.)
- 3 garlic cloves, minced
- ½ cup port wine
- 2 cartons (32 oz. each) beef broth
- ½ tsp. pepper
- ¼ tsp. salt
- 24 slices French bread baguette (½ in. thick)
- 2 large garlic cloves, peeled and halved
- ¾ cup shredded Gruyere or Swiss cheese

1. In a Dutch oven, heat 2 Tbsp. oil and the butter over medium heat. Add onions; cook and stir until softened, 10-13 minutes. Reduce the heat to medium-low; cook, stirring occasionally, until deep golden brown, 30-40 minutes. Add minced garlic; cook 2 minutes longer.
2. Stir in the wine. Bring to a boil; cook until liquid is reduced by half. Add the broth, pepper and salt; return to a boil. Reduce heat. Simmer, covered, stirring occasionally, for 1 hour.
3. Meanwhile, preheat oven to 400°. Place baguette slices on a baking sheet; brush both sides with the remaining oil. Bake until toasted, 3-5 minutes on each side. Rub toasts with halved garlic.
4. To serve, place twelve 8-oz. broiler-safe bowls or ramekins on baking sheets; place 2 toasts in each. Ladle with soup; top with cheese. Broil 4 in. from heat until cheese is melted.

¾ cup soup with 1 slice bread and 1 Tbsp. cheese: 172 cal., 9g fat (3g sat. fat), 10mg chol., 773mg sod., 16g carb. (3g sugars, 1g fiber), 6g pro.

1. Use lots of onions
Don't skimp on the onions! It might look like too many, but they'll cook down during caramelizing.

2. Choose the right wine
A hearty, full-bodied wine adds complex flavor. Port pairs well with onion and Gruyere cheese.

3. Flavor the toast
Scraping garlic over the bread slices adds another layer of flavor.

4-6. Bread on top? Sure!
Ladling the soup over the bread keeps it moist. If you prefer a crunchy topping, top soup with the baguette slices and cheese, then broil.

HAVARTI TURKEY HERO

This is not your ordinary sandwich! Everyone loves the combination of chutney and chopped peanuts. I like to make this when I have company in the afternoon or at night after a game of cards.
—Agnes Ward, Stratford, ON

Takes: 15 min. • **Makes:** 8 servings

- ⅓ cup mango chutney
- 2 Tbsp. reduced-fat mayonnaise
- 2 Tbsp. chopped unsalted peanuts
  Dash cayenne pepper
- 1 loaf (1 lb.) French bread, halved lengthwise
- ¾ lb. thinly sliced deli turkey
- 6 lettuce leaves
- 2 oz. thinly sliced Havarti cheese
- 1 medium Red Delicious apple, cored and cut into thin rings

In a small bowl, combine the chutney, mayonnaise, peanuts and cayenne; spread evenly over the cut side of bread bottom. Layer with turkey, lettuce, cheese and apple. Replace bread top. Cut into 8 slices.
1 serving: 302 cal., 7g fat (2g sat. fat), 27mg chol., 973mg sod., 45g carb. (9g sugars, 2g fiber), 16g pro. **Diabetic exchanges:** 3 starch, 1 lean meat, ½ fat.

CREAMY WHITE CHILI

When I was a child, white beans were a staple at our table. My husband, Bill, also loves them. Our four children, six grandchildren and one great-grandchild are not as fond of beans, but they still enjoy this tempting chili! You can make a shortcut version of this soup by using canned beans and skipping the soaking stage, but I prefer dried.
—Gloria Hutchings, Troy, MI

Prep: 20 min. + standing • **Cook:** 1 hour
Makes: 10 servings (2½ qt.)

- 1 lb. dried navy beans
- 1 medium onion, chopped
- 2 garlic cloves, minced
- 1 Tbsp. canola oil
- 1 can (10¾ oz.) condensed cream of chicken soup, undiluted
- 1 can (10¾ oz.) condensed cream of celery soup, undiluted
- 1 cup water
- 1 medium potato, peeled and cubed
- 2 Tbsp. chili powder
- 1 tsp. chicken bouillon granules
- ½ tsp. salt
- 1½ cups half-and-half cream
- 1 can (15 oz.) garbanzo beans or chickpeas, rinsed and drained

1. Place navy beans in a Dutch oven or soup kettle; add water to cover by 2 in. Bring to a boil; boil for 2 minutes. Remove from the heat; cover and let stand for 1 hour. Drain beans, discarding liquid; return beans to pan. Add water to cover by 2 in. Bring to a boil; cover and simmer until beans are tender, about 45 minutes. Drain beans, discarding liquid; set the beans aside.
2. In the same Dutch oven, saute onion and garlic in oil until tender. Add soups, 1 cup water, potato, chili powder, bouillon and salt; cover and cook over medium-low heat for 10 minutes.
3. Add cream, garbanzo beans and navy beans. Cook over medium heat until heated through (do not boil), about 10 minutes.
1 cup: 331 cal., 10g fat (4g sat. fat), 22mg chol., 779mg sod., 46g carb. (6g sugars, 14g fiber), 15g pro.

HAVARTI TURKEY HERO

CREAMY CHICKEN CORN CHOWDER

My 10-year-old son helped me create this recipe! It's the perfect way to enjoy a home-cooked meal in record time.
—Terrie Sowders, Carthage, IN

Prep: 10 min. • **Cook:** 25 min.
Makes: 2 servings

- 1 cup chicken broth
- ⅔ cup cubed peeled potato
- ½ cup frozen corn
- ¼ tsp. minced garlic
- ⅛ tsp. dried marjoram
- ⅛ tsp. dried thyme
- ⅛ tsp. pepper
- 2 Tbsp. all-purpose flour
- ⅔ cup 2% milk
- 2 oz. Velveeta, cubed
- ⅔ cup cubed cooked chicken breast

1. In a large saucepan, combine the broth, potato, corn, garlic, marjoram, thyme and pepper. Bring to a boil. Reduce heat; cover and simmer until potatoes are tender, 15-20 minutes.

2. Combine flour and milk until smooth; gradually add to the vegetable mixture. Bring to a boil; cook and stir until slightly thickened, about 2 minutes. Reduce heat; stir in the cheese until melted. Add the chicken; heat through.

1½ cups: 317 cal., 11g fat (6g sat. fat), 73mg chol., 926mg sod., 31g carb. (7g sugars, 2g fiber), 24g pro.

SLOW-COOKED CHICKEN CAESAR WRAPS

SLOW-COOKED CHICKEN CAESAR WRAPS

I first created this recipe for our daughter who loves Caesar salads. It's such an easy meal—perfect for vacations when you'd rather be outside than inside cooking.
—Christine Hadden, Whitman, MA

Prep: 10 min. • **Cook:** 3 hours
Makes: 6 servings

- 1½ lbs. boneless skinless chicken breast halves
- 2 cups chicken broth
- ¾ cup creamy Caesar salad dressing
- ½ cup shredded Parmesan cheese
- ¼ cup minced fresh parsley
- ½ tsp. pepper
- 6 flour tortillas (8 in.)
- 2 cups shredded lettuce
- Optional: Salad croutons, cooked crumbled bacon and additional shredded Parmesan cheese

1. Place the chicken and broth in a 1½- or 3-qt. slow cooker. Cook, covered, on low 3-4 hours or until a thermometer inserted in chicken reads 165°. Remove chicken and discard cooking juices. Shred chicken with 2 forks; return to slow cooker.

2. Stir in dressing, Parmesan, parsley and pepper; heat through. Serve in tortillas with lettuce and, if desired, salad croutons, crumbled bacon and additional shredded Parmesan cheese.

1 wrap: 476 cal., 25g fat (5g sat. fat), 81mg chol., 1089mg sod., 29g carb. (1g sugars, 2g fiber), 31g pro.

STEAK SANDWICHES WITH QUICK-PICKLED VEGETABLES

This recipe is a Cambodian version of the classic Vietnamese banh mi. This sandwich has acidity from the pickled vegetables, freshness from the cucumber, spiciness from the Sriracha mayo and sweetness from the marinated beef.
—Hudson Stiver, Bowen Island, BC

Prep: 30 min. + marinating
Cook: 15 min. + standing
Makes: 6 servings

- 1 cup white vinegar
- 1 Tbsp. sugar
- 1½ cups thinly sliced fresh carrots
- 1 small daikon radish, thinly sliced
- ¼ cup packed brown sugar
- ¼ cup rice vinegar
- ¼ cup soy sauce
- 1 beef top sirloin steak (1¼ lbs.)
- 1 Tbsp. olive oil
- 1 French bread baguette (10½ oz.), halved lengthwise
- ½ cup mayonnaise
- 2 Tbsp. Sriracha chili sauce
- ½ cup thinly sliced English cucumber
  Fresh cilantro leaves

1. In a large bowl, whisk white vinegar and sugar until sugar is dissolved. Add carrots and radish. Refrigerate at least 2 hours. Meanwhile, in a shallow dish, combine brown sugar, rice vinegar and soy sauce. Add beef and turn to coat. Refrigerate 1 hour, turning once.

2. Drain beef, discarding marinade. In a large cast-iron or other heavy skillet, heat oil over medium-high heat. Cook steak until meat reaches desired doneness (for medium-rare, a thermometer should read 135°; medium, 140°; medium-well, 145°), 7-10 minutes on each side. Let rest 10 minutes before slicing.

3. Meanwhile, place baguette on an ungreased baking sheet, cut sides up. Broil 3-4 in. from heat until golden brown, 3-4 minutes.

4. Drain carrots and radish, reserving 1½ tsp. vinegar marinade. In a small bowl, combine the mayonnaise, chili sauce and reserved vinegar marinade; spread half over cut sides of baguette. Top with steak, cucumber, pickled vegetables and cilantro; replace top. Cut crosswise into 6 slices. Serve with remaining mayonnaise mixture.

1 sandwich: 430 cal., 20g fat (4g sat. fat), 40mg chol., 888mg sod., 37g carb. (9g sugars, 2g fiber), 25g pro.

STEAK SANDWICHES WITH QUICK-PICKLED VEGETABLES

FENNEL CARROT SOUP

FENNEL CARROT SOUP

This smooth, richly colored soup is elegant enough to serve as the first course of a formal Christmas dinner— but it's so easy to make, why not dish it up when there's nothing special about the date at all? The fennel seed and curry complement the carrots, apple and sweet potato.
—Marlene Bursey, Waverly, NS

Prep: 10 min. • **Cook:** 45 min.
Makes: 8 servings

- 1 Tbsp. butter
- ½ tsp. fennel seed
- 1½ lbs. carrots, sliced
- 1 medium sweet potato, peeled and cubed
- 1 medium apple, peeled and cubed
- 3 cans (14½ oz. each) vegetable broth
- 2 Tbsp. uncooked long grain rice
- 1 bay leaf
- ¼ tsp. curry powder
- 1 Tbsp. lemon juice
- ½ tsp. salt
- ¼ tsp. white pepper
- 2 Tbsp. minced fresh parsley

1. In a large saucepan, melt butter over medium-high heat. Add fennel; cook and stir 2-3 minutes or until lightly toasted. Add carrots, sweet potato and apple; cook and stir 5 minutes longer.
2. Stir in broth, rice, bay leaf and curry powder; bring to a boil. Reduce heat; simmer, covered, 30 minutes or until the vegetables and rice are soft.
3. Remove from the heat; cool slightly. Discard bay leaf. Process in batches in a blender until smooth; return to pan.
4. Stir in the lemon juice, salt and pepper. Cook over medium heat 5 minutes or until heated through, stirring occasionally. Sprinkle with parsley.
1 cup: 117 cal., 2g fat (1g sat. fat), 4mg chol., 989mg sod., 23g carb. (0 sugars, 3g fiber), 3g pro. **Diabetic exchanges:** 2 vegetable, 1 starch.

GRILLED CHEESE STEAKHOUSE BURGER

GRILLED CHEESE STEAKHOUSE BURGER

My husband loves both my grilled cheese and my iron-skillet burgers, so one night I decided to combine them. He said it was the best burger he ever ate!
—Lisa Allen, Joppa, AL

Prep: 35 min. • **Cook:** 25 min.
Makes: 4 servings

- 1 lb. lean ground beef (90% lean)
- 2 Tbsp. Worcestershire sauce
- 1 tsp. garlic powder
- ½ tsp. salt
- ¼ tsp. pepper
- 1 Tbsp. liquid smoke, optional
- 1 Tbsp. olive oil
- 5 Tbsp. butter, softened, divided
- 1 large onion, thinly sliced
- 16 slices American cheese
- 16 slices sandwich bread

1. In a large bowl, combine the beef, Worcestershire sauce, garlic powder, salt, pepper and liquid smoke if desired, mixing lightly but thoroughly. Shape into four 4-in. square patties.
2. In a large nonstick skillet, cook the burgers in oil over medium heat until a thermometer reads 160°, 4-5 minutes on each side. Remove and keep warm.
3. In the same skillet, heat 1 Tbsp. butter over medium-high heat. Add onion; cook and stir until tender, 6-8 minutes. Remove and keep warm. Place cheese on 8 bread slices; top with remaining bread. Spread outsides of sandwiches with the remaining 4 Tbsp. butter.
4. In the same skillet, toast sandwiches over medium heat until golden brown and the cheese is melted, 1-2 minutes on each side. Top 4 sandwiches with burgers and onions. Top with remaining sandwiches.
1 sandwich: 900 cal., 50g fat (27g sat. fat), 129mg chol., 1954mg sod., 56g carb. (12g sugars, 3g fiber), 47g pro.

SLOW-COOKER MEATBALL SANDWICHES

Our approach to meatball sandwiches is a simple one: Cook the meatballs low and slow, load them into hoagie buns, and top them with provolone and pepperoncini.
—Stacie Nicholls, Spring Creek, NV

Prep: 5 min. • **Cook:** 3 hours
Makes: 8 servings

- 2 pkg. (12 oz. each) frozen fully cooked Italian meatballs, thawed
- 2 jars (24 oz. each) marinara sauce
- 8 hoagie buns, split
- 8 slices provolone cheese
  Sliced pepperoncini, optional

1. Place meatballs and sauce in a 3- or 4-qt. slow cooker. Cook, covered, on low for 3-4 hours or until the meatballs are heated through.
2. On each bun bottom, layer cheese, meatballs and, if desired, pepperoncini; replace tops.

1 sandwich: 526 cal., 20g fat (7g sat. fat), 93mg chol., 1674mg sod., 55g carb. (15g sugars, 4g fiber), 32g pro.

BROCCOLI BEER CHEESE SOUP

BROCCOLI BEER CHEESE SOUP

Whether you include the beer or not, this soup tastes wonderful. I always make extra and pop individual servings into the freezer.
—Lori Lee, Brooksville, FL

Prep: 20 min. • **Cook:** 30 min.
Makes: 10 servings (2½ qt.)

- 3 Tbsp. butter
- 5 celery ribs, finely chopped
- 3 medium carrots, finely chopped
- 1 small onion, finely chopped
- 4 cups fresh broccoli florets, chopped
- ¼ cup chopped sweet red pepper
- 4 cans (14½ oz. each) chicken broth
- ½ tsp. pepper
- ½ cup all-purpose flour
- ½ cup water
- 3 cups shredded cheddar cheese
- 1 pkg. (8 oz.) cream cheese, cubed
- 1 bottle (12 oz.) beer or nonalcoholic beer
  Optional: Additional shredded cheddar cheese, cooked and crumbled bacon strips, chopped green onions, sour cream and salad croutons

1. In a Dutch oven, melt butter over medium-high heat. Add celery, carrots and onion; saute until crisp-tender. Add broccoli and red pepper; stir in broth and pepper.
2. Combine the flour and water until smooth; gradually stir into pan. Bring to a boil. Reduce heat; simmer, uncovered, until soup is thickened and vegetables are tender, 25-30 minutes.
3. Stir in cheeses and beer until the cheeses are melted (do not boil). Top with additional shredded cheese, bacon, green onions, sour cream and croutons as desired.

Freeze option: Before adding toppings, cool soup; transfer to freezer containers. Freeze up to 3 months. To use, partially thaw in the refrigerator overnight; heat through in a large saucepan over medium-low heat, stirring occasionally (do not boil). Add toppings as desired.

1 cup: 316 cal., 23g fat (13g sat. fat), 69mg chol., 1068mg sod., 13g carb. (5g sugars, 2g fiber), 12g pro.

CHIPOTLE BEEF SANDWICHES

A jar of chipotle salsa makes it easy to spice up savory beef sirloin for these mouthwatering sandwiches. Keep this no-stress recipe in mind the next time you have to feed a hungry crowd.
—Jessica Ring, Madison, WI

....

Prep: 25 min. • **Cook:** 7 hours
Makes: 10 servings

- 1 large sweet onion,
   halved and thinly sliced
- 1 beef sirloin tip roast (3 lbs.)
- 1 jar (16 oz.) chipotle salsa
- ½ cup beer or nonalcoholic beer
- 1 envelope Lipton
   beefy onion soup mix
- 10 kaiser rolls, split

1. Place onion in a 5-qt. slow cooker. Cut roast in half; place over onion. Combine the salsa, beer and soup mix. Pour over top. Cover and cook on low for 7-8 hours or until the meat is tender.

2. Remove the roast. Shred meat with 2 forks and return to the slow cooker; heat through. Using a slotted spoon, spoon shredded meat onto rolls.

1 sandwich: 362 cal., 9g fat (3g sat. fat), 72mg chol., 524mg sod., 37g carb. (6g sugars, 2g fiber), 31g pro. **Diabetic exchanges:** 3 lean meat, 2½ starch.

ASIAN TOFU NOODLE SOUP
PICTURED ON P. 51

Ginger, garlic and sherry jazz up this soup loaded with veggies and noodles. We like to accent ours with peanuts and green onions.
—Diana Rios, Lytle, TX

....

Takes: 30 min. • **Makes:** 4 servings

- 1 Tbsp. canola oil
- 1 Tbsp. minced fresh gingerroot
- 2 garlic cloves, minced
- ¼ tsp. crushed red pepper flakes, optional
- ½ lb. sliced fresh mushrooms
- 1 carton (32 oz.) reduced-sodium chicken broth
- ¼ cup sherry or reduced-sodium chicken broth
- ¼ cup reduced-sodium soy sauce
- 7 oz. firm tofu, drained and cut into ½-in. cubes
- 1 cup fresh snow peas, julienned
- 1 large carrot, shredded
- 2 green onions, thinly sliced
- 8 oz. uncooked Chinese egg noodles or uncooked spaghetti
   Optional: Finely chopped peanuts and additional green onions

1. In a large saucepan, heat oil over medium heat. Add ginger, garlic and, if desired, pepper flakes; cook and stir 1 minute or until fragrant.

2. Add mushrooms, broth, sherry and soy sauce; bring to a boil. Cook, uncovered, 5 minutes. Add tofu, snow peas, carrot and green onions. Reduce heat; simmer, uncovered, 4-6 minutes longer or until vegetables are crisp-tender.

3. Meanwhile, cook noodles according to package directions; drain and divide among 4 bowls. Pour soup over noodles. If desired, sprinkle with peanuts and green onions.

1 serving: 339 cal., 7g fat (1g sat. fat), 0 chol., 1961mg sod., 49g carb. (6g sugars, 4g fiber), 19g pro.

CHIPOTLE BEEF SANDWICHES

RUSTIC FISH CHOWDER

In my version of this classic New England specialty, I use fresh halibut that my brother-in-law, a commercial fisherman, catches in Kodiak, Alaska. Given the price of halibut these days, cod will make a perfectly good—and budget-friendly— substitution. Top individual servings with grated Parmesan, minced green onions or a few drops of hot sauce.
—Diana Lassen, Eugene, OR

Prep: 15 min. • **Cook:** 30 min.
Makes: 12 servings (3 qt.)

- ¼ cup butter, cubed
- 1 small onion, finely chopped
- 1 garlic clove, minced
- 3 lbs. potatoes (about 6 medium), cut into ½-in. cubes
- 1½ cups fresh or frozen corn
- 5 cups chicken broth
- 1½ tsp. salt
- ¾ tsp. celery salt
- ¾ tsp. pepper
- ½ tsp. dried thyme
- 1 lb. cod or halibut fillets, cut into ¾-in. pieces
- 1 cup heavy whipping cream

1. In a 6-qt. stockpot, heat butter over medium heat. Add onion; cook and stir 3-4 minutes or until tender. Add garlic; cook 1 minute longer. Add the potatoes, corn, broth, salt, celery salt, pepper and thyme; bring to a boil. Reduce the heat; simmer, covered, 10-15 minutes or until potatoes are tender. Mash the potatoes slightly.

2. Stir in the cod and cream; bring to a boil. Reduce heat; simmer, covered, 6-8 minutes or until the fish just begins to flake easily with a fork.

1 cup: 242 cal., 12g fat (7g sat. fat), 49mg chol., 842mg sod., 25g carb. (3g sugars, 3g fiber), 10g pro.

BISTRO BEEF SANDWICH

Red pepper lends a nice crunch to this satisfying roast beef sandwich. If you enjoy garlic, you'll love the zing added by the garlic-herb spread.
—David Locke, Woburn, MA

Takes: 15 min. • **Makes:** 1 serving

- 2 slices rye bread
- 1 Tbsp. garlic-herb spreadable cheese
- 3 slices deli roast beef
- 2 slices tomato
- 1 romaine leaf
- ¼ cup julienned sweet red pepper
- 2 tsp. French salad dressing

Spread 1 bread slice with the spreadable cheese. Layer with beef, tomato, romaine and red pepper. Spread remaining bread with salad dressing; place on top.

1 sandwich: 362 cal., 16g fat (6g sat. fat), 53mg chol., 957mg sod., 37g carb. (7g sugars, 5g fiber), 20g pro.

RUSTIC FISH CHOWDER

**SWEET & SPICY
SLOPPY JOES**

SPICY TOUCHDOWN CHILI
PICTURED ON P. 51

Football, cool weather and chili just seem to go together. Whether I'm cheering on the local team on a Friday night or enjoying a Saturday afternoon of Oklahoma Sooner football with friends, I enjoy serving this chili on game day.
—Chris Neal, Quapaw, OK

Prep: 30 min. • **Cook:** 4 hours
Makes: 12 servings (3 qt.)

- 1 lb. ground beef
- 1 lb. bulk pork sausage
- 2 cans (16 oz. each) kidney beans, rinsed and drained
- 2 cans (15 oz. each) pinto beans, rinsed and drained
- 2 cans (14½ oz. each) diced tomatoes with mild green chiles, undrained
- 1 can (14½ oz.) diced tomatoes with onions, undrained
- 1 can (12 oz.) beer
- 6 bacon strips, cooked and crumbled
- 1 small onion, chopped
- ¼ cup chili powder
- ¼ cup chopped pickled jalapeno slices
- 2 tsp. ground cumin
- 2 garlic cloves, minced
- 1 tsp. dried basil
- ¾ tsp. cayenne pepper
  Optional: Shredded cheddar cheese, sour cream and chopped green onions

1. In a large skillet, cook the beef over medium heat for 6-8 minutes or until no longer pink, breaking into crumbles; drain. Transfer to a 6-qt. slow cooker. Repeat with sausage.
2. Stir in the next 13 ingredients. Cook, covered, on low for 4-5 hours or until heated through. If desired, top individual servings with shredded cheddar cheese, sour cream and chopped green onions.
1 cup: 365 cal., 15g fat (5g sat. fat), 48mg chol., 901mg sod., 34g carb. (7g sugars, 9g fiber), 22g pro.

SWEET & SPICY SLOPPY JOES

These sandwiches are the go-to meal for my son's basketball team. Turkey is a wonderful change from ground beef and really absorbs all the flavors. I have also used this for a Friday the 13th celebration at work, calling it "13-Ingredient Sloppy Joes." (If people ask, I count salt and pepper separately to get to 13!)
—Karen Hildebrand, Labelle, FL

Prep: 30 min. • **Cook:** 4 hours
Makes: 12 servings

- 2 tsp. canola oil
- 3 lbs. ground turkey
- 1 large onion, chopped
- ½ medium green pepper, chopped
- 3 garlic cloves, minced
- 1 tsp. crushed red pepper flakes
- 2 Tbsp. Worcestershire sauce
- 3 cups ketchup
- ⅔ cup water
- ⅓ cup packed brown sugar
- 3 Tbsp. spicy brown mustard
- ½ tsp. salt
- ¼ tsp. pepper

- 12 hamburger buns, split
  Optional: Coleslaw or dill pickle slices

1. Heat oil in a large nonstick skillet over medium-high heat. Cook turkey in batches until no longer pink, 8-10 minutes per batch, breaking into crumbles. Transfer meat to a 5- or 6-qt. slow cooker. In same skillet, cook onion and green pepper until tender, 2-3 minutes. Add the garlic, red pepper flakes and Worcestershire; cook 1 minute longer. Transfer to slow cooker.
2. In a bowl, combine the ketchup, water, brown sugar, mustard, salt and pepper; pour over meat. Cover and cook on low until the flavors are blended, 4-5 hours. Serve on buns with toppings as desired.
1 sandwich: 390 cal., 11g fat (3g sat. fat), 75mg chol., 1206mg sod., 46g carb. (26g sugars, 1g fiber), 27g pro.

> **TEST KITCHEN TIP**
> For more spice or crunch, try topping with pickled jalapenos or fried onions.

MEXICAN LEEK SOUP

SAUSAGE & PEPPER SHEET-PAN SANDWICHES

Sausage with peppers was always on the table when I was growing up. Here's how to do it the easy way: Just grab a sheet pan and the ingredients, then let the oven do the work!
—Debbie Glasscock, Conway, AR

Prep: 20 min. • **Bake:** 35 min.
Makes: 6 servings

- 1 lb. uncooked sweet Italian turkey sausage links, roughly chopped
- 3 medium sweet red peppers, seeded and sliced
- 1 large onion, halved and sliced
- 1 Tbsp. olive oil
- 6 hot dog buns, split
- 6 slices provolone cheese

1. Preheat the oven to 375°. Place the sausage pieces in a 15x10x1-in. baking pan, arranging peppers and onion around the sausage. Drizzle olive oil over sausage and vegetables; bake, stirring mixture after 15 minutes, until sausage is no longer pink and vegetables are tender, 30-35 minutes.
2. During the last 5 minutes of baking, arrange buns cut side up in a second pan; top each bun bottom with a cheese slice. Bake until buns are golden brown and cheese is melted. Spoon sausage and pepper mixture onto bun bottoms. Replace tops.

1 sandwich: 315 cal., 15g fat (5g sat. fat), 43mg chol., 672mg sod., 28g carb. (7g sugars, 2g fiber), 18g pro.

TEST KITCHEN TIP
Top these sandwiches with warmed-up leftover pasta sauce to instantly transform them into pizza sandwiches!

MEXICAN LEEK SOUP

This quick and easy soup is so satisfying. You can substitute other beans or kale and even add leftover corn. For brunch, I add a fried egg on top. For dinner, my husband adds lots of hot sauce!
—Donna Ahnert, Scotia, NY

Takes: 20 min. • **Makes:** 2 servings

- 1 can (15 oz.) pinto beans, rinsed and drained
- 2 medium leeks (white portion only), chopped
- ½ cup water
- ¾ cup coarsely chopped fresh spinach
- 1 cup shredded cheddar cheese
- 2 Tbsp. grated Parmesan cheese
- 2 Tbsp. grated Romano cheese
- ½ tsp. ground cumin
- ½ tsp. coarsely ground pepper
- ¼ tsp. cayenne pepper
- ⅛ tsp. salt
- ¼ cup heavy whipping cream
- ¼ cup french-fried onions
- 2 bacon strips, cooked and crumbled
  Chopped fresh cilantro, optional

1. Place the beans, leeks and water in a 1-qt. microwave-safe bowl. Cover and microwave on high until tender, 4-5 minutes.
2. In a blender, process the bean mixture and spinach until smooth. Return to the bowl; add cheeses and seasonings. Whisk in the cream. Cover and microwave on high until heated through, stirring once, 2-3 minutes. Sprinkle with onions and bacon and, if desired, chopped cilantro.

1½ cups: 641 cal., 34g fat (19g sat. fat), 100mg chol., 1240mg sod., 54g carb. (9g sugars, 11g fiber), 34g pro.

**SAUSAGE & PEPPER
SHEET-PAN SANDWICHES**

THAI SHRIMP SOUP

This tasty, crowd-pleasing soup comes together in minutes, and I really appreciate the fact that the ingredients are available in my little local grocery store.
—*Jessie Grearson, Falmouth, ME*

Prep: 20 min. • **Cook:** 20 min.
Makes: 8 servings (2 qt.)

- 1 medium onion, chopped
- 1 Tbsp. olive oil
- 3 cups reduced-sodium chicken broth
- 1 cup water
- 1 Tbsp. brown sugar
- 1 Tbsp. minced fresh gingerroot
- 1 Tbsp. fish sauce or soy sauce
- 1 Tbsp. red curry paste
- 1 lemongrass stalk
- 1 lb. uncooked large shrimp, peeled and deveined
- 1½ cups frozen shelled edamame
- 1 can (13.66 oz.) light coconut milk
- 1 can (8¾ oz.) whole baby corn, drained and cut in half
- ½ cup bamboo shoots
- ¼ cup fresh basil leaves, julienned
- ¼ cup minced fresh cilantro
- 2 Tbsp. lime juice
- 1½ tsp. grated lime zest
- 1 tsp. curry powder

1. In a Dutch oven, saute onion in oil until tender. Add broth, water, brown sugar, ginger, fish sauce, curry paste and lemongrass. Bring to a boil. Reduce heat; stir in shrimp and edamame. Cook, uncovered, for 5-6 minutes or until the shrimp turn pink.

2. Add the coconut milk, corn, bamboo shoots, basil, cilantro, lime juice, lime zest and curry powder; heat through. Discard the lemongrass.

1 cup: 163 cal., 7g fat (3g sat. fat), 69mg chol., 505mg sod., 9g carb. (5g sugars, 2g fiber), 14g pro. **Diabetic exchanges:** 2 lean meat, 1 vegetable, 1 fat.

LOBSTER ROLLS

Mayonnaise infused with dill and lemon lends refreshing flavor to these super sandwiches. Try pan-toasting the buns in butter for something special.
—Taste of Home *Test Kitchen*

Takes: 30 min. • **Makes:** 8 sandwiches

- 1 cup chopped celery
- ⅓ cup mayonnaise
- 2 Tbsp. lemon juice
- ½ tsp. dill weed
- 5 cups cubed cooked lobster meat (about 4 small lobsters)
- 8 hoagie rolls, split and toasted

In a large bowl, combine the celery, mayonnaise, lemon juice and dill weed. Gently stir in lobster. Serve on rolls.

1 sandwich: 354 cal., 12g fat (2g sat. fat), 133mg chol., 887mg sod., 36g carb. (5g sugars, 1g fiber), 25g pro.

READER REVIEW

"Delicious. I served the filling on a bed of chopped lettuce with toast on the side. What a nice treat!"

DUBLINLAB, TASTEOFHOME.COM

THAI SHRIMP SOUP

GREENS & BEANS TURKEY SOUP

On winter evenings, we like nothing better than a steaming bowl of soup. This one starts with a slow-simmered turkey carcass to make a flavorful stock—then creating the soup is a snap!
—Susan Albert, Jonesburg, MO

Prep: 15 min. • **Cook:** 2½ hours
Makes: 10 servings (2½ qt.)

- 1   leftover turkey carcass (from a 12-lb. turkey)
- 9   cups water
- 2   celery ribs, cut into ½-in. pieces
- 1   medium onion, cut into chunks
- 1   can (15½ oz.) great northern beans, rinsed and drained
- 1   pkg. (10 oz.) frozen chopped spinach, thawed and squeezed dry
- 3   Tbsp. chopped onion
- 2   tsp. chicken bouillon granules
- 1   tsp. salt
- ¼   tsp. pepper

1.   Place turkey carcass in a stockpot; add water, celery and onion. Slowly bring to a boil. Reduce heat; simmer, covered, 2 hours.
2.   Remove carcass and cool. Strain broth through a cheesecloth-lined colander; discard vegetables. Skim fat. Remove meat from bones and cut into bite-sized pieces; discard bones. Return broth and meat to the pot.
3.   Add the beans, spinach, chopped onion, bouillon, salt and pepper. Bring to a boil. Reduce heat; simmer, covered, 10 minutes.

1 cup: 105 cal., 2g fat (0 sat. fat), 22mg chol., 568mg sod., 10g carb. (1g sugars, 3g fiber), 10g pro. **Diabetic exchanges:** 1 lean meat, ½ starch.

GRILLED CHICKPEA SALAD SANDWICH

GRILLED CHICKPEA SALAD SANDWICH

When my mother comes to visit, she enjoys a good old-fashioned chicken salad sandwich. As a vegetarian, I make chickpea salad sandwiches all the time and finally had the guts to make one for her. After some hesitation, she tasted it and was instantly hooked!
—Dannika Stevenson, Akron, OH

Prep: 20 min. • **Cook:** 5 min./batch
Makes: 4 servings

- 1   can (16 oz.) chickpeas or garbanzo beans, rinsed and drained
- 1   celery rib, finely chopped
- 2   sweet pickles, finely chopped
- 2   Tbsp. dried cranberries
- 2   Tbsp. finely chopped red onion
- 2   Tbsp. reduced-fat mayonnaise
- 2   tsp. sweet pickle juice
- ½   tsp. minced fresh parsley
- ¼   tsp. salt
- ¼   tsp. pepper
- 4   slices provolone cheese
- 8   slices multigrain bread

In a small bowl, mix the first 10 ingredients. Place cheese on 4 bread slices; top with chickpea mixture and the remaining bread. Preheat panini maker or indoor electric grill. Cook sandwiches, covered, until the bread is browned and cheese is melted, 3-5 minutes.

1 sandwich: 370 cal., 13g fat (4g sat. fat), 18mg chol., 753mg sod., 49g carb. (13g sugars, 9g fiber), 17g pro.

CARROT-PARSNIP BISQUE

Warm and comforting, this fabulous soup makes a pretty presentation. Easy to prepare, it's a treat to serve for family dinners and special enough for guests.
—Lisa Speer, Palm Beach, FL

Prep: 15 min. • **Cook:** 20 min.
Makes: 4 servings

- 2 Tbsp. plus 1 cup peanut oil, divided
- 1 medium onion, chopped
- ¾ tsp. ground cinnamon
- ¼ tsp. salt
- ¼ tsp. ground nutmeg
- ⅛ tsp. coarsely ground pepper
- 2 garlic cloves, minced
- 1 lb. medium carrots
- 2 medium parsnips, peeled and chopped
- 4 cups chicken stock
- ½ cup half-and-half cream
  Minced chives, optional

1. In a large saucepan, heat 2 Tbsp. oil over medium-high heat. Add the onion, cinnamon, salt, nutmeg and pepper. Cook and stir 6-8 minutes or until the onion is tender. Add garlic; cook and stir 1 minute.
2. Set aside 1 carrot; chop the remaining carrots. Add chopped carrots, parsnips and stock to onion mixture; bring to a boil. Reduce heat; simmer, covered, until vegetables are tender, 20-25 minutes.
3. Remove soup from heat; cool slightly. Process in batches in a blender until smooth. Return soup to pan; keep warm.
4. Using a vegetable peeler, shave the remaining carrot lengthwise into very thin strips. In a small saucepan, heat remaining oil over medium-high heat. Fry the carrot strips 2-3 minutes or until crispy, stirring occasionally. Drain on paper towels.
5. Gently reheat soup; stir in cream. Top individual servings with carrot strips and, if desired, chives.
1 cup: 241 cal., 11g fat (3g sat. fat), 15mg chol., 760mg sod., 30g carb. (12g sugars, 7g fiber), 8g pro.

GRILLED CHEESE, HAM & APPLE SANDWICH

GRILLED CHEESE & APPLE SANDWICH

In this stepped-up version of a grilled cheese, melty cheeses, crispy apples and smoky ham are the ultimate combination.
—Josh Rink, Milwaukee, WI

Takes: 25 min. • **Makes:** 4 servings

- 6 Tbsp. butter, softened, divided
- 8 slices sourdough bread
- 3 Tbsp. mayonnaise
- 3 Tbsp. finely shredded Manchego or Parmesan cheese
- ⅛ tsp. onion powder
- ½ cup shredded sharp white cheddar cheese
- ½ cup shredded Monterey Jack cheese
- ½ cup shredded Gruyere cheese
- 4 oz. Brie cheese, rind removed and sliced
- 12 slices deli ham
- 1 thinly sliced tart apple

1. Spread 3 Tbsp. butter on 1 side of each bread slice. Toast bread, butter side down, in a large skillet or electric griddle over medium-low heat until golden brown, 2-3 minutes; remove.
2. In a small bowl, combine mayonnaise, Manchego cheese, onion powder and the remaining 3 Tbsp. butter. In another bowl, combine cheddar, Monterey Jack and Gruyere.
3. Top toasted sides of 4 of the bread slices with sliced Brie. Sprinkle cheddar cheese mixture evenly over Brie, then layer with ham and apple slices; top with the remaining bread slices, toasted side facing inward.
4. Spread mayonnaise mixture on the outsides of each sandwich. Place in the same skillet and cook until golden brown and cheese is melted, 5-6 minutes on each side. Serve immediately.
1 sandwich: 725 cal., 50g fat (27g sat. fat), 141mg chol., 1415mg sod., 37g carb. (9g sugars, 2g fiber), 32g pro.

COCONUT CURRY CHICKEN SOUP

Similar to a Vietnamese pho rice noodle soup, coconut curry chicken soup packs big flavor and a bit of heat. The crisp raw vegetables help cool things down.
—Monnie Norasing, Mansfield, TX

Prep: 20 min. • **Cook:** 35 min.
Makes: 6 servings

- 2 cans (13.66 oz. each) coconut milk
- ⅓ to ½ cup red curry paste
- 1 pkg. (8.8 oz.) thin rice noodles
- 2 cans (14½ oz. each) chicken broth
- ¼ cup packed brown sugar
- 2 Tbsp. fish sauce or soy sauce
- ¾ tsp. garlic salt
- 3 cups shredded rotisserie chicken
- 1½ cups shredded cabbage
- 1½ cups shredded carrots
- ¾ cup bean sprouts
  Fresh basil and cilantro leaves

1. In a Dutch oven, bring coconut milk to a boil. Cook, uncovered, 10-12 minutes or until liquid is reduced to 3 cups. Stir in curry paste until completely dissolved.
2. Meanwhile, prepare noodles according to package directions.
3. Add broth, brown sugar, fish sauce and garlic salt to the curry mixture; return to a boil. Reduce heat; simmer, uncovered, 10 minutes, stirring occasionally. Stir in chicken; heat through.
4. Drain noodles; divide among 6 large soup bowls. Ladle soup over noodles; top servings with vegetables, basil and cilantro.

1 serving: 601 cal., 34g fat (26g sat. fat), 65mg chol., 1722mg sod., 50g carb. (12g sugars, 4g fiber), 27g pro.

COCONUT CURRY CHICKEN SOUP

OPEN-FACED BRATWURST SANDWICHES WITH BEER GRAVY

PICTURED ON P. 51

A nod to my Volga German heritage, this classic diner fare comes together in a snap and can be made all in one skillet! I serve it with a green vegetable and french fries or mashed potatoes on the side. Cook the sausages in lager or stout beer for a deeper flavor profile.
—Allison Ochoa, Hays, KS

Takes: 30 min. • **Makes:** 5 servings

- ¼ cup butter, divided
- 1 pkg. uncooked bratwurst links (20 oz.)
- 1 medium onion, thinly sliced
- 1 bottle (12 oz.) beer or nonalcoholic beer
- 2 Tbsp. all-purpose flour
- ⅛ tsp. dill weed
- ⅛ tsp. pepper
- 5 slices thick bread

1. In a Dutch oven, heat 2 Tbsp. butter over medium-high heat. Add bratwurst and onion; cook and stir until bratwurst starts to brown and onion softens. Stir in beer. Bring to a boil. Reduce heat; simmer, covered, turning occasionally, until a thermometer inserted in bratwurst reads 165° and the brats are no longer pink, 12-14 minutes.
2. Remove brats and onions; keep warm. Add the remaining butter to pot; whisk in the flour, dill weed and pepper. Bring to a boil, stirring constantly until thickened, 3-5 minutes.
3. To serve, place 1 brat on each slice of bread; top evenly with onions and gravy.

1 sandwich with ¼ cup gravy: 567 cal., 43g fat (17g sat. fat), 108mg chol., 1176mg sod., 23g carb. (3g sugars, 1g fiber), 19g pro.

TEST KITCHEN TIP
Try serving the sausage, onions and gravy over mashed potatoes, noodles or spaetzel. Using a dark beer will give the gravy a more deep and rich flavor, but watch out for intense dark beers since you don't want to make the gravy bitter.

GIVE ME 5 OR FEWER

This popular chapter is back with all the fast, fresh and full-flavored specialties you've come to expect. Each of these dishes calls for five ingredients, excluding water, salt, pepper, oils or optional ingredients. Turn here for speedy, succulent success even when a home-cooked meal seems out of reach.

GIVE ME 5 OR FEWER

FRUITED POT ROAST

Here's a wonderful variation of classic pot roast. The fruit is a nice change from the vegetables that usually accompany this dish. My family really enjoys it.
—Linda South, Pineville, NC

Prep: 15 min. • **Cook:** 6 hours
Makes: 6 servings

- 1 pkg. (7 oz.) mixed dried fruit
- 1 large onion, cut into wedges
- 1 can (5½ oz.) unsweetened apple juice
- 1 boneless beef chuck roast (2 lbs.)
- ½ tsp. salt
- ¼ tsp. ground allspice
- ¼ tsp. pepper

1. Place fruit and onion in a 3- or 4-qt. slow cooker; add apple juice. Top with roast; sprinkle with seasonings.
2. Cover and cook on low until meat is tender, 6-8 hours. Serve beef with the fruit mixture.

4 oz. cooked beef with ½ cup fruit mixture: 394 cal., 15g fat (6g sat. fat), 98mg chol., 302mg sod., 32g carb. (28g sugars, 2g fiber), 30g pro.

CHICKEN PESTO ROLL-UPS

One night I looked in the refrigerator and pondered what I could make with chicken, cheese, mushrooms and a little pesto. This impressive-looking dish was the result. Add Italian bread and a fast fruit salad for a complete meal!
—Melissa Nordmann, Mobile, AL

Prep: 15 min. • **Bake:** 30 min.
Makes: 4 servings

- 4 boneless skinless chicken breast halves (6 oz. each)
- ½ cup prepared pesto, divided
- 1 lb. medium fresh mushrooms, sliced
- 4 slices reduced-fat provolone cheese, halved

1. Preheat oven to 350°. Pound the chicken breasts with a meat mallet to ¼-in. thickness. Spread ¼ cup pesto over chicken breasts.

2. Coarsely chop half the sliced mushrooms; scatter remaining sliced mushrooms in a 15x10x1-in. baking pan coated with cooking spray. Top each chicken breast with a fourth of the chopped mushrooms and a halved cheese slice. Roll up chicken from a short side; secure with toothpicks. Place rolls seam side down on top of the sliced mushrooms.
3. Bake, covered, until chicken is no longer pink, 25-30 minutes. Preheat broiler; top chicken with remaining pesto and remaining cheese. Broil until cheese is melted and browned, 3-5 minutes longer. Discard toothpicks.

1 stuffed chicken breast half: 374 cal., 17g fat (5g sat. fat), 104mg chol., 582mg sod., 7g carb. (1g sugars, 1g fiber), 44g pro. **Diabetic exchanges:** 5 lean meat, 2 fat.

SHRIMP PASTA ALFREDO

My son just loves any recipe with Alfredo sauce. When he was a bachelor, this shrimp and pasta entree was one of the first recipes he learned to prepare. Now his children ask for it regularly.
—Gail Lucas, Olive Branch, MS

Takes: 25 min. • **Makes:** 4 servings

- 3 cups uncooked bow tie pasta
- 2 cups frozen peas
- 1 lb. peeled and deveined cooked medium shrimp, tails removed
- 1 jar (15 oz.) Alfredo sauce
- ¼ cup shredded Parmesan cheese

1. In a Dutch oven, cook pasta according to package directions, adding peas during the last 3 minutes of cooking; drain and return to pan.

2. Stir in shrimp and sauce; heat through over medium heat, stirring occasionally. Sprinkle with cheese.

2 cups: 545 cal., 16g fat (9g sat. fat), 206mg chol., 750mg sod., 60g carb. (5g sugars, 6g fiber), 41g pro.

TEST KITCHEN TIP
Your favorite homemade Alfredo sauce would work well in this recipe in place of store bought.

SHRIMP PASTA ALFREDO

COD WITH RASPBERRY SAUCE
PICTURED ON P. 77

My sister-in-law shared this recipe with me. I am not usually crazy about fish, but the fresh raspberry sauce makes this cod simply scrumptious.
—Angela Leinenbach, Mechanicsville, VA

Takes: 30 min.
Makes: 4 servings (½ cup sauce)

- 1½ pints fresh raspberries
- ¼ cup water
- 2 Tbsp. brown sugar
- 1 Tbsp. balsamic vinegar
- 1 tsp. salt, divided
- ⅛ tsp. plus ½ tsp. coarsely ground pepper, divided
- ¼ cup butter, softened
- 4 cod fillets (6 oz. each)
- 2 Tbsp. canola oil
  Fresh minced mint leaves, optional

1. Preheat oven to 375°. Reserve ½ cup raspberries. In a small saucepan, combine water, brown sugar, vinegar and remaining raspberries; bring to a boil. Reduce heat; simmer, covered, until sugar is dissolved and raspberries have broken down, about 4-6 minutes, stirring occasionally. Press raspberry mixture through a fine-mesh strainer into a bowl; discard seeds. Stir in ½ tsp. salt and ⅛ tsp. pepper; return to pan. Bring to a boil. Reduce heat; simmer, uncovered, until the liquid is reduced to ½ cup, 2-3 minutes.

2. In a small bowl, stir butter until smooth. Stir in remaining salt and pepper. Spread butter mixture over fillets.

3. In a large cast-iron or other ovenproof skillet, heat oil over medium heat. Add the fillets; cook 1-2 minutes on each side. Bake until fish just begins to flake easily with a fork, 6-8 minutes. Serve with sauce. Top with the reserved raspberries and, if desired, mint.

1 fillet with 2 Tbsp. sauce: 363 cal., 20g fat (8g sat. fat), 95mg chol., 776mg sod., 19g carb. (11g sugars, 2g fiber), 28g pro.

SAUCY RASPBERRY CHICKEN

SAUCY RASPBERRY CHICKEN

I first had this dish as a teenage babysitter, when the children's mom prepared it for us to eat while she was out. The kids loved it, and so did I! Now I make it for my own little ones.
—Melissa Wales, Elephant Butte, NM

Prep: 15 min. • **Cook:** 5 hours
Makes: 5 servings

- 5 chicken leg quarters, skin removed
- ⅓ cup seedless raspberry spreadable fruit
- 3 Tbsp. reduced-sodium soy sauce
- 1 tsp. spicy brown mustard
- ¼ tsp. pepper
- 2 Tbsp. cornstarch
- 2 Tbsp. cold water

1. Place the chicken in a 3-qt. slow cooker. In a small bowl, combine the spreadable fruit, soy sauce, mustard and pepper; pour over the chicken. Cover and cook on low for 5-6 hours or until meat is tender.

2. Remove chicken to a serving platter; keep warm. Skim fat from cooking juices; transfer to a small saucepan. Bring to a boil. Combine cornstarch and water until smooth; gradually stir into the pan. Bring to a boil; cook and stir for 2 minutes or until thickened. Serve with chicken.

1 chicken leg quarter with ⅓ cup sauce: 337 cal., 16g fat (4g sat. fat), 105mg chol., 468mg sod., 14g carb. (9g sugars, 0 fiber), 31g pro.

SKILLET PORK CHOPS WITH APPLES & ONION

Simple recipes that land on the table fast are a lifesaver. I serve skillet pork chops with veggies and, when there's time, cornbread stuffing.
—Tracey Karst, Ponderay, ID

Takes: 20 min. • **Makes:** 4 servings

- 4 boneless pork loin chops (6 oz. each)
- 3 medium apples, cut into wedges
- 1 large onion, cut into thin wedges
- ¼ cup water
- ⅓ cup balsamic vinaigrette
- ½ tsp. salt
- ¼ tsp. pepper

1. Place a large nonstick skillet over medium heat; brown pork chops on both sides, about 4 minutes. Remove from pan.
2. In the same skillet, combine apples, onion and water. Place pork chops over the apple mixture; drizzle chops with vinaigrette. Sprinkle with salt and pepper. Reduce heat; simmer, covered, until a thermometer inserted in chops reads 145°, 3-5 minutes.

1 pork chop with ¾ cup apple mixture: 360 cal., 15g fat (4g sat. fat), 82mg chol., 545mg sod., 22g carb. (15g sugars, 3g fiber), 33g pro. **Diabetic exchanges:** 5 lean meat, 1 fruit, 1 fat.

HERB-ROASTED SALMON FILLETS

Roasted salmon is so simple, but it is elegant enough to serve to company. I make it on days when I have less than an hour to cook.

—Luanne Asta, Hampton Bays, NY

Takes: 30 min. • **Makes:** 4 servings

- 4 salmon fillets (6 oz. each)
- 4 garlic cloves, minced
- 1 Tbsp. minced fresh rosemary or 1 tsp. dried rosemary, crushed
- 1 Tbsp. olive oil
- 2 tsp. minced fresh thyme or ½ tsp. dried thyme
- ¾ tsp. salt
- ½ tsp. pepper

Preheat oven to 425°. Place salmon in a greased 15x10x1-in. baking pan, skin side down. Combine remaining ingredients; spread over the fillets. Roast to desired doneness, 15-18 minutes.

1 fillet: 301 cal., 19g fat (4g sat. fat), 85mg chol., 529mg sod., 1g carb. (0 sugars, 0 fiber), 29g pro. **Diabetic exchanges:** 4 lean meat, 1 fat.

HERB-ROASTED SALMON FILLETS

LAMB MARSALA

PICTURED ON P. 77

Lamb was a special treat for my family when I was growing up. I have had this recipe for more than 30 years. I hope it becomes a favorite for your family, too.

—Bonnie Silverstein, Denver, CO

Prep: 10 min. • **Bake:** 1 hour
Makes: 6 servings

- ¾ cup Marsala wine or ½ cup chicken broth, ¼ cup white grape juice and 1 Tbsp. white wine vinegar
- 1 garlic clove, minced
- 1 Tbsp. dried oregano
- 1 Tbsp. olive oil
- 1 boneless leg of lamb (2½ lbs.), rolled and tied
- ½ tsp. salt
- ¼ tsp. pepper
- 1 lb. fresh mushrooms, quartered

1. In a small bowl, combine the wine, garlic and oregano; set aside. Rub oil over lamb, then sprinkle with salt and pepper. Place roast on a rack in a shallow roasting pan; spoon some wine mixture over roast. Set aside the remaining wine mixture.

2. Bake, uncovered, at 325° for 1-1½ hours or until the meat reaches desired doneness (for medium-rare, a thermometer should read 135°; medium, 140°; medium-well, 145°), basting occasionally with some of the remaining wine mixture. Remove from the oven; cover loosely with foil for 10-15 minutes.

3. Meanwhile, pour pan drippings into a measuring cup; skim fat. In a large skillet coated with cooking spray, saute the mushrooms until tender. Add the pan drippings and any remaining wine mixture; heat through. Slice lamb and serve with mushroom sauce.

1 serving: 330 cal., 13g fat (5g sat. fat), 114mg chol., 296mg sod., 7g carb. (4g sugars, 1g fiber), 38g pro. **Diabetic exchanges:** 5 lean meat, 1 vegetable.

SALMON WITH HONEY PECAN SAUCE

SIMPLE MARINATED GRILLED PORK CHOPS

This marinade is so simple that I use it for all kinds of meat. Looking for an even more robust flavor? Simply let the meat marinate in the refrigerator overnight.
—*Lori Daniels, Beverly, WV*

Prep: 10 min. + marinating • **Grill:** 10 min.
Makes: 4 servings

- ½ cup packed brown sugar
- ½ cup soy sauce
- 2 garlic cloves, minced
- ¼ tsp. pepper
- 4 bone-in pork loin chops
  (1 in. thick and 8 oz. each)

1. In a bowl or shallow dish, combine the brown sugar, soy sauce, garlic and pepper. Add pork chops and turn to coat. Cover and refrigerate for 8 hours or overnight.
2. Drain pork chops, discarding marinade. Grill chops on greased grill rack, covered, over medium heat or broil 4-5 in. from the heat for 4-5 minutes on each side or until meat reaches desired doneness (for medium-rare, a thermometer should read 145°; medium, 160°). Let meat stand for 5 minutes before serving.
1 serving: 362 cal., 18g fat (7g sat. fat), 111mg chol., 695mg sod., 9g carb. (9g sugars, 0 fiber), 37g pro.

READER REVIEW

"This recipe is a grilling staple in our home. I use boneless pork chops, and they turn out moist and delicious every time!"
HOPMOMOF3, TASTEOFHOME.COM

SALMON WITH HONEY PECAN SAUCE

I love the explosion of sweet and buttery flavors in every bite of this entree. In the summer, I make sauteed zucchini ribbons for a perfect side.
—*Alice Stanko, Warren, MI*

Takes: 30 min. • **Makes:** 4 servings

- 4 salmon fillets (4 oz. each)
- ½ tsp. seasoned salt
- ¼ tsp. pepper
- ¼ cup finely chopped pecans, toasted
- ¼ cup honey
- 3 Tbsp. reduced-fat butter

1. Sprinkle salmon with seasoned salt and pepper. Place fish on oiled grill rack, skin side down. Grill, covered, over medium-high heat or broil 4 in. from heat until the fish just begins to flake easily with a fork, about 6-8 minutes.
2. Meanwhile, in a small saucepan, cook pecans, honey and butter over medium heat until bubbly, 5-7 minutes. Serve with the salmon.
1 fillet with 2 Tbsp. sauce: 330 cal., 20g fat (5g sat. fat), 68mg chol., 319mg sod., 19g carb. (18g sugars, 1g fiber), 20g pro.
Diabetic exchanges: 3 lean meat, 2½ fat, 1 starch.

**SIMPLE MARINATED
GRILLED PORK CHOPS**

MAPLE PORK RIBS

A luscious maple-mustard sauce will take your next plate of ribs to a new level.
—*Phyllis Schmalz, Kansas City, KS*

Prep: 10 min. • **Cook:** 5 hours
Makes: 2 servings

- 1 lb. boneless country-style pork ribs, trimmed and cut into 3-in. pieces
- 2 tsp. canola oil
- 1 medium onion, sliced and separated into rings
- 3 Tbsp. maple syrup
- 2 Tbsp. spicy brown or Dijon mustard

In a large skillet, brown ribs in oil on all sides; drain. Place ribs and onion in a 1½-qt. slow cooker. Combine syrup and mustard; pour over ribs. Cover and cook on low until meat is tender, 5-6 hours.

4 oz. cooked pork: 428 cal., 20g fat (6g sat. fat), 98mg chol., 272mg sod., 27g carb. (24g sugars, 2g fiber), 31g pro.

PEPPER-CRUSTED SIRLOIN ROAST

Dinner guests will be surprised to hear that this exquisite entree calls for only a handful of items. It's a fabulous choice for serving a large group.
—*Mary Ann Griffin, Bowling Green, KY*

Prep: 15 min. • **Bake:** 2 hours + standing
Makes: 16 servings

- 2 Tbsp. Dijon mustard
- 1 Tbsp. coarsely ground pepper
- 1 Tbsp. minced fresh mint or 1 tsp. dried mint
- 1 Tbsp. minced fresh rosemary or 1 tsp. dried rosemary, crushed
- 1 beef sirloin tip roast (4 lbs.)

1. Preheat oven to 350°. Mix the first 4 ingredients.
2. Place the roast on a rack in a roasting pan; spread with mustard mixture. Roast until desired doneness (a thermometer should read 135° for medium-rare, 140° for medium and 145° for medium-well), about 2 hours.
3. Remove from oven; tent with foil. Let stand 15 minutes before slicing.

3 oz. cooked beef: 146 cal., 5g fat (2g sat. fat), 72mg chol., 78mg sod., 1g carb. (0 sugars, 0 fiber), 23g pro.
Diabetic exchanges: 3 lean meat.

MAPLE PORK RIBS

BREADED RANCH CHICKEN

POLISH KRAUT WITH APPLES

The combination of apples, sauerkraut and smoked sausage gives this hearty dinner an Old World flavor. I enjoy making it because it's so easy.
—Caren Markee, Cary, IL

Prep: 10 min. • **Cook:** 3 hours
Makes: 2 servings

- 1 cup sauerkraut, rinsed and well drained
- ½ lb. smoked Polish sausage or kielbasa, cut up
- 1 large tart apple, peeled and cut into eighths
- ¼ cup packed brown sugar
- ¼ tsp. caraway seeds, optional
  Dash pepper
- ⅓ cup apple juice

Place half the sauerkraut in an ungreased 1½-qt. slow cooker. Top with sausage, apples, brown sugar, caraway seeds if desired, and pepper. Top with remaining sauerkraut. Pour apple juice over all. Cover and cook on low until apples are tender, 3-4 hours.

1 cup: 522 cal., 30g fat (10g sat. fat), 81mg chol., 1440mg sod., 49g carb. (41g sugars, 3g fiber), 15g pro.

BREADED RANCH CHICKEN

A crunchy coating of cornflakes and Parmesan cheese adds delectable flavor to this zesty ranch chicken. The golden, crispy chicken is a mainstay dish I can always count on when time is tight.
—Launa Shoemaker, Landrum, SC

Prep: 10 min. • **Bake:** 45 min.
Makes: 8 servings

- ¼ cup unsalted butter, melted
- ¾ cup crushed cornflakes
- ¾ cup grated Parmesan cheese
- 1 envelope ranch salad dressing mix
- 8 boneless skinless chicken breast halves (4 oz. each)

1. Place butter in a shallow bowl. In another shallow bowl, combine the cornflakes, cheese and salad dressing mix. Dip chicken in butter, then roll in cornflake mixture to coat.

2. Place chicken in a greased 13x9-in. baking dish. Bake, uncovered, at 350° until a thermometer reads 165°, about 45 minutes.

1 chicken breast half: 254 cal., 10g fat (5g sat. fat), 84mg chol., 959mg sod., 13g carb. (1g sugars, 0 fiber), 26g pro.

TEST KITCHEN TIP
In Europe, Parmigiano-Reggiano and Parmesan are considered the same cheese. In the U.S., Parmesan is a generic term and may not come from Italy's Parmigiano-Reggiano region. Using authentic Italian cheese (in a lesser amount than the original's ½ cup) ensures a cheesy richness with less fat and calories.

CHOCOLATE-CHIPOTLE SIRLOIN STEAK

5i 🍎 🌶️

Looking to do something a little different for dinner tonight? Add smoky heat and chocolaty rich color to sirloin steak with this easy five-ingredient rub.
—Taste of Home *Test Kitchen*

Prep: 10 min. + chilling • **Grill:** 20 min.
Makes: 4 servings

- 3 Tbsp. baking cocoa
- 2 Tbsp. chopped chipotle peppers in adobo sauce
- 4 tsp. Worcestershire sauce
- 2 tsp. brown sugar
- ½ tsp. salt
- 1½ lbs. beef top sirloin steak

1. Place the first 5 ingredients in a blender; cover and process until blended. Rub over beef. Cover and refrigerate for at least 2 hours.
2. Grill beef, covered, over medium heat or broil 4 in. from heat for 8-10 minutes on each side or until the meat reaches desired doneness (for medium-rare, a thermometer should read 135°; medium, 140°; medium-well, 145°).

5 oz. cooked beef: 246 cal., 7g fat (3g sat. fat), 69mg chol., 477mg sod., 6g carb. (3g sugars, 1g fiber), 37g pro. **Diabetic exchanges:** 5 lean meat.

LEMON-GARLIC SALMON STEAKS

5i

I always enjoy making this easy recipe for my husband, Jim. He absolutely loves salmon and garlic, and they go together so well in this recipe.
—Mary Lynn Baronett, Waynesburg, PA

Prep: 10 min. • **Bake:** 25 min.
Makes: 6 servings

- 6 to 8 garlic cloves, minced
- 4 Tbsp. olive oil, divided
- 6 salmon steaks (6 oz. each)
- ⅔ cup lemon juice
- ¼ cup minced fresh parsley
  Salt and pepper to taste

1. Preheat oven to 350°. In a small skillet, saute garlic in 1 Tbsp. oil for 1 minute.
2. Arrange salmon steaks in a greased 13x9-in. baking dish. Combine lemon juice, parsley, salt, pepper and remaining oil; pour over salmon. Top with garlic mixture.
3. Bake, uncovered, 25-30 minutes or until fish flakes easily with a fork.

1 steak: 403 cal., 27g fat (5g sat. fat), 100mg chol., 103mg sod., 3g carb. (1g sugars, 0 fiber), 34g pro.

Tarragon Salmon Steaks: Omit garlic and olive oil. Stir 3 Tbsp. melted butter and 3 Tbsp. minced fresh tarragon into the lemon juice mixture. Proceed as directed.

CHOCOLATE-CHIPOTLE SIRLOIN STEAK

Time-Saving Technique

Lean how to spatchcock and beat the clock.

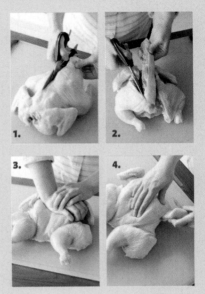

HOW TO
Spatchcock a Chicken

1. **2.**

3. **4.**

1. Cut along backbone
Use kitchen shears to cut as close along the spine as possible. If you feel any resistance cutting through rib bones, press down on the shears with both hands.

2. Remove the backbone
Rotate the chicken 180° so the uncut side is closer to your dominant hand. Cut along the bone again and remove the backbone.

3. Flatten the bird
Flip the chicken over so the breast side is facing upward. With two hands, press down firmly on the center of the bird until you hear the wishbone crack.

4. Tuck the wings under
Give the wings a quick twist and tuck them underneath the body of the bird so the chicken lies flat.

5i

GLAZED
SPATCHCOCKED CHICKEN

A few pantry items inspired this recipe, which I've since made for small weeknight meals and weekend parties alike.
—James Schend, Pleasant Prairie, WI

Prep: 15 min.
Grill: 45 minutes + standing
Makes: 6 servings

- 1 **cup white wine or chicken broth**
- 1 **cup apricot preserves or quince jelly**
- 1 **Tbsp. stone-ground mustard**
- 1 **broiler/fryer chicken (3 to 4 lbs.)**
- ¾ **tsp. salt**
- ½ **tsp. pepper**

1. In a small saucepan, bring the wine to a boil; cook 3-4 minutes or until wine is reduced by half. Stir in the preserves and mustard. Reserve half the glaze for basting.

2. Cut the chicken along each side of the backbone with shears. Remove the backbone. Turn the chicken breast side down, and press to flatten. Sprinkle with salt and pepper.

3. Prepare grill for indirect medium heat. Place chicken on greased grill grate, skin-side down, covered, over direct heat 10-15 minutes or until nicely browned. Turn chicken and place over indirect heat until a thermometer reads 170°-175° in the thickest part of the thigh, brushing occasionally with the reserved glaze mixture, about 30 minutes.

4. Remove chicken from grill. Let stand 15 minutes before carving; serve with the remaining glaze.

5 oz. cooked chicken: 437 cal., 17g fat (5g sat. fat), 104mg chol., 458mg sod., 35g carb. (23g sugars, 0 fiber), 34g pro.

SESAME NOODLES WITH SHRIMP & SNAP PEAS

Stir-fries and busy nights are a match made in heaven. For a boost of vibrant color and freshness, I sometimes stir chopped cilantro into this stir-fry before I serve it directly from the pan.
—Nedra Schell, Fort Worth, TX

Takes: 25 min. • **Makes:** 4 servings

- 8 oz. uncooked whole wheat linguine
- 1 Tbsp. canola oil
- 1 lb. uncooked medium shrimp, peeled and deveined
- 2 cups fresh sugar snap peas, trimmed
- ⅛ tsp. salt
- ⅛ tsp. crushed red pepper flakes
- ¾ cup reduced-fat Asian toasted sesame salad dressing

1. Cook linguine according to package directions for al dente.
2. Meanwhile, in a large skillet, heat the oil over medium-high heat. Add shrimp, peas, salt and pepper flakes; stir-fry 2-3 minutes or until the shrimp turn pink and the peas are crisp-tender.
3. Drain the linguine, reserving ¼ cup pasta water. Add the pasta, pasta water and salad dressing to the shrimp mixture; toss to combine.

1½ cups: 418 cal., 10g fat (1g sat. fat), 138mg chol., 646mg sod., 60g carb. (13g sugars, 8g fiber), 29g pro.

SAUSAGE HASH

SAUSAGE HASH

We always have plenty of pork sausage around, so when I need a quick supper, I turn to this handy recipe. The colorful vegetables give the hash a bold look that matches its flavor.
—Virginia Krites, Cridersville, OH

Prep: 10 min. • **Cook:** 30 min.
Makes: 6 servings

- 1 lb. bulk pork sausage
- 1 medium onion, chopped
- 2 medium carrots, grated
- 1 medium green pepper, chopped
- 3 cups diced cooked potatoes
- ½ tsp. salt
- ¼ tsp. pepper

In a large cast-iron or other heavy skillet, cook sausage over medium heat until no longer pink; drain. Add the onion, carrots and green pepper; cook until tender. Stir in the potatoes, salt and pepper. Reduce heat; cook and stir until lightly browned and heated through, about 20 minutes.

1 cup: 245 cal., 14g fat (5g sat. fat), 27mg chol., 519mg sod., 22g carb. (5g sugars, 3g fiber), 8g pro.

ORANGE POMEGRANATE SALMON

A colorful, festive salmon dish makes a delightful addition to any table—and it is as delicious as it is beautiful. What will no one guess? How easy it is to cook. I serve this with roasted baby potatoes and asparagus for a showstopping meal that is wonderful for special occasions.
—Thomas Faglon, Somerset, NJ

Prep: 10 min. • **Bake:** 25 min.
Makes: 4 servings

- 1   small red onion, thinly sliced
- 1   skinned salmon fillet (about 2 lbs.)
- ½   tsp. salt
- 1   medium navel orange, thinly sliced
- 1   cup pomegranate seeds
- 2   Tbsp. extra virgin olive oil
- 1   Tbsp. minced fresh dill, optional

1. Preheat oven to 375°. Place a 28x18-in. piece of heavy-duty foil in a 15x10x1-in. baking pan. Place onion slices in a single layer on foil. Top with salmon; sprinkle with salt. Arrange orange slices over top. Sprinkle with pomegranate seeds; drizzle with oil. Top with a second piece of foil. Bring edges of foil together on all sides and crimp to seal, forming a large packet.

2. Bake until the fish just begins to flake easily with a fork, 25-30 minutes. Be careful of the escaping steam when opening packet. Remove to a serving platter; sprinkle with dill, if desired.

4 oz. cooked salmon: 307 cal., 19g fat (3g sat. fat), 76mg chol., 274mg sod., 8g carb. (6g sugars, 1g fiber), 26g pro.
Diabetic exchanges: 4 lean meat, 1½ fat, ½ fruit.

SOUTHWEST CHICKEN PIZZA

I turn four ingredients into this fast bite whenever I'm running short on time.
—Guy Turnbull, Arlington, MA

Takes: 20 min. • **Makes:** 4 servings

- 1   prebaked 12-in. pizza crust
- 2   cups (8 oz.) shredded cheddar cheese, divided
- 1⅓ cups black bean and corn salsa
- 1   cup cubed cooked chicken

Place the pizza crust on an ungreased 12-in. pizza pan. Sprinkle with ¾ cup cheese. Top with the salsa, chicken and remaining cheese. Bake at 450° for 8-10 minutes or until cheese is bubbly.
1 slice: 579 cal., 24g fat (14g sat. fat), 91mg chol., 1261mg sod., 59g carb. (5g sugars, 7g fiber), 35g pro.

ORANGE POMEGRANATE SALMON

**SAUTEED PORK CHOPS
WITH GARLIC SPINACH**

SAUTEED PORK CHOPS WITH GARLIC SPINACH

My family adores cooking quick and delicious meals. This meal-in-one pork chop dish is also inexpensive, which helps make it a real keeper. Be sure to watch the spinach because it cooks fast!
—Joe Valerio, Whitinsville, MA

Takes: 20 min. • **Makes:** 4 servings

- 1 Tbsp. olive oil
- 4 bone-in pork loin chops (8 oz. each)
- ¼ tsp. salt
- ¼ tsp. pepper
- 1 medium lemon

GARLIC SPINACH
- 1 Tbsp. olive oil
- 3 garlic cloves, thinly sliced
- 2 pkg. (5 oz. each) fresh spinach, stems removed
- ½ tsp. salt
- ¼ tsp. coarsely ground pepper
- 1 tsp. lemon juice

1. In a large skillet, heat oil over medium-high heat. Sprinkle the pork chops with salt and pepper; add to skillet. Saute until a thermometer reads 145°, about 5 minutes per side. Remove to a serving platter; squeeze juice from lemon over chops. Tent with foil; let stand at least 5 minutes before serving.
2. For the garlic spinach, heat oil over medium-high heat in same skillet. Add garlic; cook until it just begins to brown, about 45 seconds. Add spinach; cook and stir just until wilted, 2-3 minutes. Sprinkle with salt and pepper. Remove from heat; add lemon juice. Transfer to serving platter. Remove foil from pork; serve spinach with chops.

1 pork chop with ½ cup spinach: 310 cal., 17g fat (5g sat. fat), 98mg chol., 607mg sod., 4g carb. (1g sugars, 1g fiber), 36g pro. **Diabetic exchanges:** 4 lean meat, 1½ fat, 1 vegetable.

TORTELLINI WITH SAUSAGE & MASCARPONE

TORTELLINI WITH SAUSAGE & MASCARPONE

When I crave Italian comfort food on a busy night and don't have a lot of time to spare, this dish is fast and yummy. You can have it on the table in less time than a takeout order.
—Gerry Vance, Millbrae, CA

Takes: 20 min. • **Makes:** 6 servings

- 1 pkg. (20 oz.) refrigerated cheese tortellini
- 8 oz. bulk Italian sausage
- 1 jar (24 oz.) pasta sauce with mushrooms
- ½ cup shredded Parmesan cheese
- 1 carton (8 oz.) mascarpone cheese
  Crushed red pepper flakes, optional

1. Prepare tortellini according to package directions. Meanwhile, in a large cast-iron or other heavy skillet, cook sausage over medium heat until no longer pink, about 6-8 minutes, breaking it into crumbles; drain. Stir in pasta sauce; heat through.
2. Drain the tortellini, reserving 1 cup cooking water. Add tortellini to sauce and enough reserved cooking water to reach desired consistency; toss to coat. Stir in the Parmesan cheese; dollop with mascarpone cheese. If desired, sprinkle with red pepper flakes.

1 cup: 637 cal., 37g fat (17g sat. fat), 113mg chol., 1040mg sod., 57g carb. (11g sugars, 4g fiber), 24g pro.

30-MINUTE DINNERS

Need dinner in a hurry? Forget the microwave dinners—these satisfying suppers all take a half-hour (or less!) from start to finish. So you'll always be sure to have a heartwarming homemade meal on the table, even on your busiest nights.

SKILLET-GRILLED CATFISH

You can use this recipe with any thick fish fillet, but I suggest catfish or haddock. The Cajun flavor is great.
—Traci Wynne, Denver, PA

Takes: 25 min. • **Makes:** 4 servings

- ¼ cup all-purpose flour
- ¼ cup cornmeal
- 1 tsp. onion powder
- 1 tsp. dried basil
- ½ tsp. garlic salt
- ½ tsp. dried thyme
- ¼ to ½ tsp. white pepper
- ¼ to ½ tsp. cayenne pepper
- ¼ to ½ tsp. pepper
- 4 catfish fillets (6 to 8 oz. each)
- ¼ cup butter

1. In a large shallow dish, combine the first 9 ingredients. Add catfish, 1 fillet at a time, and turn to coat.

2. Place a large cast-iron skillet on a grill rack over medium-high heat. Melt butter in the skillet; add the catfish in batches, if necessary. Grill, covered, until the fish just begins to flake easily with a fork, 5-10 minutes on each side.

1 fillet: 222 cal., 15g fat (8g sat. fat), 51mg chol., 366mg sod., 14g carb. (0 sugars, 1g fiber), 8g pro.

ANGEL HAIR PASTA WITH SAUSAGE & SPINACH

ANGEL HAIR PASTA WITH SAUSAGE & SPINACH

You won't miss the marinara once you taste this pasta dish flavored with chicken broth and Italian sausage. The sauce simmers away without much work on your part. My husband likes it so much that I make it twice a week.
—Daphine Smith, Baytown, TX

Takes: 30 min. • **Makes:** 4 servings

- 4 Italian sausage links (4 oz. each), sliced
- 1 medium onion, chopped
- 2 garlic cloves, minced
- 2 tsp. olive oil
- 2 cans (14½ oz. each) chicken broth
- 8 oz. uncooked angel hair pasta, broken in half
- 2 pkg. (9 oz. each) fresh spinach, trimmed and coarsely chopped
- 2 Tbsp. all-purpose flour
- ¼ tsp. pepper
- ⅓ cup heavy whipping cream

1. In a Dutch oven, cook the sausage, onion and garlic in oil over medium heat until meat is no longer pink; drain. Add broth; bring to a boil. Add pasta; cook for 3 minutes, stirring frequently.

2. Gradually add spinach. Cook and stir until pasta is tender and spinach is wilted, 2-3 minutes. In a small bowl, combine the flour, pepper and heavy whipping cream until smooth; gradually stir into the pasta mixture. Bring to a boil; cook and stir until thickened, 1-2 minutes.

1½ cups: 563 cal., 26g fat (10g sat. fat), 77mg chol., 1546mg sod., 57g carb. (6g sugars, 6g fiber), 25g pro.

EASY BEEF TACO SKILLET

Busy day? Save time and money with this stovetop supper the whole family will love. It calls for handy convenience products, so it can be on the table in minutes.
—Kelly Roder, Fairfax, VA

Takes: 20 min. • **Makes:** 6 servings

- 1 lb. ground beef
- 1 small red onion, chopped
- 1 can (15¼ oz.) whole kernel corn, drained
- 10 corn tortillas (6 in.), cut into 1-in. pieces
- 1 bottle (8 oz.) taco sauce
- 1¼ cups shredded cheddar cheese, divided
  Hot pepper sauce, optional

In a large skillet, cook beef and onion over medium heat until meat is no longer pink; drain. Add the corn, tortillas, taco sauce and 1 cup cheese; heat through. Sprinkle with remaining cheese. Serve with pepper sauce if desired.

1 cup: 415 cal., 19g fat (9g sat. fat), 82mg chol., 705mg sod., 34g carb. (6g sugars, 4g fiber), 25g pro.

EASY BEEF TACO SKILLET

ROSEMARY PORK MEDALLIONS WITH PEAS

PICTURED ON P. 97

It's nice to have a quick meal to fix after coming home from work. This meal is simple to prepare and doesn't use a lot of ingredients, so it's a great choice for beginner cooks.
—Laura McAllister, Morganton, NC

Takes: 25 min. • **Makes:** 4 servings

- 1 lb. pork tenderloin, cut into ½-in. slices
- ½ tsp. salt
- ¼ tsp. pepper
- ¼ cup all-purpose flour
- 1 Tbsp. olive oil
- 2 tsp. butter
- 1 cup reduced-sodium chicken broth
- 1 garlic clove, minced
- 1 tsp. dried rosemary, crushed
- 2 cups frozen peas

1. Sprinkle pork slices with salt and pepper. Toss with flour to coat lightly; shake off excess.
2. In a large skillet, heat oil and butter over medium heat. Add pork; cook until tender, 1-2 minutes on each side. Remove from pan; keep warm.
3. In same pan, add chicken broth, garlic and rosemary; bring to a boil, stirring to loosen browned bits from pan. Cook until liquid is reduced by a third, 2-3 minutes. Stir in peas; cook until heated through, 2-3 minutes longer. Serve with pork.

3 oz. cooked pork with ⅓ cup peas: 260 cal., 10g fat (3g sat. fat), 69mg chol., 571mg sod., 15g carb. (4g sugars, 3g fiber), 28g pro. **Diabetic exchanges:** 3 lean meat, 1 starch, ½ fat.

TURKEY A LA KING

TURKEY A LA KING

This is a smart way to use up leftover turkey. You might want to make a double batch!
—Mary Gaylord, Balsam Lake, WI

Takes: 25 min. • **Makes:** 6 servings

- 1 medium onion, chopped
- ¾ cup sliced celery
- ¼ cup diced green pepper
- ¼ cup butter, cubed
- ¼ cup all-purpose flour
- 1 tsp. sugar
- 1½ cups chicken broth
- ¼ cup half-and-half cream
- 3 cups cubed cooked turkey or chicken
- 1 can (4 oz.) sliced mushrooms, drained
- 6 slices bread, toasted

1. In a large skillet, saute the onion, celery and green pepper in butter until tender. Stir in flour and sugar until a paste forms.
2. Gradually stir in chicken broth. Bring to a boil; boil until thickened, about 1 minute. Reduce heat. Add half-and-half cream, turkey and mushrooms; heat through. Serve with toast.

1 serving: 297 cal., 13g fat (7g sat. fat), 98mg chol., 591mg sod., 21g carb. (4g sugars, 2g fiber), 24g pro.

LEMON HERBED SALMON

We sometimes send our delicious Washington salmon all the way to Michigan for my sister to use in this family-favorite dish! The topping can be used on other fish, too. Fresh thyme from the garden really sparks the flavor.
—Perlene Hoekema, Lynden, WA

Takes: 30 min. • **Makes:** 8 servings

- 2½ cups fresh bread crumbs
- 4 garlic cloves, minced
- ½ cup chopped fresh parsley
- 6 Tbsp. grated Parmesan cheese
- ¼ cup chopped fresh thyme or 1 Tbsp. dried thyme
- 2 tsp. grated lemon zest
- ½ tsp. salt
- 6 Tbsp. butter, melted, divided
- 1 salmon fillet (3 to 4 lbs.)

1. In a shallow bowl, combine bread crumbs, garlic, parsley, Parmesan cheese, thyme, lemon zest and salt; mix well. Add 4 Tbsp. melted butter and toss lightly to coat; set aside.
2. Pat salmon dry. Place skin side down in a greased baking dish. Brush with remaining butter; cover with crumb mixture. Bake at 350° for 20 to 25 minutes or until salmon flakes easily with a fork.

6 oz. cooked salmon: 446 cal., 29g fat (10g sat. fat), 126mg chol., 483mg sod., 8g carb. (1g sugars, 1g fiber), 37g pro.

CILANTRO SHRIMP & RICE

I created this one-dish wonder for my son, who has the pickiest palate. The aroma of fresh herbs is so appetizing, he can't resist!

—*Nibedita Das, Fort Worth, TX*

Takes: 30 min. • **Makes:** 8 servings

- 2 pkg. (8½ oz. each) ready-to-serve basmati rice
- 2 Tbsp. olive oil
- 2 cups frozen corn, thawed
- 2 medium zucchini, quartered and sliced
- 1 large sweet red pepper, chopped
- ½ tsp. crushed red pepper flakes
- 3 garlic cloves, minced
- 1 lb. peeled and deveined cooked large shrimp, tails removed
- ½ cup chopped fresh cilantro
- 1 Tbsp. grated lime zest
- 2 Tbsp. lime juice
- ¾ tsp. salt
  Lime wedges, optional

1. Prepare rice according to package directions.
2. Meanwhile, in a large skillet, heat olive oil over medium-high heat. Add the corn, zucchini, red pepper and pepper flakes; cook and stir 3-5 minutes or until zucchini is crisp-tender. Add garlic; cook 1 minute longer. Add shrimp; cook and stir until heated through, 3-5 minutes.
3. Stir in rice, cilantro, lime zest, lime juice and salt. If desired, serve with lime wedges.

1½ cups: 243 cal., 6g fat (1g sat. fat), 86mg chol., 324mg sod., 28g carb. (3g sugars, 3g fiber), 16g pro. **Diabetic exchanges:** 2 lean meat, 1½ starch, ½ fat.

TOMATO WALNUT TILAPIA

PICTURED ON P. 97

Tomato, bread crumbs and crunchy walnuts dress up tilapia fillets in this delightful main dish. I often serve it with cooked green beans and some julienned carrots.

—*Phyl Broich-Wessling, Garner, IA*

Takes: 20 min. • **Makes:** 4 servings

- 4 tilapia fillets (4 oz. each)
- ¼ tsp. salt
- ¼ tsp. pepper
- 1 Tbsp. butter
- 1 medium tomato, thinly sliced

TOPPING
- ½ cup soft bread crumbs
- ¼ cup chopped walnuts
- 2 Tbsp. lemon juice
- 1½ tsp. butter, melted

1. Sprinkle fillets with salt and pepper. In a large skillet coated with cooking spray, cook fillets in butter over medium-high heat until lightly browned, 2-3 minutes on each side.
2. Transfer fish to a broiler pan or baking sheet; top with tomato. Combine topping ingredients; spoon over the tomato slices.
3. Broil 3-4 in. from the heat until topping is lightly browned and fish just begins to flake easily with a fork, 2-3 minutes.

1 fillet: 202 cal., 10g fat (4g sat. fat), 67mg chol., 251mg sod., 6g carb. (2g sugars, 1g fiber), 23g pro. **Diabetic exchanges:** 3 lean meat, 2 fat, ½ starch.

CILANTRO SHRIMP & RICE

SALMON DILL SOUP

CHINESE CASHEW CHICKEN PIZZA

I make this quick weeknight dinner recipe whenever I'm craving take-out pizza as well as Chinese food. I like using shortcuts like premade pizza crust and rotisserie chicken to cut down on the time I have to spend in the kitchen.

—Joseph Sciascia, San Mateo, CA

Takes: 30 min. • **Makes:** 8 servings

- 1 prebaked 12-in. pizza crust or flatbread
- 1 Tbsp. sesame oil
- ¾ cup hoisin sauce
- 2 tsp. chili garlic sauce
- 1½ cups shredded cooked chicken
- 4 green onions, chopped, divided
- ½ cup chopped sweet red pepper
- ⅓ cup shredded carrots
- ½ cup chopped cashews
- 3 Tbsp. chopped fresh cilantro
- 1¼ cups shredded mozzarella cheese

1. Preheat oven to 425°. Place pizza crust on a pizza pan; brush with sesame oil. In small bowl, combine hoisin sauce and chili garlic sauce; brush ⅓ cup over crust. Toss remaining mixture with chicken; sprinkle over crust. Top with 2 green onions, red pepper, carrots, cashews and cilantro. Sprinkle mozzarella over top.
2. Bake until cheese is lightly browned, 12-15 minutes. Let stand for 5 minutes; sprinkle with remaining 2 green onions.

1 slice: 357 cal., 15g fat (5g sat. fat), 38mg chol., 876mg sod., 37g carb. (9g sugars, 2g fiber), 19g pro.

DID YOU KNOW?
Hoisin sauce is a thick, sweet and somewhat spicy condiment popular in Chinese cooking. It's often made with fermented soybeans (miso), garlic, spices and sweet ingredients such as plums or sweet potatoes.

SALMON DILL SOUP

This is the best soup I have ever made, according to my husband, who loves salmon so much that he could eat it every day. When I get salmon, I try to make it a very special dish because salmon is a treat for both of us.

—Hidemi Walsh, Plainfield, IN

Takes: 30 min. • **Makes:** 2 servings

- 1 large potato, peeled and cut into 1½-in. pieces
- 1 large carrot, cut into ½-in.-thick slices
- 1½ cups water
- 1 cup reduced-sodium chicken broth
- 5 medium fresh mushrooms, halved
- 1 Tbsp. all-purpose flour
- ¼ cup reduced-fat evaporated milk
- ¼ cup shredded part-skim mozzarella cheese
- ½ lb. salmon fillet, cut into 1½-in. pieces
- ¼ tsp. pepper
- ⅛ tsp. salt
- 1 Tbsp. chopped fresh dill

1. Place first 4 ingredients in a saucepan; bring to a boil. Reduce heat to medium; cook, uncovered, until vegetables are tender, 10-15 minutes.
2. Add mushrooms. In a small bowl, mix flour and milk until smooth; stir into soup. Return to a boil; cook and stir until the mushrooms are tender. Reduce heat to medium; stir in cheese until melted.
3. Reduce heat to medium-low. Add the salmon; cook, uncovered, until the fish just begins to flake easily with a fork, 3-4 minutes. Stir in pepper and salt. Sprinkle with dill.

2½ cups: 398 cal., 14g fat (4g sat. fat), 71mg chol., 647mg sod., 37g carb. (7g sugars, 3g fiber), 30g pro. **Diabetic exchanges:** 3 lean meat, 2½ starch.

**CHINESE CASHEW
CHICKEN PIZZA**

Oh-So-Easy Eggs

A perfectly made omelet is just the thing for a specai brunch or a light dinner!

Make a Simple Mediterranean Omelet

1. Mix the eggs

Whisk eggs, water, salt and pepper until blended. Heat butter over medium-high heat and pour in the egg mixture. Mixture should set immediately at the edge.

2. Be sure to cook evenly

As the eggs set, push cooked portions toward the center, letting uncooked eggs flow underneath.

3. Add the fillings

When the eggs are thickened and no liquid egg remains, add cheese, tomato and green onion to 1 side.

4. Fold and serve!

Fold the omelet in half and slide out of the pan. Cut the omelet in half and and serve. It couldn't be simpler!

MEDITERRANEAN OMELET

This fluffy omelet gives us reason to rush to the breakfast table. For extra flair, add a chopped fresh herb such as basil, oregano or tarragon.
—Milynne Charlton, Scarborough, ON

½ omelet: 236 cal., 18g fat (8g sat. fat), 395mg chol., 472mg sod., 3g carb. (1g sugars, 1g fiber), 15g pro.

Takes: 10 min. • **Makes:** 2 servings

- 4 large eggs
- ¼ cup water
- ⅛ tsp. salt
- Dash pepper
- 1 Tbsp. butter
- ¼ cup crumbled feta or goat cheese
- ¼ cup chopped tomato
- 1 green onion, chopped

SAUSAGE & ASPARAGUS PASTA WITH CAJUN CREAM SAUCE

I needed to use up some ingredients in my refrigerator, so I threw together this dish. It's delicious and everyone loves it. I only use Tony Chachere's Creole seasoning mix.
—Angela Lively, Conroe, TX

Takes: 25 min. • **Makes:** 8 servings

- 1 pkg. (16 oz.) spiral pasta
- 1 lb. fresh asparagus, trimmed and cut into 2-in. pieces
- 1 pkg. (14 oz.) smoked sausage, sliced
- 2 garlic cloves, minced
- 1 cup heavy whipping cream
- ½ cup shredded Parmesan cheese
- 1 Tbsp. Creole seasoning
- ¼ tsp. pepper

1. In a Dutch oven, cook pasta according to package directions, adding asparagus during the last 4 minutes of cooking. Meanwhile, in a large nonstick skillet, cook sausage over medium heat until browned. Add garlic; cook 1 minute longer. Stir in heavy cream, Parmesan cheese, Creole seasoning and pepper; cook and stir until slightly thickened, about 3 minutes.

2. Drain pasta mixture, reserving ½ cup cooking water; add to sausage mixture. Toss to coat, gradually adding enough of the reserved cooking water to reach desired consistency.

1¼ cups: 496 cal., 26g fat (14g sat. fat), 71mg chol., 909mg sod., 46g carb. (4g sugars, 2g fiber), 18g pro.

QUICK SHRIMP CURRY
PICTURED ON P. 97

I like to serve the optional toppings in bowls on the table. That way, everyone can take what they like.
—Sharon Tipton, Casselberry, FL

Takes: 30 min. • **Makes:** 6 servings

- 2 Tbsp. butter
- 1 large onion, chopped
- 1 medium tart apple, peeled and finely chopped
- 1 celery rib, chopped
- 1 garlic clove, minced
- 2 Tbsp. all-purpose flour
- 2 cups chicken stock
- ½ cup heavy whipping cream
- 2 tsp. curry powder
- ½ tsp. salt
- ¼ tsp. ground mustard
- 1 bay leaf
- 1½ lbs. uncooked medium shrimp, peeled and deveined
  Hot cooked rice
  Optional: Lime wedges, toasted coconut and chopped green onions

1. In a large saucepan, heat butter over medium-high heat. Add onion, apple and celery; cook and stir until tender, 3-4 minutes. Add garlic; cook 1 minute longer. Stir in flour until blended; gradually whisk in stock, cream, curry powder, salt, ground mustard and bay leaf. Bring to a boil, stirring constantly; cook and stir until thickened, 2-3 minutes.

2. Reduce heat; simmer, uncovered, until slightly reduced, 6-8 minutes, stirring occasionally. Add shrimp; cook until shrimp turn pink, 6-8 minutes. Serve with rice and, if desired, optional toppings.

⅔ cup: 239 cal., 13g fat (7g sat. fat), 171mg chol., 544mg sod., 10g carb. (4g sugars, 1g fiber), 21g pro.

SAUSAGE & ASPARAGUS PASTA WITH CAJUN CREAM SAUCE

PINTO BEAN ZUCCHINI BOATS

Zucchini shells take center stage when filled with vegetables, beans and sauce.
—Taste of Home *Test Kitchen*

Takes: 30 min. • **Makes:** 4 servings

- 4 large zucchini
- 8 cups water
- 1 tsp. salt
- ½ cup chopped red onion
- 1 Tbsp. olive oil
- 1 can (15 oz.) pinto beans, rinsed and drained
- 1 can (11 oz.) Mexicorn, drained
- 1 can (8 oz.) tomato sauce
- ½ cup chili sauce
- 1 tsp. dried cilantro flakes
- ½ tsp. ground cumin
- 3 oz. Gouda cheese, shredded
- ½ cup chopped tomato

1. Cut zucchini in half lengthwise. Scoop out pulp, leaving a ⅜-in. shell. Chop pulp and set aside. In a Dutch oven, bring water and salt to a boil. Add zucchini shells; cook until crisp-tender, 5-8 minutes. Drain and set aside.

2. In a large skillet, saute the onion and zucchini pulp in oil until crisp-tender. Stir in the beans, corn, tomato sauce, chili sauce, cilantro and cumin. Cook over medium heat until heated through, about 5 minutes. Sprinkle with cheese; cover and cook until cheese is melted, about 1 minute. Spoon into zucchini shells; sprinkle with tomato.

2 zucchini halves: 377 cal., 11g fat (4g sat. fat), 24mg chol., 1310mg sod., 55g carb. (22g sugars, 9g fiber), 17g pro.

QUICK ITALIAN VEGGIE SKILLET

QUICK ITALIAN VEGGIE SKILLET

When you don't know what to serve, Italian flavors are always a good starting point. We combine cannellini and garbanzo beans for this snappy dish.
—Sonya Labbe, West Hollywood, CA

Takes: 25 min. • **Makes:** 4 servings

- 1 can (15 oz.) no-salt-added garbanzo beans or chickpeas, rinsed and drained
- 1 can (15 oz.) no-salt-added cannellini beans, rinsed and drained
- 1 can (14½ oz.) no-salt-added stewed tomatoes, undrained
- 1 cup vegetable broth
- ¾ cup uncooked instant rice
- 1 tsp. Italian seasoning
- ¼ tsp. crushed red pepper flakes, optional
- 1 cup marinara sauce
- ¼ cup grated Parmesan cheese
  Minced fresh basil

In a large skillet, combine the first 6 ingredients and, if desired, pepper flakes; bring to a boil. Reduce heat; simmer, covered, until rice is tender, 7-9 minutes. Stir in marinara sauce; heat through, stirring occasionally. Top with cheese and basil.

1⅓ cups: 342 cal., 4g fat (1g sat. fat), 6mg chol., 660mg sod., 59g carb. (10g sugars, 11g fiber), 16g pro.

HALIBUT SOFT TACOS

I sometimes serve the fish wrapped in lettuce instead of tortillas. Either way, the mango salsa tastes amazing with grilled halibut. This warm-weather favorite is quick, colorful and full of nutrients.
—Kristin Kossak, Bozeman, MT

Takes: 30 min. • **Makes:** 4 servings

- 1 medium mango, peeled and cubed
- ½ cup cubed avocado
- ¼ cup chopped red onion
- 2 Tbsp. chopped seeded jalapeno pepper
- 1 Tbsp. minced fresh cilantro
- 3 tsp. olive oil, divided
- 1 tsp. lemon juice
- 1 tsp. honey
- 1 lb. halibut steaks (¾ in. thick)
- ½ tsp. salt
- ¼ tsp. pepper
- 4 Bibb lettuce leaves
- 4 flour tortillas (6 in.), warmed
- 4 tsp. sweet Thai chili sauce

1. In a small bowl, combine the mango, avocado, onion, jalapeno, cilantro, 2 tsp. oil, lemon juice and honey; set aside. Brush halibut with remaining oil; sprinkle with salt and pepper.

2. Grill halibut on greased rack, covered, over high heat or broil 3-4 in. from the heat until the fish flakes easily with a fork, 3-5 minutes on each side.

3. Place lettuce leaves on tortillas; top with fish and mango mixture. Drizzle with chili sauce.

1 taco with ⅓ cup mango mixture : 330 cal., 12g fat (1g sat. fat), 36mg chol., 648mg sod., 28g carb. (12g sugars, 2g fiber), 28g pro. **Diabetic exchanges:** 3 lean meat, 2 starch, 1 fat.

HALIBUT SOFT TACOS

LEMONY GREEK BEEF & VEGETABLES

PICTURED ON P. 97

I love the lemon in this recipe, which is the latest addition to my collection of quick, healthy dinners. I'm sensitive to cow's milk, so I use goat cheese crumbles on my portion instead of the Parmesan.
—Alice Neff, Lake Worth, FL

Takes: 30 min. • **Makes:** 4 servings

- 1 bunch baby bok choy
- 1 lb. ground beef
- 1 Tbsp. olive oil
- 5 medium carrots, sliced
- 3 garlic cloves, minced
- ¼ cup plus 2 Tbsp. white wine, divided
- 1 can (15 to 16 oz.) navy beans, rinsed and drained
- 2 Tbsp. minced fresh oregano or 2 tsp. dried oregano
- ¼ tsp. salt
- 2 Tbsp. lemon juice
- ½ cup shredded Parmesan cheese

1. Trim and discard root end of bok choy. Coarsely chop leaves. Cut stalks into 1-in. pieces. Set aside.

2. In a large skillet, cook ground beef over medium-high heat until no longer pink, breaking into crumbles, 5-7 minutes; drain. Remove from skillet and set aside.

3. In same skillet, heat oil over medium-high heat. Add the carrots and bok choy stalks; cook and stir until crisp-tender, 5-7 minutes. Stir in garlic, bok choy leaves and ¼ cup wine; increase heat to medium-high. Cook, stirring to loosen browned bits from pan, until greens wilt, 3-5 minutes.

4. Stir in ground beef, beans, oregano, salt and enough remaining wine to keep mixture moist. Reduce heat; simmer about 3 minutes. Stir in lemon juice; sprinkle with Parmesan cheese.

1½ cups: 478 cal., 21g fat (7g sat. fat), 77mg chol., 856mg sod., 36g carb. (7g sugars, 10g fiber), 36g pro.

> **TEST KITCHEN TIP**
> Can't find bok choy? Any hearty greens, like kale or collards, will be just as delicious. If you don't have white wine on hand, try beer, water or broth instead.

THAI CHICKEN PASTA

I try to buy fresh chicken when it's on sale. I cook a big batch in the slow cooker, then cut it up and package it in small amounts suitable for recipes like this. When I want it, I just need to be pull it out of the freezer and let it thaw.

—Jeni Pittard, Statham, GA

Takes: 25 min. • **Makes:** 2 servings

- 3 oz. uncooked whole wheat linguine
- ½ cup salsa
- 2 Tbsp. reduced-fat creamy peanut butter
- 1 Tbsp. orange juice
- 1½ tsp. honey
- 1 tsp. reduced-sodium soy sauce
- 1 cup cubed cooked chicken breast
- 1 Tbsp. chopped unsalted peanuts
- 1 Tbsp. minced fresh cilantro

1. Cook linguine according to package directions.
2. Meanwhile, in a microwave-safe dish, combine the salsa, peanut butter, orange juice, honey and soy sauce. Cover and microwave on high for 1 minute; stir. Add the chicken; heat through.
3. Drain linguine. Serve with the chicken mixture. Garnish with chopped peanuts and cilantro.

1 serving: 409 cal., 10g fat (2g sat. fat), 54mg chol., 474mg sod., 46g carb. (10g sugars, 6g fiber), 33g pro.

PORK CHOPS WITH NECTARINE SALSA

My special pork dish has so much flavor and is a snap to prepare. A sweet, fruity salsa perfectly balances the spicy rub that coats the pan-fried chops.

—Bonnie Bufford, Nicholson, PA

Takes: 20 min. • **Makes:** 4 servings

- 2 tsp. chili powder
- 1 tsp. ground coriander
- ½ tsp. ground cumin
- ½ tsp. paprika
- ¼ tsp. salt
- ¼ tsp. pepper
- 4 boneless pork loin chops (4 oz. each and ½ in. thick)
- 1 Tbsp. olive oil
- ¼ cup salsa
- 2 Tbsp. apricot spreadable fruit
- 2 cups sliced peeled nectarines or peaches
- 2 Tbsp. minced fresh cilantro
- 1 Tbsp. minced fresh oregano or 1 tsp. dried oregano

1. In a small bowl, combine the first 6 ingredients. Rub over both sides of pork chops. In a large nonstick skillet, cook the pork chops in oil over medium-high heat until juices run clear, 5-6 minutes on each side. Remove chops to a serving platter and keep warm.
2. In the same skillet, combine salsa and spreadable fruit. Bring to a boil. Reduce heat; cook and stir over medium heat for 1 minute. Stir in nectarines, cilantro and oregano; cook until heated through, 2-3 minutes. Serve with pork.

1 pork chop with ½ cup salsa: 246 cal., 10g fat (3g sat. fat), 55mg chol., 279mg sod., 15g carb. (10g sugars, 2g fiber), 23g pro. **Diabetic exchanges:** 3 lean meat, 1 fruit.

PORK CHOPS WITH NECTARINE SALSA

LEMONY SHRIMP & ARUGULA ORZO

LEMONY SHRIMP & ARUGULA ORZO

What I love about this recipe is that it's so tasty and can be eaten hot or cold. If you're allergic to shrimp, it tastes great with chicken, too.
—Aleni Salcedo, East Elmhurst, NY

Takes: 30 min. • **Makes:** 8 servings

- 2 Tbsp. olive oil
- 1 small onion, chopped
- 2 garlic cloves, minced
- 3½ cups reduced-sodium chicken broth
- 1 lb. uncooked whole wheat orzo pasta
- 1 cup water
- 1 lb. uncooked shrimp (31-40 per lb.), peeled and deveined
- 4 cups fresh arugula
- 3 Tbsp. lemon juice
- ½ tsp. salt
- ¼ tsp. pepper
- ½ cup pitted Greek olives, halved
- 1½ cups crumbled feta cheese
  Fresh basil leaves

1. In a large skillet, heat oil over medium-high heat. Add onion; cook and stir until crisp-tender, 3-4 minutes. Add garlic; cook 1 minute longer. Stir in the chicken broth, orzo and water. Bring to a boil; reduce heat. Simmer, uncovered, until orzo is al dente, 8-10 minutes.
2. Stir in shrimp, arugula, lemon juice, salt and pepper. Cook and stir until the shrimp turn pink, 4-5 minutes. Stir in olives. Sprinkle with feta and basil leaves.
1 cup: 367 cal., 11g fat (3g sat. fat), 80mg chol., 808mg sod., 44g carb. (1g sugars, 10g fiber), 22g pro.

BLUE CHEESE-STUFFED STEAKS

For a fast, fancy dinner, try this tender beef with a mild blue cheese stuffing. Grape tomatoes sauteed in garlic make a colorful and flavorful accompaniment.
—Teddy Devico, Warren, NJ

Takes: 30 min. • **Makes:** 4 servings

- 10 garlic cloves, peeled
- 2 Tbsp. canola oil
- 4 cups grape tomatoes
- 4 boneless beef top loin steaks (8 oz. each)
- ½ cup crumbled blue cheese
- ½ tsp. salt
- ¼ tsp. pepper

1. In a large skillet, saute garlic in oil until tender. Cover and cook over low heat for 5-7 minutes or until golden and softened. Add grape tomatoes; cook and stir until tomatoes just begin to burst. Remove from the skillet; set aside and keep warm.
2. Cut a pocket in the thickest part of each steak; fill with blue cheese. Sprinkle with salt and pepper.
3. In the same skillet, cook steaks over medium heat for 4-5 minutes on each side or until meat reaches desired doneness (for medium-rare, a thermometer should read 135°; medium, 140°; medium-well, 145°). Serve with tomato mixture.
1 steak with 1 cup tomato mixture: 463 cal., 23g fat (8g sat. fat), 113mg chol., 644mg sod., 10g carb. (4g sugars, 2g fiber), 53g pro.

**SKILLET CHICKEN
FAJITAS**

SKILLET CHICKEN FAJITAS

Fresh flavor with a flair describes this quick and easy recipe. Fajitas are just right for hot summer evenings when you want to serve something fun and tasty, yet keep cooking to a minimum. Try topping them with sour cream, guacamole or both. My family loves them!
—Lindsay St. John, Plainfield, IN

Takes: 30 min. • **Makes:** 6 servings

- ¼ cup lime juice
- 1 garlic clove, minced
- 1 tsp. chili powder
- ½ tsp. salt
- ½ tsp. ground cumin
- 2 Tbsp. olive oil, divided
- 1½ lbs. boneless skinless chicken breasts, cut into strips
- 1 medium onion, cut into thin wedges
- ½ medium sweet red pepper, cut into strips
- ½ medium yellow pepper, cut into strips
- ½ medium green pepper, cut into strips
- ½ cup salsa
- 12 flour tortillas (8 in.), warmed
- 1½ cups shredded cheddar cheese or Monterey Jack cheese

1. Mix first 5 ingredients and 1 Tbsp. oil. Add chicken breast strips; toss to coat. Let stand 15 minutes.
2. In a large nonstick skillet, heat the remaining oil over medium-high heat; saute onion and peppers until crisp-tender, 3-4 minutes. Remove from pan.
3. In same skillet, saute chicken mixture until no longer pink, 3-4 minutes. Stir in salsa and pepper mixture; heat through. Serve in tortillas. Sprinkle with cheese.
1 serving: 621 cal., 24g fat (8g sat. fat), 91mg chol., 999mg sod., 61g carb. (3g sugars, 4g fiber), 38g pro.

SMOKED SALMON PASTA

SMOKED SALMON PASTA

This pasta originally came to be from the miscellaneous ingredients in my fridge, and depending on whom I'm cooking for, it changes a little each time I make it. The recipe makes enough for a party or for leftovers, which is a bonus because it's excellent the next day, whether you serve it cold or reheated.
—Jackie Hennon, Boise, ID

Takes: 25 min. • **Makes:** 8 servings

- 1 lb. uncooked spiral or penne pasta
- 2 Tbsp. olive oil
- 2 large tomatoes, diced
- 2 cups water-packed artichoke hearts, drained and chopped
- 1½ cups kalamata olives, pitted and halved
- 1 cup chopped oil-packed sun-dried tomatoes
- ¾ cup chopped onion
- 8 oz. smoked salmon fillets
- 2 Tbsp. sun-dried tomato pesto
- 2 tsp. dried basil
- ¾ tsp. crushed red pepper flakes
- ¼ cup grated Parmesan cheese
- ¼ cup crumbled feta cheese

1. In a large saucepan, cook the pasta according to package directions for al dente. Meanwhile, in a Dutch oven, heat olive oil over medium-low heat. Add next 5 ingredients. Break salmon into bite-sized pieces; add to the tomato mixture. Stir in pesto, basil and red pepper flakes. Cook, stirring occasionally, until vegetables are crisp-tender, 8-10 minutes.
2. Drain pasta. Add to salmon mixture; stir to combine. Top with cheeses.
¾ cup: 433 cal., 16g fat (3g sat. fat), 11mg chol., 924mg sod., 55g carb. (4g sugars, 4g fiber), 17g pro.

TEST KITCHEN TIP
This is a very forgiving recipe, so use more of the ingredients you like! If you love salmon, add more. If you're not fond of olives, cut back.

SKILLET ZUCCHINI & SAUSAGE

I lived on the Oregon coast for 20 years and had plenty of guests dropping by. I often turned to this quick and easy dish, serving it up with skillet cornbread or garlic bread. Judging by the requests for the recipe, everyone loved it!
—LaBelle Doster, Vancouver, WA

Takes: 30 min. • **Makes:** 4 servings

- 2 Tbsp. vegetable oil
- ½ lb. fully cooked smoked Polish sausage, cut into ½-in. diagonal slices
- 1 cup chopped onion
- 1 cup sliced celery
- ½ cup chopped green pepper
- 1 garlic clove, minced
- ½ tsp. dried oregano
- ½ tsp. pepper
- 4 to 5 medium zucchini, sliced
- 4 to 5 medium tomatoes, coarsely chopped
  Herb seasoning blend to taste

Heat oil in a large skillet; add sausage and lightly brown. Add onion, celery, green pepper, garlic, oregano and pepper. Cook and stir until vegetables are almost tender. Add zucchini and tomatoes; cook and stir until zucchini is just tender. Sprinkle with seasoning blend.

1 serving: 313 cal., 23g fat (6g sat. fat), 40mg chol., 525mg sod., 18g carb. (10g sugars, 5g fiber), 11g pro.

GINGER PORK STIR-FRY

GINGER PORK STIR-FRY

My recipe box is full of delicious pork recipes, but this quick stir-fry really stands out from all the rest. My family loves the citrus glaze that coats the tender pork and vegetables. Ginger, garlic and orange juice provide its terrific taste.
—Jackie Hannahs, Cedar Springs, MI

Takes: 25 min. • **Makes:** 4 servings

- 1 Tbsp. cornstarch
- 1 cup orange juice
- 2 Tbsp. soy sauce
- 2 garlic cloves, minced
- ¼ tsp. ground ginger
- 1 lb. pork tenderloin, cut into thin strips
- 1 Tbsp. canola oil
- 1 small onion, sliced
- ¼ lb. fresh snow peas
- ½ sweet red pepper, julienned
  Hot cooked rice
  Optional: Chopped green onion and sesame seeds

1. In a small bowl, combine cornstarch, orange juice, soy sauce, garlic and ginger until smooth; set aside.
2. In a large skillet or wok, stir-fry pork in oil until lightly browned, about 5 minutes; drain. Add vegetables; cook and stir until crisp-tender, 3-5 minutes.
3. Stir orange juice mixture and add to pan. Bring to a boil; cook and stir until thickened, about 2 minutes. Serve with rice. Garnish with green onion and sesame seeds, if desired.

1 serving: 228 cal., 7g fat (2g sat. fat), 64mg chol., 508mg sod., 13g carb. (8g sugars, 1g fiber), 25g pro. **Diabetic exchanges:** 3 lean meat, 1 vegetable, ½ starch, ½ fat.

QUICK CHICKEN & DUMPLINGS

Oh, the things you can make with frozen biscuit dough. I like to use buttermilk biscuits to make this easy dumpling dish.
—Lakeya Astwood, Schenectady, NY

Takes: 30 min.
Makes: 6 servings (2¼ qt.)

- 6 individually frozen biscuits
- ¼ cup chopped onion
- ¼ cup chopped green pepper
- 1 Tbsp. olive oil
- 4 cups shredded rotisserie chicken
- 3 cans (14½ oz. each) reduced-sodium chicken broth
- 1 can (4 oz.) mushroom stems and pieces, drained
- 1 tsp. chicken bouillon granules
- 1 tsp. minced fresh parsley
- ½ tsp. dried sage leaves
- ¼ tsp. dried rosemary, crushed
- ¼ tsp. pepper

1. Cut each biscuit into fourths; set aside. In a large saucepan, saute onion and green pepper in olive oil until tender. Stir in the shredded chicken, broth, mushrooms, bouillon granules, parsley, sage, rosemary and pepper.

2. Bring to a boil. Reduce heat; add the biscuits for dumplings. Cover and simmer (do not lift cover while simmering) for 10 minutes or until a toothpick inserted in the center of a dumpling comes out clean.

1½ cups: 420 cal., 20g fat (5g sat. fat), 83mg chol., 1443mg sod., 26g carb. (6g sugars, 1g fiber), 34g pro.

MAHI MAHI & VEGGIE SKILLET

Cooking mahi mahi with a mixture of vegetables may seem complex, but I developed a skillet recipe to bring out the wow factor without the hassle and fuss.
—Solomon Wang, Arlington, TX

Takes: 30 min. • **Makes:** 4 servings

- 3 Tbsp. olive oil, divided
- 4 mahi mahi or salmon fillets (6 oz. each)
- 3 medium sweet red peppers, cut into thick strips
- ½ lb. sliced baby portobello mushrooms
- 1 large sweet onion, cut into thick rings and separated
- ⅓ cup lemon juice
- ¾ tsp. salt, divided
- ½ tsp. pepper
- ¼ cup minced fresh chives
- ⅓ cup pine nuts, optional

1. In a large skillet, heat 2 Tbsp. oil over medium-high heat. Add fillets; cook until fish just begins to flake easily with a fork, 4-5 minutes on each side. Remove fish from pan.

2. Add the remaining olive oil, peppers, mushrooms, onion, lemon juice and ¼ tsp. salt. Cook, covered, over medium heat until the vegetables are tender, stirring occasionally, 6-8 minutes.

3. Place fish over vegetables; sprinkle with pepper and remaining salt. Cook, covered, until heated through, about 2 minutes longer. Sprinkle with chives and, if desired, pine nuts before serving.

1 serving: 307 cal., 12g fat (2g sat. fat), 124mg chol., 606mg sod., 15g carb. (9g sugars, 3g fiber), 35g pro. **Diabetic exchanges:** 4 lean meat, 3 vegetable, 2 fat.

QUICK CHICKEN & DUMPLINGS

MEDITERRANEAN TURKEY SKILLET

I've always heard that it's important to eat a rainbow of colors to get all of the nutrients we need. Thanks to my garden-grown veggies, this healthy dish is in my regular rotation.
—Nicole Ehlert, Burlington, WI

Takes: 30 min. • **Makes:** 6 servings

- 1 Tbsp. olive oil
- 1 pkg. (20 oz.) lean ground turkey
- 2 medium zucchini, quartered lengthwise and cut into ½-in. slices
- 1 medium onion, chopped
- 2 banana peppers, seeded and chopped
- 3 garlic cloves, minced
- ½ tsp. dried oregano
- 1 can (15 oz.) black beans, rinsed and drained
- 1 can (14½ oz.) diced tomatoes, undrained
- 1 Tbsp. balsamic vinegar
- ½ tsp. salt

In a large skillet, heat the olive oil over medium-high heat. Add turkey, zucchini, onion, peppers, garlic and oregano; cook until the turkey is no longer pink and vegetables are tender, 10-12 minutes, breaking up turkey into crumbles; drain. Stir in remaining ingredients and heat through, stirring occasionally.

1 cup: 259 cal., 10g fat (2g sat. fat), 65mg chol., 504mg sod., 20g carb. (6g sugars, 6g fiber), 24g pro. **Diabetic exchanges:** 3 lean meat, 1 vegetable, ½ starch, ½ fat.

COCONUT CITRUS SAUCED COD

I love to make this fusion weeknight meal when I'm short on time, but want something big in flavor.
—Roxanne Chan, Albany, CA

Takes: 30 min. • **Makes:** 4 servings

- 4 cod fillets (6 oz. each)
- 1 Tbsp. cornstarch
- 1 cup canned coconut milk
- ½ cup orange juice
- 2 Tbsp. sweet chili sauce
- 1 tsp. minced fresh gingerroot
- 1 tsp. soy sauce
- 1 can (11 oz.) mandarin oranges, drained
- 1 green onion, chopped
- 2 Tbsp. sliced almonds
- 1 Tbsp. sesame oil
   Minced fresh cilantro

1. In a large saucepan, place a steamer basket over 1 in. of water. Place cod in basket. Bring water to a boil. Reduce heat to maintain a low boil; steam, covered, until fish just begins to flake easily with a fork, 8-10 minutes.

2. Meanwhile, in small saucepan, whisk cornstarch, coconut milk and orange juice until smooth. Add chili sauce, ginger and soy sauce. Cook and stir over medium heat until thickened, 1-2 minutes. Stir in next 4 ingredients; heat through. Serve with cod; sprinkle with cilantro.

1 serving: 330 cal., 15g fat (10g sat. fat), 65mg chol., 316mg sod., 19g carb. (15g sugars, 1g fiber), 29g pro.

COCONUT CITRUS SAUCED COD

PESTO VEGETABLE PIZZA

SOUTHWEST SMOTHERED CHICKEN

There's a fiesta in every bite of this tasty chicken dish. Let it spice up your dinner tonight! If you're worried about the heat, simply reduce the amount of jalapenos.
—Debbie Schaefer, Durand, MI

Takes: 30 min. • **Makes:** 4 servings

- 4 boneless skinless chicken breast halves (6 oz. each)
- ½ tsp. ground cumin
- ½ tsp. cayenne pepper
- 1 Tbsp. canola oil
- 1 cup fresh or frozen corn
- 1 cup salsa
- 1 cup shredded pepper Jack cheese
- ¼ cup pickled jalapeno slices
- ¼ cup sour cream

1. Flatten chicken to ½-in. thickness. Sprinkle both sides with cumin and cayenne. In a large skillet, cook chicken in oil over medium heat until no longer pink, 4-5 minutes on each side.
2. Meanwhile, combine corn and salsa; spoon over chicken. Top with cheese and jalapeno slices. Cover and cook until heated through and cheese is melted, 3-5 minutes. Top each chicken breast with a dollop of sour cream.

1 chicken breast half: 409 cal., 20g fat (8g sat. fat), 127mg chol., 593mg sod., 13g carb. (5g sugars, 1g fiber), 43g pro.

PESTO VEGETABLE PIZZA

My family loves pizza, but we rarely have it delivered since I created this fresh and flavorful version. Always a winner in my house, it is a fast and delicious meal.
—Kate Selner, Lino Lakes, MN

Takes: 30 min. • **Makes:** 6 servings

- 1 prebaked 12-in. thin pizza crust
- 2 garlic cloves, halved
- ½ cup pesto sauce
- ¾ cup packed fresh spinach, chopped
- 2 large portobello mushrooms, thinly sliced
- 1 medium sweet yellow pepper, julienned
- 2 plum tomatoes, seeded and sliced
- ⅓ cup packed fresh basil, chopped
- 1 cup shredded part-skim mozzarella cheese
- ¼ cup grated Parmesan cheese
- ½ tsp. fresh or dried oregano

1. Preheat oven to 450°. Place crust on an ungreased 12-in. pizza pan. Rub cut side of garlic cloves over crust; discard garlic. Spread pesto over crust. Top with spinach, mushrooms, yellow pepper, tomatoes and basil. Sprinkle with cheeses and oregano.
2. Bake until pizza is heated through and cheese is melted, 10-15 minutes.

1 slice: 310 cal., 15g fat (4g sat. fat), 15mg chol., 707mg sod., 31g carb. (4g sugars, 2g fiber), 13g pro. **Diabetic exchanges:** 2 starch, 2 fat, 1 medium-fat meat.

AVOCADO CRAB BOATS

These boats are wonderful with tortilla chips, beans or rice. You can also cover them, pack them on ice, and take them to a picnic or potluck. Straight from the oven or cold, they're always delicious.
—Frances Benthin, Scio, OR

Takes: 20 min. • **Makes:** 8 servings

- 5 medium ripe avocados, peeled and halved
- ½ cup mayonnaise
- 2 Tbsp. lemon juice
- 2 cans (6 oz. each) lump crabmeat, drained
- 4 Tbsp. chopped fresh cilantro, divided
- 2 Tbsp. minced chives
- 1 serrano pepper, seeded and minced
- 1 Tbsp. capers, drained
- ¼ tsp. pepper
- 1 cup shredded pepper jack cheese
- ½ tsp. paprika
  Lemon wedges

1. Preheat broiler. Place 2 avocado halves in a large bowl; mash lightly with a fork. Add mayonnaise and lemon juice; mix until well blended. Stir in crab, 3 Tbsp. cilantro, minced chives, serrano pepper, capers and pepper. Spoon into remaining avocado halves.
2. Transfer to a 15x10x1-in. baking pan. Sprinkle with cheese and paprika. Broil 4-5 in. from heat until cheese is melted, 3-5 minutes. Sprinkle with remaining cilantro; serve with lemon wedges.
1 filled avocado half: 325 cal., 28g fat (6g sat. fat), 57mg chol., 427mg sod., 8g carb. (0 sugars, 6g fiber), 13g pro.

CREAMY PUMPKIN SPAGHETTI WITH CHICKEN

CREAMY PUMPKIN SPAGHETTI WITH CHICKEN

This delicious pasta is very fast to prepare, and its mild taste appeals to both adults and children. Eliminate the meat and serve it as a side dish, or try it with browned sliced sausage.
—Blair Lonergan, Rochelle, VA

Takes: 25 min. • **Makes:** 6 servings

- 1 pkg. (16 oz.) spaghetti
- 1 Tbsp. olive oil
- 1 small onion, chopped
- 3 garlic cloves, minced
- 1 can (15 oz.) pumpkin
- 1 cup chicken broth
- ¾ cup half-and-half cream
- ½ cup grated Parmesan cheese
- 1 Tbsp. minced fresh parsley
- ½ tsp. minced fresh rosemary or ¼ tsp. dried rosemary, crushed
- ¼ tsp. ground nutmeg
- ¼ tsp. salt
- ¼ tsp. pepper
- ½ rotisserie chicken, shredded (about 2½ cups)
  Additional minced fresh parsley and rosemary

1. Cook spaghetti according to package directions. Drain spaghetti.
2. Meanwhile, in a large skillet, heat oil over medium heat. Add onion; cook and stir 4-6 minutes or until tender. Add garlic; cook 1 minute longer. Stir in pumpkin, broth, cream, cheese, parsley, rosemary, nutmeg, salt and pepper; heat through.
3. Add the spaghetti and chicken; heat through. Sprinkle with additional parsley and rosemary.
1⅓ cups: 481 cal., 12g fat (4g sat. fat), 58mg chol., 339mg sod., 66g carb. (6g sugars, 5g fiber), 26g pro.

BULGUR JAMBALAYA

I like making this dish because it allows me to stay on track for my weight loss without giving up foods I love.
—Nicholas Monfre, Oak Ridge, NJ

Takes: 30 min. • **Makes:** 4 servings

- 8 oz. boneless skinless chicken breasts, cut into ¾-in. pieces
- 1 tsp. Cajun seasoning
- 2 tsp. olive oil
- 6 oz. smoked turkey sausage, sliced
- 1 medium sweet red pepper, diced
- 2 celery ribs, diced
- 1 small onion, chopped
- ½ cup no-salt-added tomato sauce
- 1 cup bulgur
- 1 cup reduced-sodium chicken broth
- ¾ cup water
- ¼ tsp. cayenne pepper, optional

1. Toss chicken with Cajun seasoning. In a large saucepan, heat oil over medium heat; saute chicken until browned, 2-3 minutes. Remove from pan.

2. In same pan, saute the sausage until browned, 1-2 minutes. Add red pepper, celery and onion; cook and stir 2 minutes. Stir in tomato sauce; cook 30 seconds. Stir in bulgur, broth, water, chicken and, if desired, cayenne; bring to a boil. Reduce the heat; simmer, covered, until bulgur is tender and liquid is almost absorbed, about 10 minutes, stirring occasionally.

1 cup: 287 cal., 6g fat (2g sat. fat), 58mg chol., 751mg sod., 34g carb. (5g sugars, 6g fiber), 24g pro. **Diabetic exchanges:** 3 lean meat, 2 starch, ½ fat.

GRILLED CHICKEN RAMEN SALAD

PICTURED ON P. 97

This is one of those recipes that I love because it's pretty much a complete meal in one bowl, and when it goes on the table, everyone says, "Yeah!"
—Karen Carlson, San Luis Obispo, CA

Takes: 30 min. • **Makes:** 8 servings

- 2 Tbsp. canola oil
- 2 pkg. (3 oz. each) ramen noodles, crumbled
- ⅔ cup canola oil
- 2 tsp. sesame oil
- ⅓ cup seasoned rice vinegar
- 1 Tbsp. sugar
- 2 Tbsp. reduced-sodium soy sauce
- 1½ lbs. boneless skinless chicken breast halves
- ½ tsp. pepper
- ¼ tsp. salt
- 1 pkg. (14 oz.) coleslaw mix
- ½ cup minced fresh cilantro
- 3 cups fresh snow peas, thinly sliced lengthwise
- 2 cups shredded carrots
- 4 cups torn mixed salad greens
- 3 thinly sliced green onions
- ⅓ cup crumbled cooked bacon, optional

1. In a large saucepan, heat oil over medium-low heat. Add ramen noodles; cook and stir until toasted, 5-8 minutes. Remove from pan; set aside.

2. In a small bowl, whisk oils, vinegar, sugar and soy sauce until blended; set aside.

3. Sprinkle chicken with pepper and salt. Place chicken on a lightly oiled grill rack. Grill, covered, over medium heat or broil 4-5 in. from heat until a thermometer reads 165°, 8-10 minutes on each side. Cool slightly and chop into ½-in. pieces.

4. In a large bowl, combine coleslaw mix and cilantro. Layer coleslaw mixture, peas, chicken, carrots, salad greens, noodles and green onions in an 8- to 10-qt. dish. Sprinkle with bacon; serve with vinaigrette.

1 serving: 458 cal., 29g fat (4g sat. fat), 47mg chol., 738mg sod., 28g carb. (10g sugars, 4g fiber), 22g pro.

BULGUR JAMBALAYA

VEGETARIAN SKILLET ENCHILADAS

HAWAIIAN PORK CHOPS

For a great meal when friends drop in unexpectedly, I recommend one of my husband's sweet-and-sour favorites. This tastes just like Hawaiian pizza, and I usually have all ingredients on hand.
—Michelle Cavalier, Hampton, VA

Takes: 30 min. • **Makes:** 4 servings

- 4 boneless pork loin chops
  (¾ in. thick and 4 oz. each)
- ¼ tsp. salt
- ¼ tsp. pepper
- 3 tsp. canola oil, divided
- ⅓ cup chopped green pepper
- ⅓ cup thinly sliced onion
- 1 can (14½ oz.) reduced-sodium beef broth
- 1 can (8 oz.) unsweetened pineapple chunks, undrained
- ¼ cup ketchup
- 2 Tbsp. brown sugar
- 1 Tbsp. cider vinegar
- 2 Tbsp. cornstarch
- 3 Tbsp. cold water
  Hot cooked rice, optional

1. Sprinkle pork chops with salt and pepper. Heat 2 tsp. oil in a large nonstick skillet over medium heat. Cook pork chops until lightly browned, 3-4 minutes on each side. Remove and keep warm.
2. In the same skillet, saute green pepper and onion in the remaining 1 tsp. oil until almost tender, about 2 minutes. Stir in broth, pineapple, ketchup, brown sugar and vinegar. Bring to a boil. Return pork to the pan. Reduce the heat; cover and simmer until a thermometer inserted in pork reads 145°, 5-7 minutes. Remove and keep warm.
3. Combine cornstarch and water until smooth; stir into skillet. Bring to a boil; cook and stir until sauce is thickened, 1-2 minutes. Serve with pork and, if desired, hot rice.
1 pork chop with ¾ cup sauce: 250 cal., 7g fat (2g sat. fat), 57mg chol., 554mg sod., 24g carb. (16g sugars, 1g fiber), 23g pro. **Diabetic exchanges:** 3 lean meat, ½ starch, ½ fruit, ½ fat.

VEGETARIAN SKILLET ENCHILADAS

Whether it's meatless Monday or your family eats vegetarian every day, everyone will be satisfied with these unconventional enchiladas. Garnish servings with the optional toppings or other favorites like tortilla chips and extra shredded cheese.
—Susan Court, Pewaukee, WI

Takes: 25 min. • **Makes:** 4 servings

- 1 Tbsp. canola oil
- 1 medium onion, chopped
- 1 medium sweet red pepper, chopped
- 2 garlic cloves, minced
- 1 can (15 oz.) black beans, rinsed and drained
- 1 can (10 oz.) enchilada sauce
- 1 cup frozen corn
- 2 tsp. chili powder
- ½ tsp. ground cumin
- ⅛ tsp. pepper
- 8 corn tortillas (6 in.), cut into ½-in. strips
- 1 cup shredded Mexican cheese blend
  Optional: Chopped fresh cilantro, sliced avocado, sliced radishes, sour cream and lime wedges

1. Preheat oven to 400°. Heat oil a 10-in. cast-iron or other ovenproof skillet over medium-high heat. Add onion and pepper; cook and stir until tender, 2-3 minutes. Add garlic; cook 1 minute longer. Stir in beans, enchilada sauce, corn, chili powder, cumin and pepper. Stir in tortillas.
2. Bring to a boil. Reduce heat; simmer, uncovered, until tortillas are softened, 3-5 minutes. Sprinkle with cheese. Bake, uncovered, until the sauce is bubbly and cheese is melted, 3-5 minutes. If desired, garnish with optional ingredients.
1½ cups: 307 cal., 14g fat (5g sat. fat), 25mg chol., 839mg sod., 33g carb. (5g sugars, 7g fiber), 14g pro.

TEST KITCHEN TIP
Enchilada sauce is a blend of tomatoes, oil and spices thickened with a little flour or cornstarch. Green enchilada sauce, which is made from tomatillos instead of tomatoes, is also available.

HAWAIIAN
PORK CHOPS

ISRAELI COUSCOUS & CHICKEN SAUSAGE SKILLET

Craving a plate full of comfort? With sausage, onion, celery, a touch of heat and a sprinkle of feta, this is hearty, satisfying and a little bit different. My family loves it.
—Angela Spengler, Niceville, FL

Takes: 30 min. • **Makes:** 4 servings

- 2 tsp. olive oil
- 1 pkg. (12 oz.) fully cooked spinach and feta chicken sausage links or flavor of your choice, sliced
- 1 small onion, finely chopped
- 1 celery rib, finely chopped
- 1 garlic clove, minced
- 1 cup reduced-sodium chicken broth
- 1 cup water
- ¼ tsp. crushed red pepper flakes
- 1¼ cups uncooked pearl (Israeli) couscous
- 2 Tbsp. minced fresh parsley
- ¼ cup crumbled feta cheese, optional

1. In a large nonstick skillet, heat oil over medium-high heat. Add sausage, onion and celery; cook and stir 6-8 minutes or until sausage is browned. Add garlic; cook 1 minute longer.
2. Stir in broth, water and pepper flakes; bring to a boil. Stir in couscous. Reduce heat; simmer, covered, 10-12 minutes or until liquid is absorbed. Remove from heat; let stand, covered, for 5 minutes. Stir in parsley. If desired, sprinkle with cheese.
1 cup: 343 cal., 10g fat (3g sat. fat), 65mg chol., 694mg sod., 41g carb. (1g sugars, 1g fiber), 22g pro. **Diabetic exchanges:** 3 starch, 3 lean meat, ½ fat.

READER REVIEW

"My husband could not stop complimenting me on this dish. I used chicken sausage with red and green peppers and added fresh spinach after the couscous. Great one-pan dinner, highly recommend."

FOURMOSHERS, TASTEOFHOME.COM

LEMON-PEPPER TILAPIA WITH MUSHROOMS

My husband and I are trying to add more fish and healthy entrees to our diet and this one makes it easy. It comes together in less than 30 minutes, so it's perfect for hectic weeknights.
—Donna McDonald, Lake Elsinore, CA

Takes: 25 min. • **Makes:** 4 servings

- 2 Tbsp. butter
- ½ lb. sliced fresh mushrooms
- ¾ tsp. lemon-pepper seasoning, divided
- 3 garlic cloves, minced
- 4 tilapia fillets (6 oz. each)
- ¼ tsp. paprika
- ⅛ tsp. cayenne pepper
- 1 medium tomato, chopped
- 3 green onions, thinly sliced

1. In a 12-in. skillet, heat the butter over medium heat. Add mushrooms and ¼ tsp. lemon pepper; cook and stir 3-5 minutes or until tender. Add the garlic and cook 30 seconds longer.
2. Place fillets over mushrooms; sprinkle with paprika, cayenne and the remaining lemon pepper. Cook, covered, 5-7 minutes or until fish just begins to flake easily with a fork. Top with tomato and green onions.
1 fillet: 216 cal., 8g fat (4g sat. fat), 98mg chol., 173mg sod., 5g carb. (2g sugars, 1g fiber), 34g pro. **Diabetic exchanges:** 4 lean meat, 1½ fat.

LEMON-PEPPER TILAPIA WITH MUSHROOMS

TACOS IN A BOWL

This easy skillet dish tastes just like tacos and makes a fun dinner for two. Garnish each serving with sour cream and salsa and top with crushed tortilla chips.
—Sue Schoening, Sheboygan, WI

Takes: 25 min. • **Makes:** 2 servings

- ½ lb. lean ground beef (90% lean)
- 2 Tbsp. finely chopped onion
- ¾ cup canned diced tomatoes, drained
- 2 Tbsp. taco seasoning
- 1 cup water
- 1 pkg. (3 oz.) ramen noodles
- ¼ cup shredded cheddar or Mexican cheese blend
  Crushed tortilla chips, optional

1. In a small skillet, cook beef and onion over medium heat until meat is no longer pink; drain. Stir in the tomatoes, taco seasoning and water. Bring to a boil. Add ramen noodles (discard seasoning packet or save for another use). Cook and stir until noodles are tender, 3-5 minutes.
2. Spoon into serving bowls; sprinkle with cheese and, if desired, tortilla chips.
1 cup: 480 cal., 21g fat (10g sat. fat), 85mg chol., 1279mg sod., 40g carb. (3g sugars, 2g fiber), 30g pro.

CAJUN BEEF & RICE

CAJUN BEEF & RICE

Dirty rice from a box or a restaurant can have a lot of sodium and fat. Here's my hearty, healthy way to trim it down.
—Raquel Haggard, Edmond, OK

Takes: 30 min. • **Makes:** 4 servings

- 1 lb. lean ground beef (90% lean)
- 3 celery ribs, chopped
- 1 small green pepper, chopped
- 1 small sweet red pepper, chopped
- ¼ cup chopped onion
- 2 cups water
- 1 cup instant brown rice
- 1 Tbsp. minced fresh parsley
- 1 Tbsp. Worcestershire sauce
- 2 tsp. reduced-sodium beef bouillon granules
- 1 tsp. Cajun seasoning
- ¼ tsp. crushed red pepper flakes
- ¼ tsp. pepper
- ⅛ tsp. garlic powder

1. In a large skillet, cook beef, celery, green and red peppers, and onion over medium heat until the beef is no longer pink, breaking up beef into crumbles, 8-10 minutes; drain.
2. Stir in remaining ingredients. Bring to a boil. Reduce heat; simmer, covered, until rice is tender, 12-15 minutes.
1½ cups: 291 cal., 10g fat (4g sat. fat), 71mg chol., 422mg sod., 23g carb. (3g sugars, 2g fiber), 25g pro. **Diabetic exchanges:** 3 lean meat, 1 starch, 1 vegetable.

CASSEROLES
& OVEN ENTREES

When you're looking for comforting, heartwarming dishes
that take center stage but not a lot of time, the recipes in
this chapter are just the answer. Minimal prep time pays off
as you let your oven do the work!

WEEKNIGHT
SKILLET
SPINACH PIE

WEEKNIGHT SKILLET SPINACH PIE

I love sneaking veggies into my kids' dinners! When I make this deceptively simple recipe, the flaky crust and extra cheese never let the kids suspect they're eating a vitamin-rich dish—and I'm not hovering over an oven for hours. Put the frozen spinach and phyllo sheets in the refrigerator the night before or early in the morning to thaw.
—Kristyne McDougle, Lorain, OH

Prep: 35 min. • **Bake:** 35 min. + cooling
Makes: 8 servings

- 2 large eggs, room temperature, lightly beaten
- 3 pkg. (10 oz. each) frozen chopped spinach, thawed and squeezed dry
- 2 cups (8 oz.) crumbled feta cheese
- 1½ cups shredded part-skim mozzarella cheese
- ¼ cup chopped walnuts, toasted
- 1½ tsp. dried oregano
- 1½ tsp. dill weed
- ½ tsp. pepper
- ¼ tsp. salt
- ¼ cup julienned soft sun-dried tomatoes (not packed in oil), optional
- ⅓ cup canola oil
- 12 sheets phyllo dough (14x9-in. size)

1. Preheat oven to 375°. In a large bowl, combine eggs, spinach, cheeses, walnuts, seasonings and, if desired, tomatoes; set aside. Brush a 10-in. cast-iron or other ovenproof skillet with some of the oil; set aside.
2. Unroll the phyllo dough. Place 1 sheet of dough on a work surface; brush with oil. (Keep the remaining phyllo covered with a damp towel to prevent it from drying out.) Place in prepared skillet, letting the edges of phyllo hang over the sides. Repeat with an additional 5 sheets of the phyllo dough, again brushing with oil and rotating sheets to cover the skillet.
3. Spread the spinach mixture over the phyllo in the skillet. Top with an additional 6 sheets of phyllo, again brushing with oil and rotating sheets. Fold ends of phyllo up over top of pie; brush with oil.
4. Using a sharp knife, cut into 8 wedges. Bake on a lower oven rack until the top is golden brown, 35-40 minutes. Cool on a wire rack. Refrigerate leftovers.

1 slice: 334 cal., 23g fat (7g sat. fat), 75mg chol., 649mg sod., 17g carb. (2g sugars, 5g fiber), 18g pro.

PORK SPANISH RICE

My family wasn't fond of pork roast—until I used it in this yummy casserole.
—Betty Unrau, MacGregor, MB

Prep: 20 min. • **Bake:** 20 min.
Makes: 4 servings

1 medium green pepper, chopped
1 small onion, chopped
2 Tbsp. butter
1 can (14½ oz.) diced tomatoes, drained
1 cup chicken broth
½ tsp. salt
¼ tsp. pepper
1¾ cups cubed cooked pork
1 cup uncooked instant rice
Optional: Lime wedges and minced cilantro

1. Preheat oven to 350°. In a large skillet, saute green pepper and onion in butter until tender. Stir in the tomatoes, broth, salt and pepper. Bring to a boil; stir in pork and rice.
2. Transfer to a greased 2-qt. baking dish. Cover and bake until rice is tender and liquid is absorbed, 20-25 minutes. Stir before serving. If desired, serve with lime wedges and top with minced cilantro.
1 cup: 304 cal., 12g fat (6g sat. fat), 71mg chol., 756mg sod., 29g carb. (5g sugars, 3g fiber), 21g pro. **Diabetic exchanges:** 3 lean meat, 2 starch, 1½ fat.

FIRECRACKER CASSEROLE
PICTURED ON P. 123

My husband and I love this Southwestern-style casserole. The flavor reminds us of enchiladas, but this handy recipe doesn't require the extra time to roll them up.
—Teressa Eastman, El Dorado, KS

Prep: 15 min. • **Bake:** 25 min.
Makes: 8 servings

2 lbs. ground beef
1 medium onion, chopped
1 can (15 oz.) black beans, rinsed and drained
1 to 2 Tbsp. chili powder
2 to 3 tsp. ground cumin
½ tsp. salt
4 flour tortillas (6 in.)
1 can (10¾ oz.) condensed cream of mushroom soup, undiluted
1 can (10 oz.) diced tomatoes and green chiles, undrained
1 cup shredded cheddar cheese

1. Preheat oven to 350°. In a large skillet, cook beef and onion until the meat is no longer pink; drain. Add the beans, chili powder, cumin and salt.
2. Transfer to a greased 13x9-in. baking dish. Arrange flour tortillas over the top. Combine soup and tomatoes; pour over tortillas. Sprinkle with cheddar cheese. Bake, uncovered, for 25-30 minutes or until heated through.
1 piece: 363 cal., 18g fat (8g sat. fat), 72mg chol., 941mg sod., 21g carb. (2g sugars, 4g fiber), 28g pro.

TEST KITCHEN TIP
You can use corn tortillas for this recipe if you like—corn tortillas are traditional for enchiladas, but many people use flour because they're easier to roll. Since rolling isn't necessary here, you can use the tortilla of your choice!

PORK SPANISH RICE

INSIDE-OUT STUFFED PEPPERS

My daughters don't care for the usual hollowed-out green peppers stuffed with meat and rice, so one of the girls dreamed up this alternative. The peppers are simply chopped and combined with the other ingredients in a casserole dish.
—Darlene Brenden, Salem, OR

Prep: 15 min. • **Bake:** 65 min.
Makes: 6 servings

- 1 lb. ground beef
- ½ cup chopped onion
- 1 can (14½ oz.) stewed tomatoes, cut up
- 1 large green pepper, chopped
- ½ cup uncooked long grain rice
- ½ cup water
- 2 tsp. Worcestershire sauce
- ½ tsp. salt
- ¼ tsp. pepper
- 1 cup shredded cheddar cheese

1. Preheat oven to 350°. In a large skillet, cook the beef over medium heat until no longer pink; drain. Transfer to a greased 2-qt. casserole. Add the next 8 ingredients.
2. Cover and bake until the rice is tender, about 1 hour. Uncover and sprinkle with cheese; cook until cheese is melted, about 5 minutes longer.
1 serving: 276 cal., 12g fat (7g sat. fat), 57mg chol., 516mg sod., 22g carb. (5g sugars, 2g fiber), 19g pro.

BAKED TERIYAKI PORK & VEGGIES

BAKED TERIYAKI PORK & VEGGIES

Minimal preparation makes this dish so easy. I use precut broccoli and boneless, trimmed pork chops to save time. And sometimes I throw in a few multicolored carrots for extra prettiness. Try it served over rice or noodles.
—Billie Davis, Spring Creek, NV

Prep: 15 min. • **Bake:** 30 min.
Makes: 4 servings

- 2 cups fresh broccoli florets
- 1 lb. fresh baby carrots, halved lengthwise
- 1 Tbsp. olive oil
- 1 tsp. minced fresh gingerroot
- ½ tsp. pepper
- ¼ tsp. salt
- 4 boneless pork loin chops (6 oz. each)
- 4 Tbsp. reduced-sodium teriyaki sauce
  Toasted sesame seeds, optional

Preheat oven to 375°. Line a 15x10x1-in. pan with foil; add broccoli and carrots. Toss with olive oil, ginger, pepper and salt; spread out into a single layer. Place pork chops on top of vegetables; drizzle with teriyaki sauce. Bake until a thermometer inserted in pork chop reads 145°, about 30 minutes. If desired, preheat broiler; broil chops and vegetables 2-4 in. from heat until browned, 1-2 minutes. Top with sesame seeds if desired.
1 pork chop with 1 cup vegetables: 322 cal., 13g fat (4g sat. fat), 82mg chol., 613mg sod., 14g carb. (9g sugars, 3g fiber), 35g pro. **Diabetic exchanges:** 5 lean meat, 2 vegetable, ½ fat.

SAUSAGE & 'SHROOM DUTCH OVEN PIZZA

We created this pizza when we were experimenting with different ways to use a Dutch oven. We couldn't believe how well it turned out.
—Taste of Home *Test Kitchen*

Prep: 10 min. • **Cook:** 20 min.
Makes: 8 servings

- 1 lb. frozen pizza dough, thawed
- 1 Tbsp. olive oil
- 1 cup marinara sauce
- 1 cup shredded Italian cheese blend
- 8 oz. bulk spicy pork sausage, cooked and drained
- ⅓ cup chopped onion
- ½ cup sliced fresh mushrooms
- Optional: Minced fresh basil, red pepper flakes and grated Parmesan cheese

1. Preheat oven to 450°. Place a 10-in. Dutch oven on the bottom rack in oven to let heat through, 2-3 minutes.
2. Roll dough on a lightly floured surface into a 12-in. circle. Fold an 18-in. piece of foil lengthwise into thirds, making a sling. Remove pan from oven; place dough on sling and gently lower dough into bottom. Using a wooden spoon, move dough into place and up the sides. Brush dough with olive oil; spread with marinara sauce. Top evenly with cheese, pork sausage, onion and mushrooms.
3. Bake until crust is lightly browned and crisp, 20 minutes. Cool slightly. Using sling, remove crust from Dutch oven. Serve with fresh basil, red pepper flakes and grated Parmesan cheese as desired.

1 slice: 273 cal., 13g fat (4g sat. fat), 25mg chol., 418mg sod., 27g carb. (1g sugars, 1g fiber), 11g pro.

REUBEN CRESCENT BAKE

OK, it may not be a true Reuben, but my recipe tastes just like one! And it's so much easier to whip up a casserole than to make individual sandwiches for eight! I like to serve it with homemade soup.
—Kathy Kittell, Lenexa, KS

Prep: 20 min. • **Bake:** 15 min.
Makes: 8 servings

- 2 tubes (8 oz. each) refrigerated crescent rolls, divided
- 1 lb. sliced Swiss cheese, divided
- 1¼ lbs. sliced deli corned beef
- 1 can (14 oz.) sauerkraut, rinsed and well drained
- ⅔ cup Thousand Island salad dressing
- 1 large egg white, lightly beaten
- 3 tsp. caraway seeds

1. Preheat oven to 375°. Unroll 1 tube of crescent dough into 1 long rectangle; seal seams and perforations. Press onto the bottom of a greased 13x9-in. baking dish. Bake until the crust is golden brown, 8-10 minutes.
2. Layer with half the cheese and all the corned beef. Combine sauerkraut and salad dressing; spread over beef. Top with remaining cheese.
3. On a lightly floured surface, press or roll the second tube of crescent dough into a 13x9-in. rectangle, sealing seams and perforations. Place over cheese. Brush with egg white; sprinkle with caraway seeds.
4. Bake until casserole is heated through and crust is golden brown, 12-16 minutes. Let stand 5 minutes before cutting.

1 piece: 610 cal., 39g fat (18g sat. fat), 108mg chol., 1905mg sod., 28g carb. (8g sugars, 2g fiber), 31g pro.

SAUSAGE & 'SHROOM DUTCH OVEN PIZZA

SAUSAGE FLORENTINE SHEPHERD'S PIE

BUTTERY HERB ROASTED CHICKEN

Roasting chicken is always such a comforting thing, especially when you can pick the herbs right from your garden and pair them with some fresh citrus to smear across the bird! My family just can't get enough of this herb-roasted chicken recipe.
—Jenn Tidwell, Fair Oaks, CA

Prep: 15 min. • **Bake:** 1½ hours + standing
Makes: 6 servings

- 1 roasting chicken (5 to 6 lbs.)
- ½ cup unsalted butter, softened, divided
- 1 cup chicken broth
- ¾ cup orange juice
- ½ cup white wine or additional chicken broth
- 2 garlic cloves, minced
- 1 tsp. salt
- ½ tsp. pepper
- 2 fresh rosemary sprigs
- 2 fresh thyme sprigs
- 2 fresh sage sprigs

1. Preheat oven to 350°. With fingers, carefully loosen skin from chicken; rub ¼ cup butter under skin. Secure skin to the underside of breast with toothpicks. Place the chicken on a rack in a shallow roasting pan, breast side up. Tuck wings under chicken; tie drumsticks together. Pour broth around chicken.
2. Melt remaining ¼ cup butter; brush over chicken. Drizzle with orange juice and wine. Combine garlic, salt and pepper; rub over skin. Place sprigs of rosemary, thyme and sage in roasting pan.
3. Roast until thermometer inserted in thickest part of thigh reads 170°-175°, 1½-2 hours (Cover loosely with foil if chicken browns too quickly.) Remove from oven; tent with foil. Let stand for 15 minutes before carving; remove toothpicks. If desired, skim fat from the pan drippings and thicken drippings with cornstarch or flour for gravy.
6 oz. cooked chicken: 599 cal., 42g fat (17g sat. fat), 191mg chol., 703mg sod., 4g carb. (3g sugars, 0 fiber), 48g pro.

5i

SAUSAGE FLORENTINE SHEPHERD'S PIE

In this Italian take on shepherd's pie, sausage takes the place of ground beef or lamb, and spinach replaces the green veggies. Zesty tomatoes, an Italian cheese blend and garlicky mashed potatoes make this dish long on flavor, even if the list of ingredients is short. Layer it up, pop it into the oven and watch the family come running at the awesome aroma!
—Leah Lyon, Ada, OK

Prep: 15 min. • **Bake:** 40 min. + standing
Makes: 6 servings

- 1 lb. bulk mild Italian sausage
- 1 can (14½ oz.) Italian diced tomatoes, lightly drained
- 1 pkg. (10 oz.) frozen chopped spinach, thawed and squeezed dry
- 3 cups shredded Italian cheese blend, divided
- 1 pkg. (24 oz.) refrigerated garlic mashed potatoes

1. Preheat oven to 375°. In a Dutch oven over medium heat, cook sausage, crumbling the meat, until no longer pink, 5-6 minutes; drain. Stir in the tomatoes, spinach and 2 cups cheese.
2. Pour sausage mixture into a greased 11x7-in. baking dish; top evenly with the mashed potatoes. Bake for 20 minutes; sprinkle with the remaining cheese. Bake until cheese is melted and the top begins to brown, about 20 minutes longer. Let stand 10 minutes before serving.
1 serving: 540 cal., 34g fat (16g sat. fat), 95mg chol., 1439mg sod., 23g carb. (6g sugars, 3g fiber), 24g pro.

TEST KITCHEN TIP
Like a little more spice in your life? Substitute your favorite hot Italian sausage for the mild version.

**BUTTERY HERB
ROASTED CHICKEN**

VEGETABLE-STUFFED PORTOBELLOS

I often like to substitute portobellos for hamburger patties, but in this open-faced recipe, they take the place of buns. My family loves this tasty, healthful dinner, and it's ready in no time.

—Elizabeth Doss, California City, CA

....

Prep: 20 min. • **Broil:** 15 min.
Makes: 4 servings

- 1 can (15 oz.) cannellini beans, rinsed and drained
- 2 Tbsp. olive oil, divided
- 1 Tbsp. water
- 1 tsp. dried rosemary, crushed
- 1 garlic clove, peeled and halved
- ¼ tsp. salt
- ¼ tsp. pepper
- 4 large portobello mushrooms (4 to 4½ in.), stems removed
- 1 medium sweet red pepper, finely chopped
- 1 medium red onion, finely chopped
- 1 medium zucchini, finely chopped
- ½ cup shredded pepper Jack cheese

1. In a food processor, combine the beans, 1 Tbsp. oil, water, rosemary, garlic, salt and pepper. Cover and process until pureed; set aside.

2. Place mushrooms on a broiler pan coated with cooking spray. Broil 4 in. from the heat for 6-8 minutes on each side or until mushrooms are tender.

3. Meanwhile, in a small nonstick skillet, saute the red pepper, red onion and zucchini in remaining oil until tender.

4. Spread about ⅓ cup of the reserved bean mixture over each mushroom; top with ½ cup vegetable mixture. Sprinkle with cheese. Broil 2-3 minutes longer or until cheese is melted.

1 serving: 252 cal., 12g fat (4g sat. fat), 15mg chol., 378mg sod., 26g carb. (5g sugars, 7g fiber), 11g pro. **Diabetic exchanges:** 2 lean meat, 2 vegetable, 1 starch, 1 fat.

TUSCAN GRAPES & SAUSAGES

This is a recipe that is always a go-to when entertaining. It is simple and elegant, and you can entertain your guests instead of spending the entire time in the kitchen. I serve this over rustic hand-mashed red potatoes. I love the pieces of garlic in this dish because they become so sweet. It is a nice complement to the sweet grapes and spicy sausage.

—Melissa Zienter, Las Vegas, NV

....

Prep: 30 min. • **Bake:** 15 min.
Makes: 8 servings

- 8 uncooked Italian sausage links (4 oz. each), hot or mild
- 2½ lbs. seedless green or red grapes, or a mixture
- 20 to 30 garlic cloves, peeled and halved
- ½ cup melted butter, divided
- ¼ cup balsamic vinegar

1. Preheat oven to 450°. Place sausage links in a large saucepan; add water to cover. Bring to a boil. Reduce the heat; simmer, covered, until the sausage is no longer pink and some of the fat has been rendered, 20-25 minutes. Drain. When cool enough to handle, cut sausage into ½-in. slices.

2. Meanwhile, remove grape stems; place grapes and garlic in a 15x10x1-in. baking pan. Add 6 Tbsp. butter; toss to coat. Top with sausage slices. Bake until sausage is browned, 15-20 minutes, stirring once.

3. Using a slotted spoon, transfer the sausage mixture to a serving dish. Keep warm. Transfer cooking juices to a small saucepan; add balsamic vinegar. Bring to a boil. Cook until liquid is reduced by half, 4-5 minutes. Reduce heat. Stir in the remaining butter; cook until slightly thickened. Drizzle sauce over sausage and grapes.

1½ cups: 498 cal., 36g fat (15g sat. fat), 92mg chol., 799mg sod., 32g carb. (25g sugars, 1g fiber), 13g pro.

> **TEST KITCHEN TIP**
> Grapes don't always get eaten before they start to age—luckily they freeze well! Keep a container in the freezer and you'll always have grapes on hand.

TUSCAN GRAPES & SAUSAGES

PERFECT FOUR-CHEESE LASAGNA

FOLD-OVER TORTILLA BAKE
PICTURED ON P. 123

Here's something a little different from the usual tacos. It's special enough for potlucks or dinner guests.
—Deborah Smith, DeWitt, NE

Prep: 20 min. • **Bake:** 20 min.
Makes: 6 servings

- 1 lb. ground beef
- 1 cup chopped onion
- 2 cans (14½ oz. each) stewed tomatoes
- 1 cup enchilada sauce
- 1 to 2 tsp. ground cumin
- ½ tsp. salt
- ¼ tsp. pepper
- 12 flour or corn tortillas (6 in.)
- 6 oz. cream cheese, softened
- 1 can (4 oz.) chopped green chiles, drained
- 1 cup shredded Monterey Jack cheese
  Minced fresh cilantro, optional

1. Preheat oven to 350°. In a large skillet, cook ground beef and onion until the beef is no longer pink, breaking it into crumbles; drain. Stir in the tomatoes, enchilada sauce and seasonings. Bring to a boil. Reduce heat and simmer, covered, for 5 minutes. Pour half the meat sauce into a 13x9-in. baking dish. Set aside.
2. Wrap the stack of tortillas in foil; warm in the oven for 8-10 minutes. Spread each warm tortilla with cream cheese and top with chiles. Fold tortillas in half. Arrange folded tortillas over meat sauce; pour remaining sauce over top.
3. Cover dish and bake for 15 minutes. Sprinkle with cheese; bake until cheese is melted, about 5 minutes longer. If desired, top with cilantro.
2 tortillas: 473 cal., 25g fat (10g sat. fat), 69mg chol., 1138mg sod., 38g carb. (7g sugars, 2g fiber), 27g pro.

PERFECT FOUR-CHEESE LASAGNA

Lasagna is one of my favorites, and this is the recipe I've been making since I was a teenager. It's a tantalizing combo of pasta, meat sauce, cheese and more cheese that really lives up to its name!
—Lauren Delaney-Wallace, Glen Carbon, IL

Prep: 25 min. • **Bake:** 50 min. + standing
Makes: 12 servings

- 1 lb. ground beef
- 1 medium onion, chopped
- 2 garlic cloves, minced
- 1 tsp. dried oregano
- 1 tsp. dried basil
- 2 cans (15 oz. each) tomato sauce
- 2 large eggs, lightly beaten
- 2 cups 4% cottage cheese
- ⅔ cup grated Parmesan cheese
- ¼ cup shredded cheddar cheese
- 1½ cups shredded part-skim mozzarella cheese, divided
- 12 no-cook lasagna noodles (about 7 oz.)
- 1 tsp. Italian seasoning

1. Preheat oven to 350°. In a large skillet, cook and crumble beef with onion and garlic over medium-high heat until meat is browned, 5-7 minutes; drain. Stir in herbs and tomato sauce. In a bowl, mix eggs, cottage cheese, Parmesan cheese, cheddar cheese and ½ cup of the mozzarella cheese.
2. Spread 1 cup meat sauce into a greased 13x9-in. baking dish; layer with 4 noodles, cottage cheese mixture, an additional 4 noodles and half of the remaining meat sauce. Repeat the last 2 layers. Sprinkle with Italian seasoning and the remaining mozzarella cheese.
3. Cover with greased foil; bake until cheese is melted, 50-55 minutes. Let stand 10 minutes before serving.
Freeze option: Cover and freeze unbaked lasagna. To use, partially thaw in the refrigerator overnight. Remove from refrigerator 30 minutes before baking. Preheat oven to 350°. Bake lasagna as directed until heated through and a thermometer inserted in center reads 165°, increasing time to 1-1½ hours.
1 piece: 279 cal., 13g fat (6g sat. fat), 72mg chol., 662mg sod., 22g carb. (4g sugars, 2g fiber), 20g pro.

MUSHROOM PENNE BAKE
PICTURED ON P. 123

This is an easy, hearty and delicious meal for a chilly evening! Its cheesy goodness will have you going back for seconds. I like serving this accompanied with a salad and garlic bread.
—Sue Aschemeier, Defiance, OH

Prep: 25 min. • **Bake:** 25 min.
Makes: 8 servings

- 1 pkg. (12 oz.) whole wheat penne pasta
- 1 Tbsp. olive oil
- 1 lb. sliced baby portobello mushrooms
- 2 garlic cloves, minced
- 1 jar (24 oz.) marinara sauce
- 1 tsp. Italian seasoning
- ½ tsp. salt
- 2 cups reduced-fat ricotta cheese
- 1 cup shredded part-skim mozzarella cheese, divided
- ½ cup grated Parmesan cheese

1. Preheat the oven to 350°. In a 6-qt. stockpot, cook pasta according to package directions. Drain and return to pot; let cool slightly.
2. In a large skillet, heat oil over medium-high heat; saute mushrooms until tender, 4-6 minutes. Add garlic; cook 1 minute. Stir in marinara sauce and seasonings. Spread half the mixture into a 13x9-in. baking dish coated with cooking spray.
3. Stir ricotta cheese and ½ cup of the mozzarella cheese into pasta; spoon over the mushroom mixture. Spread with the remaining mushroom mixture.
4. Sprinkle with remaining mozzarella cheese and Parmesan cheese. Bake, uncovered, until bubbly, 25-30 minutes.
1 cup: 353 cal., 11g fat (4g sat. fat), 30mg chol., 748mg sod., 44g carb. (10g sugars, 7g fiber), 20g pro. **Diabetic exchanges:** 3 starch, 2 lean meat, 1 fat.

SEAFOOD CASSEROLE

SEAFOOD CASSEROLE

A family favorite, this rice casserole is filled with plenty of seafood and veggies. It's hearty, homey and so easy to make!
—Nancy Billups, Princeton, IA

Prep: 20 min. • **Bake:** 40 min.
Makes: 6 servings

- 1 pkg. (6 oz.) long grain and wild rice
- 1 lb. frozen crabmeat, thawed, or 2½ cups canned lump crabmeat, drained
- 1 lb. cooked shrimp, peeled, deveined and cut into ½-in. pieces
- 2 celery ribs, chopped
- 1 medium onion, finely chopped
- ½ cup finely chopped green pepper
- 1 can (4 oz.) mushroom stems and pieces, drained
- 1 jar (2 oz.) diced pimientos, drained
- 1 cup mayonnaise
- 1 cup 2% milk
- ½ tsp. pepper
  Dash Worcestershire sauce
- ¼ cup dry bread crumbs

1. Cook rice according to package directions. Meanwhile, preheat oven to 375°.
2. In a large bowl, combine the crab, shrimp, celery, onion, green pepper, mushrooms and pimientos. In a small bowl, whisk mayonnaise, milk, pepper and Worcestershire sauce; stir into the seafood mixture. Stir in rice.
3. Transfer to a greased 13x9-in. baking dish. Sprinkle with bread crumbs. Bake, uncovered, until bubbly, 40-50 minutes.
1½ cups: 585 cal., 34g fat (5g sat. fat), 209mg chol., 1045mg sod., 31g carb. (5g sugars, 2g fiber), 37g pro.

MATTHEW'S BEST EVER MEAT LOAF

This entree is comfort food at its best. Mushrooms, beef stock, tomato paste, Worcestershire and soy sauce help boost the meaty flavor of this classic diner staple.

—Matthew Hass, Ellison Bay, WI

Prep: 30 min. • **Bake:** 1¼ hours + standing
Makes: 8 servings

- 3 slices white bread, torn into small pieces
- ½ cup beef stock
- 2 large portobello mushrooms (about 6 oz.), cut into chunks
- 1 medium onion, cut into wedges
- 1 medium carrot, cut into chunks
- 1 celery rib, cut into chunks
- 3 garlic cloves, halved
- 1 Tbsp. olive oil
- 2 Tbsp. tomato paste
- 2 large eggs, lightly beaten
- 1¼ lbs. ground beef
- ¾ lb. ground pork
- 1 Tbsp. Worcestershire sauce
- 1 Tbsp. reduced-sodium soy sauce
- 1¼ tsp. salt
- ¾ tsp. pepper

GLAZE
- ½ cup ketchup
- 2 Tbsp. tomato paste
- 2 Tbsp. brown sugar
- 1 tsp. ground mustard

1. Preheat oven to 350°. Combine the bread and stock; let stand until the liquid is absorbed.

2. Meanwhile, pulse the mushrooms, onion, carrot, celery and garlic in a food processor until finely chopped. In a large skillet, heat oil over medium heat. Add the mushroom mixture; cook and stir until vegetables are tender and the liquid is evaporated, 5-6 minutes. Stir in tomato paste; cook 1 minute longer. Cool slightly.

3. Add the next 7 ingredients and the cooked vegetables to the bread mixture; mix thoroughly. Place a 12x7-in. piece of foil on a rack in a foil-lined rimmed baking pan. Transfer meat mixture to the foil and shape into a 10x6-in. loaf.

4. Bake 1 hour. Mix together the glaze ingredients; spread over loaf. Bake until a thermometer reads 160°, 15-25 minutes longer. Let stand 10 minutes before slicing.

Freeze option: Shape the meat loaf on a plastic wrap-lined baking sheet; wrap and freeze until firm. Remove from pan and wrap securely in foil; return to freezer. To use, unwrap meat loaf and bake as directed, increasing initial baking time to 2 hours. Mix together glaze ingredients; spread over loaf. Bake until a thermometer inserted in center reads 160°, 15-25 minutes longer. Let stand 10 minutes before slicing.

1 slice: 341 cal., 18g fat (6g sat. fat), 119mg chol., 832mg sod., 19g carb. (11g sugars, 2g fiber), 25g pro.

MATTHEW'S BEST EVER MEAT LOAF

BALSAMIC ROASTED CHICKEN THIGHS WITH ROOT VEGETABLES

PICTURED ON P. 123

I will always remember the way my grandmother's house smelled when she made this chicken every Sunday. Ever since she gave me the recipe, the heartwarming flavors always take me back to childhood.
—Erin Chilcoat, Central Islip, NY

Prep: 15 min. + marinating
Bake: 35 min. • **Makes:** 6 servings

- 4 Tbsp. olive oil, divided
- 3 Tbsp. stone-ground mustard
- 2 Tbsp. balsamic vinaigrette
- ¾ tsp. kosher salt, divided
- ¾ tsp. freshly ground pepper, divided
- 6 bone-in chicken thighs (about 2¼ lbs.)
- 4 medium parsnips, peeled and cut into ½-in. pieces
- 1 medium sweet potato, peeled and cut into ½-in. pieces
- 4 shallots, chopped
- ¼ tsp. caraway seeds
- 4 Tbsp. minced fresh parsley, divided
- 3 bacon strips, cooked and crumbled, divided

1. In a bowl, whisk 3 Tbsp. olive oil, the mustard, vinaigrette and ½ tsp. each salt and pepper until blended. Add chicken, turning to coat. Refrigerate, covered, for 6 hours or overnight.
2. Preheat oven to 425°. Place chicken thighs, skin side up, on half of a greased 15x10x1-in. baking pan. Place parsnips and sweet potato in a large bowl; add shallots, caraway seeds and the remaining oil, salt and pepper and toss to combine. Arrange in a single layer on remaining half of pan.
3. Roast the chicken and vegetables for 20 minutes. Stir vegetables; roast until a thermometer inserted in chicken reads 170°-175° and vegetables are tender, 15-20 minutes longer.
4. Transfer vegetables to a bowl; toss with 2 Tbsp. parsley and half the bacon. Serve chicken with vegetables; sprinkle chicken with the remaining parsley and bacon.
1 serving: 480 cal., 27g fat (6g sat. fat), 85mg chol., 604mg sod., 33g carb. (10g sugars, 5g fiber), 27g pro.

CHILI MAC CASSEROLE

This nicely spiced entree uses several of my family's favorite ingredients, including macaroni, kidney beans, tomatoes and cheese. Just add a nice green salad for a complete meal.
—Marlene Wilson, Rolla, ND

Prep: 15 min. • **Bake:** 30 min.
Makes: 10 servings

- 1 cup uncooked elbow macaroni
- 2 lbs. lean ground beef (90% lean)
- 1 medium onion, chopped
- 2 garlic cloves, minced
- 1 can (28 oz.) diced tomatoes, undrained
- 1 can (16 oz.) kidney beans, rinsed and drained
- 1 can (6 oz.) tomato paste
- 1 can (4 oz.) chopped green chiles
- 1¼ tsp. salt
- 1 tsp. chili powder
- ½ tsp. ground cumin
- ½ tsp. pepper
- 2 cups shredded reduced-fat Mexican cheese blend
  Thinly sliced green onions, optional

1. Preheat oven to 375°. Cook macaroni according to the package directions. Meanwhile, in a large nonstick skillet, cook beef, onion and garlic over medium heat until meat is no longer pink, breaking into crumbles; drain. Stir in tomatoes, beans, tomato paste, chiles and seasonings. Drain macaroni; add to the beef mixture.
2. Transfer to a 13x9-in. baking dish coated with cooking spray. Cover and bake until bubbly, 25-30 minutes. Uncover; sprinkle with cheese. Bake until cheese is melted, 5-8 minutes longer. If desired, top with sliced green onions.
1 cup: 313 cal., 13g fat (6g sat. fat), 69mg chol., 758mg sod., 22g carb. (6g sugars, 5g fiber), 30g pro. **Diabetic exchanges:** 3 lean meat, 1½ starch, 1 fat.

CHILI MAC CASSEROLE

QUICK & EASY
VEGETABLE POTPIE

5i

WARM CHICKEN TORTELLINI AU GRATIN

I have a number of easy planned leftover meals in my recipe arsenal, and this is one of my favorites. Pasta from Monday plus roasted chicken from Tuesday equals this delicious dish on Wednesday! It's fast and delicious, and paired with a green salad and toasty bread, you have a meal that's fancy enough for company.
—Brenda Cole, Reisterstown, MD

Prep: 15 min. • **Bake:** 30 min.
Makes: 6 servings

2 cans (14 oz. each) water-packed artichoke hearts
3 cups shredded cooked chicken
3 cups refrigerated spinach tortellini, cooked
1½ cups mayonnaise
1½ cups grated Asiago cheese, divided
   Fresh basil, optional

Preheat oven to 350°. Drain artichoke hearts, reserving ¼ cup of juices. Coarsely chop; combine with chicken, tortellini, mayonnaise, 1 cup cheese and reserved artichoke liquid. Place artichoke mixture in a greased 13x9-in. baking dish; sprinkle with remaining cheese. Bake until bubbly and starting to brown, about 30 minutes. If desired, garnish with basil.
1⅓ cups: 709 cal., 54g fat (13g sat. fat), 101mg chol., 859mg sod., 19g carb. (1g sugars, 0 fiber), 34g pro.

QUICK & EASY VEGETABLE POTPIE

This meatless Monday superstar comes together quickly and is inexpensive as well. My 4-year-old always asks for seconds! You can substitute any canned or frozen beans for the canned lentils in this easy vegetable potpie. We also like using frozen edamame.
—Maggie Torsney-Weir, Los Angeles, CA

Prep: 30 min. • **Bake:** 30 min.
Makes: 6 servings

2 Tbsp. butter
3 cups frozen mixed vegetables, thawed
1 can (15 oz.) lentils, drained
2 Tbsp. all-purpose flour
1 cup vegetable or chicken broth
1 Tbsp. Dijon mustard
1 tsp. quatre epices (French four spice)
½ tsp. salt
1 sheet refrigerated pie crust
1 Tbsp. olive oil
¼ cup grated Parmesan cheese

1. Preheat oven to 375°. In a large skillet, melt the butter over medium heat. Add vegetables and lentils; cook and stir until heated through, 3-5 minutes. Stir in flour until blended; gradually whisk in broth. Bring to a boil, stirring constantly; cook and stir until thickened, 1-2 minutes. Stir in mustard, quatre epices and salt.
2. Transfer to a greased 9-in. pie plate. Place pie crust over filling. Trim; cut slits in top. Brush with olive oil; sprinkle with Parmesan. Bake until golden brown, 30-35 minutes. Cool 5 minutes before serving.
1 serving: 356 cal., 17g fat (7g sat. fat), 20mg chol., 705mg sod., 41g carb. (5g sugars, 9g fiber), 10g pro.

TEST KITCHEN TIP
If you can't find French four spice, make your own by mixing 2 parts ground pepper to 1 part each of nutmeg, cloves and ginger.

**HEALTHY CHIPOTLE
CHICKEN PUMPKIN PIZZA**

HEALTHY CHIPOTLE CHICKEN PUMPKIN PIZZA

Think pizza and pumpkin can't go together? Think again! The sweetness of pumpkin paired with the spice of chipotle peppers makes for a delicious, balanced sauce. I love that this recipe incorporates healthy ingredients in a fun, family-friendly way.
—Julie Peterson, Crofton, MD

Prep: 20 min. • **Bake:** 15 min./batch
Makes: 2 pizzas (4 slices each)

- 2 pkg. (7½ oz. each) frozen cauliflower pizza crust or 2 prebaked 12-in. thin whole wheat pizza crusts
- 1 Tbsp. olive oil
- ¾ cup canned pumpkin
- 2 chipotle peppers in adobo sauce, minced
- ¼ tsp. salt
- ⅛ tsp. pepper
- 1½ cups cubed cooked chicken
- ½ cup mild chunky salsa
- 1½ cups shredded part-skim mozzarella cheese
- ¼ cup thinly sliced red onion
  Minced fresh cilantro, optional

1. Preheat oven to 425°. Place crusts on ungreased baking sheets; brush with oil. Combine the pumpkin, minced chipotle peppers, salt and pepper; spread over crusts. Combine chicken and salsa; spoon over pumpkin layer. Top with cheese and red onion.
2. Bake until edges are lightly browned and cheese is melted, 12-15 minutes. Let stand 5 minutes before cutting. If desired, sprinkle with cilantro.

1 slice: 225 cal., 9g fat (3g sat. fat), 37mg chol., 504mg sod., 21g carb. (4g sugars, 3g fiber), 15g pro. **Diabetic exchanges:** 2 lean meat, 1 starch, 1 vegetable, ½ fat.

BAKED CHIMICHANGAS

BAKED CHIMICHANGAS

My baked chimichanga recipe is healthier than a deep-fried version, but it's just as delicious. If you like, you can omit the chiles for less heat.
—Angela Oelschlaeger, Tonganoxie, KS

Takes: 30 min. • **Makes:** 6 servings

- 2½ cups shredded cooked chicken breast
- 1 cup salsa
- 1 small onion, chopped
- ¾ tsp. ground cumin
- ½ tsp. dried oregano
- 6 flour tortillas (10 in.), warmed
- ¾ cup shredded reduced-fat cheddar cheese
- 1 cup reduced-sodium chicken broth
- 2 tsp. chicken bouillon granules
- ⅛ tsp. pepper
- ¼ cup all-purpose flour
- 1 cup fat-free half-and-half
- 1 can (4 oz.) chopped green chiles

1. Preheat oven to 425°. In a nonstick skillet, simmer the chicken, salsa, onion, cumin and oregano until ingredients are heated through and most of the liquid has evaporated.
2. Place ½ cup of the chicken mixture down the center of each tortilla; top with 2 Tbsp. cheese. Fold sides and ends over filling and roll up.
3. Place seam side down in a 13x9-in. baking dish coated with cooking spray. Bake, uncovered, until lightly browned, about 15 minutes.
4. Meanwhile, in a small saucepan, combine the broth, bouillon and pepper. Cook until bouillon is dissolved. In a small bowl, combine flour and half-and-half until smooth; gradually stir into broth. Bring to a boil; cook and stir for 2 minutes or until thickened. Stir in chiles; cook until heated through. Serve with chimichangas.

1 chimichanga: 427 cal., 11g fat (4g sat. fat), 55mg chol., 1306mg sod., 49g carb. (7g sugars, 3g fiber), 30g pro.

LIGHTENED-UP DELIGHTS

Looking for healthier options that will still keep your family satisfied? Look no further! Light and healthy eating doesn't mean you need to scrimp on the flavors you love.

TENDER SALSA BEEF

This is my Mexican-style twist on an ultimate comfort food—beef stew. To keep it kid-friendly, use a mild salsa.
—Stacie Stamper, North Wilkesboro, NC

Prep: 15 min. • **Cook:** 8 hours
Makes: 8 servings

- 1½ lbs. beef stew meat, cut into ¾-in. cubes
- 2 cups salsa
- 1 Tbsp. brown sugar
- 1 Tbsp. reduced-sodium soy sauce
- 1 garlic clove, minced
- 4 cups hot cooked brown rice
  Sliced jalapeno peppers, optional

In a 3-qt. slow cooker, combine the beef, salsa, brown sugar, soy sauce and garlic. Cover and cook on low 8-10 hours, until meat is tender. Using a slotted spoon, serve beef with rice and, if desired, sliced jalapeno peppers.

Freeze option: Freeze individual portions of cooled stew in freezer containers. To use, partially thaw in refrigerator overnight. Heat through in a saucepan, stirring occasionally and adding water if necessary.

½ cup beef mixture with ½ cup rice : 259 cal., 7g fat (2g sat. fat), 53mg chol., 356mg sod., 28g carb. (4g sugars, 2g fiber), 19g pro. **Diabetic exchanges:** 2 starch, 2 lean meat.

MOROCCAN LAMB LETTUCE WRAPS

MOROCCAN LAMB LETTUCE WRAPS

I am a huge fan of both lettuce wraps and lamb, and combining the two this way with the creamy and crunchy cucumber makes a tasty slow cooked dish. Wine and chili powder add extra flavor elements to the sauce and make this dish extra special.
—Arlene Erlbach, Morton Grove, IL

Prep: 25 min. • **Cook:** 5 hours
Makes: 8 servings

- 2 lbs. lamb stew meat
- 1 cup chunky salsa
- ⅓ cup apricot preserves
- 6 Tbsp. dry red wine, divided
- 1 to 2 Tbsp. Moroccan seasoning (ras el hanout)
- 2 tsp. chili powder
- ½ tsp. garlic powder
- 1 English cucumber, very thinly sliced
- 2 Tbsp. prepared ranch salad dressing
- 16 Bibb or Boston lettuce leaves

1. Combine lamb, salsa, preserves, 4 Tbsp. wine, the Moroccan seasoning, chili powder and garlic powder. Transfer to a 3-qt. slow cooker. Cook, covered, on low for 5-6 hours, until the lamb is tender. Remove lamb; shred with 2 forks. Strain cooking juices and skim fat. Return lamb and cooking juices to slow cooker; heat through. Stir in remaining 2 Tbsp. wine; heat through.

2. Combine the cucumber slices and ranch dressing; toss to coat. Serve lamb mixture in lettuce leaves; top with cucumber mixture.

2 filled lettuce wraps: 221 cal., 8g fat (2g sat. fat), 74mg chol., 257mg sod., 13g carb. (8g sugars, 1g fiber), 24g pro. **Diabetic exchanges:** 3 lean meat, 1 starch.

TURKEY-STUFFED BELL PEPPERS

This lactose-free meal is so tasty, you won't even miss having real cheddar cheese. Round out the dinner with a salad or a side of rice.
—Judy Hand-Truitt, Birmingham, AL

Prep: 30 min. • **Bake:** 20 min.
Makes: 5 servings

- 5 medium green, red or yellow peppers
- 2 tsp. olive oil
- 1¼ lbs. extra-lean ground turkey (99% lean)
- 1 large onion, chopped
- 1 garlic clove, minced
- 2 tsp. ground cumin
- 1 tsp. Italian seasoning
- ½ tsp. salt
- ½ tsp. pepper
- 2 medium tomatoes, finely chopped
- 1¾ cups shredded cheddar-flavored lactose-free or other cheese
- 1½ cups soft bread crumbs
- ¼ tsp. paprika

1. Preheat oven to 325°. Cut peppers lengthwise in half; remove seeds. Place in a 15x10x1-in. pan coated with cooking spray.
2. In a large skillet, heat oil over medium-high heat. Cook and crumble turkey with onion, garlic and seasonings over medium-high heat until the meat is no longer pink, 6-8 minutes. Cool slightly. Stir in tomatoes, cheese and bread crumbs.
3. Fill the peppers with turkey mixture. Sprinkle with paprika. Bake, uncovered, until filling is heated through and peppers are tender, 20-25 minutes.

2 stuffed pepper halves: 323 cal., 10g fat (0 sat. fat), 45mg chol., 771mg sod., 20g carb. (6g sugars, 4g fiber), 40g pro. **Diabetic exchanges:** 5 lean meat, 2 vegetable, 1 starch, ½ fat.

TURKEY-STUFFED BELL PEPPERS

STOVETOP TARRAGON CHICKEN

PICTURED ON P. 139

My oldest daughter can't get enough of the tarragon sauce with this chicken. She uses biscuits to soak up every drop. My husband and I like it best served up over mashed potatoes.
—Tina Westover, La Mesa, CA

Prep: 10 min. • **Cook:** 30 min.
Makes: 4 servings

- 4 boneless skinless chicken breast halves (5 oz. each)
- 2 tsp. paprika
- 1 Tbsp. olive oil
- 1 pkg. (10 oz.) julienned carrots
- ½ lb. sliced fresh mushrooms
- 2 cans (10¾ oz. each) reduced-fat reduced-sodium condensed cream of chicken soup, undiluted
- 3 tsp. dried tarragon
- 1 Tbsp. lemon juice
- 3 small zucchini, thinly sliced

1. Sprinkle chicken with paprika. In a Dutch oven, heat oil over medium heat. Cook chicken until lightly browned, about 2 minutes on each side; remove from pan.
2. Add carrots and mushrooms to the same pan; cook, covered, until carrots are crisp-tender, 6-8 minutes, stirring occasionally.
3. In a small bowl, mix soup, tarragon and lemon juice until blended; pour over vegetables. Return chicken to pan. Bring to a boil; reduce heat to low. Cook, covered, 8 minutes. Top with zucchini; cook, covered, until a thermometer inserted in the chicken reads 165° and vegetables are tender, 6-8 minutes longer.

1 chicken breast with 1 cup vegetables: 345 cal., 11g fat (3g sat. fat), 85mg chol., 649mg sod., 28g carb. (16g sugars, 5g fiber), 35g pro. **Diabetic exchanges:** 4 lean meat, 2 vegetable, 1 starch, 1 fat.

TURKEY MEDALLIONS WITH TOMATO SALAD

In this quick and healthy meal, turkey medallions with a crisp coating are enhanced by the bright, fresh flavors of a summer garden tomato salad.

—Gilda Lester, Millsboro, DE

Prep: 30 min. • **Cook:** 15 min.
Makes: 6 servings

2   Tbsp. olive oil
1   Tbsp. red wine vinegar
½   tsp. sugar
¼   tsp. dried oregano
¼   tsp. salt
1   medium green pepper, coarsely chopped
1   celery rib, coarsely chopped
¼   cup chopped red onion
1   Tbsp. thinly sliced fresh basil
3   medium tomatoes

TURKEY

1   large egg
2   Tbsp. lemon juice
1   cup panko bread crumbs
½   cup grated Parmesan cheese
½   cup finely chopped walnuts
1   tsp. lemon-pepper seasoning
1   pkg. (20 oz.) turkey breast tenderloins
¼   tsp. salt
¼   tsp. pepper
3   Tbsp. olive oil
    Additional fresh basil

1. Whisk together the first 5 ingredients. Stir in green pepper, celery, onion and basil. Cut tomatoes into wedges; cut wedges in half. Stir tomatoes into the pepper mixture.

2. In a shallow bowl, whisk together egg and lemon juice. In another shallow bowl, toss bread crumbs with cheese, walnuts and lemon pepper.

3. Cut tenderloins crosswise into 1-in. slices; flatten slices with a meat mallet to ½-in. thickness. Sprinkle with salt and pepper. Dip in the egg mixture, then in the crumb mixture, patting to adhere.

4. In a large skillet, heat 1 Tbsp. oil over medium-high heat. Add a third of the turkey medallions; cook until golden brown, 2-3 minutes per side. Repeat twice with the remaining oil and turkey. Serve with tomato mixture; sprinkle with basil.

1 serving: 351 cal., 21g fat (3g sat. fat), 68mg chol., 458mg sod., 13g carb. (4g sugars, 2g fiber), 29g pro.

SALMON WITH MANGO-CITRUS SALSA

My mother would make this recipe for us on weeknights in the summer—it was the only way we would eat fish! To save time, you can make the salsa a day ahead. Just keep it in the refrigerator in a covered container until ready to use.

—Najmussahar Ahmed, Ypsilanti, MI

Takes: 30 min.
Makes: 4 servings (2 cups salsa)

- 1 large navel orange
- 1 medium lemon
- 2 Tbsp. olive oil
- 1 Tbsp. capers, drained and coarsely chopped
- 1½ tsp. minced fresh mint
- 1½ tsp. minced fresh parsley
- ¼ tsp. crushed red pepper flakes
- ⅛ tsp. plus ½ tsp. salt, divided
- ⅛ tsp. plus ¼ tsp. pepper, divided
- 1 medium mango, peeled and chopped
- 1 green onion, thinly sliced
- 4 salmon fillets (6 oz. each)
- 1 Tbsp. canola oil

1. For salsa, finely grate enough peel from orange to measure 2 tsp. and finely grate enough peel from lemon to measure ½ tsp.; place citrus zest in a small bowl. Cut lemon crosswise in half; squeeze 2 Tbsp. lemon juice and add to bowl.
2. Cut a thin slice from the top and bottom of orange; stand orange upright on a cutting board. With a knife, cut off peel and outer membrane from orange. Cut along the membrane of each segment to remove fruit.
3. Add olive oil, capers, mint, parsley, pepper flakes and ⅛ tsp. each salt and pepper to the lemon juice mixture. Gently stir in the mango, green onion and the orange sections.
4. Sprinkle salmon with the remaining salt and pepper. In a large skillet, heat canola oil over medium heat. Add salmon; cook 5-6 minutes on each side or until fish just begins to flake easily with a fork. Serve with salsa.

1 fillet with ½ cup salsa: 433 cal., 26g fat (4g sat. fat), 85mg chol., 516mg sod., 19g carb. (16g sugars, 3g fiber), 30g pro.
Diabetic exchanges: 5 lean meat, 1½ fat, 1 fruit.

SALMON WITH MANGO-CITRUS SALSA

CURRIED ZOODLES WITH GOLDEN RAISINS & APPLES

These curried zoodles are a quick and easy dish packed with flavor. A little heat from jalapeno is nicely balanced with the sweet golden raisins and tart apples. All of it is bathed in a delicious coconut curry sauce dotted with red pepper and basil, then topped with crunchy honey-roasted peanuts. Serve it as a healthy, delicious vegan main dish or side.

—Pamela Gelsomini, Wrentham, MA

Prep: 30 min. • **Cook:** 10 min.
Makes: 5 servings

- 2 Tbsp. olive oil
- 1 medium onion, chopped
- 1 medium sweet red pepper, julienned
- 1 jalapeno pepper, seeded and chopped
- 6 garlic cloves, minced
- 1 Tbsp. grated fresh gingerroot
- 1 can (13.66 oz.) coconut milk
- 2 to 3 tsp. curry powder
- 1 tsp. salt
- ½ tsp. pepper
- 2 medium zucchini, spiralized (about 4 cups)
- 1 cup golden raisins
- 2 medium Granny Smith apples, julienned
- ½ cup loosely packed basil leaves, chopped
- ½ cup honey-roasted peanuts, chopped

1. In a large skillet, heat oil over medium-high heat. Add onion, red pepper and jalapeno; cook and stir until crisp-tender, 3-4 minutes. Add garlic and ginger; cook 1 minute longer.
2. Stir in coconut milk, curry, salt and pepper. Bring to a boil; reduce heat. Add zucchini and raisins. Simmer until zucchini is crisp-tender, 3-4 minutes.
3. Remove from heat; stir in apples and basil. Garnish with peanuts and additional chopped basil.

1½ cups: 411 cal., 25g fat (14g sat. fat), 0 chol., 554mg sod., 45g carb. (31g sugars, 6g fiber), 8g pro.

FISH & FRIES

ARRABBIATA SAUCE WITH ZUCCHINI NOODLES

We re-created one of our favorite spicy Italian sauces and served it over zucchini pasta for a healthier meal that's naturally gluten-free. The results were amazing!
—Courtney Stultz, Weir, KS

Prep: 10 min. • **Cook:** 35 min.
Makes: 4 servings

- 1 lb. lean ground beef (90% lean)
- ½ cup finely chopped onion
- 2 garlic cloves, minced
- 1 can (14½ oz.) petite diced tomatoes, undrained
- ¼ cup dry red wine or beef broth
- 3 Tbsp. tomato paste
- 2 tsp. honey
- 1 tsp. cider vinegar
- ¾ tsp. dried basil
- ½ to 1 tsp. crushed red pepper flakes
- ½ tsp. salt
- ¼ tsp. dried oregano
- ¼ tsp. dried thyme

ZUCCHINI NOODLES
- 2 large zucchini
- 1 Tbsp. olive oil
- ¼ tsp. salt
  Chopped fresh parsley, optional

1. In a large saucepan, cook and crumble beef with onion and garlic over medium-high heat until no longer pink, 5-7 minutes. Stir in tomatoes, red wine, tomato paste, honey, vinegar and seasonings; bring to a boil. Reduce heat; simmer, uncovered, until the flavors are blended, about 25 minutes, stirring occasionally.
2. For noodles, trim ends of zucchini. Using a spiralizer, cut zucchini into thin strands. In a large cast-iron or other heavy skillet, heat oil over medium-high heat. Add zucchini; cook until slightly softened, 1-2 minutes, tossing constantly with tongs (do not overcook). Sprinkle with salt. Serve with sauce. If desired, sprinkle with parsley.

1 cup sauce with 1 cup zucchini noodles:
287 cal., 13g fat (4g sat. fat), 71mg chol., 708mg sod., 17g carb. (11g sugars, 4g fiber), 26g pro. **Diabetic exchanges:** 3 lean meat, 2 vegetable, ½ starch.

FISH & FRIES

Dine like you're in a traditional British pub! These moist fish fillets from the oven have a fuss-free coating that's healthier but just as crunchy and golden as the deep-fried kind. The crispy, simply seasoned baked fries are perfect on the side.
—Janice Mitchell, Aurora, CO

Prep: 10 min. • **Bake:** 35 min.
Makes: 4 servings

- 1 lb. potatoes (about 2 medium)
- 2 Tbsp. olive oil
- ¼ tsp. pepper

FISH
- ⅓ cup all-purpose flour
- ¼ tsp. pepper
- 1 large egg
- 2 Tbsp. water
- ⅔ cup crushed cornflakes
- 1 Tbsp. grated Parmesan cheese
- ⅛ tsp. cayenne pepper
- 1 lb. haddock or cod fillets
  Tartar sauce, optional

1. Preheat oven to 425°. Peel potatoes and cut lengthwise into ½-in.-thick slices; cut slices into ½-in.-thick sticks.
2. In a large bowl, toss potatoes with oil and pepper. Transfer to a 15x10x1-in. baking pan coated with cooking spray. Bake, uncovered, 25-30 minutes or until golden brown and crisp, stirring once.
3. Meanwhile, in a shallow bowl, mix the flour and pepper. In another shallow bowl, whisk egg with water. In a third bowl, toss cornflakes with cheese and cayenne. Dip fish in flour mixture to coat both sides; shake off excess. Dip in egg mixture, then in the cornflake mixture, patting to help coating adhere.
4. Place fish on a baking sheet coated with cooking spray. Bake 10-12 minutes or until fish just begins to flake easily with a fork. Serve with potatoes and, if desired, tartar sauce.

1 serving: 376 cal., 9g fat (2g sat. fat), 120mg chol., 228mg sod., 44g carb. (3g sugars, 2g fiber), 28g pro. **Diabetic exchanges:** 3 starch, 3 lean meat, 1½ fat.

ARRABBIATA SAUCE
WITH ZUCCHINI NOODLES

SOUTHWEST TURKEY STEW

I prefer main dishes that enable me to stay on my diet but still eat what the rest of the family eats. This healthy stew is a hit with my husband and our young children.
—Stephanie Hutchinson, Helix, OR

Prep: 15 min. • **Cook:** 5 hours
Makes: 6 servings

- 1½ lbs. turkey breast tenderloins, cubed
- 2 tsp. canola oil
- 1 can (15 oz.) turkey chili with beans, undrained
- 1 can (14½ oz.) diced tomatoes, undrained
- 1 medium sweet red pepper, chopped
- 1 medium green pepper, chopped
- ¾ cup chopped onion
- ¾ cup salsa
- 3 garlic cloves, minced
- 1½ tsp. chili powder
- ½ tsp. ground cumin
- ¼ tsp. salt
- 1 Tbsp. minced fresh cilantro, optional

1. In a nonstick skillet, brown turkey in oil; transfer to a 3-qt. slow cooker. Stir in the chili, tomatoes, peppers, onion, salsa, garlic, chili powder, cumin and salt.
2. Cover and cook on low for 5-6 hours, until the turkey is no longer pink and the vegetables are tender. Garnish with cilantro if desired.

1¼ cups: 238 cal., 4g fat (1g sat. fat), 65mg chol., 837mg sod., 17g carb. (7g sugars, 5g fiber), 33g pro. **Diabetic exchanges:** 4 lean meat, 1 vegetable, ½ starch.

LIME-CHIPOTLE CARNITAS TOSTADAS

LIME-CHIPOTLE CARNITAS TOSTADAS

Here's a terrific recipe for your next party! Set out various toppings and garnishes so guests can customize their own tostadas with the lime-kissed shredded pork.
—Jan Valdez, Chicago, IL

Prep: 20 min. • **Cook:** 8 hours
Makes: 16 servings

- ½ cup chicken broth
- 4 tsp. ground chipotle pepper
- 4 tsp. ground cumin
- 1 tsp. salt
- 1 boneless pork shoulder roast (4 to 5 lbs.), halved
- 1 large onion, peeled and halved
- 8 garlic cloves, peeled
- 1 to 2 limes, halved
- 16 tostada shells
   Optional : Warmed refried beans, salsa, sour cream, shredded lettuce, chopped avocado, crumbled queso fresco and minced fresh cilantro
   Lime wedges

1. Add broth to a 5-qt. slow cooker. Mix chipotle, cumin and salt; rub over all sides of pork. Place in slow cooker. Add onion and garlic cloves. Cook, covered, on low 8-10 hours, until meat is tender.
2. Remove pork; cool slightly. Strain cooking juices, reserving garlic cloves; discard onion. Skim fat from the cooking juices. Mash garlic with a fork. Shred pork with 2 forks.
3. Return cooking juices, garlic and pork to the slow cooker. Squeeze lime juice over the pork; heat through, stirring to combine. Layer tostada shells with pork mixture and toppings as desired. Serve with lime wedges.

1 tostada: 269 cal., 15g fat (5g sat. fat), 76mg chol., 279mg sod., 9g carb. (1g sugars, 1g fiber), 23g pro. **Diabetic exchanges:** 3 medium-fat meat, ½ starch.

SIMPLE CHICKEN ENCHILADAS

This quick, easy recipe instantly becomes a favorite with friends whenever I share a batch. Modify the spiciness to suit your taste by varying the intensity of the salsa and chiles.

—Kristi Black, Harrison Township, MI

Prep: 20 min. • **Bake:** 25 min.
Makes: 5 servings

- 1 can (10 oz.) enchilada sauce, divided
- 4 oz. cream cheese, cubed
- 1½ cups salsa
- 2 cups cubed cooked chicken
- 1 can (15 oz.) pinto beans, rinsed and drained
- 1 can (4 oz.) chopped green chiles
- 10 flour tortillas (6 in.)
- 1 cup shredded Mexican cheese blend

Optional: Shredded lettuce, chopped tomato, sour cream and sliced ripe olives

1. Preheat oven to 350°. Spoon ½ cup enchilada sauce into a greased 13x9-in. baking dish. In a large saucepan, cook and stir the cream cheese and salsa over medium heat until blended, 2-3 minutes. Stir in the chicken, beans and chiles.
2. Place about ⅓ cup of the chicken mixture down the center of each tortilla. Roll up and place seam side down over the sauce in baking dish. Top with the remaining enchilada sauce; sprinkle with cheese.
3. Cover and bake until heated through, 25-30 minutes. If desired, serve with lettuce, tomato, sour cream and olives.

2 enchiladas: 468 cal., 13g fat (6g sat. fat), 75mg chol., 1394mg sod., 51g carb. (6g sugars, 8g fiber), 34g pro.

SIMPLE CHICKEN ENCHILADAS

SHRIMP & VEGETABLE BOIL
PICTURED ON P. 139

When my children were small, they liked picking out the ingredients for making this supper. When there's no shrimp on hand, we like to use crab or chicken.

—Joyce Guth, Mohnton, PA

Prep: 20 min. • **Cook:** 30 min.
Makes: 6 servings

- 4 cups water
- 4 cups chicken broth
- 2 tsp. salt
- 2 tsp. ground nutmeg
- ½ tsp. sugar
- 2 lbs. red potatoes (about 8 medium), cut into wedges
- 1 medium head cauliflower, broken into florets
- 2 large onions, quartered
- 3 medium carrots, sliced
- 1 lb. fresh peas, shelled (about 1 cup)
- 2 lbs. uncooked shell-on shrimp (26-30 per lb.), deveined
- 6 oz. fresh baby spinach (about 8 cups)
- 1 Tbsp. minced fresh parsley
  Salt and pepper to taste

1. In a stockpot, combine the first 5 ingredients; add potatoes, cauliflower, onions, carrots and peas. Bring to a boil. Reduce heat; simmer, uncovered, until the vegetables are tender, 12-15 minutes.
2. Stir in the shrimp and spinach; cook 3-5 minutes longer or until the shrimp turn pink. Drain; transfer to a large serving bowl. Sprinkle with parsley; season with salt and pepper.

2⅔ cups: 367 cal., 3g fat (1g sat. fat), 185mg chol., 721mg sod., 50g carb. (12g sugars, 11g fiber), 35g pro.
Diabetic exchanges: 4 lean meat, 3 starch.

SPICY LAMB CURRY

PICTURED ON P. 139

I've tweaked this curry recipe over the years with a blend of aromatic spices. Fenugreek seeds can be found in specialty spice stores and are common in Middle Eastern curries and chutneys, but you can leave them out of this recipe if you desire.

—Janis Kracht, Slaterville Springs, NY

Prep: 25 min. + marinating • **Cook:** 1 hour
Makes: 6 servings

- 3 Tbsp. ground cumin
- 2 Tbsp. ground ginger
- 1 Tbsp. ground coriander
- 1 Tbsp. ground fenugreek
- 4 garlic cloves, minced
- 1 tsp. ground cloves
- ½ tsp. ground cinnamon
- 2 lbs. lamb stew meat, cut into ¾-in. pieces
- 1 Tbsp. olive oil
- 2 large onions, chopped
- ½ cup water
- 2 Tbsp. paprika
- 2 Tbsp. tomato paste
- 1 tsp. salt
- 1 tsp. ground mustard
- 1 tsp. chili powder
- 1 cup plain yogurt
- 3 cups hot cooked brown rice
  Optional: Cubed fresh pineapple, flaked coconut and toasted sliced almonds

1. In a large bowl, combine the first 7 ingredients. Add the lamb; turn to coat. Cover; refrigerate for 8 hours or overnight.
2. In a Dutch oven, brown meat in oil in batches; remove and keep warm. In the same pan, cook onions in drippings until tender. Add the water, paprika, tomato paste, salt, mustard and chili powder.
3. Return lamb to pan. Bring to a boil. Reduce heat; cover and simmer for 1-1½ hours or until the meat is tender. Remove from the heat; stir in yogurt. Serve with rice. Top with pineapple, coconut and almonds if desired.

¾ cup curry with ½ cup rice: 419 cal., 14g fat (4g sat. fat), 104mg chol., 534mg sod., 36g carb. (5g sugars, 6g fiber), 37g pro. **Diabetic exchanges:** 4 lean meat, 2 starch, 1 vegetable, 1 fat.:

TANDOORI-STYLE CHICKEN WITH CUCUMBER MELON RELISH

We all need a quick meal that's deliciously healthy. For this one, I can marinate the chicken before I leave for work; when I get home, I grill the chicken and make the relish. My husband loves the spicy flavor. If you want a bit more heat, just add more crushed red pepper flakes.

—Naylet LaRochelle, Miami, FL

Prep: 20 min. + marinating • **Grill:** 15 min.
Makes: 4 servings

- 1½ cups reduced-fat plain yogurt
- 2 Tbsp. lemon juice, divided
- 1½ tsp. garam masala or curry powder
- ½ tsp. salt
- ¼ to ½ tsp. crushed red pepper flakes
- 4 boneless skinless chicken breast halves (6 oz. each)
- 1½ cups chopped cantaloupe
- ½ cup chopped seeded peeled cucumber
- 2 green onions, finely chopped
- 2 Tbsp. minced fresh cilantro
- 1 Tbsp. minced fresh mint
- ¼ cup toasted sliced almonds, optional

1. In a small bowl, whisk yogurt, 1 Tbsp. lemon juice, the garam masala, salt and pepper flakes until blended. Pour 1 cup marinade into a large bowl. Add chicken; turn to coat. Cover; refrigerate for up to 6 hours. Cover and refrigerate the remaining marinade.
2. For relish, in a small bowl, mix the cantaloupe, cucumber, green onions, cilantro, mint and remaining lemon juice.
3. Drain chicken, discarding marinade. Grill chicken, covered, on a lightly oiled rack over medium heat or broil 4 in. from heat until a thermometer reads 165°, 6-8 minutes on each side. Serve with the relish and reserved marinade. If desired, sprinkle with almonds.

1 serving: 247 cal., 5g fat (2g sat. fat), 98mg chol., 332mg sod., 10g carb. (9g sugars, 1g fiber), 38g pro. **Diabetic exchanges:** 5 lean meat, ½ starch.

TANDOORI-STYLE
CHICKEN WITH
CUCUMBER
MELON RELISH

GREEK-STYLE STUFFED PEPPERS

LENTIL & CHICKEN SAUSAGE STEW

This hearty and healthy set-it-and-forget-it stew will warm your family right down to their toes! Serve with cornbread or rolls to soak up every last morsel.
—*Jan Valdez, Chicago, IL*

Prep: 15 min. • **Cook:** 8 hours
Makes: 6 servings

- 1 carton (32 oz.) reduced-sodium chicken broth
- 1 can (28 oz.) diced tomatoes, undrained
- 3 fully cooked spicy chicken sausage links (3 oz. each), cut into ½-in. slices
- 1 cup dried lentils, rinsed
- 1 medium onion, chopped
- 1 medium carrot, chopped
- 1 celery rib, chopped
- 2 garlic cloves, minced
- ½ tsp. dried thyme

In a 4- or 5-qt. slow cooker, combine all ingredients. Cover and cook on low for 8-10 hours, until lentils are tender.

1½ cups: 231 cal., 4g fat (1g sat. fat), 33mg chol., 803mg sod., 31g carb. (8g sugars, 13g fiber), 19g pro. **Diabetic exchanges:** 2 lean meat, 2 vegetable, 1 starch.

GREEK-STYLE STUFFED PEPPERS

The bounty of peppers found you can find at the local farmers market in the early fall, combined with classic Greek ingredients, creates a dish that just bursts with bright color and fresh flavor.
—*Renee Murby, Johnston, RI*

Prep: 30 min. • **Cook:** 4½ hours
Makes: 8 servings

- 2 Tbsp. olive oil
- 1 small fennel bulb, chopped
- 1 small red onion, chopped
- 1 pkg. (10 oz.) frozen chopped spinach, thawed and squeezed dry
- 3 garlic cloves, minced
- 2 each medium sweet yellow, orange, red and green peppers
- 1 can (28 oz.) crushed tomatoes, divided
- 1 lb. ground lamb
- 1 cup cooked barley
- 1 cup crumbled feta cheese,
- ½ cup Greek olives, chopped
- 1½ tsp. dried oregano
- ½ tsp. salt
- ½ tsp. crushed red pepper flakes
- ½ tsp. pepper
  - Additional crumbled feta cheese
  - Chopped fresh parsley, optional

1. In a large skillet, heat oil over medium-high heat. Add fennel and onion; cook and stir until tender, 6-8 minutes. Add spinach and minced garlic; cook 1 minute longer. Let cool slightly.
2. Cut and reserve tops from peppers; remove and discard seeds. Pour 1 cup crushed tomatoes into bottom of a 6- or 7-qt. slow cooker. In a large bowl, combine lamb, barley, 1 cup feta cheese, olives and seasonings; add fennel mixture. Spoon the mixture into peppers; place in slow cooker. Pour remaining crushed tomatoes over peppers; replace pepper tops. Cook, covered, on low for 4½-5½ hours, until peppers are tender. Serve with additional feta and, if desired, chopped parsley.

1 stuffed pepper: 313 cal., 16g fat (6g sat. fat), 45mg chol., 684mg sod., 26g carb. (11g sugars, 8g fiber), 17g pro. **Diabetic exchanges:** 2 starch, 2 medium-fat meat, 1 fat.

SIMPLE POACHED SALMON

This recipe is a favorite because it's healthy and almost effortless. And the salmon fillets always cook to perfection!

—Erin Chilcoat, Central Islip, NY

Prep: 10 min. • **Cook:** 1½ hours
Makes: 4 servings

- 2 cups water
- 1 cup white wine
- 1 medium onion, sliced
- 1 celery rib, sliced
- 1 medium carrot, sliced
- 2 Tbsp. lemon juice
- 3 fresh thyme sprigs
- 1 fresh rosemary sprig
- 1 bay leaf
- ½ tsp. salt
- ¼ tsp. pepper
- 4 salmon fillets (1¼ in. thick and 6 oz. each)
  Lemon wedges

1. In a 3-qt. slow cooker, combine the first 11 ingredients. Cook, covered, on low 45 minutes.

2. Carefully place fillets in liquid; add additional warm water (120° to 130°) to cover if needed. Cook, covered, for 45-55 minutes, just until fish flakes easily with a fork (a thermometer inserted in fish should read at least 145°). Remove fish from cooking liquid. Serve warm or cold with lemon wedges.

1 salmon fillet: 272 cal., 16g fat (3g sat. fat), 85mg chol., 115mg sod., 1g carb. (0 sugars, 0 fiber), 29g pro. **Diabetic exchanges:** 4 lean meat.

HEARTY PITA TACOS

HEARTY PITA TACOS

These tasty tacos prove you don't need to skimp on flavor when trying to eat healthy. Our 9-year-old daughter enjoys helping us make these—and she likes eating them even more!

—Jamie Valocchi, Mesa, AZ

Takes: 30 min. • **Makes:** 6 servings

- 1 lb. lean ground beef (90% lean)
- 1 small sweet red pepper, chopped
- 2 green onions, chopped
- 1 can (16 oz.) kidney beans, rinsed and drained
- ¾ cup frozen corn
- ⅔ cup taco sauce
- 1 can (2¼ oz.) sliced ripe olives, drained
- ½ tsp. garlic salt
- ¼ tsp. onion powder
- ¼ tsp. dried oregano
- ¼ tsp. paprika
- ¼ tsp. pepper
- 6 whole wheat pita pocket halves
- 6 Tbsp. shredded reduced-fat cheddar cheese
  Optional: Sliced avocado and additional taco sauce

1. In a large skillet, cook the beef, red pepper and onions over medium heat until meat is no longer pink; drain. Stir in the beans, corn, taco sauce, olives and seasonings; heat through.

2. Spoon ¾ cup beef mixture into each pita half. Sprinkle with cheese. Serve with sliced avocado and additional taco sauce if desired.

1 serving: 339 cal., 10g fat (4g sat. fat), 52mg chol., 787mg sod., 38g carb. (4g sugars, 8g fiber), 26g pro. **Diabetic exchanges:** 3 lean meat, 2½ starch.

WILD MUSHROOM PIZZA

What's great about this pizza is that you don't need to worry about finding the right toppings. Whatever wild mushrooms are in season or at your market will work beautifully. I like to get as many different ones as possible.
—James Schend, Pleasant Prairie, WI

Prep: 30 min. + rising • **Bake:** 15 min.
Makes: 6 slices

- 1 pkg. (¼ oz.) active dry yeast
- ¾ cup warm water (110° to 115°)
- 1 tsp. olive oil
- ½ tsp. sugar
- ½ cup whole wheat flour
- ½ tsp. salt
- 1½ cups all-purpose flour

TOPPINGS

- 2 tsp. olive oil, divided
- 1 lb. sliced fresh wild mushrooms
- ¼ cup chopped shallot
- 4 garlic cloves, minced
- 2 oz. cream cheese, softened
- 1½ tsp. salt
- ½ cup shredded Gruyere cheese
- ¼ cup shredded Parmesan cheese
- 6 fresh thyme sprigs, stems removed
  Fresh basil, optional

1. In a bowl, dissolve yeast in warm water. Add olive oil and sugar; mix well. Combine whole wheat flour and salt; stir into the yeast mixture until smooth. Stir in enough all-purpose flour to form a soft dough.
2. Turn onto a floured surface; knead until smooth and elastic, 6-8 minutes. Place in a bowl coated with cooking spray, turning once to coat top. Cover and let rise in a warm place until doubled, about 1½ hours. Preheat oven to 425°.
3. Punch down the dough; press onto a 12-in. pizza pan coated with cooking spray. Prick dough several times with a fork. Bake until the edges are light golden brown, 10-12 minutes.
4. Meanwhile, in a large skillet, heat 1 tsp. oil over medium-high heat; saute mushrooms in a single layer, in batches, until golden brown, about 8 minutes. Add onion and garlic; cook until onion is tender.
5. In a food processor, process half of the sauteed mushrooms with cream cheese, the remaining olive oil and salt. Spread on crust. Top with the remaining mushroom mixture, cheeses and thyme. Bake until the crust is golden brown and cheese is melted, 12-14 minutes. If desired, garnish with additional fresh thyme and basil.

1 slice: 284 cal., 10g fat (5g sat. fat), 22mg chol., 357mg sod., 37g carb. (3g sugars, 3g fiber), 12g pro. **Diabetic exchanges:** 2½ starch, 2 medium-fat meat, ½ fat.

READER REVIEW

"We love mushroom-topped pizza, and this recipe did not disappoint! I used fresh pizza dough from the market and dried thyme. Fantastic! Will make this recipe again."

ANNRMS, TASTEOFHOME.COM

WILD MUSHROOM PIZZA

CONTEST-WINNING
GREEK PASTA BAKE

CONTEST-WINNING GREEK PASTA BAKE

When I take this dish to potlucks, there is never so much as a morsel left! It's a simple, healthy, hearty supper made with ingredients that are easy to find. Add a salad of field greens and a crusty loaf of artisan bread for a quick workweek meal solution.

—Anne Taglienti, Kennett Square, PA

....

Prep: 20 min. • **Bake:** 25 min.
Makes: 8 servings

- 3⅓ cups uncooked whole grain spiral or penne pasta
- 4 cups cubed cooked chicken breast
- 1 can (29 oz.) tomato sauce
- 1 can (14½ oz.) no-salt-added diced tomatoes, drained
- 1 pkg. (10 oz.) frozen chopped spinach, thawed and squeezed dry
- 2 cans (2¼ oz. each) sliced ripe olives, drained
- ¼ cup thinly sliced red onion
- ¼ cup chopped green pepper
- 1 tsp. dried basil
- 1 tsp. dried oregano
- 1 cup shredded mozzarella cheese
- ½ cup crumbled feta cheese
  Optional: Chopped fresh oregano or fresh basil

1. Preheat oven to 400°. Cook pasta according to package directions; drain. In a large bowl, combine pasta, chicken, tomato sauce, tomatoes, spinach, olives, onion, green pepper, basil and oregano.
2. Transfer to a 13x9-in. baking dish coated with cooking spray. Sprinkle with cheeses. Bake, uncovered, until heated through and cheese is melted, 25-30 minutes. If desired, sprinkle with fresh oregano or basil.
Freeze option: Cool unbaked casserole; cover and freeze. To use, partially thaw in refrigerator overnight. Remove from refrigerator 30 minutes before baking. Preheat oven to 400°. Bake casserole as directed, increasing time as necessary to heat through and for a thermometer inserted in center to read 165°.
1½ cups: 398 cal., 10g fat (3g sat. fat), 67mg chol., 832mg sod., 47g carb. (5g sugars, 9g fiber), 34g pro. **Diabetic exchanges:** 3 lean meat, 3 very lean meat, 2½ starch, 1 vegetable, ½ fat.

TERIYAKI BEEF STEW

TERIYAKI BEEF STEW

As they say, necessity is the mother of invention. I created this recipe because I had a package of stew meat I needed to use. I spotted the ginger beer in the fridge and rest was history. This stew has a delicious sweet-tangy flavor. It's nice to have a different way to serve an inexpensive meal.

—Leslie Simms, Sherman Oaks, CA

....

Prep: 20 min. • **Cook:** 6½ hours
Makes: 8 servings

- 2 lbs. beef stew meat
- 1 bottle (12 oz.) ginger beer or ginger ale
- ¼ cup teriyaki sauce
- 2 garlic cloves, minced
- 2 Tbsp. sesame seeds
- 2 Tbsp. cornstarch
- 2 Tbsp. cold water
- 2 cups frozen peas, thawed
  Hot cooked rice, optional

1. In a large nonstick skillet, brown beef in batches. Transfer to a 3-qt. slow cooker.
2. In a small bowl, combine the ginger beer, teriyaki sauce, garlic and sesame seeds; pour over beef. Cover and cook on low for 6-8 hours, until meat is tender.
3. Combine cornstarch and cold water until smooth; gradually stir into stew. Stir in peas. Cover and cook on high for 30 minutes or until thickened. Serve with rice if desired.
1 cup stew: 310 cal., 12g fat (4g sat. fat), 94mg chol., 528mg sod., 17g carb. (9g sugars, 2g fiber), 33g pro. **Diabetic exchanges:** 4 lean meat, 1 starch.

CHARD & WHITE BEAN PASTA
PICTURED ON P. 139

I love to prepare dishes without gluten or dairy products, and this recipe meets the criteria when you use gluten-free pasta. It's proof you can use delicious, healthy products to create a crowd-pleasing meal. It's also soy-free, nut-free and vegetarian.
—Amie Valpone, New York, NY

Prep: 20 min. • **Cook:** 20 min.
Makes: 8 servings

- 1 pkg. (12 oz.) uncooked whole wheat or brown rice penne pasta
- 2 Tbsp. olive oil
- 4 cups sliced leeks (white portion only)
- 1 cup sliced sweet onion
- 4 garlic cloves, sliced
- 1 Tbsp. minced fresh sage or 1 tsp. rubbed sage
- 1 large sweet potato, peeled and cut into ½-in. cubes
- 1 medium bunch Swiss chard (about 1 lb.), cut into 1-in. slices
- 1 can (15½ oz.) great northern beans, rinsed and drained
- ¾ tsp. salt
- ¼ tsp. chili powder
- ¼ tsp. crushed red pepper flakes
- ⅛ tsp. ground nutmeg
- ⅛ tsp. pepper
- ⅓ cup finely chopped fresh basil
- 1 Tbsp. balsamic vinegar
- 2 cups marinara sauce, warmed

1. Cook pasta according to package directions. Drain, reserving ¾ cup of the pasta water.
2. In a 6-qt. stockpot, heat olive oil over medium heat; saute leeks and onion until tender, 5-7 minutes. Add garlic and sage; cook and stir 2 minutes.
3. Add potato and chard; cook, covered, over medium-low heat 5 minutes. Stir in beans, dry seasonings and reserved pasta water; cook, covered, until potato and chard are tender, about 5 minutes.
4. Add pasta, basil and vinegar; toss and heat through. Serve with sauce.
1⅓ cups pasta mixture with ½ cup sauce: 369 cal., 6g fat (1g sat. fat), 1mg chol., 801mg sod., 67g carb. (13g sugars, 13g fiber), 14g pro.

LEMON CHICKEN PASTA

LEMON CHICKEN PASTA
This dish reminds me of the lemony chicken and rice my mom used to make. In my speedier update, I saute lightly breaded chicken breasts and serve them over capellini pasta.
—Aileen Rivera, Bronx, NY

Prep: 30 min. • **Cook:** 15 min.
Makes: 6 servings

- 4 boneless skinless chicken breast halves (6 oz. each)
- 1 tsp. salt, divided
- ¼ tsp. plus ⅛ tsp. pepper, divided
- ½ cup all-purpose flour
- 8 oz. uncooked capellini or angel hair pasta
- 3 Tbsp. olive oil, divided
- ¼ cup peeled and thinly sliced garlic cloves (about 12 cloves)
- 1 cup white wine or chicken broth
- 2 Tbsp. lemon juice
- ½ cup grated Parmigiano-Reggiano cheese
- ⅓ cup plus 3 Tbsp. minced fresh parsley, divided
  Lemon wedges, optional

1. Pound chicken breasts with a meat mallet to ¼-in. thickness. Sprinkle with ½ tsp. salt and ¼ tsp. pepper. Place flour in a shallow bowl. Dip chicken in flour to coat both sides; shake off excess.
2. Cook pasta according to package directions for al dente. Meanwhile, in a large skillet, heat 2 Tbsp. oil over medium heat. Add chicken; cook 2-3 minutes on each side or until no longer pink. Remove and keep warm.
3. In the same pan, heat remaining oil over medium heat; add garlic. Cook and stir 30-60 seconds or until garlic is lightly browned. Add wine to pan; increase heat to medium-high. Cook, stirring to loosen browned bits from pan, until the liquid is reduced by half. Stir in lemon juice.
4. Drain pasta, reserving ½ cup of the pasta water; place in a large bowl. Add cheese, ⅓ cup parsley, half the garlic mixture, and remaining salt and pepper; toss to combine, adding enough reserved pasta water to moisten the pasta. Serve with chicken. Drizzle with remaining garlic mixture; sprinkle with remaining parsley. If desired, serve with lemon wedges.
1 serving: 403 cal., 12g fat (3g sat. fat), 68mg chol., 577mg sod., 35g carb. (2g sugars, 2g fiber), 31g pro. **Diabetic exchanges:** 4 lean meat, 2 starch, 1½ fat.

SPINACH, SHRIMP & RICOTTA TACOS

I was looking for a new recipe for tacos, and this version was a perfect solution. With shrimp, green chiles, spinach and ricotta, it's made up of ingredients I love that aren't normally associated with traditional tacos.

—Priscilla Gilbert, Indian Harbour Beach, FL

Takes: 30 min. • **Makes:** 6 servings

- 1 carton (15 oz.) part-skim ricotta cheese
- 2 Tbsp. minced fresh cilantro
- 4 garlic cloves, minced, divided
- ¼ tsp. salt
- ⅛ tsp. pepper
- 1 Tbsp. canola oil
- 1 medium onion, chopped
- 1 lb. uncooked shrimp (31-40 per lb.), peeled and deveined
- 2 cans (4 oz. each) chopped green chiles
- ¼ tsp. crushed red pepper flakes
- 10 oz. fresh baby spinach (about 12 cups)
- 12 corn tortillas (6 in.), warmed Salsa and lime wedges

1. In a large bowl, combine the ricotta, cilantro, half the minced garlic, the salt and pepper; set aside.
2. In a large skillet, heat oil over medium-high heat. Add onion; cook and stir until softened, 4-5 minutes. Add shrimp, green chiles and pepper flakes; cook 1 minute longer. Add spinach and the remaining garlic; cook and stir until shrimp turn pink and spinach is wilted, 4-5 minutes.
3. Serve shrimp mixture in tortillas with ricotta mixture, salsa and lime wedges.

2 tacos: 317 cal., 11g fat (4g sat. fat), 114mg chol., 468mg sod., 32g carb. (2g sugars, 5g fiber), 25g pro. **Diabetic exchanges:** 3 lean meat, 1½ starch, 1 vegetable, ½ fat.

TEST KITCHEN TIP
If you have any of the shrimp mixture left over, serve it over hot cooked pasta, polenta or quinoa.

CHICKEN IN TOMATO-BASIL CREAM SAUCE

Our fresh garden tomatoes and herbs inspired this recipe. During summer, I grill the chicken with Italian seasonings and a bit of garlic powder, but on rainy days or in winter, I cook it on the stovetop.

—Rachel Kowasic, Valrico, FL

Prep: 20 min. • **Cook:** 30 min.
Makes: 4 servings

- 1 lb. boneless skinless chicken breasts, cut into ½-in. cubes
- 3 tsp. butter, divided
- 8 plum tomatoes, seeded and chopped
- 1 small onion, finely chopped
- 1 garlic clove, minced
- ½ cup reduced-sodium chicken broth
- 1 cup uncooked whole wheat orzo pasta
- 1 cup evaporated milk
- ½ cup loosely packed basil leaves, julienned
- ¾ tsp. salt
- ¼ tsp. pepper
- ¼ cup crumbled feta cheese

1. In a large nonstick skillet, cook the chicken in 2 tsp. butter until no longer pink. Remove and keep warm. In same skillet, saute tomatoes and onion in the remaining 1 tsp. butter until the onion is softened. Add garlic; cook 1 minute longer.
2. Stir in broth. Bring to a boil; add the orzo. Reduce heat. Cover and simmer for 10-12 minutes or until orzo is tender. Stir in the chicken, milk, basil, salt and pepper; heat through (do not boil). Sprinkle with cheese just before serving.

1½ cups: 417 cal., 12g fat (6g sat. fat), 94mg chol., 723mg sod., 41g carb. (10g sugars, 9g fiber), 35g pro. **Diabetic exchanges:** 3 lean meat, 2 starch, 1 vegetable, ½ whole milk, ½ fat.

SPINACH, SHRIMP & RICOTTA TACOS

CURRY POMEGRANATE PROTEIN BOWL

CURRY POMEGRANATE PROTEIN BOWL

This recipe is simple and beautiful. It uses a lot of distinct flavors that, when blended together, create a taste sensation that is out of this world. You can substitute other roasted, salted nuts for the soy nuts, and can use warmed berry jam in place of the pomegranate molasses.
—Mary Baker, Wauwatosa, WI

Prep: 25 min. • **Cook:** 25 min.
Makes: 6 servings

- 3 cups cubed peeled butternut squash (½-in. cubes)
- 2 Tbsp. olive oil, divided
- ½ tsp. salt, divided
- ¼ tsp. pepper
- ½ small onion, chopped
- 1 Tbsp. curry powder
- 1 Tbsp. ground cumin
- 1 garlic clove, minced
- 1 tsp. ground coriander
- 3 cups water
- 1 cup dried red lentils, rinsed
- ½ cup salted soy nuts
- ½ cup dried cranberries
- ⅓ cup thinly sliced green onions
- ⅓ cup pomegranate molasses
- ½ cup crumbled feta cheese
- ½ cup pomegranate seeds
- ¼ cup chopped fresh cilantro

1. Preheat oven to 375°. Place squash on a greased 15x10x1-in. baking pan. Drizzle with 1 Tbsp. oil; sprinkle with ¼ tsp. salt and pepper. Roast until tender, 25-30 minutes, turning once.

2. Meanwhile, in a large skillet, heat the remaining 1 Tbsp. oil over medium-high heat. Add onion; cook and stir until crisp-tender, 4-6 minutes. Add curry powder, cumin, garlic, coriander and remaining ¼ tsp. salt; cook 1 minute longer. Add water and lentils; bring to boil. Reduce heat; simmer, covered, until lentils are tender and water is absorbed, about 15 minutes.

3. Gently stir in soy nuts, cranberries, green onions and roasted squash. Divide among 6 serving bowls. Drizzle with the molasses and top with feta, pomegranate seeds and cilantro.

¾ cup: 367 cal., 9g fat (2g sat. fat), 5mg chol., 327mg sod., 60g carb. (23g sugars, 9g fiber), 14g pro.

FRUITED PORK CHOPS

Here's one of my favorite slow-cooker recipes. When I have guests, I'll often prepare these tender pineapple pork chops and serve them with brown rice.
—Cindy Ragan, North Huntingdon, PA

Prep: 10 min. • **Cook:** 4¼ hours
Makes: 6 servings

- 3 Tbsp. all-purpose flour
- 1½ tsp. dried oregano
- ¾ tsp. salt
- ¼ tsp. garlic powder
- ¼ tsp. pepper
- 6 boneless pork loin chops (5 oz. each)
- 1 Tbsp. olive oil
- 1 can (20 oz.) unsweetened pineapple chunks
- ¾ cup unsweetened pineapple juice
- ¼ cup water
- 2 Tbsp. brown sugar
- 2 Tbsp. dried minced onion
- 2 Tbsp. tomato paste
- ¼ cup raisins

1. Combine the flour, oregano, salt, garlic powder and pepper in a shallow dish; coat chops, 1 at a time. In a nonstick skillet, brown the chops in olive oil on both sides. Transfer to a 5-qt. slow cooker.
2. Drain pineapple, reserving juice; set pineapple aside. In a bowl, combine the ¾ cup pineapple juice with the reserved pineapple juice. Stir in the water, brown sugar, onion and tomato paste; pour over chops. Sprinkle with raisins.
3. Cover and cook on low 4-5 hours, until meat is tender. Stir in pineapple chunks. Cover and cook 15 minutes longer or until heated through.

1 pork chop: 342 cal., 10g fat (3g sat. fat), 68mg chol., 341mg sod., 31g carb. (24g sugars, 2g fiber), 29g pro. **Diabetic exchanges:** 4 lean meat, 1 starch, 1 fruit, ½ fat.

LIGHT & LEMONY SCAMPI

A touch more lemon helped me trim the calories in our favorite shrimp scampi recipe. For those who want to indulge...pass around the Parmesan!
—Ann Sheehy, Lawrence, MA

Prep: 20 min. • **Cook:** 15 min.
Makes: 4 servings

- 1 lb. uncooked shrimp (26-30 per lb.)
- 8 oz. uncooked multigrain angel hair pasta
- 1 Tbsp. butter
- 1 Tbsp. olive oil
- 2 green onions, thinly sliced
- 4 garlic cloves, minced
- ½ cup reduced-sodium chicken broth
- 2 tsp. grated lemon zest
- 3 Tbsp. lemon juice
- ½ tsp. freshly ground pepper
- ¼ tsp. salt
- ¼ tsp. crushed red pepper flakes
- ¼ cup minced fresh parsley
  Grated Parmesan cheese, optional

1. Peel and devein shrimp, removing tails. Cut each shrimp lengthwise in half. Cook pasta according to package directions.
2. In a large nonstick skillet, heat butter and olive oil over medium-high heat. Add shrimp, green onions and garlic; cook and stir until shrimp turn pink, 2-3 minutes. Remove from pan with a slotted spoon.
3. Add broth, lemon zest, lemon juice, pepper, salt and red pepper flakes to the same pan. Bring to a boil; cook until liquid is slightly reduced, about 1 minute. Return shrimp to pan; heat through. Remove from heat.
4. Drain pasta; divide among 4 bowls. Top with shrimp mixture; sprinkle with parsley. If desired, serve with cheese.

1 serving: 378 cal., 10g fat (3g sat. fat), 146mg chol., 405mg sod., 42g carb. (3g sugars, 5g fiber), 29g pro. **Diabetic exchanges:** 3 very lean meat, 2½ starch, 1½ fat.

FRUITED PORK CHOPS

CHICKEN JAMBALAYA

CREOLE PORK TENDERLOIN WITH VEGETABLES

Fresh summer vegetables are paired with lean pork and tasty Greek olives for this healthy and quick dinner that's great for family or friends.
—Judy Armstrong, Prairieville, LA

Prep: 30 min. • **Bake:** 20 min.
Makes: 8 servings

- 3½ tsp. reduced-sodium Creole seasoning, divided
- 2 pork tenderloins (1 lb. each)
- 2 Tbsp. canola oil
- 2 medium fennel bulbs, trimmed and cut into 1-in. wedges
- 1 medium eggplant, cut into 1-in. cubes
- 2 medium yellow summer squash, halved and cut into ½-in. slices
- 1 large sweet red pepper, cut into 1-in. pieces
- 2 shallots, thinly sliced
- ½ cup pitted Greek olives, coarsely chopped
- 3 garlic cloves, minced
- ½ cup vegetable broth
- 4 tsp. minced fresh thyme or 1¼ tsp. dried thyme

1. Preheat oven to 350°. Sprinkle 3 tsp. Creole seasoning over tenderloins. In a 6-qt. stockpot, heat oil over medium-high heat. Brown tenderloins on all sides. Transfer to a roasting pan.
2. Add fennel, eggplant, squash, pepper and shallots to stockpot; cook and stir over medium heat 3-4 minutes or until lightly browned. Add olives and garlic; cook and stir 1 minute longer. Stir in broth, thyme and remaining Creole seasoning; bring to a boil. Reduce heat; simmer, covered, 6-8 minutes or until fennel is crisp-tender. Spoon vegetables and liquid around pork.
3. Bake, uncovered, 20-25 minutes or until vegetables are tender and a thermometer inserted in pork reads 145°. Let stand 5 minutes before serving. Cut pork into slices; serve with vegetables.
3 oz. cooked pork with 1 cup vegetables: 247 cal., 10g fat (2g sat. fat), 64mg chol., 575mg sod., 15g carb. (7g sugars, 5g fiber), 25g pro.

CHICKEN JAMBALAYA

This is a great dish to serve at parties. It's just as good as, if not tastier than, most high-fat versions. And it reheats well.
—Lynn Desjardins, Atkinson, NH

Prep: 20 min. • **Cook:** 1 hour
Makes: 6 servings

- ¾ lb. boneless skinless chicken breasts, cubed
- 3 cups reduced-sodium chicken broth
- 1½ cups uncooked brown rice
- 4 oz. reduced-fat smoked turkey sausage, diced
- ½ cup thinly sliced celery with leaves
- ½ cup chopped onion
- ½ cup chopped green pepper
- 2 to 3 tsp. Cajun or Creole seasoning
- 1 to 2 garlic cloves, minced
- ⅛ tsp. hot pepper sauce
- 1 bay leaf
- 1 can (14½ oz.) no-salt-added diced tomatoes, undrained
  Chopped green onions, optional

1. In a large skillet lightly coated with cooking spray, saute the chicken for 2-3 minutes or until no longer pink. Stir in the next 10 ingredients. Bring to a boil. Reduce heat; cover and simmer for 50-60 minutes or until heated through.
2. Stir in tomatoes; cover and simmer 10 minutes longer or until the liquid is absorbed and rice is tender. Remove from heat; let stand for 5 minutes. Discard bay leaf. Serve with green onions if desired.
1 cup: 285 cal., 4g fat (1g sat. fat), 43mg chol., 654mg sod., 41g carb. (4g sugars, 4g fiber), 21g pro. **Diabetic exchanges:** 2½ starch, 2 lean meat.

CREOLE PORK TENDERLOIN WITH VEGETABLES

BLACK BEAN & CORN TACOS

We eat meatless meals a few times a week, so I replaced the beef with nutty brown rice to bulk up these tacos. I also like to substitute quinoa for the rice.
—Kristin Rimkus, Snohomish, WA

Takes: 30 min. • **Makes:** 4 servings

- 1 medium onion, finely chopped
- 1 medium green pepper, finely chopped
- 1 small sweet red pepper, finely chopped
- 1 can (15 oz.) black beans, rinsed and drained
- 2 large tomatoes, seeded and chopped
- 2 cups shredded cabbage
- 1 cup fresh or frozen corn
- 2 Tbsp. reduced-sodium taco seasoning
- 2 Tbsp. lime juice
- 2 garlic cloves, minced
- 1 cup ready-to-serve brown rice
- 8 taco shells, warmed
- ½ cup shredded reduced-fat Mexican cheese blend
- ½ cup reduced-fat sour cream

1. In a lightly oiled large nonstick skillet, saute onion and peppers until crisp-tender. Add the beans, tomatoes, cabbage, corn, taco seasoning, lime juice and garlic. Cook and stir over medium heat until vegetables are tender, 8-10 minutes. Stir in rice; heat through.
2. Spoon bean mixture into taco shells. Top with cheese and sour cream.
2 tacos: 423 cal., 12g fat (4g sat. fat), 20mg chol., 682mg sod., 64g carb. (12g sugars, 10g fiber), 17g pro.

TUSCAN PORK STEW

TUSCAN PORK STEW

Tender chunks of pork slowly cook in a nicely seasoned, wine-infused sauce. Add some crushed red pepper flakes for a little extra kick.
—Penny Hawkins, Mebane, NC

Prep: 15 min. • **Cook:** 8½ hours
Makes: 8 servings (2 qt.)

- 1½ lbs. boneless pork loin roast, cut into 1-in. cubes
- 2 Tbsp. olive oil
- 2 cans (14½ oz. each) Italian diced tomatoes, undrained
- 2 cups reduced-sodium chicken broth
- 2 cups frozen pepper stir-fry vegetable blend, thawed
- ½ cup dry red wine or additional reduced-sodium chicken broth
- ¼ cup orange marmalade
- 2 garlic cloves, minced
- 1 tsp. dried oregano
- ½ tsp. fennel seed
- ½ tsp. pepper
- ⅛ tsp. crushed red pepper flakes, optional
- 2 Tbsp. cornstarch
- 2 Tbsp. cold water
  Hot cooked fettuccine, optional

1. In a large skillet, brown pork in oil; drain. Transfer to a 5-qt. slow cooker.
2. Stir in the tomatoes, broth, vegetable blend, wine, marmalade, garlic, oregano, fennel seed, pepper and, if desired, pepper flakes. Cover and cook on low 8-10 hours, until meat is tender.
3. Combine cornstarch and water until smooth; gradually stir into stew. Cover and cook on high, about 30 minutes longer, until thickened. Serve with fettuccine if desired.
1 cup: 232 cal., 7g fat (2g sat. fat), 42mg chol., 614mg sod., 19g carb. (12g sugars, 1g fiber), 19g pro. **Diabetic exchanges:** 2 lean meat, 1 starch, 1 vegetable, ½ fat.

TEST KITCHEN TIP
To make a fresh garlic clove easy to peel, gently crush it with the flat side of a large knife blade to loosen the skin. If you don't have a large knife, you can crush the garlic with a small can. The peel will come right off.

MEDITERRANEAN SOLE

Steaming in parchment is an easy and healthy way to cook fish and vegetables. This is a simple recipe, but it's elegant and incredibly flavorful. Any white fish will work in place of the sole.
—Andrea Potischman, Menlo Park, CA

Takes: 25 min. • **Makes:** 4 servings

- 1 lb. sole fillets, cut into 4 portions
- ¼ tsp. pepper
- 1 medium lemon, sliced
- 2 Tbsp. dry white wine or chicken broth
- 2 Tbsp. olive oil, divided
- 2 cups cherry tomatoes, halved
- ½ cup Greek olives, halved
- 1 Tbsp. capers, drained
- 1 Tbsp. lemon juice
- 2 garlic cloves, minced
- 2 Tbsp. minced fresh parsley

1. Preheat oven to 400°. Place each fillet on a piece of heavy-duty foil or parchment (about 12 in. square). Sprinkle fillets with pepper; top with lemon slices. Drizzle with wine and 1 Tbsp. oil.
2. In a small bowl, combine tomatoes, olives, capers, lemon juice, garlic and remaining 1 Tbsp. oil; spoon over fillets. Fold the foil or parchment around fish, sealing tightly.
3. Place the packets on a baking sheet. Bake until fish just begins to flake easily with a fork, 10-12 minutes. Open packets carefully to allow the steam to escape. Sprinkle with parsley.

1 packet: 211 cal., 14g fat (2g sat. fat), 51mg chol., 669mg sod., 7g carb. (2g sugars, 2g fiber), 15g pro.
Diabetic exchanges: 3 lean meat, 3 fat, 1 vegetable.

CHICKEN WITH SUGAR PUMPKINS & APRICOTS
PICTURED ON P. 139

When we have family gatherings, we give the slow cooker kitchen duty. This yummy chicken dish with pumpkin and apricots has the warm flavors of Morocco.
—Nancy Heishman, Las Vegas, NV

Prep: 20 min. • **Cook:** 4 hours
Makes: 8 servings

- 3 Sugar Baby pumpkins, peeled and cubed (5 to 6 cups each)
- 1 Tbsp. canola oil
- 8 boneless skinless chicken thighs (4 oz. each)
- 1 medium red onion, chopped
- 2 garlic cloves, minced
- ¾ cup dried Turkish apricots, diced
- ½ cup apricot nectar
- ⅓ cup apricot preserves
- 2 Tbsp. lemon juice
- 1 tsp. ground ginger
- 1 tsp. ground cinnamon
- 1 tsp. salt
- ½ tsp. pepper
- 3 Tbsp. minced fresh parsley
  Hot cooked rice, optional
- ½ cup pomegranate seeds, optional

1. Place pumpkin in a 5-qt. slow cooker coated with cooking spray.
2. In a large nonstick skillet, heat oil over medium-high heat; brown chicken thighs on all sides. Transfer chicken to slow cooker. In same skillet, saute onion and garlic 1-2 minutes; transfer to slow cooker.
3. Add next 8 ingredients to slow cooker. Cook, covered, on low 4-5 hours, until chicken is tender. Top with parsley. If desired, serve with hot cooked rice and sprinkle with pomegranate seeds.
Note: If Sugar Baby pumpkins are not available, you may substitute one large (5- to 6-lb.) butternut squash, peeled and cut into 1-in. cubes. You should have 15-18 cups of cubed squash.
1 chicken thigh with 1 cup pumpkin: 318 cal., 10g fat (3g sat. fat), 76mg chol., 376mg sod., 36g carb. (20g sugars, 3g fiber), 24g pro. **Diabetic exchanges:** 2 starch, 3 lean meat, ½ fat.

MEDITERRANEAN SOLE

BLACKENED CATFISH WITH MANGO AVOCADO SALSA

A delightful and tasty rub makes this quick recipe fantastic. While the fish is sitting to allow the flavors to blend, you can easily assemble the salsa. My family thinks this dish is marvelous.
—Laura Fisher, Westfield, MA

Prep: 20 min. + chilling • **Cook:** 10 min.
Makes: 4 servings (2 cups salsa)

- 2 tsp. dried oregano
- 2 tsp. ground cumin
- 2 tsp. paprika
- 2¼ tsp. pepper, divided
- ¾ tsp. salt, divided
- 4 catfish fillets (6 oz. each)
- 1 medium mango, peeled and cubed
- 1 medium ripe avocado, peeled and cubed
- ⅓ cup finely chopped red onion
- 2 Tbsp. minced fresh cilantro
- 2 Tbsp. lime juice
- 2 tsp. olive oil

1. Combine the oregano, cumin, paprika, 2 tsp. pepper and ½ tsp. salt; rub over the fillets. Refrigerate for at least 30 minutes.
2. Meanwhile, in a small bowl, combine the mango, avocado, red onion, cilantro, lime juice and remaining salt and pepper. Chill until serving.
3. In a large cast-iron skillet, cook fillets in oil over medium heat until fish flakes easily with a fork, 5-7 minutes on each side. Serve with salsa.
1 fillet with ½ cup salsa: 376 cal., 22g fat (4g sat. fat), 80mg chol., 541mg sod., 17g carb. (9g sugars, 6g fiber), 28g pro.
Diabetic exchanges: 5 lean meat, 1 starch, ½ fat.

CURRIED SWEET POTATO PINEAPPLE CHICKEN

This dish is a delicious combination of sweet and savory flavors with pineapple, curry and sweet potatoes. Cutting the sweet potatoes in chunks lets them cook at the same rate as the chicken—but be sure to keep them large so they keep their integrity over the long cooking time. I always add a bit more curry powder and garlic—feel free to add to taste!
—Trisha Kruse, Eagle, ID

Prep: 25 min. • **Cook:** 5 hours 20 min.
Makes: 8 servings

- 8 boneless skinless chicken thighs (about 2 lbs.)
- 2 to 3 tsp. curry powder
- 1 tsp. granulated garlic
- ½ tsp. salt
- 2 Tbsp. canola oil
- 2 large sweet potatoes, peeled and cut into 1-in. pieces
- 1 medium onion, chopped
- 1 can (8 oz.) unsweetened crushed pineapple
- 1 cup apricot-pineapple preserves or ½ cup each apricot and pineapple preserves
- 1 Tbsp. soy sauce
- 2 Tbsp. cornstarch
  Minced fresh parsley, optional

1. Sprinkle chicken with curry powder, garlic and salt. In a large nonstick skillet, heat oil over medium heat. Add chicken and cook until golden brown, 3-4 minutes on each side.
2. Place sweet potatoes and onion in a 5- or 6-qt. slow cooker; top with chicken. Drain pineapple, reserving juice. Add pineapple, preserves and soy sauce to the slow cooker. Cook, covered, on low 5-6 hours, until the chicken and potatoes are tender.
3. Mix cornstarch and the reserved pineapple juice until smooth; gradually stir into slow cooker. Cook, covered, on high 20-25 minutes, until sauce is thickened. If desired, sprinkle with parsley.
1 serving: 383 cal., 8g fat (2g sat. fat), 76mg chol., 352mg sod., 55g carb. (31g sugars, 3g fiber), 23g pro.

CURRIED SWEET POTATO PINEAPPLE CHICKEN

KIMCHI CAULIFLOWER FRIED RICE

TURKEY TENDERLOINS WITH SHALLOT BERRY SAUCE

The original recipe called for chicken and apricot, but I decided to try turkey and berry jam to use up some leftovers. I was so thrilled with how well it turned out.
—Kendra Doss, Colorado Springs, CO

Prep: 15 min. • **Cook:** 25 min.
Makes: 8 servings

- 4 turkey breast tenderloins (12 oz. each)
- ½ tsp. salt
- ½ tsp. pepper
- 1 Tbsp. olive oil
- ¼ cup chicken broth
- SAUCE
- 1 Tbsp. olive oil
- 5 shallots, thinly sliced
- ¼ tsp. salt
- ¼ tsp. pepper
- ½ cup chicken broth
- ¼ cup balsamic vinegar
- 3 Tbsp. seedless raspberry jam

1. Sprinkle turkey with salt and pepper. In a large skillet, heat olive oil over medium heat; brown tenderloins in batches. Cook, covered, until a thermometer inserted in pork reads 165°, 8-10 minutes longer. Remove from pan; keep warm.
2. Add chicken broth to skillet; increase heat to medium-high. Cook, stirring to loosen browned bits from pan; remove from heat.
3. For the sauce, in another skillet, heat oil over medium-high heat. Add shallots, salt and pepper; cook and stir until the shallots are tender. Add broth, stirring to loosen browned bits from pan. Stir in vinegar and jam. Bring to a boil; cook until slightly thickened, 4-5 minutes, stirring occasionally.
4. Slice tenderloins; drizzle with pan juices. Serve with berry sauce.
1 serving: 258 cal., 6g fat (0 sat. fat), 68mg chol., 414mg sod., 12g carb. (8g sugars, 0 fiber), 43g pro. **Diabetic exchanges:** 5 lean meat, 1 starch, ½ fat.

KIMCHI CAULIFLOWER FRIED RICE

This is one of my favorite recipes, because it is customizable. If there's a vegetarian in the family, leave out the bacon and add your favorite veggies.
—Stefanie Schaldenbrand, Los Angeles, CA

Takes: 30 min. • **Makes:** 2 servings

- 2 bacon strips, chopped
- 1 green onion, chopped
- 2 garlic cloves, minced
- 1 cup kimchi, chopped
- 3 cups frozen riced cauliflower
- 2 large eggs
- 1 to 3 Tbsp. kimchi juice
  Optional: Sesame oil and sesame seeds

1. In a large skillet, cook bacon over medium heat until partially cooked but not crisp, stirring occasionally. Add green onion and garlic; cook 1 minute longer. Add kimchi; cook and stir until heated through, 2-3 minutes. Add cauliflower; cook and stir until tender, 8-10 minutes.
2. Meanwhile, heat a large nonstick skillet over medium-high heat. Break eggs, 1 at a time, into the pan; reduce heat to low. Cook until whites are set and yolks begin to thicken, turning once if desired. Stir enough kimchi juice into the cauliflower mixture to moisten. Divide between 2 serving bowls. Top with fried eggs, additional green onions and, if desired, sesame seeds and oil.
1 serving: 254 cal., 17g fat (5g sat. fat), 204mg chol., 715mg sod., 13g carb. (6g sugars, 6g fiber), 15g pro. **Diabetic exchanges:** 2 high-fat meat, 2 vegetable.

FAMILY-FRIENDLY
FARE

Dig in to the good old-fashioned favorites that kids of all ages love. Get ready for frosty floats, creamy mac and cheese, corn dogs, dessert pizza, muffin-tin dinners and much, more more. Turn to this chapter for a fun, family-pleasing meal.

FAMILY-FRIENDLY FARE

5i

CORN DOGS

It's super easy to make homemade corn dogs that taste just like those sold at carnivals and fairs.
—Ruby Williams, Bogalusa, LA

Takes: 25 min. • **Makes:** 10 servings

- ¾ cup yellow cornmeal
- ¾ cup self-rising flour
- 1 large egg, lightly beaten
- ⅔ cup 2% milk
- 10 pop sticks
- 10 hot dogs
  Oil for deep-fat frying

1. In a large bowl, combine cornmeal, flour and egg. Stir in milk to make a thick batter; let stand 4 minutes. Insert sticks into hot dogs; dip into batter.

2. In an electric skillet or deep-fat fryer, heat oil to 375°. Fry corn dogs, a few at a time, until golden brown, 6-8 minutes, turning occasionally. Drain corn dogs on paper towels.

1 corn dog: 316 cal., 23g fat (7g sat. fat), 45mg chol., 588mg sod., 18g carb. (2g sugars, 1g fiber), 8g pro.

> **TEST KITCHEN TIP**
> To help the batter stick to the hot dog, make sure the dogs are thoroughly dry before dipping them. The batter won't adhere to any part that's wet.

RAINBOW FRUIT SALAD

When my children were young, I would often dress up fresh fruit in this easy salad. Decades later, my grandchildren and great-grandchildren still love digging in to the fruity layers. The salad goes really well with barbecued meats or cold sandwiches.
—Jonnie Adams Sisler, Stevensville, MT

Prep: 20 min. + chilling
Makes: 20 servings

- 2 large firm bananas, sliced
- 2 Tbsp. lemon juice
- 2 cups seeded cubed watermelon
- 2 cups fresh or canned pineapple chunks
- 1 pint fresh blueberries
- 3 kiwifruit, peeled and sliced
- 1 pint fresh strawberries, halved
- 6 oz. cream cheese, softened
- ⅓ cup confectioners' sugar
- 2 Tbsp. fresh lime juice
- ½ tsp. grated lime zest
- 1 cup heavy whipping cream, whipped

1. Toss bananas and lemon juice; place in a 4-qt. glass serving bowl. Add remaining fruit in layers.

2. In a bowl, beat cream cheese until smooth. Gradually add sugar, lime juice and zest. Stir in a small amount of whipped cream; mix well. Fold in the remaining whipped cream. Spread over fruit. Chill until serving.

¾ cup: 123 cal., 7g fat (5g sat. fat), 22mg chol., 31mg sod., 14g carb. (10g sugars, 2g fiber), 1g pro.

TURTLE SKILLET

This caramel-chocolate dip with buttery biscuit dippers is delicious! You can use refrigerated croissants instead of biscuits for a flakier texture and caramel dip in place of the ice cream topping.

—Betsy Tankersley, Flat Rock, NC

Prep: 20 min. • **Bake:** 25 min.
Makes: 8 servings

- 3 Tbsp. melted butter, divided
- 1 tube (16.3 oz.) large refrigerated flaky biscuits
- 1 pkg. (8 oz.) cream cheese, softened
- ½ cup caramel ice cream topping
- ½ cup semisweet chocolate chips
- ¼ cup confectioners' sugar

1. Preheat oven to 350°. Coat bottom and sides of a 10-in. cast-iron or other ovenproof skillet with 1 Tbsp. butter. Cut each biscuit in half; roll each piece into a ball. Place along outer edge of prepared skillet, leaving center open. Brush biscuit balls with remaining 2 Tbsp. butter.

2. Beat the cream cheese and caramel topping until blended. Pour into center of skillet; sprinkle with chocolate chips.

3. Bake until biscuits are browned and chocolate is softened, 25-30 minutes. If desired, stir cream cheese mixture until combined. Sprinkle with confectioners' sugar; serve warm.

1 serving: 416 cal., 23g fat (13g sat. fat), 40mg chol., 653mg sod., 49g carb. (26g sugars, 2g fiber), 5g pro.

DAD'S BAKED BEANS

I always use this recipe whenever I make beans for a potluck. Everybody loves the sweet-tangy flavor and bits of sliced hot dogs.

—Kimberly Wallace, Dennison, OH

Prep: 15 min. • **Bake:** 1 hour
Makes: 8 servings

- 3 cans (15½ oz. each) great northern beans, rinsed and drained
- 5 hot dogs, sliced
- 1½ cups ketchup
- ½ cup packed brown sugar
- 2 Tbsp. molasses
- 1 medium onion, chopped
- ½ tsp. ground mustard
- ¼ tsp. salt
- ¼ tsp. pepper

Preheat oven to 350°. In an ungreased 2-qt. baking dish, combine all ingredients. Cover and bake for 1-1½ hours or until heated through.

¾ cup: 344 cal., 9g fat (4g sat. fat), 16mg chol., 1322mg sod., 55g carb. (30g sugars, 8g fiber), 11g pro.

TURTLE SKILLET

CHILLY SNOW DAY FLOATS

On your next snow day, pass out these frothy floats and everybody will be glad they're cooped up indoors with you. Cream soda works with the peppermint ice cream, too.
—Julianne Schnuck, Milwaukee, WI

Takes: 10 min. • **Makes:** 2 servings

- ½ cup lemon-lime soda
- 1 cup peppermint ice cream
- ½ cup whipped cream
  Peppermint candy, optional

Pour lemon-lime soda into 2 glasses; add ice cream. Top with whipped cream. If desired, sprinkle floats with crushed peppermint candy. Serve immediately with straws and spoons.

1 float: 248 cal., 15g fat (9g sat. fat), 44mg chol., 59mg sod., 27g carb. (19g sugars, 0 fiber), 3g pro.

HOMEMADE
POTATO CHIPS

HOMEMADE POTATO CHIPS

Forget buying potato chips at the grocery store when you can make these at home. This quick and easy recipe will delight everyone in the family.
—Taste of Home *Test Kitchen*

Prep: 30 min. + soaking
Cook: 5 min./batch • **Makes:** 8½ cups

- 7 unpeeled medium potatoes (about 2 lbs.)
- 2 qt. ice water
- 5 tsp. salt
- 2 tsp. garlic powder
- 1½ tsp. celery salt
- 1½ tsp. pepper
  Oil for deep-fat frying

1. Using a vegetable peeler or a metal cheese slicer, cut potatoes into very thin slices. Place in a large bowl; add ice water and salt. Soak for 30 minutes.

2. Drain potatoes; place on paper towels and pat dry. In a small bowl, combine the garlic powder, celery salt and pepper; set mixture aside.

3. In a cast-iron or other heavy skillet, heat 1½ in. oil to 375°. Fry potatoes in batches until golden brown, 3-4 minutes, stirring frequently.

4. Remove with a slotted spoon; drain on paper towels. Immediately sprinkle with seasoning mixture. Store in an airtight container.

¾ cup: 176 cal., 8g fat (1g sat. fat), 0 chol., 703mg sod., 24g carb. (1g sugars, 3g fiber), 3g pro.

READER REVIEW

"Excellent! I used a mandoline to slice the potatoes extra thin. I hesitated to use the spice mix, but went ahead with it and was very glad that I did."

MASKUSLM, TASTEOFHOME.COM

DOUBLE JACK MAC

This recipe came about when I asked my two sisters what they would like to see added to traditional mac and cheese to make it a little more special. One of them said pepper jack cheese and the other said black beans. I liked both ideas, and this is the result. The black beans add color and nutrition. The pepper jack cheese adds zip and fun.
—Andrea Johnson, Freeport, IL

Prep: 25 min. • **Bake:** 25 min.
Makes: 6 servings

- 1 lb. small pasta shells
- ¼ cup chopped onion
- ¼ cup butter, cubed
- 2 garlic cloves, minced
- ¼ cup all-purpose flour
- 2½ cups 2% milk
- 4 oz. cream cheese, cubed
- 1 cup shredded Monterey Jack cheese
- 1 cup shredded pepper jack cheese
- 1 cup shredded sharp cheddar cheese
- 1 tsp. salt
- 1 tsp. ground cumin
- ⅛ tsp. pepper
- 1 can (15 oz.) black beans, rinsed and drained
- 8 bacon strips, cooked and crumbled
- 2 Tbsp. minced fresh cilantro
- ½ cup shredded Mexican cheese blend
  Additional minced fresh cilantro

1. Preheat oven to 375°. Cook shells according to the package directions.
2. Meanwhile, in a Dutch oven, saute the onion in butter. Add garlic; cook 1 minute longer. Stir in flour until blended; gradually add milk. Bring to a boil; cook and stir for 2 minutes or until thickened.
3. Add the cream cheese, Monterey Jack cheese, pepper jack cheese, cheddar cheese, salt, cumin and pepper; cook and stir until cheese is melted.
4. Drain pasta. Add the beans, bacon, cilantro and pasta to the cheese sauce. Transfer to a greased 13x9-in. baking dish. Sprinkle with the Mexican cheese blend.
5. Bake, uncovered, until bubbly and golden brown, 25-30 minutes. Garnish with additional cilantro.

1½ cups: 837 cal., 41g fat (24g sat. fat), 123mg chol., 1283mg sod., 79g carb. (8g sugars, 6g fiber), 37g pro.

SNACKIN' GRANOLA

Granola's a popular treat with children, and this one couldn't be easier to prepare. I flavor it with lots of tasty, good-for-you ingredients. It's perfect to send in bag lunches or to serve after school. I've also brought it along as a snack in the car when we take family vacations.
—Marlene Mohr, Cincinnati, OH

Prep: 15 min. • **Bake:** 25 min. + cooling
Makes: 7 cups

- 2⅔ cups sweetened shredded coconut
- 1 cup quick-cooking oats
- ¼ cup packed brown sugar
- ¼ cup raisins or chopped pitted dried plums
- ¼ cup chopped dried apricots
- 2 Tbsp. sesame seeds
- ¼ cup vegetable oil
- ¼ cup honey
- ¼ cup semisweet chocolate chips or M&M's

1. Preheat oven to 325°. In a large metal bowl, combine the first 6 ingredients. In a small saucepan, bring the oil and honey just to a boil. Immediately remove from heat; pour over the coconut mixture, stirring to coat evenly.
2. Spread in an ungreased 13x9-in. baking pan. Bake for 25 minutes, stirring several times. Pour onto waxed paper to cool. Sprinkle with chocolate chips or M&M's. Store the granola in an airtight container.

¼ cup: 106 cal., 6g fat (3g sat. fat), 0 chol., 25mg sod., 13g carb. (10g sugars, 1g fiber), 1g pro.

DOUBLE JACK MAC

ABC SALAD TOSS

BERRY BROWNIE PIZZA

How could you not love pizza for dessert? A fudgy brownie base is layered with whipped topping sauce, fresh berries, nuts and a drizzle of chocolate syrup.
—Karen Heleski, Ubly, MI

Prep: 15 min. • **Bake:** 15 min. + chilling
Makes: 12 servings

- 1 pkg. fudge brownie mix (8-in. square pan size)
- 1¼ cups cold 2% milk
- 1 pkg. (3.4 oz.) instant vanilla pudding mix
- 2½ cups whipped topping
- 2 cups mixed fresh berries
  Chocolate syrup and chopped pecans

1. Preheat oven to 350°. Prepare the brownie batter according to package directions; spread onto a greased 12-in. pizza pan. Bake until a toothpick inserted in the center comes out almost clean, 18-22 minutes. Cool for 15 minutes on a wire rack.
2. Meanwhile, in a large bowl, whisk milk and pudding mix for 2 minutes. Let stand until soft-set, about 2 minutes. Fold in the whipped topping. Spread over the brownie crust.
3. Top with berries and drizzle with chocolate syrup. Sprinkle with pecans. Refrigerate until chilled.
1 piece: 312 cal., 14g fat (5g sat. fat), 19mg chol., 215mg sod., 44g carb. (31g sugars, 2g fiber), 4g pro.

> **TEST KITCHEN TIP**
> Get creative with this brownie-crust version of fruit pizza. Use your favorite fruits, candies and syrups.

ABC SALAD TOSS

Getting kids to eat their veggies, fruit and protein is as easy as ABC—that's apples, bananas and cheese. This is a slightly sweet salad that appeals to kids' taste buds while still delivering the vitamins and nutrition Mom demands.
—Christine Maddux, Council Bluffs, IA

Takes: 25 min. • **Makes:** 16 servings

- 1 pkg. (12 oz.) broccoli coleslaw mix
- 1 pkg. (8 oz.) ready-to-serve salad greens
- ½ cup mayonnaise
- 1 Tbsp. sugar
- 2 tsp. olive oil
- 8 oz. Colby-Monterey Jack cheese, cut into ½-in. cubes
- 1 medium apple, chopped
- 1 cup seedless red grapes, halved
- ¼ cup raisins
- 1 medium banana, sliced

In a large bowl, combine the coleslaw mix and salad greens. Whisk together mayonnaise, sugar and oil; stir in cheese, apple, grapes and raisins. Pour over salad; toss to coat. Top with bananas.
1 cup: 143 cal., 10g fat (4g sat. fat), 14mg chol., 135mg sod., 10g carb. (6g sugars, 1g fiber), 4g pro.

BERRY BROWNIE PIZZA

Chocolate Fruit Dip

This sweet, light dip is perfect paired with practically any fruit you like!

*Beat one 8-oz. package of cream cheese with ⅓ cup sugar until smooth. Beat in ⅓ cup cocoa and 1 tsp. vanilla. Beat in 2 cups whipped topping, and serve with fruit.

FAMILY-FAVORITE CHEESEBURGER PASTA

I created this recipe to satisfy a cheeseburger craving. The result was a delicious, healthy classic. It's great for a weeknight.
—Raquel Haggard, Edmond, OK

Takes: 30 min. • **Makes:** 4 servings

- 1½ cups uncooked whole wheat penne pasta
- ¾ lb. lean ground beef (90% lean)
- 2 Tbsp. finely chopped onion
- 1 can (14½ oz.) no-salt-added diced tomatoes
- 2 Tbsp. dill pickle relish
- 2 Tbsp. prepared mustard
- 2 Tbsp. ketchup
- 1 tsp. steak seasoning
- ¼ tsp. seasoned salt
- ¾ cup shredded reduced-fat cheddar cheese
  Chopped green onions, optional

1. Cook pasta according to package directions. Meanwhile, in a large skillet, cook beef and onion over medium heat until meat is no longer pink; drain. Drain pasta; add to meat mixture.
2. Stir in the tomatoes, relish, mustard, ketchup, steak seasoning and seasoned salt. Bring to a boil. Reduce heat; simmer, uncovered, for 5 minutes.
3. Sprinkle with cheese. Remove from heat; cover and let stand until cheese is melted. Sprinkle with onions if desired.

1½ cups: 391 cal., 12g fat (6g sat. fat), 57mg chol., 759mg sod., 43g carb. (10g sugars, 4g fiber), 28g pro. **Diabetic exchanges:** 3 lean meat, 2 starch, 1 vegetable, ½ fat.

BACON & EGGS PIZZA

I tried a breakfast pizza at a resort in Florida and wanted to adapt it for home. I'm pleased with the results! It's a fun alternative to typical egg bakes.
—Noelle Myers, Grand Forks, ND

Takes: 30 min. • **Makes:** 6 slices

- 8 thick-sliced bacon strips, chopped
- ¼ cup finely chopped onion
- 4 large eggs
- ¼ cup grated Parmesan cheese
- 1 tsp. Italian seasoning
- ¼ tsp. salt
- ¼ tsp. pepper
- 1 Tbsp. butter
- 1 prebaked 12-in. pizza crust
- ½ cup Alfredo sauce
- ½ cup chopped roasted sweet red peppers
- ⅔ cup shredded cheddar cheese
- ½ cup crumbled queso fresco or shredded part-skim mozzarella cheese

1. Preheat oven to 425°. In a large skillet, cook chopped bacon over medium heat until crisp, stirring occasionally. Remove with a slotted spoon; drain the bacon on paper towels. Discard drippings, reserving 1 Tbsp. in pan.
2. Add onion to drippings; cook and stir over medium-high heat until tender. Remove from pan. Wipe skillet clean if necessary.
3. In a small bowl, whisk eggs, Parmesan cheese and seasonings until blended. In same pan, heat butter over medium-high heat. Pour in egg mixture; cook and stir until eggs are almost set.
4. Place pizza crust on an ungreased baking sheet. Spread with Alfredo sauce. Top with red peppers, bacon, onion and scrambled eggs. Sprinkle with cheeses. Bake 6-8 minutes or until cheese is melted and eggs are set.

1 slice: 465 cal., 26g fat (12g sat. fat), 190mg chol., 1152mg sod., 34g carb. (3g sugars, 2g fiber), 24g pro.

FAMILY-FAVORITE CHEESEBURGER PASTA

5i **L**

PEANUT BUTTER-BANANA YOGURT PARFAITS

For a lightning-fast breakfast, I layer vanilla yogurt with bananas, peanuts and multigrain cereal. It's crunchy, easy, fun and perfect for kids.
—Teresa Miller, Hamilton, IN

Takes: 5 min. • **Makes:** 4 servings

- 3 cups vanilla yogurt
- 1 cup dried banana chips, crushed
- 1 cup Peanut Butter Multi Grain Cheerios
- 2 large ripe bananas, sliced
- ¼ cup unsalted dry roasted peanuts, chopped

Layer ¾ cup yogurt, ¼ cup banana chips and ¼ cup cereal into each of 4 parfait glasses. Top with bananas and peanuts.
1 parfait: 457 cal., 17g fat (11g sat. fat), 9mg chol., 152mg sod., 67g carb. (47g sugars, 5g fiber), 14g pro.

MAKEOVER LI'L CHEDDAR MEAT LOAVES

MAKEOVER LI'L CHEDDAR MEAT LOAVES

My husband absolutely loves my mini meat loaves, but this family-favorite recipe wasn't very healthy when I first received it. The Taste of Home *Test Kitchen experts slashed the calories and fat while keeping the original recipe's tender texture and delicious taste.*
—Jodie Mitchell, Denver, PA

Prep: 15 min. • **Bake:** 25 min.
Makes: 8 servings

- 2 large egg whites, beaten
- ¾ cup fat-free milk
- 1 cup shredded reduced-fat cheddar cheese
- ¾ cup quick-cooking oats
- 1 medium onion, chopped
- 1 medium carrot, shredded
- ½ tsp. salt
- ¾ lb. lean ground beef (90% lean)
- ⅔ cup ketchup
- 2 Tbsp. brown sugar
- 1½ tsp. prepared mustard

1. Preheat oven to 350°. In a large bowl, whisk egg whites and milk. Stir in the cheese, oats, onion, carrot and salt. Crumble beef over mixture and mix well.
2. Shape into 8 loaves; place in a 13x9-in. baking dish coated with cooking spray. In a small bowl, combine the ketchup, brown sugar and mustard; spoon over the loaves.
3. Bake, uncovered, for 25-30 minutes or until no pink remains and a thermometer reads 160°.
1 meat loaf: 187 cal., 7g fat (3g sat. fat), 36mg chol., 550mg sod., 18g carb. (11g sugars, 1g fiber), 15g pro. **Diabetic exchanges:** 2 lean meat, 1 starch.

MINI PIZZA MUFFIN CUPS

I had no sooner baked a batch of these mini pizzas than the kids were already asking for more. With no-cook pizza sauce and convenient refrigerated pizza dough, making this meal is a snap.
—Melissa Haines, Valparaiso, IN

Prep: 25 min. • **Bake:** 10 min.
Makes: 8 servings

- 1 can (15 oz.) tomato sauce
- 1 can (6 oz.) tomato paste
- 1 tsp. dried basil
- ½ tsp. garlic salt
- ¼ tsp. onion powder
- ¼ tsp. sugar
- 1 tube (11 oz.) refrigerated thin pizza crust
- 1½ cups shredded part-skim mozzarella cheese

OPTIONAL TOPPINGS
Pepperoni, olives, sausage, onion, green pepper, Canadian bacon, pineapple, tomatoes, fresh basil and crushed red pepper flakes

1. Preheat oven to 425°. In a small bowl, mix the first 6 ingredients.
2. Unroll pizza crust; cut into 16 squares. Press squares onto bottom and up sides of 16 ungreased muffin cups, allowing corners to hang over edges.
3. Spoon 1 Tbsp. sauce mixture into each cup. Top with cheese; add toppings as desired. Bake 10-12 minutes or until crust is golden brown. Serve remaining sauce mixture with pizzas.

Freeze option: Freeze cooled baked pizzas in a freezer container. To use, reheat pizzas on a baking sheet in a preheated 425° oven until heated through.

2 pizzas with 2 Tbsp. sauce: 209 cal., 8g fat (3g sat. fat), 14mg chol., 747mg sod., 26g carb. (5g sugars, 2g fiber), 10g pro.

PEANUT BUTTER & JELLY FRENCH TOAST

I've always tried to make cooking fun for myself, as well as for my daughters and my grandchildren. If people see you're having a good time, they'll want to join in. Cooking also teaches children the importance of following directions and being organized. This recipe is easy to make, and kids really like it.
—Flo Burtnett, Gage, OK

Takes: 20 min. • **Makes:** 6 servings

- ¾ cup peanut butter
- 12 slices bread
- 6 Tbsp. jelly or jam
- 3 large eggs
- ¾ cup 2% milk
- ¼ tsp. salt
- 2 Tbsp. butter

1. Spread peanut butter on 6 slices of bread; spread jelly on the remaining 6 slices of bread. Put 1 slice of each together to form sandwiches. In a large bowl, whisk the eggs, milk and salt. Dip both sides of sandwiches in egg mixture.
2. In a large skillet, melt butter over medium heat. Cook the sandwiches for 2-3 minutes on each side or until golden brown.

1 piece: 450 cal., 22g fat (5g sat. fat), 96mg chol., 567mg sod., 50g carb. (20g sugars, 3g fiber), 16g pro.

**MINI PIZZA
MUFFIN CUPS**

BREAKFAST & BRUNCH FAVORITES

From sweet to savory, healthy to decadent, we have your morning meal covered with the dishes in this chapter. Whether you're making breakfast for family, putting on a brunch for friends or whipping up breakfast for dinner, these recipes shine!

ASPARAGUS HAM STRATA

You can easily prepare this the night before for a luncheon, or in the morning for dinner. I serve it year-round for large groups, like my card and garden clubs, and make it for other occasions. Nearly every time, someone requests the recipe!
—Ethel Pressel, New Oxford, PA

Prep: 20 min. + chilling
Bake: 55 min. + standing
Makes: 8 servings

- 12 slices white bread
- 12 oz. Velveeta, diced
- 1½ lbs. fresh asparagus, trimmed
- 2 cups diced cooked ham
- 6 large eggs
- 3 cups 2% milk
- 2 Tbsp. finely chopped onion
- ½ tsp. salt
- ¼ tsp. ground mustard

1. Using a doughnut cutter, cut 12 circles and holes from bread; set aside. Tear the remaining bread in pieces and place in a greased 13x9-in. baking dish.
2. Layer with cheese, asparagus and ham; arrange the bread circles and holes on top. Lightly beat eggs with milk. Add onion, salt and mustard; mix well. Pour egg mixture over bread circles and holes. Cover and refrigerate at least 6 hours or overnight.
3. Bake, uncovered, at 325° until top is light golden brown, 55 minutes. Let stand for 10 minutes before serving.
1 piece: 420 cal., 21g fat (10g sat. fat), 211mg chol., 1427mg sod., 32g carb. (10g sugars, 2g fiber), 27g pro.

CHEESE &
RED PEPPER
LATKES

CHEESE & RED PEPPER LATKES

These zesty latkes combine three cheeses with a handful of garlic and a colorful burst of red peppers.
—Christine Montalvo, Windsor Heights, IA

Prep: 30 min. • **Cook:** 5 min./batch
Makes: 3 dozen

- 3 large onions, finely chopped
- 3 medium sweet red peppers, finely chopped
- ⅓ cup butter, cubed
- 18 medium garlic cloves, minced, divided
- 1 Tbsp. celery salt
- 1 Tbsp. coarsely ground pepper
- 3 lbs. russet potatoes, peeled and shredded
- 1½ cups grated Parmesan cheese
- 1½ cups shredded cheddar cheese
- 1 cup shredded part-skim mozzarella cheese
- 1 cup all-purpose flour
- ¾ cup sour cream
  Canola oil for frying
  Minced fresh parsley

1. In a large cast-iron or other heavy skillet, saute the onions and red peppers in butter until tender. Add ¼ cup garlic, celery salt and the pepper; cook 1 minute longer.
2. Transfer to a large bowl. Add the potatoes, cheeses, flour, sour cream and remaining garlic; mix well.
3. Heat ¼ in. of oil in the same skillet over medium heat. Working in batches, drop batter by ¼ cupfuls into hot oil. Press lightly to flatten. Fry until golden brown, carefully turning once. Drain on paper towels. Sprinkle with parsley.
3 potato pancakes: 437 cal., 29g fat (11g sat. fat), 46mg chol., 677mg sod., 33g carb. (5g sugars, 3g fiber), 12g pro.

TEST KITCHEN TIP
Lay shredded potatoes on a layer of paper towels to remove excess moisture. This will give you crisper latkes.

BUTTERMILK BUCKWHEAT PANCAKES

This flapjack recipe uses buckwheat flour instead of the wheat-based variety. The light and tender pancakes offer a nutty flavor and hearty texture.
—Taste of Home *Test Kitchen*

Takes: 25 min. • **Makes:** 8 pancakes

- 1 cup buckwheat flour
- 2 Tbsp. brown sugar
- 1 tsp. baking powder
- ½ tsp. baking soda
- ½ tsp. salt
- ⅛ tsp. ground cinnamon
- ⅛ tsp. ground nutmeg
- ⅛ tsp. ground cloves
- 1 large egg, room temperature
- 1 cup buttermilk
- 1 Tbsp. butter, melted
  Maple syrup, optional
  Additional butter, optional

1. Combine the first 8 ingredients. Whisk the egg, buttermilk and butter; stir into the dry ingredients just until moistened.
2. Preheat a lightly greased griddle over medium heat. Pour batter by ¼ cupfuls onto griddle; turn when bubbles on top begin to pop. Cook until second side is golden brown. If desired, serve with syrup and additional butter.

2 pancakes: 195 cal., 6g fat (3g sat. fat), 63mg chol., 667mg sod., 31g carb. (11g sugars, 3g fiber), 7g pro. **Diabetic exchanges:** 2 starch, 1 fat.

BUTTERMILK BUCKWHEAT PANCAKES

EGGS BENEDICT BRUNCH BRAID

PICTURED ON P. 177

I like serving this for special-occasion breakfasts. Classic eggs Benedict components are encased in puff pastry to create a beautiful presentation for a family group or for visiting friends.
—Sarah Strohl, Commerce Township, MI

Prep: 45 min. • **Bake:** 20 min.
Makes: 8 servings

- 3 large egg yolks
- 1 Tbsp. lemon juice
- ¼ tsp. salt
- ¼ tsp. Dijon mustard
  Dash cayenne pepper
- ½ cup unsalted butter, melted

BRAID

- 1 Tbsp. unsalted butter
- 6 large eggs, divided use
- ½ tsp. salt
- ¼ tsp. pepper
- 1 sheet frozen puff pastry, thawed
- 6 slices Canadian bacon
- 2 Tbsp. minced chives, divided
- 1 tsp. water

1. Preheat oven to 375°. In a blender, combine the first 5 ingredients. Cover and process on high. While processing, gradually add the melted butter in a steady stream until combined. Set aside.
2. For braid, in a large skillet, melt butter over medium-high heat. Whisk 5 eggs, salt and the pepper; add to skillet. Cook and stir until barely set; stir in sauce.
3. On a lightly greased baking sheet, roll out pastry into a 12x10-in. rectangle. Layer Canadian bacon and the egg mixture down the center of the rectangle; sprinkle with 1 Tbsp. chives.
4. On each long side, cut ½-in.-wide strips. Starting at 1 end, fold alternating strips at an angle across the filling; pinch ends to seal. Whisk the remaining egg and the water; brush over braid.
5. Bake until braid is golden brown and eggs are completely set, 20-25 minutes. Let stand for 5 minutes before cutting. Sprinkle with the remaining chives.

1 slice: 354 cal., 27g fat (12g sat. fat), 275mg chol., 523mg sod., 18g carb. (1g sugars, 2g fiber), 10g pro.

**CARNITAS HUEVOS
RANCHEROS**

CARNITAS HUEVOS RANCHEROS

*In college, I spent a
summer in Colorado as a
church counselor and had
my first taste of Mexican
food. Over the next
50-plus years, I lived in Nebraska and
Iowa, and authentic Mexican food was not
to be found much of that time. In the past
decade, though, I have become friends
with people from Texas and have learned
to make more authentic Mexican food.
This is one of my favorites. You may have
extra pork left over and this is a plus—
there are so many ways to serve this meat!*
—Lonnie Hartstack, Clarinda, IA

Prep: 35 min. • **Cook:** 7¼ hours
Makes: 12 servings

- 1 boneless pork shoulder butt roast
  (3 lbs.), halved
- 2 tsp. olive oil
- 3 garlic cloves, thinly sliced
- ½ tsp. salt
- ½ tsp. pepper
- 1 medium onion, chopped
- 2 cans (4 oz. each) chopped
  green chiles
- 1 cup salsa
- ½ cup minced fresh cilantro
- ½ cup chicken broth
- ½ cup tequila or additional
  chicken broth
- 1 can (15 oz.) black beans,
  rinsed and drained

ASSEMBLY
- 12 large eggs
- 1 jar (16 oz.) salsa
- 12 flour tortillas (6 in.), warmed
  and quartered
- 4 medium ripe avocados, peeled
  and sliced
  Additional minced cilantro

1. Rub roast with oil, garlic, salt and
pepper. Place in a 4- or 5-qt. slow cooker.
Top with the onion, green chiles, salsa,
cilantro, broth and tequila. Cook, covered,
on low until the meat is tender, 7-8 hours.

2. Remove roast; shred with 2 forks.
Discard cooking juices, reserving 1 cup.
Return cooking juices and meat to slow
cooker. Stir in beans; heat through.
3. Meanwhile, coat a large skillet with
cooking spray; place over medium-high
heat. Working in batches, break eggs,
1 at a time, into pan; reduce heat to low.
Cook until whites are set and yolks begin
to thicken, turning once if desired. Divide
pork mixture among 12 serving bowls.
Top with salsa, eggs, avocado slices and
additional cilantro. Serve with tortillas.
Freeze option: Freeze cooled meat
mixture and juices in freezer containers. To
use, partially thaw in refrigerator overnight.
Heat through in a saucepan, stirring
occasionally; add a little water if necessary.
1 serving: 509 cal., 27g fat (8g sat. fat),
254mg chol., 858mg sod., 32g carb.
(3g sugars, 7g fiber), 31g pro.

SWISS & CHIVE QUICHE

I used to make this quiche recipe using two cans of corned beef hash, but I switched to a meatless version. I don't miss the meat a bit, and my family loves generous portions.
—Theresa Jerger, Holland, IN

Prep: 15 min. • **Bake:** 25 min.
Makes: 6 servings

- 5 large eggs, divided use
- ½ tsp. salt
- ¼ tsp. pepper
- 2 cups frozen cubed hash brown potatoes, thawed
- 1 cup shredded Swiss cheese
- ¼ cup chopped fresh chives
- 1 cup 2% milk
- ½ cup biscuit/baking mix

1. Preheat oven to 400°. In a large bowl, beat 1 egg, salt and pepper; stir in the potatoes. Transfer to a 10-in. greased cast-iron or other ovenproof skillet. Sprinkle with cheese and chives.
2. In the same bowl, beat the remaining 4 eggs and the milk. Stir in biscuit mix; pour over the potatoes.
3. Bake on a lower oven rack until a knife inserted in center comes out clean, 25-30 minutes. Let stand 5 minutes before cutting.

1 piece: 208 cal., 11g fat (5g sat. fat), 175mg chol., 418mg sod., 14g carb. (3g sugars, 1g fiber), 13g pro.

GRANOLA-TO-GO BARS

Hand-held goodies can become a portable breakfast or a hearty snack for a long day out. Sweet and chewy, these fruity oat bars really satisfy. Any dried fruit or nuts will work in this recipe, so customize to your heart's desire!
—Sally Haen, Menomonee Falls, WI

Prep: 30 min. • **Bake:** 15 min. + cooling
Makes: 3 dozen

- 3½ cups quick-cooking oats
- 1 cup chopped almonds
- 1 large egg, room temperature, lightly beaten
- ⅔ cup butter, melted
- ½ cup honey
- 1 tsp. vanilla extract
- ½ cup sunflower kernels
- ½ cup sweetened shredded coconut
- ½ cup chopped dried apples
- ½ cup dried cranberries
- ½ cup packed brown sugar
- ½ tsp. ground cinnamon

1. Preheat oven to 350°. Combine oats and almonds in a 15x10x1-in. baking pan coated with cooking spray. Bake for 15 minutes or until lightly toasted, stirring occasionally.
2. In a large bowl, combine egg, butter, honey and vanilla. Stir in sunflower kernels, coconut, apples, cranberries, brown sugar and cinnamon. Stir in oat mixture.
3. Firmly press into a 15x10x1-in. baking pan coated with cooking spray. Bake 13-18 minutes or until set and edges are lightly browned. Cool on a wire rack. Cut into bars. Store in an airtight container.

1 bar: 130 cal., 7g fat (3g sat. fat), 15mg chol., 40mg sod., 16g carb. (9g sugars, 2g fiber), 2g pro.

TEST KITCHEN TIP
For an easy and healthy egg substitute, mix 1 Tbsp. ground flax seeds with 2½ Tbsp. water. Let stand for 5 minutes before adding with butter, honey and vanilla.

SWISS & CHIVE QUICHE

LOADED HUEVOS RANCHEROS WITH ROASTED POBLANO PEPPERS

PICTURED ON P. 177

This is a unique but very tasty version of huevos rancheros. It's similar to a cowboy hash, as the potatoes take the place of the corn tortillas.
—Joan Hallford, N. Richland Hills, TX

Prep: 15 min. + standing • **Cook:** 20 min.
Makes: 4 servings

- 1 poblano pepper
- ½ lb. fresh chorizo or bulk spicy pork sausage
- 4 cups frozen O'Brien potatoes, thawed
- ½ cup shredded pepper jack cheese
- 1 tsp. smoked paprika
- ½ tsp. kosher salt
- ½ tsp. garlic powder
- ½ tsp. pepper
- 4 large eggs
  Salsa, sour cream and minced fresh cilantro

1. Place poblano pepper in a 12-in. cast-iron or other ovenproof skillet. Broil 4 in. from heat until skins blister, rotating with tongs until all sides are blistered and blackened, about 5 minutes. Immediately place pepper in a small bowl; let stand, covered, 20 minutes.
2. Peel off and discard charred skin. Remove stems and seeds. Finely chop pepper; set aside.
3. In the same skillet, cook chorizo over medium heat until cooked through, 6-8 minutes, breaking into crumbles; drain. Add potatoes; cook and stir until potatoes are tender, 8-10 minutes. Stir in cheese, smoked paprika, kosher salt, garlic powder and pepper.
4. With the back of a spoon, make 4 wells in the potato mixture. Break an egg into each well. Cook, covered, on medium-low until the egg whites are completely set and yolks begin to thicken but are not hard, 5-7 minutes. Serve with roasted poblano pepper, salsa, sour cream and cilantro.
1 serving: 426 cal., 26g fat (10g sat. fat), 251mg chol., 1114mg sod., 20g carb. (2g sugars, 3g fiber), 24g pro.

BERRY PUFF PANCAKE

Breakfast is my husband's favorite meal of the day. I use our homegrown blueberries in this sweet morning treat.
—Cecilia Morgan, Milwaukie, OR

Takes: 25 min. • **Makes:** 6 servings

- 1 Tbsp. butter
- 3 large eggs
- ¾ cup 2% milk
- ¾ cup all-purpose flour
- ½ tsp. salt

BERRY TOPPING
- 1 cup fresh raspberries
- 1 cup fresh blueberries
- 1 cup sliced fresh strawberries
- ⅓ cup orange marmalade
- 2 Tbsp. confectioners' sugar
  Whipped cream, optional

1. Preheat oven to 400°. Place the butter in a 9-in. pie plate; place in oven for 4-5 minutes or until melted. Tilt pie plate to evenly coat bottom and sides with butter.
2. In a small bowl, whisk the eggs and milk. In another small bowl, combine the flour and salt; whisk in the egg mixture until smooth. Pour batter into prepared pie plate. Bake until sides are crisp and golden brown, 15-20 minutes.
3. Meanwhile, in a large bowl, gently combine the berries and marmalade. Sprinkle pancake with confectioners' sugar; fill with the berry mixture. Serve immediately. If desired, serve with whipped cream.
1 piece: 215 cal., 6g fat (3g sat. fat), 116mg chol., 273mg sod., 36g carb. (21g sugars, 3g fiber), 6g pro.

BERRY PUFF PANCAKE

BLT EGG BAKE

FRUITY WAFFLE PARFAITS

This recipe satisfied all of my cravings for breakfast when I was pregnant. I knew I was getting plenty of nutrition in each serving, and it tasted wonderful.
—Penelope Wyllie, San Francisco, CA

Takes: 10 min. • **Makes:** 4 servings

- 4 frozen low-fat multigrain waffles
- ½ cup almond butter or creamy peanut butter
- 2 cups strawberry yogurt
- 2 large bananas, sliced
- 2 cups sliced fresh strawberries
  Optional: Toasted chopped almonds, maple syrup

Toast waffles according to package directions. Spread each waffle with 2 Tbsp. almond butter. Cut waffles into bite-sized pieces. Layer half the yogurt, bananas, strawberries and waffle pieces into 4 parfait glasses. Repeat layers. If desired, top with toasted almonds and maple syrup. Serve immediately.
1 serving: 469 cal., 20g fat (4g sat. fat), 6mg chol., 337mg sod., 65g carb. (39g sugars, 8g fiber), 15g pro.

BLT EGG BAKE

BLTs are a favorite at my house, so I created this recipe to combine those flavors into a warm, cozy casserole. It was such a hit, I served it to my church ladies group at a brunch I hosted.
—Priscilla Detrick, Catoosa, OK

Takes: 30 min. • **Makes:** 4 servings

- ¼ cup mayonnaise
- 5 slices bread, toasted
- 4 slices process American cheese
- 12 bacon strips, cooked and crumbled
- 2 Tbsp. butter
- 2 Tbsp. all-purpose flour
- ¼ tsp. salt
- ⅛ tsp. pepper
- 1 cup 2% milk
- 4 large eggs
- 1 medium tomato, halved and sliced
- ½ cup shredded cheddar cheese
- 2 green onions, thinly sliced
  Shredded lettuce

1. Preheat oven to 325°. Spread the mayonnaise on 1 side of each slice of toast and cut toast into small pieces. Arrange toast pieces, mayonnaise side up, in a greased 8-in. square baking dish. Top with cheese slices and bacon.
2. In a small saucepan, melt butter. Stir in flour, salt and pepper until smooth. Gradually add milk. Bring to a boil; cook and stir until thickened, 2 minutes. Pour over bacon.
3. In a large skillet, fry eggs over medium heat until they reach desired doneness; place over bacon. Top with tomato slices; sprinkle with cheddar cheese and onions. Bake, uncovered, 10 minutes. Cut into squares; serve with lettuce.
1 serving: 594 cal., 42g fat (16g sat. fat), 251mg chol., 1262mg sod., 25g carb. (7g sugars, 1g fiber), 27g pro.

BAKED CHEDDAR
EGGS & POTATOES

BANANA BLUEBERRY PANCAKES

This recipe is a favorite in our home. My kids don't even realize how healthy it is!
—Kelly Reinicke, Wisconsin Rapids, WI

Prep: 15 min. • **Cook:** 5 min./batch
Makes: 14 pancakes

- 1 cup whole wheat flour
- ½ cup all-purpose flour
- 2 Tbsp. sugar
- 2 tsp. baking powder
- ½ tsp. salt
- 1 large egg, room temperature, lightly beaten
- 1¼ cups fat-free milk
- 3 medium ripe bananas, mashed
- 1 tsp. vanilla extract
- 1½ cups fresh or frozen blueberries
  Optional: Maple syrup and sliced bananas

1. In a large bowl, combine the flours, sugar, baking powder and salt. In a second bowl, combine the egg, milk, bananas and vanilla; stir into the dry ingredients just until moistened.

2. Pour batter by ¼ cupfuls onto a hot griddle coated with cooking spray; sprinkle with blueberries. Turn when bubbles form on top; cook until the second side is golden brown. If desired, serve with syrup and sliced bananas.

Freeze option: Freeze cooled pancakes between layers of waxed paper in a resealable freezer container. To use, place pancakes on an ungreased baking sheet, cover with foil, and reheat in a preheated 375° oven 6-10 minutes. Or, place a stack of 3 pancakes on a microwave-safe plate and microwave on high until heated through, 1¼-1½ minutes.

2 pancakes: 195 cal., 2g fat (0 sat. fat), 31mg chol., 317mg sod., 41g carb. (19g sugars, 4g fiber), 6g pro. **Diabetic exchanges:** 1½ starch, 1 fruit.

BAKED CHEDDAR EGGS & POTATOES

This combo of eggs, potatoes and cheese makes a hearty breakfast—or a great breakfast for dinner. It starts in a skillet on the stovetop and then I pop it into the oven to bake.
—Nadine Merheb, Tucson, AZ

Takes: 30 min. • **Makes:** 4 servings

- 3 Tbsp. butter
- 1½ lbs. red potatoes, chopped
- ¼ cup minced fresh parsley
- 2 garlic cloves, minced
- ¾ tsp. kosher salt
- ⅛ tsp. pepper
- 8 large eggs
- ½ cup shredded extra sharp cheddar cheese

1. Preheat oven to 400°. In a 10-in. cast-iron or other ovenproof skillet, heat butter over medium-high heat. Add the potatoes; cook and stir until golden brown and tender. Stir in parsley, garlic, salt and pepper. With the back of a spoon, make 4 wells in the potato mixture; break 2 eggs into each well.

2. Bake until egg whites are completely set and yolks begin to thicken but are not hard, 9-11 minutes. Sprinkle with cheese; bake until cheese is melted, 1 minute.

1 serving: 395 cal., 23g fat (12g sat. fat), 461mg chol., 651mg sod., 29g carb. (3g sugars, 3g fiber), 19g pro.

BANANA
BLUEBERRY
PANCAKES

Creamy, Crunchy & Easy

This brunch favorite could not be easier to make!
The keys: a perfectly ripe avocado and quality oil.

HOW TO
Make Avocado Toast

1. Toast and top...
Spread a slice of hearty multigrain toast with a teaspoon of a light, flavorful oil; top with avocado slices.

2. Mash and drizzle!
Mash the avocado slightly or, if you prefer, leave the slices whole. Drizzle with additional oil and sprinkle with a coarse sea salt.

TEST KITCHEN TIP
Once you've made the basic toast, experiment by adding eggs, herbs, vegetables, smoked salmon, lemon or lime juice—any of your favorites!

CLASSIC AVOCADO TOAST

This is such an easy way to add avocados to your diet. Use healthy multigrain bread and top with sliced radishes and cracked pepper or lime zest, or with chipotle peppers and cilantro.
—Taste of Home *Test Kitchen*

Takes: 5 min. • **Makes:** 1 serving

1 slice hearty bread, toasted
1 to 2 tsp. extra virgin olive oil or coconut oil
¼ medium ripe avocado, sliced
⅛ tsp. sea salt

1 slice: 160 cal., 11g fat (2g sat. fat), 0 chol., 361mg sod., 15g carb. (1g sugars, 3g fiber), 3g pro. **Diabetic exchanges:** 2 fat, 1 starch.

TUSCAN CHICKEN FRITTATA

The pecorino Romano cheese in this sunny dish makes it feel that much more elevated.
—Michael Cohen, Los Angeles, CA

Prep: 20 min. • **Bake:** 15 min.
Makes: 6 servings

- 8 large eggs
- ½ cup heavy whipping cream
- ½ cup minced fresh basil
- ¼ cup grated pecorino Romano cheese or grated Parmesan cheese, divided
- ½ tsp. salt
- ¼ tsp. pepper
- 1 pkg. (8 oz.) cream cheese, softened and cubed
- ⅓ cup oil-packed sun-dried tomatoes, patted dry and chopped
- 1 cup shredded cooked chicken

1. Preheat the oven to 400°. In a large bowl, whisk the eggs, whipping cream, basil, 2 Tbsp. pecorino Romano cheese, salt and pepper. Stir in the cream cheese and sun-dried tomatoes.

2. Heat a greased 10-in. cast-iron or other ovenproof skillet over medium heat; pour in the egg mixture. As the eggs set, lift edges to allow the uncooked portion to flow underneath. Cook until frittata begins to set, 3-4 minutes.

3. Sprinkle with chicken and the remaining pecorino Romano cheese. Bake, uncovered, at 400° until eggs are completely set, 15-20 minutes. Let stand for 5 minutes. Cut into wedges.

1 piece: 374 cal., 31g fat (17g sat. fat), 377mg chol., 531mg sod., 4g carb. (1g sugars, 1g fiber), 21g pro.

SALMON CROQUETTE BREAKFAST SANDWICH

I just love smoked salmon on bagels with all the accouterments—I could seriously eat it every day for breakfast! But smoked salmon can get pricey, so I found a cheaper alternative without losing the flavor.
—Jessi Hampton, Richmond Hill, GA

Prep: 25 min. • **Cook:** 10 min.
Makes: 2 servings

- 1 large egg, lightly beaten
- ¼ cup dry bread crumbs
- 1 tsp. garlic powder
- 1 tsp. smoked paprika
- 1 pouch (6 oz.) boneless skinless pink salmon
- 1 Tbsp. olive oil
- 2 everything bagels, split and toasted
- 4 Tbsp. cream cheese, softened
- 1 Tbsp. capers, drained
- 1 medium tomato, sliced
- ½ medium red onion, thinly sliced into rings
  Snipped fresh dill, optional

1. In a small bowl, combine egg, bread crumbs, garlic powder and smoked paprika. Add salmon and mix well. Shape into 2 patties.

2. In a large skillet, cook patties in oil over medium heat until browned, 5-6 minutes on each side.

3. Spread cut sides of bagels with cream cheese; sprinkle with capers. Serve salmon patties on bagels with tomato, red onion and, if desired, dill.

1 sandwich: 656 cal., 25g fat (10g sat. fat), 152mg chol., 1205mg sod., 75g carb. (14g sugars, 4g fiber), 34g pro.

TUSCAN CHICKEN FRITTATA

BRUNCH PIZZA

Whenever I entertain guests, this zippy pizza is a definite crowd-pleaser. It also makes a superb late-night snack when you are in the middle of a good movie!
—Janelle Lee, Appleton, WI

Prep: 15 min. • **Bake:** 25 min.
Makes: 8 servings

- 1 tube (8 oz.) refrigerated crescent rolls
- 1 lb. bulk pork sausage
- 5 large eggs
- ¼ cup 2% milk
- ½ tsp. salt
- ¼ tsp. pepper
- 1 cup frozen shredded hash browns
- 1 cup shredded cheddar cheese
- 2 Tbsp. grated Parmesan cheese

1. Preheat oven to 375°. Separate crescent roll dough into 8 triangles and place on an ungreased 12-in. round pizza pan with points toward center. Press over the bottom and up the sides to form a crust; seal perforations. Set aside.
2. In a large nonstick skillet, cook sausage over medium heat until no longer pink, 5-7 minutes, breaking up sausage into crumbles. Drain and transfer to pizza crust. Wipe out skillet. In a bowl, beat eggs, milk, salt and pepper; pour into same skillet. Cook and stir over medium heat until almost set; spoon over sausage.
3. Sprinkle pizza with hash browns, cheddar cheese and Parmesan. Bake until crust is golden, 25-30 minutes.

1 slice: 340 cal., 24g fat (10g sat. fat), 170mg chol., 756mg sod., 15g carb. (4g sugars, 0 fiber), 14g pro.

MIXED BERRY FRENCH TOAST BAKE

MIXED BERRY FRENCH TOAST BAKE

I love this recipe! It's perfect for fuss-free holiday breakfasts or company because it's scrumptious and so easy to put together the night before.
—Amy Berry, Poland, ME

Prep: 20 min. + chilling • **Bake:** 45 min.
Makes: 8 servings

- 6 large eggs
- 1¾ cups fat-free milk
- 1 tsp. sugar
- 1 tsp. ground cinnamon
- 1 tsp. vanilla extract
- ¼ tsp. salt
- 1 loaf (1 lb.) French bread, cubed
- 1 pkg. (12 oz.) frozen unsweetened mixed berries
- 2 Tbsp. cold butter
- ⅓ cup packed brown sugar
  Optional: Confectioners' sugar and maple syrup

1. Whisk together first 6 ingredients. Place bread cubes in a 13x9-in. or 3-qt. baking dish coated with cooking spray. Pour egg mixture over top. Refrigerate, covered, 8 hours or overnight.
2. Preheat oven to 350°. Remove berries from the freezer and French toast from the refrigerator and let stand while the oven heats. Bake, covered, 30 minutes.
3. In a small bowl, cut butter into brown sugar until crumbly. Top French toast with berries; sprinkle with the brown sugar mixture. Bake, uncovered, until a knife inserted in the center comes out clean, 15-20 minutes. If desired, dust with confectioners' sugar and serve with syrup.

1 serving: 310 cal., 8g fat (3g sat. fat), 148mg chol., 517mg sod., 46g carb. (17g sugars, 3g fiber), 13g pro.

CAST-IRON LOADED BREAKFAST BISCUITS

These biscuits are full of hearty breakfast ingredients like eggs, bacon, mushrooms and cheese! I like to bake up a batch on the weekend, then freeze some for quick weekday breakfasts. A gluten-free flour blend can be substituted for the all-purpose flour if needed.
—Courtney Stultz, Weir, KS

....

Prep: 35 min. • **Bake:** 20 min.
Makes: 8 servings

- 4 bacon strips, chopped
- 1 cup chopped fresh mushrooms
- ⅓ cup chopped onion
- 1 garlic clove, minced
- 4 large eggs
- 2 cups all-purpose flour
- 3 tsp. baking powder
- ½ tsp. salt
- ½ cup cold butter, cubed
- 1 cup buttermilk
- ½ cup shredded cheddar cheese

1. Preheat oven to 400°. In a 10-in. cast-iron or other ovenproof skillet, cook bacon over medium heat until crisp, stirring occasionally. Remove with a slotted spoon; drain on paper towels.

2. Cook and stir mushrooms, onion and garlic in the bacon drippings until tender, 4-5 minutes. Remove from pan.

3. In a small bowl, whisk eggs until blended. Pour eggs into same pan; cook and stir over medium heat until eggs are thickened and no liquid egg remains. Remove from pan.

4. In a large bowl, whisk flour, baking powder and salt. Cut in butter until mixture resembles coarse crumbs. Add buttermilk; stir just until moistened. Gently stir in mushroom mixture, eggs, bacon and cheese.

5. Drop dough by ½ cupfuls 1 in. apart into same skillet. Bake until bottoms are golden brown, 20-25 minutes.

1 biscuit: 356 cal., 22g fat (11g sat. fat), 141mg chol., 653mg sod., 27g carb. (2g sugars, 1g fiber), 11g pro.

CAST-IRON LOADED BREAKFAST BISCUITS

SWEET POTATO DUTCH BABY

I love a traditional Dutch baby, so I created a savory version to serve for breakfast or brunch. Top it with poached eggs, smoked salmon or sour cream. I also like to serve it with mixed greens tossed in olive oil and lemon juice.
—Tom Doyle, Pittsburgh, PA

Prep: 15 min. • **Bake:** 20 min.
Makes: 6 servings

- ¾ cup cubed peeled sweet potato
- 1 Tbsp. water
- ¼ cup butter, cubed
- ½ cup all-purpose flour
- ¼ cup grated Parmesan cheese, divided
- 2 Tbsp. sugar
- 2 tsp. minced fresh tarragon or ¾ tsp. dried tarragon
- 1 tsp. kosher salt
- ½ tsp. pepper
- 4 large eggs, room temperature
- 1 cup 2% milk

1. Preheat oven to 425°. Place sweet potato and water in a microwave-safe bowl; microwave, covered, on high until potato is tender, 3-4 minutes; drain.
2. Place butter in a 10-in. cast-iron or other ovenproof skillet. Place in oven until butter is melted, 4-5 minutes; carefully swirl to coat evenly.
3. Meanwhile, in a large bowl, whisk together flour, 2 Tbsp. Parmesan, the sugar, tarragon, kosher salt and pepper. Place eggs, milk and sweet potato in a blender; process until blended. Add the flour mixture; pulse until combined. Pour into hot skillet. Bake until puffed and the sides are golden brown and crisp, 20-25 minutes. Sprinkle with remaining 2 Tbsp. Parmesan. Serve immediately.
1 serving: 219 cal., 13g fat (7g sat. fat), 150mg chol., 517mg sod., 18g carb. (7g sugars, 1g fiber), 8g pro.

SHRIMP & TOMATO MIGAS

My friends and family know I adore shrimp, especially when it's mixed with spices. Staple ingredients in my house are corn tortillas, eggs and cheese, and I've found that this cast-iron combo is a match made in heaven.
—Kim Banick, Turner, OR

Prep: 25 min. • **Cook:** 25 min.
Makes: 6 servings

- 6 Tbsp. canola oil, divided
- 8 corn tortillas (6 in.), cut into ½-in. pieces
- 2 cups cherry tomatoes
- 1 lb. uncooked shrimp (31-40 per lb.), peeled and deveined
- ¾ tsp. salt, divided
- ⅛ tsp. pepper
- 1 medium onion, chopped
- 1 can (15¼ oz.) southwest corn with poblano and red peppers, drained
- 8 large eggs, beaten
- 2 cups shredded pepper jack cheese
- 4 Tbsp. minced fresh cilantro, divided
- 1 cup sour cream
- 3 Tbsp. queso fresco, crumbled
- 2 medium limes, cut into wedges

1. In a 12-in. cast-iron or other heavy skillet, heat 3 Tbsp. oil over medium-high heat. Add tortillas; cook and stir until crisp, 4-5 minutes. Remove and set aside.
2. In the same skillet, heat 2 Tbsp. oil. Add tomatoes; cook and stir 3 minutes. Add shrimp, ¼ tsp. salt and the pepper; cook until shrimp turn pink, 6-8 minutes. Remove and keep warm.
3. In the same skillet, heat remaining 1 Tbsp. oil. Add onion; cook and stir until crisp-tender, 6-7 minutes. Add corn; heat through. Whisk eggs and remaining ½ tsp. salt. Pour into skillet; cook and stir until eggs are thickened and no liquid egg remains. Stir in shredded cheese, 2 Tbsp. cilantro and the tortilla pieces.
4. Serve shrimp mixture with eggs, sour cream, queso fresco, limes and remaining 2 Tbsp. cilantro.
1 serving: 648 cal., 44g fat (15g sat. fat), 392mg chol., 933mg sod., 31g carb. (6g sugars, 5g fiber), 35g pro.

SHRIMP & TOMATO MIGAS

**SWEET ORANGE
CROISSANT PUDDING**

TOFFEE COFFEE CAKE

*This coffee cake is good on its own with
a cup of morning coffee. In the afternoon
or evening, serve it up with a scoop of
your favorite ice cream!*
—Edie DeSpain, Logan, UT

Prep: 15 min. • **Bake:** 30 min. + cooling
Makes: 16 servings

- ½ cup butter or margarine, softened
- 1 cup packed brown sugar
- ½ cup sugar
- 2 cups all-purpose flour
- 1 cup buttermilk
- 1 large egg, room temperature
- 1 tsp. baking soda
- 1 tsp. vanilla extract
- 3 chocolate English toffee candy bars
  (1.4 oz. each), chopped
- ¼ cup chopped pecans

Preheat oven to 350°. Blend butter,
sugars and flour; set aside ½ cup. To the
remaining sugar mixture, add buttermilk,
egg, baking soda and vanilla; mix well. Pour
into a greased and floured 13x9-in. baking
pan. Combine candy and pecans with
the reserved sugar mixture; sprinkle over
batter. Bake at 350° until a toothpick
inserted in the center comes out clean,
30-35 minutes. Cool on a wire rack.
1 piece: 247 cal., 10g fat (5g sat. fat),
33mg chol., 186mg sod., 37g carb.
(25g sugars, 1g fiber), 3g pro.

SWEET ORANGE
CROISSANT PUDDING

*Time-crunched cooks will appreciate the
make-ahead convenience of this delightful
dish. Feel free to replace the orange
marmalade with any jam or jelly that
suits your taste.*
—Mary Gabriel, Las Vegas, NV

Prep: 15 min. + chilling
Bake: 40 min. + cooling
Makes: 8 servings

- 4 croissants, split
- 1 cup orange marmalade, divided
- 3 large eggs
- 1¼ cups whole milk
- 1 cup heavy whipping cream
- ½ cup sugar
- 1 tsp. grated orange zest, optional
- ½ tsp. almond extract

1. Spread croissant bottoms with 3 Tbsp.
marmalade; replace the tops. Cut each
croissant into 5 slices; place in a greased
11x7-in. baking dish.
2. Whisk together the next 4 ingredients,
orange zest if desired, and the extract.
Pour over croissants. Refrigerate, covered,
overnight.
3. Remove from refrigerator 30 minutes
before baking. Preheat the oven to 350°.
Place dish in a larger baking dish; fill the
larger dish with 1 in. boiling water.
4. Bake, uncovered, until a knife inserted
in center comes out clean, 40-45 minutes.
Remove pan from water bath; cool on a
wire rack 10 minutes. Brush the remaining
marmalade over top. Cut and serve warm.
1 piece: 416 cal., 20g fat (11g sat. fat),
143mg chol., 287mg sod., 55g carb.
(42g sugars, 1g fiber), 7g pro.

BREADS
IN A JIFFY

You can treat your family to fresh-from-the-oven bread even if you don't have a lot of time! In this chapter, quick breads come together in a snap, convenience breads shorten work time, and even yeast breads are short on prep time and rise while you get on with other things.

PERFECT DINNER ROLLS

These rolls melt in your mouth. I loved them as a child, and I'm happy to make them for my kids now because I know I am creating those same wonderful memories my mom made for me!
—Gayleen Grote, Battleview, ND

Prep: 30 min. + rising • **Bake:** 15 min.
Makes: 2 dozen

- 1 Tbsp. active dry yeast
- 2¼ cups warm water (110° to 115°)
- ⅓ cup sugar
- ⅓ cup shortening
- ¼ cup powdered nondairy creamer
- 2¼ tsp. salt
- 6 to 7 cups bread flour

1. In a large bowl, dissolve yeast in warm water. Add the sugar, shortening, creamer, salt and 5 cups flour. Beat until smooth. Stir in enough of the remaining flour to form a soft dough (dough will be sticky).
2. Turn onto a floured surface; knead until smooth and elastic, 6-8 minutes. Place in a bowl coated with cooking spray, turning once to coat the top. Cover and let rise in a warm place until doubled, about 1 hour.
3. Punch dough down. Turn onto a lightly floured surface; divide into 24 pieces. Shape each into a roll. Place 2 in. apart on baking sheets coated with cooking spray. Cover and let rise until doubled, about 30 minutes.
4. Meanwhile, preheat oven to 350°. Bake until lightly browned, 12-15 minutes. Remove from pans to wire racks.
1 roll: 142 cal., 3g fat (1g sat. fat), 0 chol., 222mg sod., 25g carb. (3g sugars, 1g fiber), 4g pro.

GARLIC BREAD

GARLIC BREAD

This wonderful accompaniment could not be tastier or simpler to make. Minced fresh garlic is key to these flavor-packed crusty slices, which our big family snaps up before they even have a chance to cool!
—Grace Yaskovic, Lake Hiawatha, NJ

Takes: 20 min. • **Makes:** 8 servings

- ½ cup butter, melted
- 3 to 4 garlic cloves, minced
- 1 loaf (1 lb.) French bread, halved lengthwise
- 2 Tbsp. minced fresh parsley

1. Preheat oven to 350°. In a small bowl, combine butter and garlic. Brush over cut sides of bread; sprinkle with parsley. Place, cut side up, on a baking sheet.
2. Bake for 8 minutes. Broil 4-6 in. from the heat for 2 minutes or until golden brown. Serve warm.
1 serving: 258 cal., 13g fat (7g sat. fat), 31mg chol., 462mg sod., 30g carb. (1g sugars, 2g fiber), 5g pro.

> **TEST KITCHEN TIP**
> How do you store garlic bread? Leftover garlic bread can be wrapped tightly in foil and stored in the refrigerator for up to 3 days. To reheat, bake the wrapped bread at 350° for 10-15 minutes.

HERB & ROMANO CHEESE WREATH

After the wreath is baked and cooled, it can be wrapped in foil, placed in an airtight plastic bag and frozen until you are ready to use it—either to serve or give away. Add a pretty jar of whipped butter on the side and it makes a perfect gift!
—Linda Padia, Wauna, WA

Prep: 30 min. + rising
Bake: 30 min. + cooling
Makes: 1 loaf (24 slices)

- 1 pkg. (¼ oz.) active dry yeast
- 2 Tbsp. honey
- 1½ cups warm water (110° to 115°)
- ½ cup nonfat dry milk powder
- 2 large eggs, room temperature
- ½ cup butter, softened
- 4 Tbsp. grated Romano cheese, divided
- 2 tsp. minced fresh rosemary or ½ tsp. dried rosemary, crushed
- 2 tsp. minced fresh thyme or ½ tsp. dried thyme
- 1½ tsp. salt
- 5½ to 6 cups bread flour
- 1 Tbsp. butter, melted

1. In a small bowl, dissolve yeast and honey in warm water; stir in milk powder. In a large bowl, combine eggs, softened butter, 2 Tbsp. cheese, rosemary, thyme, salt, yeast mixture and 2 cups flour; beat on medium speed until smooth. Stir in enough of the remaining flour to form a soft dough (dough will be sticky).
2. Turn the dough onto a floured surface; knead until smooth and elastic, 6-8 minutes. Place in a greased bowl, turning once to grease the top. Cover and let rise in a warm place until doubled, about 1 hour.
3. Punch down dough. Turn onto a lightly floured surface; divide into thirds. Roll each into a 30-in. rope. Place ropes on a greased baking sheet and braid. Shape into a wreath and pinch ends to seal.
4. Cover with a kitchen towel; let rise in a warm place until almost doubled, about 45 minutes. Preheat oven to 375°.
5. Brush braid with melted butter; sprinkle with remaining cheese. Bake 30-35 minutes or until golden brown. Remove from pan to a wire rack to cool.

1 slice: 174 cal., 6g fat (3g sat. fat), 27mg chol., 215mg sod., 25g carb. (2g sugars, 1g fiber), 5g pro.

HERB & ROMANO CHEESE WREATH

PARMESAN-SAGE BEER BREAD

I'm asked to bring this savory loaf to nearly every function I attend. It's great as a side dish, but if you're in the mood for an extraordinary sandwich, start with two slices of beer bread.
—Elizabeth King, Duluth, MN

Prep: 10 min. • **Bake:** 45 min. + cooling
Makes: 1 loaf (12 slices)

2½ cups all-purpose flour
1 cup grated Parmesan cheese
2 Tbsp. sugar
3 tsp. baking powder
1 Tbsp. chopped fresh sage
1 tsp. salt
1½ cups beer
¼ cup melted butter, divided

1. Preheat oven to 375°. In a small bowl, whisk the first 6 ingredients. Add beer and 3 Tbsp. melted butter; stir just until moistened.
2. Transfer to a greased 8x4-in. loaf pan. Drizzle with the remaining butter. Bake for 45-50 minutes or until a toothpick inserted in center comes out clean. Cool in pan 5 minutes before removing to a wire rack to cool.
1 slice: 177 cal., 6g fat (4g sat. fat), 16mg chol., 469mg sod., 24g carb. (3g sugars, 1g fiber), 5g pro.

BACON PARMESAN POPOVERS

My popovers are a nice change from ordinary toast or muffins. This recipe proves that simple ingredients often result in the best-tasting dishes.
—Donna Gaston, Coplay, PA

Prep: 10 min. • **Bake:** 30 min.
Makes: 6 popovers

2 large eggs, room temperature
1 cup 2% milk
1 cup all-purpose flour
2 Tbsp. grated Parmesan cheese
¼ tsp. salt
3 bacon strips, diced

1. In a large bowl, beat eggs and milk. Combine flour, cheese and salt; add to egg mixture and mix well. Cover and let stand at room temperature for 45 minutes.
2. Preheat oven to 450°. In a large skillet, cook bacon over medium heat until crisp. Using a slotted spoon, remove to paper towels to drain. Grease cups of a nonstick popover pan well with some of the bacon drippings; set aside. Stir bacon into batter; fill prepared cups two-thirds full.
3. Bake 15 minutes. Reduce heat to 350° (do not open oven door). Bake until deep golden brown, about 15 minutes longer (do not underbake).
4. Run a table knife or a small metal spatula around edges of cups to loosen if necessary. Immediately remove popovers from pan; prick with a small sharp knife to allow steam to escape. Serve immediately.
1 popover: 167 cal., 7g fat (3g sat. fat), 73mg chol., 248mg sod., 18g carb. (2g sugars, 1g fiber), 7g pro.

TEST KITCHEN TIP
You may use greased muffin tins instead of a popover pan. Fill every other cup two-thirds full with batter to avoid crowding the popovers; fill the remaining cups with water. Bake at 450° for 15 minutes, then 350° for 10 minutes. Makes: 9 popovers.

BACON PARMESAN POPOVERS

CHOCOLATE PINWHEEL BREAD

CHOCOLATE PINWHEEL BREAD

This swirled yeast bread is brimming with chocolate chips, so the sweet, moist slices don't need any butter. This recipe makes two loaves, so you can keep one and share the other with a neighbor!
—Dawn Onuffer, Crestview, FL

Prep: 30 min. + rising
Bake: 40 min. + cooling
Makes: 2 loaves (16 slices each)

- 1 pkg. (¼ oz.) active dry yeast
- 1 cup warm 2% milk (110° to 115°)
- ¼ cup sugar
- 1 tsp. salt
- 2 large eggs, room temperature
- 4 oz. cream cheese, softened
- 4 to 4½ cups bread flour

FILLING
- 4 oz. cream cheese, softened
- ½ cup confectioners' sugar
- 2 Tbsp. baking cocoa
- 1 cup semisweet chocolate chips
- 1 large egg, beaten

1. In a large bowl, dissolve the yeast in warm milk. Add the sugar, salt, eggs, cream cheese and 2 cups flour; beat until smooth. Stir in enough of the remaining flour to form a soft dough.
2. Turn onto a floured surface; knead until smooth and elastic, 6-8 minutes. Place in a greased bowl, turning once to grease the top. Cover; let rise in a warm place until doubled, about 1 hour.
3. Punch dough down. Turn onto a floured surface; divide in half. Roll each portion into a 12x8-in. rectangle. For the filling, in a small bowl, beat cream cheese, confectioners' sugar and cocoa until smooth. Spread over each rectangle to within ½ in. of edges. Sprinkle with chocolate chips. Roll up jelly-roll style, starting with a short side; pinch seam to seal. Place seam side down in 2 greased 9x5-in. loaf pans. Cover and let rise until doubled, about 45 minutes.
4. Brush tops of loaves with egg. Bake at 350° for 25 minutes. Cover loosely with foil. Bake 15-20 minutes longer or until the loaves sound hollow when tapped. Remove from pans to wire racks to cool.
1 slice: 127 cal., 5g fat (3g sat. fat), 29mg chol., 105mg sod., 19g carb. (7g sugars, 1g fiber), 4g pro.

40-MINUTE HAMBURGER BUNS

Here on our ranch, I cook for three men who love hamburgers. These fluffy yet hearty buns are just right for their big appetites. They're so good, I sometimes serve them plain with a meal.
—Jessie McKenney, Twodot, MT

Prep: 20 min. + resting • **Bake:** 10 min.
Makes: 1 dozen

- 2 Tbsp. active dry yeast
- 1 cup plus 2 Tbsp. warm water (110° to 115°)
- ⅓ cup vegetable oil
- ¼ cup sugar
- 1 large egg, room temperature
- 1 tsp. salt
- 3 to 3½ cups all-purpose flour

1. In a large bowl, dissolve the yeast in warm water. Add the oil and sugar; let stand for 5 minutes. Add egg, salt and enough flour to form a soft dough.
2. Turn the dough onto a floured surface; knead until smooth and elastic, 3-5 minutes. Do not let rise. Divide into 12 pieces; shape each into a ball. Place 3 in. apart on greased baking sheets. Preheat oven to 425°.
3. Cover and let rest for 10 minutes. Bake until golden brown, 8-12 minutes. Remove from pans to wire racks to cool.
1 serving: 195 cal., 7g fat (1g sat. fat), 18mg chol., 204mg sod., 29g carb. (5g sugars, 1g fiber), 5g pro.

LEMON BLUEBERRY BREAD

VEGETABLE & CHEESE FOCACCIA

My family eats up this flavorful bread as fast as I can make it. Sometimes I add different herbs, red onion or crumbled bacon. It's one of my best recipes!
—Mary Cass, Baltimore, MD

Prep: 20 min. + rising • **Bake:** 30 min.
Makes: 15 servings

- 1 cup water (70° to 80°)
- 4½ tsp. olive oil
- 4½ tsp. sugar
- 2 tsp. dried oregano
- 1¼ tsp. salt
- 3¾ cups bread flour
- 1½ tsp. active dry yeast

TOPPING
- 1 Tbsp. olive oil
- 1 Tbsp. dried basil
- 2 medium tomatoes, thinly sliced
- 1 medium onion, thinly sliced
- 1 cup frozen chopped broccoli, thawed
- ¼ tsp. salt
- ¼ tsp. pepper
- ¾ cup grated Parmesan cheese
- 1 cup shredded part-skim mozzarella cheese

1. In bread machine pan, place the first 7 ingredients in the order suggested by the manufacturer. Select dough setting (check dough after 5 minutes of mixing; add 1-2 Tbsp. water or flour if needed).
2. When cycle is completed, turn dough onto a lightly floured surface. Punch the dough down. Roll into a 13x9-in. rectangle; transfer to a 13x9-in. baking dish coated with cooking spray.
3. For topping, brush dough with olive oil; sprinkle with basil. Layer with the tomatoes, onion and broccoli; sprinkle with salt, pepper and Parmesan cheese. Cover and let rise in a warm place until doubled, about 30 minutes.
4. Bake at 350° for 20 minutes. Sprinkle with the mozzarella cheese; bake until bread is golden brown and cheese is melted, 10-15 minutes longer.
1 piece: 151 cal., 4g fat (2g sat. fat), 7mg chol., 315mg sod., 22g carb. (3g sugars, 2g fiber), 7g pro.

LEMON BLUEBERRY BREAD

Of all the quick breads we had growing up, this beautifully glazed berry-studded loaf is the best! The lemon glaze adds a lustrous finish and locks in moisture.
—Julianne Johnson, Grove City, MN

Prep: 15 min. • **Bake:** 1 hour + cooling
Makes: 1 loaf (16 slices)

- ⅓ cup butter, melted
- 1 cup sugar
- 3 Tbsp. lemon juice
- 2 large eggs, room temperature
- 1½ cups all-purpose flour
- 1 tsp. baking powder
- ½ tsp. salt
- ½ cup 2% milk
- 1 cup fresh or frozen blueberries
- ½ cup chopped nuts
- 2 Tbsp. grated lemon zest

GLAZE
- 2 Tbsp. lemon juice
- ¼ cup sugar

1. Preheat oven to 350°. In a large bowl, beat butter, sugar, lemon juice and eggs. Combine the flour, baking powder and salt; stir into the egg mixture alternately with milk, beating well after each addition. Fold in blueberries, nuts and lemon zest.
2. Transfer to a greased 8x4-in. loaf pan. Bake 60-70 minutes or until a toothpick inserted in the center comes out clean. Cool for 10 minutes before removing from pan to a wire rack.
3. Combine glaze ingredients; drizzle over warm bread. Cool completely.
1 slice: 181 cal., 7g fat (3g sat. fat), 38mg chol., 149mg sod., 27g carb. (17g sugars, 1g fiber), 3g pro.

TEST KITCHEN TIP
To keep this quick bread moist, avoid using low-fat milk; stick to 2% or whole milk. Also, bring the eggs to room temperature before using. The glaze absorbs into the warm bread, providing even more moisture. When cool, store the bread in an airtight container to keep it from drying out.

VEGETABLE &
CHEESE FOCACCIA

Make Better Butters

Why settle for plain butter? Doesn't your home-baked bread deserve something special?

DAIRY STATE BUTTER

SOUTHWEST BUTTER

CALIFORNIA-STYLE BUTTER

HEARTLAND BUTTER

EAST COAST BUTTER

CALIFORNIA-STYLE BUTTER

Turn a stick of butter into a showstopping spread with fresh herbs, a sprinkle of spice, or any other mix-in you like.
—Taste of Home *Test Kitchen*

Takes: 5 min. • **Makes:** 8 servings

- 1 Tbsp. minced ripe olives
- 2 tsp. minced fresh rosemary
- ½ cup butter, softened

Stir ripe olives and minced rosemary into softened butter.

1 Tbsp.: 103 cal., 12g fat (7g sat. fat), 31mg chol., 99mg sod., 0 carb. (0 sugars, 0 fiber), 0 pro.

Dairy State Butter: Stir 2 Tbsp. grated Parmesan cheese and 2 Tbsp. finely grated cheddar cheese into ½ cup softened butter.

East Coast Butter: Stir 2 tsp. Old Bay seasoning and 1½- 2 tsp. grated lemon zest into ½ cup softened butter.

Southwest Butter: Stir 1½ tsp. grated lime zest, 1 tsp. minced fresh cilantro and ½ tsp. ground chipotle pepper into ½ cup softened butter.

Heartland Butter: Stir 2 Tbsp. crumbled Maytag blue cheese into ½ cup softened butter.

HOMEMADE ENGLISH MUFFIN BREAD

Most of my baking is from scratch— and with only 20 minutes of prep time, the clock is no reason not to treat your family to this delicious homemade bread!
—Elsie Trippett, Jackson, MI

Prep: 20 min. + rising • **Bake:** 35 min.
Makes: 2 loaves

- 5 cups all-purpose flour, divided
- 2 pkg. (¼ oz. each) active dry yeast
- 1 Tbsp. sugar
- 2 tsp. salt
- ¼ tsp. baking soda
- 2 cups warm 2% milk (110° to 115°)
- ½ cup warm water (120° to 130°)
  Cornmeal

1. In a large bowl, combine 2 cups flour, yeast, sugar, salt and baking soda. Add warm milk and water; beat on low speed 30 seconds, scraping bowl occasionally. Beat on high 3 minutes. Stir in remaining flour (batter will be stiff). Do not knead.

2. Grease two 8x4-in. loaf pans. Sprinkle pans with cornmeal. Spoon batter into pans and sprinkle cornmeal on top. Cover and let rise in a warm place until doubled, about 45 minutes.

3. Preheat oven to 375°. Bake 35 minutes or until golden brown. Remove from pans to wire racks to cool.

1 slice: 83 cal., 1g fat (0 sat. fat), 2mg chol., 165mg sod., 16g carb. (1g sugars, 1g fiber), 3g pro.

HERB QUICK BREAD
PICTURED ON P. 193

This simple bread is especially good with soups and stews, but slices are also tasty alongside fresh green salads. The herbs make this a flavorful treat any time of the year.
—Donna Roberts, Manhattan, KS

Prep: 15 min. • **Bake:** 40 min. + cooling
Makes: 1 loaf (16 slices)

- 3 cups all-purpose flour
- 3 Tbsp. sugar
- 1 Tbsp. baking powder
- 3 tsp. caraway seeds
- ½ tsp. salt
- ½ tsp. ground nutmeg
- ½ tsp. dried thyme
- 1 large egg, room temperature
- 1 cup fat-free milk
- ⅓ cup canola oil

1. Preheat oven to 350°. In a large bowl, whisk together the first 7 ingredients. In another bowl, whisk together egg, milk and oil. Add to flour mixture; stir just until moistened.

2. Transfer to a 9x5-in. loaf pan coated with cooking spray. Bake until a toothpick inserted in the center comes out clean, 40-50 minutes. Cool in pan 10 minutes before removing to a wire rack to cool.

1 slice: 147 cal., 5g fat (1g sat. fat), 12mg chol., 160mg sod., 21g carb. (3g sugars, 1g fiber), 3g pro. **Diabetic exchanges:** 1½ starch, 1 fat.

Skillet Bread: Prepare batter as directed. Spoon batter into a greased 8-in. cast-iron skillet and bake at 350° until a toothpick inserted in the center comes out clean, 45-50 minutes.

Muffins: Prepare batter as directed. Spoon batter into 9 greased muffin tins and bake at 350° until a toothpick inserted in center comes out clean, 25-30 minutes.

HOMEMADE ENGLISH MUFFIN BREAD

CHEESE & GARLIC BISCUITS

My biscuits won the prize for best quick bread at my county fair. One judge liked them so much, she asked for the recipe! These buttery, savory biscuits go with just about anything.
—Gloria Jarrett, Loveland, OH

Takes: 20 min. • **Makes:** 2½ dozen

- 2½ cups biscuit/baking mix
- ¾ cup shredded sharp cheddar cheese
- 1 tsp. garlic powder
- 1 tsp. ranch salad dressing mix
- 1 cup buttermilk

TOPPING

- ½ cup butter, melted
- 1 Tbsp. minced chives
- ½ tsp. garlic powder
- ½ tsp. ranch salad dressing mix
- ¼ tsp. pepper

1. Preheat oven to 450°. In a large bowl, combine the baking mix, cheese, garlic powder and salad dressing mix. Stir in the buttermilk just until moistened. Drop by tablespoonfuls onto greased baking sheets.

2. Bake until golden brown, 6-8 minutes. Meanwhile, combine topping ingredients. Brush over biscuits. Serve warm.

1 biscuit: 81 cal., 5g fat (3g sat. fat), 11mg chol., 176mg sod., 7g carb. (1g sugars, 0 fiber), 2g pro.

HOMEMADE BAGELS

HOMEMADE BAGELS

Instead of going to a baker, head to the kitchen and surprise your family with homemade bagels. For variation and flavor, sprinkle the tops with cinnamon sugar instead of sesame and poppy seeds.
—Rebecca Phillips, Burlington, CT

Prep: 30 min. + rising
Bake: 20 min. + cooling • **Makes:** 1 dozen

- 1 tsp. active dry yeast
- 1¼ cups warm 2% milk (110° to 115°)
- ½ cup butter, softened
- 2 Tbsp. sugar
- 1 tsp. salt
- 1 egg yolk
- 3¾ to 4¼ cups all-purpose flour
  Sesame or poppy seeds, optional

1. In a large bowl, dissolve yeast in warm milk. Add the butter, sugar, salt and egg yolk; mix well. Stir in enough flour to form a soft dough.

2. Turn onto a floured surface; knead until smooth and elastic, 6-8 minutes. Place in a greased bowl, turning once to grease top. Cover and let rise in a warm place until doubled, about 1 hour.

3. Punch the dough down. Shape into 12 balls. Push thumb through centers to form a 1½-in. hole. Stretch and shape dough to form an even ring. Place on a floured surface. Cover and let rest for 10 minutes; flatten bagels slightly.

4. Preheat oven to 400°. Fill a Dutch oven two-thirds full with water; bring to a boil. Drop bagels, 2 at a time, into boiling water. Cook for 45 seconds; turn and cook for 45 seconds longer. Remove with a slotted spoon; drain well on paper towels.

5. Sprinkle with sesame or poppy seeds if desired. Place 2 in. apart on greased baking sheets. Bake for 20-25 minutes or until golden brown. Remove from pans to wire racks to cool.

1 bagel: 237 cal., 9g fat (5g sat. fat), 38mg chol., 271mg sod., 33g carb. (3g sugars, 1g fiber), 5g pro.

TEST KITCHEN TIP
The key to making fluffy bagels is to avoid overboiling. Doing so will cause them to sink and lose the air you incorporated during the rise.

CINNAMON-SUGAR SWEET POTATO PASTRIES

We always have leftover mashed sweet potatoes after our Thanksgiving meal. I use what's left to make an indulgent filling for empanadas. Convenient crescent roll dough makes this recipe easy as pie.
—Sarah Vasques, Milford, NH

Prep: 25 min. • **Bake:** 10 min.
Makes: 32 appetizers

- ½ cup mashed sweet potato
- 2 oz. cream cheese, softened
- 1 Tbsp. brown sugar
- ½ tsp. grated orange zest
- 2 tubes (8 oz. each) refrigerated crescent rolls
- ½ cup sugar
- 2 tsp. ground cinnamon
- ¼ cup butter, melted

1. Preheat oven to 375°. In a small bowl, combine sweet potato, cream cheese, brown sugar and orange zest. Unroll the crescent dough and separate into 4 rectangles; press perforations to seal. Cut each rectangle into 4 triangles. Repeat with remaining dough. Place 1 tsp. potato filling in center of each triangle. Fold the dough over filling and pinch seams to seal.
2. Place 2 in. apart on parchment-lined baking sheets. Bake 10-12 minutes or until golden brown. Cool slightly. In a small bowl, mix sugar and cinnamon. Brush the pastries with butter; coat with the cinnamon-sugar mixture.

1 appetizer: 88 cal., 5g fat (1g sat. fat), 6mg chol., 125mg sod., 11g carb. (5g sugars, 0 fiber), 1g pro.

ZESTY HAM & CHEESE MUFFINS

Since I developed this recipe, it has become one of my mother's favorites. I often make a batch for the two of us to share. The muffins are great for brunch or an on-the-go breakfast.
—Julie Hess, Lititz, PA

Takes: 30 min. • **Makes:** 14 muffins

- 2 cups all-purpose flour
- ¼ cup minced fresh chives
- 1 tsp. baking powder
- 1 tsp. dried parsley flakes
- ½ tsp. baking soda
- ½ tsp. salt
- ½ tsp. dried minced onion
- ½ tsp. ground mustard
- 1 large egg, room temperature
- 1 cup plus 2 Tbsp. buttermilk
- 6 drops hot pepper sauce
- 1 cup cubed fully cooked ham
- ¾ cup shredded cheddar cheese
- ¾ cup shredded Velveeta

TOPPING
- 5 Tbsp. shredded Parmesan cheese
- 3½ tsp. butter
- ½ tsp. paprika
- ½ tsp. dried parsley flakes
- ¼ tsp. pepper

1. Preheat oven to 450°. In a large bowl, combine the first 8 ingredients. In another bowl, beat the egg, buttermilk and pepper sauce. Stir into the dry ingredients just until moistened. Fold in the ham, cheddar cheese and Velveeta.
2. Fill greased muffin cups three-fourths full. Top each muffin with about 1 tsp. Parmesan cheese and ¼ tsp. butter. Combine the paprika, parsley and pepper; sprinkle over muffins.
3. Bake 10-14 minutes or until a toothpick comes out clean. Cool for 5 minutes before removing from pans to wire racks. Serve warm. Refrigerate leftovers.

1 muffin: 153 cal., 6g fat (4g sat. fat), 36mg chol., 462mg sod., 16g carb. (2g sugars, 1g fiber), 8g pro.

CINNAMON-SUGAR SWEET POTATO PASTRIES

SLOW-COOKER SENSATIONS

Turn to these easy slow-cooker recipes for the best set-it-and-forget-it meals. You'll find exceptional ideas for simple but delicious dinners, no-fuss side dishes and luscious desserts.

SLOW-COOKER LAVA CAKE

I love chocolate. Perhaps that's why this decadent slow-cooker cake has long been one of my favorites. The cake can also be served cold.
—*Elizabeth Farrell, Hamilton, MT*

Prep: 15 min. • **Cook:** 2 hours + standing
Makes: 8 servings

- 1 cup all-purpose flour
- 1 cup packed brown sugar, divided
- 5 Tbsp. baking cocoa, divided
- 2 tsp. baking powder
- ¼ tsp. salt
- ½ cup fat-free milk
- 2 Tbsp. canola oil
- ½ tsp. vanilla extract
- ⅛ tsp. ground cinnamon
- 1¼ cups hot water

1. In a large bowl, whisk flour, ½ cup brown sugar, 3 Tbsp. cocoa, baking powder and salt. In another bowl, whisk milk, oil and vanilla until blended. Add to flour mixture; stir just until moistened.
2. Spread into a 3-qt. slow cooker coated with cooking spray. In a small bowl, mix cinnamon and the remaining brown sugar and cocoa; stir in hot water. Pour over batter (do not stir).
3. Cook, covered, on high 2-2½ hours or until a toothpick inserted in cake portion comes out clean. Turn off slow cooker; let stand 15 minutes before serving.
1 serving: 207 cal., 4g fat (0 sat. fat), 0 chol., 191mg sod., 41g carb. (28g sugars, 1g fiber), 3g pro.

CARROT & LENTIL CHILI

CARROT & LENTIL CHILI

I make this meatless chili in the spring and fall. I love the satisfying combination of fresh bright orange carrots and hearty, earthy lentils. Filled with flavor and color, it leaves me energized and nourished. It's also affordable and a terrific way to fit in extra veggies and legumes. I serve this with yogurt, sour cream or plant-based cheese. It also makes a fun dip for your favorite crackers or cubes of bread.
—*Rebekah Ranes, Sedona, AZ*

Prep: 30 min. • **Cook:** 4 hours
Makes: 8 servings

- 2 Tbsp. olive oil
- 1 medium onion, chopped
- ¾ cup dried green lentils, rinsed
- ¾ cup dried red lentils, rinsed
- 6 garlic cloves, minced
- 6 cups chopped carrots (about 10 medium carrots)
- 1 carton (32 oz.) reduced-sodium vegetable broth
- 1 Tbsp. ground cumin
- 1 tsp. salt
- 2 tsp. paprika
- 1 tsp. chili powder
- 1 can (15 oz.) crushed tomatoes, undrained
- 2 medium ripe avocados, peeled and cubed
  Optional: Sour cream, sliced red onion and additional paprika

1. In a large skillet, heat oil over medium-high heat. Add onion; cook and stir until tender, 4-5 minutes. Add lentils and garlic; cook 1 minute longer. Transfer to a 5- or 6-qt. slow cooker. Stir in the carrots, broth and seasonings. Cook, covered, on low 4-6 hours or until the vegetables and lentils are tender.
2. Stir in crushed tomatoes; cook, covered, 30 minutes longer. Serve with avocados and, if desired, sour cream, red onion and additional paprika.
Freeze option: Freeze cooled chili in freezer containers. To use, partially thaw in refrigerator overnight. Heat through in a saucepan, stirring occasionally; add a little broth or water if necessary.
1¼ cups: 310 cal., 10g fat (1g sat. fat), 0 chol., 574mg sod., 47g carb. (11g sugars, 12g fiber), 13g pro.

EASY LEMON-ROSEMARY CHICKEN

With its light, fresh lemon and rosemary flavor, this fragrant chicken is perfect for spring. It pairs well with a variety of sides, and I love that the slow cooker does most of the work!
—*Courtney Stultz, Weir, KS*

Prep: 10 min. • **Cook:** 4 hours + standing
Makes: 6 servings

- 1 broiler/fryer chicken (3 to 4 lbs.)
- 2 celery ribs, cut into 1-in. pieces
- 1 medium onion, chopped
- 1 medium apple, sliced
- 1 Tbsp. olive oil
- 1 Tbsp. minced fresh rosemary or
   1 tsp. dried rosemary, crushed
- 2 tsp. sea salt
- 1½ tsp. minced fresh thyme or
   ½ tsp. dried thyme
- 1½ tsp. paprika
- 1 garlic clove, minced
- 1 tsp. pepper
- 1 medium lemon, sliced

1. Fill chicken cavity with celery, onion and apple. Tuck wings under chicken; tie drumsticks together. Place in a 6-qt. slow cooker, breast side up. Rub the chicken with oil; rub with rosemary, salt, thyme, paprika, garlic and pepper. Top with the lemon slices.

2. Cook chicken, covered, on low until a thermometer inserted in thickest part of thigh reads at least 170°-175°, 4-5 hours. Remove chicken from slow cooker; tent with foil. Discard vegetables and apple. Let chicken stand 15 minutes before carving.

5 oz. cooked chicken: 318 cal., 19g fat (5g sat. fat), 104mg chol., 730mg sod., 1g carb. (0 sugars, 0 fiber), 33g pro.

CONTEST-WINNING BRAISED SHORT RIBS

PICTURED ON P. 205

I've been relying on this recipe ever since I bought my first slow cooker nearly two decades ago. The fall-off-the-bone-tender ribs are so good to come home to after a busy day.
—*Peggy Edwards, Heber City, UT*

Prep: 20 min. • **Cook:** 6 hours
Makes: 7 servings

- ½ cup all-purpose flour
- 1½ tsp. salt
- 1½ tsp. paprika
- ½ tsp. ground mustard
- 4 lbs. bone-in beef short ribs
- 2 Tbsp. canola oil
- 2 medium onions, sliced
- 1 cup beer or beef broth
- 1 garlic clove, minced

GRAVY
- 2 tsp. all-purpose flour
- 1 Tbsp. cold water

1. In a shallow dish, combine the flour, salt, paprika and mustard. Add the ribs in batches and turn to coat. In a large skillet, brown ribs in oil; drain.

2. Place onions in a 5-qt. slow cooker; add ribs. Top with beer and garlic. Cover and cook on low for 6-7 hours or until meat is tender.

3. Remove ribs and onions to a serving platter; keep warm. Skim fat from cooking juices; transfer to a small saucepan. Bring to a boil. Combine flour and water until smooth; gradually stir into the pan. Bring to a boil; cook and stir for 2 minutes or until thickened. Serve with ribs.

1 serving: 281 cal., 14g fat (5g sat. fat), 62mg chol., 547mg sod., 12g carb. (4g sugars, 1g fiber), 22g pro.

READER REVIEW

"Gotta love slow-cooker meals, and this one is amazing! The meat is mouthwatering and tender. I served it with wide egg noodles for a stick-to-your-ribs meal."

SUEFALK, TASTEOFHOME.COM

EASY LEMON-ROSEMARY CHICKEN

SLOW-COOKED
ROPA VIEJA

SLOW-COOKED ROPA VIEJA

*I tasted some of the best food on a trip
to Cuba. One dish stuck out more than
all the others: ropa vieja. I had multiple
variations of this staple, and when I
returned home, I experimented to make
my own version. I went through roughly
five trials before coming to this recipe.*
—Joshua Boyer, Traverse City, MI

Prep: 35 min. • **Cook:** 8 hours
Makes: 6 servings

- 1 **beef flank steak (2 lbs.)**
- ½ **tsp. salt**
- ½ **tsp. pepper**
- 2 **cups beef broth**
- ½ **cup dry vermouth**
- ½ **cup dry red wine or**
  additional beef broth
- 1 **can (6 oz.) tomato paste**

- 1 **large onion, thinly sliced**
- 1 **large carrot, sliced**
- 1 **small sweet red pepper, thinly sliced**
- 1 **Cubanelle or mild banana pepper,**
  thinly sliced
- 3 **springs fresh oregano**
  Hot cooked rice
  Optional: Additional fresh oregano,
    lime wedges and sliced green olives
    with pimientos

1. Cut steak into 6 pieces; sprinkle with
salt and pepper. Heat a large skillet over
medium-high heat; brown the meat in
batches. Transfer meat to a 5- or 6-qt.
slow cooker. Add broth, vermouth, wine
and tomato paste to the pan. Cook for
2-3 minutes, stirring to loosen browned
bits from pan. Pour over meat.
2. Top with onion, carrot, red pepper,
Cubanelle pepper and oregano. Cook,
covered, on low until meat is tender,

8-10 hours. Remove the oregano sprigs;
discard. Remove meat; shred with 2 forks.
Return to the slow cooker; heat through.
Serve with rice and, if desired, additional
oregano, lime wedges and green olives.
1 serving: 278 cal., 11g fat (5g sat. fat),
72mg chol., 611mg sod., 10g carb.
(5g sugars, 2g fiber), 32g pro. **Diabetic
exchanges:** 4 lean meat, 1 vegetable.

TEST KITCHEN TIP
For a spicier version, add sliced
serrano or jalapeno peppers. For
a tangier version, add 2 Tbsp. of
lemon juice or apple cider vinegar.
For a sweeter version, add more
carrots. For a heartier broth, add
more tomato paste.

BROWN SUGAR SWEET POTATOES WITH APPLES

This foolproof side is easy to prepare and makes a beautiful alternative to traditional sweet potatoes. To save time, make it in advance, allow it to cool and refrigerate it up to two days. Put the mashed potatoes back in the slow cooker set to low for about two hours before serving. Add a bit of apple cider or water if needed.
—Judy Batson, Tampa, FL

Prep: 25 min. • **Cook:** 5 hours
Makes: 12 servings

- 5 lbs. sweet potatoes (about 10 medium)
- 3 medium Granny Smith apples, peeled and cut into 1-in. slices
- ¾ cup butter, cubed
- 1 cup packed brown sugar
- 2 tsp. pumpkin pie spice

1. Peel and cut potatoes lengthwise in half; cut crosswise into ½-in. slices. Place the potatoes and apples in a 6-qt. slow cooker. In a small saucepan, mix butter, brown sugar and pie spice. Bring to a boil over medium heat; cook until blended, 1-2 minutes. Pour over potato mixture. Cook, covered, on low until potatoes are tender, 5-6 hours.
2. With a slotted spoon, remove potatoes and apples to a bowl, reserving cooking liquid. Mash the potato mixture, gradually adding enough reserved cooking liquid, if necessary, to reach desired consistency.
⅔ cup: 383 cal., 12g fat (7g sat. fat), 31mg chol., 116mg sod., 68g carb. (40g sugars, 6g fiber), 3g pro.

SLOW-COOKER BERRY COBBLER

It doesn't matter if it's hot or cold outside. This homespun recipe lets you enjoy the amazing flavor of warm homemade cobbler without heating up the kitchen.
—Karen Jarocki, Yuma, AZ

Prep: 15 min. • **Cook:** 1¾ hours
Makes: 8 servings

- 1¼ cups all-purpose flour, divided
- 2 Tbsp. plus 1 cup sugar, divided
- 1 tsp. baking powder
- ¼ tsp. ground cinnamon
- 1 large egg
- ¼ cup fat-free milk
- 2 Tbsp. canola oil
- ⅛ tsp. salt
- 2 cups fresh or frozen raspberries, thawed
- 2 cups fresh or frozen blueberries, thawed
  Low-fat frozen yogurt, optional

1. Whisk together 1 cup flour, 2 Tbsp. sugar, baking powder and cinnamon. In another bowl, whisk together egg, milk and oil; add to dry ingredients, stirring just until moistened (batter will be thick). Spread onto bottom of a 5-qt. slow cooker coated with cooking spray.
2. Mix salt and the remaining flour and sugar; toss with the berries. Spoon over batter. Cook, covered, on high until berry mixture is bubbly, 1¾-2 hours. If desired, serve with frozen yogurt.
1 serving: 260 cal., 5g fat (1g sat. fat), 23mg chol., 110mg sod., 53g carb. (34g sugars, 3g fiber), 4g pro.

BROWN SUGAR
SWEET POTATOES
WITH APPLES

GREEK SAUSAGE & PEPPERS

BEERGARITA CHICKEN TACOS

I was at my friend's bachelorette party the first time I had a beergarita, and I loved it! It was the inspiration for these delicious chicken tacos. I love that they have traditional taco flavors with a fun twist from the margarita!
—Ashley Lecker, Green Bay, WI

Prep: 20 min. • **Cook:** 2½ hours
Makes: 6 servings

- 1 bottle (12 oz.) Mexican beer or chicken broth
- 1 cup thawed nonalcoholic margarita mix
- 1 can (4 oz.) chopped green chiles, undrained
- 2 Tbsp. lime juice
- 1 tsp. grated lime zest
- 1 tsp. salt
- 1 tsp. garlic powder
- 1 tsp. onion powder
- 1 tsp. chili powder
- ½ tsp. ground cumin
- ½ tsp. pepper
- 1½ lbs. boneless skinless chicken breast halves
- 12 taco shells
  Optional: Shredded pepper jack cheese, minced fresh cilantro, thinly sliced radishes and sour cream

1. Combine the first 11 ingredients in a 3- or 4-qt. slow cooker; top with chicken breast halves. Cook, covered, on low until a thermometer inserted in chicken reads 165°, 2½-3 hours.
2. Remove chicken; shred with 2 forks. Return to slow cooker; heat through. Using a slotted spoon, serve in taco shells with toppings as desired.
Freeze option: Freeze the cooled meat mixture and juices in freezer containers. To use, partially thaw in the refrigerator overnight. Heat through in a saucepan, stirring occasionally; add broth if necessary.
2 tacos: 294 cal., 7g fat (3g sat. fat), 63mg chol., 627mg sod., 32g carb. (16g sugars, 1g fiber), 25g pro.

GREEK SAUSAGE & PEPPERS

This recipe is an old family favorite. My grandmother, mother and I make it every year for Christmas Eve. Just toss all the ingredients in your slow cooker and let the meal cook all day on low. It makes the house smell amazing and is wonderful comfort food for a chilly holiday. You can double the recipe and freeze the other portion for a quick hot meal in the future.
—Debbie Vair, Wake Forest, NC

Prep: 30 min. • **Cook:** 5 hours
Makes: 12 servings

- 4 lbs. Loukaniko or other smoked sausage, cut into ½ in. slices
- 1 each large sweet yellow, orange and red pepper, chopped
- 1 large sweet onion, chopped
- 2 cups beef stock
- 1 whole garlic bulb, minced
- 1 Tbsp. minced fresh oregano or 1 tsp. dried oregano
- 1 tsp. coarse sea salt
- 1 tsp. coarsely ground pepper
- 60 cherry tomatoes
  Hot cooked rice, optional

In a 7- or 8-qt. slow cooker, combine sausage, sweet peppers, onion, stock, garlic, oregano, salt and pepper. Cook, covered, on low until the vegetables are tender, 5-6 hours. Add tomatoes; cook until wilted, about 30 minutes longer. If desired, serve with rice.
1¼ cups: 504 cal., 41g fat (17g sat. fat), 101mg chol., 1958mg sod., 10g carb. (7g sugars, 1g fiber), 23g pro.

CHOCOLATE MALT PUDDING CAKE

PICTURED ON P. 205

When I make this warm, comforting cake, I chop the malted milk balls by putting them in a bag and pounding them with a rubber mallet. Doing this completely eliminates the mess.
—Sarah Skubinna, Cascade, MT

Prep: 25 min. • **Cook:** 2 hours + standing
Makes: 8 servings

- ½ cup 2% milk
- 2 Tbsp. canola oil
- ½ tsp. almond extract
- 1 cup all-purpose flour
- ½ cup packed brown sugar
- 2 Tbsp. baking cocoa
- 1½ tsp. baking powder
- ½ cup coarsely chopped malted milk balls
- ½ cup semisweet chocolate chips
- ¾ cup sugar
- ¼ cup malted milk powder
- 1¼ cups boiling water
- 4 oz. cream cheese, softened and cubed
  Optional: Vanilla ice cream and sliced almonds

1. In a large bowl, combine milk, oil and extract. Combine the flour, brown sugar, cocoa and baking powder; gradually beat into milk mixture until blended. Stir in milk balls and chocolate chips.
2. Spoon into a greased 3-qt. slow cooker. In a small bowl, combine sugar and milk powder; stir in water and cream cheese. Pour over batter (do not stir).
3. Cover and cook on high for 2-3 hours or until a toothpick inserted in center of cake comes out clean. Turn off heat. Let stand 15 minutes. Serve warm. If desired, serve with the ice cream and sprinkle with almonds.

1 serving: 430 cal., 17g fat (8g sat. fat), 19mg chol., 167mg sod., 67g carb. (50g sugars, 2g fiber), 6g pro.

BRAZILIAN PORK & BLACK BEAN STEW

During high school, I spent a year in Brazil and fell in love with the culture and food. One of my favorite dishes was feijoada, a chili/stew served over hot white rice. I introduced my family to this easy recipe, and it has since become one of our most-requested dinners.
—Andrea Romanczyk, Magna, UT

Prep: 15 min. + soaking • **Cook:** 7 hours
Makes: 8 servings

- 1½ cups dried black beans
- 1 lb. smoked kielbasa or Polish sausage, sliced
- 1 lb. boneless country-style pork ribs
- 1 pkg. (12 oz.) fully cooked Spanish chorizo links, sliced
- 1 smoked ham hock
- 1 large onion, chopped
- 3 garlic cloves, minced
- 2 bay leaves
- ¾ tsp. salt
- ½ tsp. pepper
- 5 cups water
  Hot cooked rice

1. Rinse and sort beans; soak according to package directions. Drain and rinse, discarding soaking liquid.
2. In a 6-qt. slow cooker, combine beans with the next 9 ingredients. Add water; cook, covered, on low until meat and beans are tender, 7-9 hours.
3. Remove the pork ribs and ham hock. When cool enough to handle, remove meat from bones; discard bones and bay leaves. Shred meat with 2 forks; return to slow cooker. Serve with hot cooked rice.

Freeze option: Freeze cooled stew in freezer containers. To use, partially thaw in refrigerator overnight. Heat through in a saucepan, stirring occasionally; add water if necessary.

1½ cups: 531 cal., 33g fat (11g sat. fat), 101mg chol., 1069mg sod., 27g carb. (3g sugars, 6g fiber), 33g pro.

BRAZILIAN PORK & BLACK BEAN STEW

CARAMEL & PEAR PUDDING

SLOW-COOKED CREAMY RICE

This wonderful side dish goes well with any entree or stew. I use fresh herbs that I have on hand, along with chopped parsley to add more flavor and color.
—Laura Crane, Leetonia, OH

....

Prep: 25 min. • **Cook:** 2½ hours
Makes: 8 servings

- 3 cups cooked rice
- 2 large eggs, lightly beaten
- 1 can (12 oz.) evaporated milk
- 1 cup shredded Swiss cheese
- 1 cup shredded cheddar cheese
- 1 medium onion, chopped
- ½ cup minced fresh parsley
- 6 Tbsp. water
- 2 Tbsp. canola oil
- 1 garlic clove, minced
- 1½ tsp. salt
- ¼ tsp. pepper

In a 3-qt. slow cooker, combine all the ingredients. Cover and cook on low for 2½-3 hours or until a thermometer reads 160°.
¾ cup: 290 cal., 15g fat (8g sat. fat), 94mg chol., 624mg sod., 24g carb. (6g sugars, 1g fiber), 13g pro.

CARAMEL & PEAR PUDDING

Here's a lovely winter dessert that uses fresh seasonal pears. It is easy to fix and a delightful treat after any meal. I enjoy it while sitting next to the fireplace.
—Diane Halferty, Corpus Christi, TX

....

Prep: 20 min. • **Cook:** 3 hours
Makes: 10 servings

- 1 cup all-purpose flour
- ½ cup sugar
- 1½ tsp. baking powder
- ½ tsp. ground cinnamon
- ¼ tsp. salt
- ⅛ tsp. ground cloves
- ½ cup 2% milk
- 4 medium pears, peeled and cubed
- ½ cup chopped pecans
- ¾ cup packed brown sugar
- ¼ cup butter, softened
- ½ cup boiling water
  Vanilla ice cream, optional

1. In a large bowl, combine flour, sugar, baking powder, cinnamon, salt and cloves. Stir in milk until smooth. Add pears and pecans. Spread evenly into a 3-qt. slow cooker coated with cooking spray.
2. In a small bowl, combine brown sugar and butter; stir in boiling water. Pour over batter (do not stir). Cover and cook on low for 3-4 hours or until pears are tender. Serve warm, with ice cream if desired.
½ cup: 274 cal., 9g fat (3g sat. fat), 13mg chol., 164mg sod., 47g carb. (33g sugars, 3g fiber), 3g pro.

SLOW-COOKED MAC & CHEESE

Slow-cooked mac and cheese—the words alone are enough to make mouths water. And this is the classic at its best: rich and extra cheesy. The slow cooker makes it so easy.
—Shelby Molina, Whitewater, WI

Prep: 25 min. • **Cook:** 2½ hours
Makes: 9 servings

- 2 cups uncooked elbow macaroni
- 1 can (12 oz.) evaporated milk
- 1½ cups whole milk
- 2 large eggs
- ¼ cup butter, melted
- 1 tsp. salt
- 2½ cups shredded cheddar cheese
- 2½ cups shredded sharp cheddar cheese, divided

1. Cook macaroni according to package directions; drain and rinse in cold water. In a large bowl, combine the evaporated milk, milk, eggs, butter and salt. Stir in the cheddar cheese, 2 cups sharp cheddar cheese and macaroni.
2. Transfer to a greased 3-qt. slow cooker. Cover and cook on low for 2½-3 hours or until center is set, stirring once. Sprinkle with remaining sharp cheddar cheese.

¾ cup: 415 cal., 28g fat (20g sat. fat), 143mg chol., 745mg sod., 20g carb. (6g sugars, 1g fiber), 21g pro.

SLOW-COOKER MIXED FRUIT & PISTACHIO CAKE

SLOW-COOKER MIXED FRUIT & PISTACHIO CAKE

This cake is easy to whip up on a lazy day and is a guaranteed delicious dessert that can be enjoyed for several days—if you can make it last that long! It's perfect for fall and the holidays.
—Nancy Heishman, Las Vegas, NV

Prep: 20 min. • **Cook:** 2½ hours + cooling
Makes: 8 servings

- 1½ cups all-purpose flour
- 1½ tsp. ground cinnamon
- ½ tsp. baking soda
- ½ tsp. baking powder
- ½ tsp. ground allspice
- ¼ tsp. salt
- 1 can (8 oz.) jellied cranberry sauce
- ⅓ cup packed brown sugar
- ⅓ cup buttermilk
- ¼ cup butter, melted
- 2 tsp. grated orange zest
- ½ tsp. orange extract
- 1 large egg, room temperature
- 1 cup mixed dried fruit bits
- 1 cup pistachios
  Sweetened whipped cream, optional

1. In a large bowl, whisk together the first 6 ingredients. In another bowl, combine the next 7 ingredients. Add the cranberry mixture to flour mixture; stir until smooth. Add the dried fruit and pistachios.
2. Pour the batter into a greased 1½-qt. baking dish; place in a 6-qt. slow cooker. Lay a 14x12-in. piece of parchment over top of slow cooker under the lid. Cook, covered, on high until a toothpick inserted in the center comes out clean, about 2½ hours. Remove dish from slow cooker to a wire rack. Cool 30 minutes before inverting onto a serving platter.
3. Cut into wedges with a serrated knife; if desired, serve with sweetened whipped cream.

1 slice: 375 cal., 14g fat (5g sat. fat), 39mg chol., 349mg sod., 57g carb. (30g sugars, 4g fiber), 7g pro.

SLOW-COOKER ASEAN SHORT RIBS

My slow cooker is my best friend. I use it at least three times a week. This recipe is one of my favorites. The sauce can be used for other cuts of meat, too.
—Carole Resnick, Cleveland, OH

Prep: 15 min. • **Cook:** 6 hours
Makes: 6 servings

¾ cup sugar
¾ cup ketchup
¾ cup reduced-sodium soy sauce
⅓ cup honey
¼ cup lemon juice
3 Tbsp. hoisin sauce
1 Tbsp. ground ginger
2 garlic cloves, minced
4 lbs. bone-in beef short ribs
  Optional: Sesame seeds and chopped green onions

In a greased 4- or 5-qt. slow cooker, whisk together the first 8 ingredients. Add short ribs and turn to coat; cook, covered, on low until the meat is tender, 6-7 hours. If desired, serve with sesame seeds and green onions.
1 serving: 460 cal., 15g fat (6g sat. fat), 73mg chol., 1706mg sod., 56g carb. (51g sugars, 0 fiber), 27g pro.

SLOW-COOKER CHICKEN BOG
PICTURED ON P. 205

Chicken bog is a South Carolina tradition with lots of variations on herbs, spices and fresh vegetables, but the key ingredients remain: sausage, chicken and rice. This slow-cooked rendition is a simple take on the classic.
—Anna Hanson, Spanish Fork, UT

Prep: 20 min. • **Cook:** 4 hours
Makes: 6 servings

1 Tbsp. canola oil
1 medium onion, chopped
8 oz. smoked sausage, halved and sliced ½-in. thick
3 garlic cloves, minced
5 cups chicken broth, divided
2 cups uncooked converted rice
1 tsp. salt
1 tsp. pepper
1 rotisserie chicken (about 3 lbs.), meat removed and shredded
  Thinly sliced green onions, optional
  Hot sauce

1. In a large skillet, heat oil over medium heat. Add onion and sausage; cook until sausage is lightly browned. Add garlic and cook 1 minute longer; transfer to a 5-qt. slow cooker.
2. Stir in 4 cups broth, rice, salt and pepper. Cook, covered, on low until rice is tender, 4-5 hours. Stir in chicken and remaining broth. Cook, covered, on low until chicken is heated through, about 30 minutes. If desired, sprinkle with green onions. Serve with hot sauce.
Freeze option: Omitting the green onions and hot sauce, freeze cooled meat mixture, juices and rice in freezer containers. To use, partially thaw in the refrigerator overnight. Microwave, covered, on high until heated through, stirring gently; add broth or water if necessary.
1⅓ cups: 681 cal., 30g fat (9g sat. fat), 134mg chol., 1728mg sod., 54g carb. (3g sugars, 0 fiber), 45g pro.

SLOW-COOKER ASIAN SHORT RIBS

COMFORTING BARLEY & PUMPKIN BEEF STEW

COMFORTING BARLEY & PUMPKIN BEEF STEW

There's nothing more comforting than a bowl of beef stew—unless, of course, it's a bowl of steaming hot beef stew loaded with lots and lots of barley. Now this is comfort food—a bowl of stew robust enough to be a meal on its own. Rinsing the barley will help remove any dust, dirt or debris.
—*Colleen Delawder, Herndon, VA*

Prep: 30 min. • **Cook:** 6 hours
Makes: 9 servings (3½ qt.)

- ¼ cup all-purpose flour
- 3 Tbsp. cornstarch
- 1½ tsp. salt, divided
- 1½ tsp. pepper, divided
- 1½ lbs. beef stew meat
- 3 Tbsp. olive oil
- 1 large sweet onion, finely chopped
- 2 cartons (32 oz. each) beef broth
- 1 can (15 oz.) pumpkin
- 1 cup medium pearl barley
- 1 tsp. dried thyme
- ¼ tsp. garlic powder
- ¼ tsp. crushed red pepper flakes
  Optional: Additional red pepper flakes and minced fresh parsley

1. In a shallow dish, mix flour, cornstarch, 1 tsp. salt and 1 tsp. pepper. Add beef, a few pieces at a time, and toss to coat. In a large skillet, heat oil over medium-high heat; brown meat in batches. Transfer meat to a 5- or 6-qt. slow cooker. In the same skillet, cook and stir onion in drippings until tender, 6-8 minutes; add to slow cooker.

2. Stir in the broth, pumpkin, barley, thyme, garlic powder and red pepper flakes. Cook, covered, on low until meat is tender, 6-8 hours. If desired, serve with additional red pepper flakes and parsley.
1½ cups: 211 cal., 8g fat (2g sat. fat), 35mg chol., 819mg sod., 20g carb. (3g sugars, 4g fiber), 15g pro. **Diabetic exchanges:** 2 lean meat, 1 starch, 1 fat.

SLOW-COOKED WILD RICE

SLOW-COOKED WILD RICE

This recipe has become such a family heirloom that I asked permission from my mother before passing it along. It has traveled to weddings, baptisms, landmark birthdays and wedding anniversaries— and it always makes people happy.
—*Janet Mahowald, Rice Lake, WI*

Prep: 15 min. • **Cook:** 4 hours
Makes: 8 cups

- 1 lb. bulk pork sausage
- 4 celery ribs, chopped
- 1 small onion, chopped
- 1 can (10¾ oz.) condensed cream of mushroom soup, undiluted
- 1 can (10¾ oz.) condensed cream of chicken soup, undiluted
- 1 cup uncooked wild rice
- 1 can (4 oz.) mushroom stems and pieces, drained
- 3 cups chicken broth

1. In a large skillet, cook and crumble sausage with celery and onion over medium heat until the sausage is no longer pink and vegetables are tender, 6-8 minutes; drain. Transfer to a 3-qt. slow cooker. Add the soups, rice and mushrooms. Stir in broth.

2. Cook, covered, on low until rice is tender, 4-5 hours.
¾ cup: 236 cal., 14g fat (4g sat. fat), 30mg chol., 1059mg sod., 19g carb. (2g sugars, 2g fiber), 9g pro.

SLOW-COOKER SENSATIONS

MEDITERRANEAN SLOW-COOKER MASHED POTATOES

I love the convenience of cooking meals in my slow cooker. These no-fuss mashed potatoes are the perfect side dish to my special Sunday meat loaf.
—Kristen Heigl, Staten Island, NY

Prep: 20 min. • **Cook:** 2 hours
Makes: 10 servings

- 4 lbs. red potatoes, cubed
- 1 cup sour cream
- ½ cup butter, softened
- 3 garlic cloves, minced
- 2 Tbsp. snipped fresh dill
- ¾ tsp. salt
- ½ tsp. pepper
- 1 cup crumbled feta cheese

Place potatoes in a 6-qt. stockpot; add water to cover. Bring to a boil. Reduce the heat; cook, uncovered, until potatoes are tender, 10-15 minutes. Drain and coarsely mash. Combine the next 6 ingredients in a greased 5-qt. slow cooker; stir in the mashed potatoes and feta until well combined. Cook, covered, on low until heated through, 2-3 hours.
¾ cup: 287 cal., 15g fat (10g sat. fat), 46mg chol., 377mg sod., 30g carb. (3g sugars, 4g fiber), 6g pro.

SLOW-COOKER CHERRY PEAR BUCKLE

SLOW-COOKER CHERRY PEAR BUCKLE

I added pears to my cherry cobbler recipe to create this delightful slow-cooked buckle. You could also add fresh summer plums and berries to your cherries. You'll love this old-fashioned, pretty dessert.
—Mary Anne Thygesen, Portland, OR

Prep: 20 min. • **Cook:** 4½ hours
Makes: 8 servings

- 6 medium pears, peeled and sliced
- 4 cups fresh or frozen pitted dark sweet cherries, thawed
- 1 cup sugar
- ¼ cup tapioca flour
- 1¾ cups all-purpose flour
- ¼ cup old-fashioned oats
- 3 tsp. baking powder
- ½ tsp. salt
- ¼ cup cold butter
- ¾ cup 2% milk
- 2 tsp. cinnamon sugar
   Sweetened whipped cream

1. Line the inside of a 5-qt. slow cooker with a double thickness of heavy-duty foil; spray the foil with cooking spray. In a large bowl, combine pears, cherries, sugar and tapioca flour; spoon into slow cooker. Cook, covered, on high 4-5 hours or until bubbly.
2. Meanwhile, combine flour, oats, baking powder and salt. Cut in the butter until crumbly. Stir in the milk. Drop batter by tablespoonfuls over pear mixture; sprinkle with cinnamon sugar. Cover and cook until a toothpick inserted in center of topping comes out clean, 30-45 minutes longer. Serve with whipped cream.
1 serving: 411 cal., 7g fat (4g sat. fat), 17mg chol., 386mg sod., 86g carb. (48g sugars, 6g fiber), 5g pro.

MEXICAN PORK & HOMINY STEW

This stew, also known as pozole, is a delicious southwestern delicacy. I moved it to the slow cooker so it can simmer away on its own. The rich, brothy soup is delicious, much like a tamale in a bowl.
—Joan Hallford, North Richland Hills, TX

Prep: 30 min. • **Cook:** 6 hours
Makes: 8 servings (2¾ qt.)

- 2 cups water
- 1 large poblano pepper, seeded and chopped
- 1 jalapeno pepper, seeded and chopped
- 1 can (14½ oz.) fire-roasted diced tomatoes, undrained
- 1 medium onion, chopped
- 4 garlic cloves, minced
- 2 tsp. ground cumin
- ½ tsp. dried oregano
- 2 lbs. boneless country-style pork ribs, cubed
- 1 can (29 oz.) hominy, rinsed and drained
- 2 cups reduced-sodium chicken broth
- 1 Tbsp. lime juice
- 1 tsp. kosher salt
- ¼ tsp. pepper
  Optional: Fried tortillas, cubed avocado, sliced radishes, lime wedges and minced cilantro

1. In a small saucepan, combine water, poblano and jalapeno. Bring to a boil. Reduce heat; simmer until tender, about 10 minutes. Remove from the heat; cool slightly. Place the mixture in a blender. Add tomatoes, onion, garlic, cumin and oregano; cover and process until smooth.
2. Transfer to a 5- or 6-qt. slow cooker. Stir in the pork, hominy, broth, lime juice, kosher salt and pepper. Cook, covered, on low 6-8 hours or until pork is tender. If desired, serve with optional ingredients.

Freeze option: Freeze cooled stew in freezer containers. To use, partially thaw in refrigerator overnight. Heat through in a saucepan, stirring occasionally; add a little broth if necessary.

1⅓ cups: 257 cal., 10g fat (4g sat. fat), 65mg chol., 1005mg sod., 16g carb. (3g sugars, 4g fiber), 22g pro.

MEXICAN PORK & HOMINY STEW

SLOW-COOKER SENSATIONS

SPICED SWEET POTATO PUDDING

One of my favorite fall desserts, this treat's rich flavors are well-suited to the chillier months. I like to serve it over a slice of pound cake or a scoop of vanilla ice cream.
—Aysha Schurman, Ammon, ID

Prep: 15 min. • **Cook:** 3 hours
Makes: 7 servings

- 2 cans (15¾ oz. each) sweet potatoes, drained and mashed
- 3 large eggs
- 1 can (12 oz.) evaporated milk
- ⅔ cup biscuit/baking mix
- ½ cup packed brown sugar
- ½ cup apple butter
- 2 Tbsp. butter, softened
- 2 tsp. vanilla extract
- ⅓ cup finely chopped pecans
  Pound cake, optional

In a large bowl, beat the first 8 ingredients until well-blended. Pour into a greased 3-qt. slow cooker. Sprinkle with pecans. Cover and cook on low for 3-4 hours or until a thermometer reads 160°. Serve with pound cake if desired.
¾ cup: 418 cal., 15g fat (6g sat. fat), 115mg chol., 309mg sod., 64g carb. (45g sugars, 4g fiber), 8g pro.

SPICE TRADE BEANS & BULGUR

SPICE TRADE BEANS & BULGUR

A rich blend of spices adds flavor to tender, nutritious bulgur and garbanzo beans in this tangy stew that has just the right amount of heat. A hint of sweetness from golden raisins is the perfect accent.
—Faith Cromwell, San Francisco, CA

Prep: 30 min. • **Cook:** 3½ hours
Makes: 10 servings

- 3 Tbsp. canola oil, divided
- 2 medium onions, chopped
- 1 medium sweet red pepper, chopped
- 5 garlic cloves, minced
- 1 Tbsp. ground cumin
- 1 Tbsp. paprika
- 2 tsp. ground ginger
- 1 tsp. pepper
- ½ tsp. ground cinnamon
- ½ tsp. cayenne pepper
- 1½ cups bulgur
- 1 can (28 oz.) crushed tomatoes
- 1 can (14½ oz.) diced tomatoes, undrained
- 1 carton (32 oz.) vegetable broth
- 2 Tbsp. brown sugar
- 2 Tbsp. soy sauce
- 1 can (15 oz.) garbanzo beans or chickpeas, rinsed and drained
- ½ cup golden raisins
  Minced fresh cilantro, optional

1. In a large skillet, heat 2 Tbsp. oil over medium-high heat. Add the onions and pepper; cook and stir until tender, 3-4 minutes. Add garlic and seasonings; cook 1 minute longer. Transfer to a 5-qt. slow cooker.
2. In the same skillet, heat remaining oil over medium-high heat. Add bulgur; cook and stir until lightly browned, 2-3 minutes.
3. Add bulgur, tomatoes, broth, brown sugar and soy sauce to slow cooker. Cook, covered, on low 3-4 hours or until bulgur is tender. Stir in beans and raisins; cook 30 minutes longer. If desired, sprinkle with cilantro.
1¼ cups: 245 cal., 6g fat (0 sat. fat), 0 chol., 752mg sod., 45g carb. (15g sugars, 8g fiber), 8g pro.

INDULGENT COCONUT RICE PUDDING

This slow-cooked winter comfort dessert is a healthier option for your family that doesn't sacrifice flavor. If you can't find turbinado or raw sugar, you can use brown sugar, adjusting to ¾ cup. This pudding can also be made in the oven.
—Teri Rasey, Cadillac, MI

Prep: 10 min. • **Cook:** 4 hours
Makes: 12 servings

- 1 cup uncooked long grain rice
- 5 cups coconut milk, divided
- 2 Tbsp. coconut oil
- 1 cup turbinado (washed raw) sugar
- 1 cup dried cranberries
- 2 tsp. vanilla extract
- 1 tsp. ground cinnamon
  Dash salt
  Optional: Toasted sweetened shredded coconut and additional coconut milk

1. Place rice in a 3- or 4-qt. slow cooker coated with cooking spray; pour in 4 cups coconut milk. Add coconut oil; distribute evenly over top. Add next 5 ingredients.
2. Cook, covered, on low until the rice is tender, 4-5 hours, adding enough of the remaining coconut milk to reach desired consistency. Let stand, uncovered, for 10 minutes. Serve warm, with toasted coconut and additional coconut milk if desired.

½ cup: 340 cal., 18g fat (17g sat. fat), 0 chol., 39mg sod., 43g carb. (28g sugars, 1g fiber), 3g pro.

TEST KITCHEN TIPS
Give it some crunch by topping it with slivered almonds, chopped walnuts or hazelnuts. For the ultimate winter morning comfort food, let the pudding cook overnight, then top it with fresh bananas right before serving.

GREEK-STYLE CHICKEN WITH GREEN BEANS
PICTURED ON P. 205

My Greek grandmother used to make the most delicious, melt-in-your-mouth Greek-style green beans with a lemon-tomato flavor. Whenever I make this slow-cooker recipe, I think of her. The juices from the chicken help flavor the green beans, but the beans can be prepared alone as a side dish without the chicken.
—Elizabeth Lindemann, Driftwood, TX

Prep: 20 min. • **Cook:** 4 hours
Makes: 4 servings

- 1 lb. fresh green beans, trimmed
- 2 large tomatoes, chopped
- 1 medium onion, chopped
- 1 cup chicken broth
- ¼ cup snipped fresh dill
- 2 to 3 Tbsp. lemon juice
- 2 garlic cloves, minced
- 4 bone-in chicken thighs (about 1½ lbs.)
- 1 Tbsp. olive oil
- ¾ tsp. salt
- ¼ tsp. pepper
  Optional: Lemon wedges and additional snipped fresh dill

1. Combine the first 7 ingredients in a 5- or 6-qt. slow cooker. Top with chicken. Drizzle with oil; sprinkle with salt and pepper. Cook, covered, on low until a thermometer inserted in chicken reads 170°-175°, 4-6 hours.
2. Preheat broiler. Place the chicken on a greased rack in a broiler pan. Broil 4-6 in. from heat until golden brown, 3-4 minutes. Serve with bean mixture and, if desired, lemon wedges and additional fresh dill.

1 serving: 324 cal., 18g fat (5g sat. fat), 82mg chol., 769mg sod., 16g carb. (7g sugars, 6g fiber), 26g pro.

INDULGENT COCONUT RICE PUDDING

HOT OFF THE GRILL

When the sun comes out and temperatures rise, these recipes will give you what you need for the perfect backyard barbecue! And when the weather turns colder, you can recapture the spirit of summer using a broiler or a grill pan.

BLACKOUT PEACH BREAD PUDDING

PICTURED ON P. 223

I bake several times a week so my kids have homemade desserts. We lost power in a storm, so I used the grill to invent this blackout pudding.
—Tina Zaccardi, Eastchester, NY

Prep: 30 min. • **Grill:** 15 min.
Makes: 6 servings

- 4 large egg yolks
- 1 cup whole milk
- ⅓ cup sugar
- ¼ cup mascarpone cheese
- ½ tsp. ground cinnamon
- 2 medium peaches, halved and pitted
- 1 Tbsp. butter, melted
- 4 potato dinner rolls, halved
- 2 Tbsp. brown sugar
- ½ cup caramel sundae syrup
  Sweetened whipped cream, optional

1. In a small bowl, whisk first 5 ingredients until blended; refrigerate until assembling.
2. Brush the peaches with butter. Grill, covered, on an oiled rack over medium heat or broil 4 in. from heat until lightly browned, 5-6 minutes, turning once. Grill rolls, uncovered, until lightly browned, 3-4 minutes, turning once. Cool slightly. Cut peaches and rolls into ¾-in. cubes.
3. In a large bowl, combine peaches and brown sugar; stir in bread cubes. Spoon into 12 well-greased disposable aluminum muffin cups. Pour the egg mixture into muffin cups.
4. Grill, covered, over indirect high heat for 12-15 minutes or until a thermometer reads at least 160°. Cool in pan 5 minutes before removing. Serve with caramel syrup and, if desired, whipped cream.
1 serving: 386 cal., 16g fat (8g sat.fat), 155mg chol., 250mg sod., 55g carb. (37g sugars, 2g fiber), 8g pro.

TEST KITCHEN TIPS
If you don't have potato dinner rolls, substitute any leftover white bread or rolls. Substitute canned peaches for fresh if peaches are out of season.

GRILLED VEGGIE PIZZA

I came up with this recipe one summer as a way to use the many vegetables from our garden. Grilling the veggies first brings out their flavors. Try sprinkling on some olives or pine nuts before adding cheese.
—Susan Marshall, Colorado Springs, CO

Prep: 30 min. • **Bake:** 10 min.
Makes: 6 servings

- 8 small fresh mushrooms, halved
- 1 small zucchini, cut into ¼-in. slices
- 1 small sweet yellow pepper, sliced
- 1 small sweet red pepper, sliced
- 1 small onion, sliced
- 1 Tbsp. white wine vinegar
- 1 Tbsp. water
- 4 tsp. olive oil, divided
- 2 tsp. minced fresh basil or ½ tsp. dried basil
- ¼ tsp. salt
- ¼ tsp. pepper
- 1 prebaked 12-in. thin whole wheat pizza crust
- 1 can (8 oz.) pizza sauce
- 2 small tomatoes, chopped
- 2 cups shredded part-skim mozzarella cheese

1. In a large bowl, combine the halved mushrooms, zucchini, peppers, onion, wine vinegar, water, 3 tsp. olive oil, basil, salt and pepper. Transfer to a grill wok or basket. Grill, covered, over medium heat for 8-10 minutes or until tender, stirring once.
2. Prepare grill for indirect heat. Brush crust with the remaining oil; spread with pizza sauce. Top with grilled vegetables, tomatoes and cheese.
3. Grill, covered, over indirect medium heat for 10-12 minutes or until edges are lightly browned and cheese is melted. Rotate pizza halfway through cooking to ensure evenly browned crust.
1 slice: 274 cal., 11g fat (5g sat. fat), 22mg chol., 634mg sod., 30g carb. (6g sugars, 5g fiber), 17g pro. **Diabetic exchanges:** 2 starch, 2 medium-fat meat, 1 vegetable.

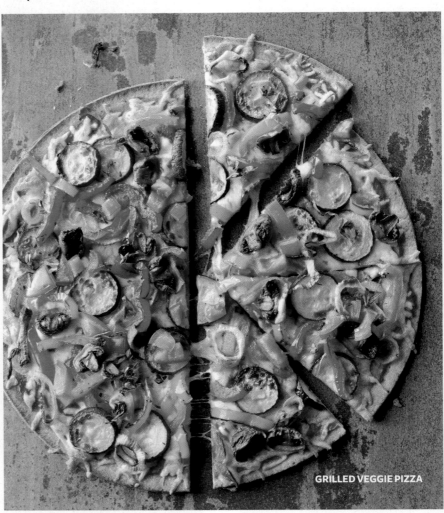

GRILLED VEGGIE PIZZA

TUNA TERIYAKI KABOBS

GRILLED CHICKEN RANCH BURGERS

This is one of the most fantastic, flavorful burgers I have ever made. Ranch is one of our favorites in dips and dressings, and believe me, it doesn't disappoint in these burgers, either!
—Kari Shifflett, Lake Mills, IA

Prep: 15 min. + chilling • **Grill:** 10 min.
Makes: 16 servings

- ¾ cup ranch salad dressing
- ¾ cup panko bread crumbs
- ¾ cup grated Parmesan cheese
- 3 Tbsp. Worcestershire sauce
- 3 garlic cloves, minced
- 3 tsp. pepper
- 4 lbs. ground chicken
- 3 Tbsp. olive oil
- 16 hamburger buns, split
  Optional: Tomato slices, lettuce leaves, sliced red onion, sliced cucumber, sliced avocado and ranch dip

1. In a large bowl, mix first 6 ingredients. Add chicken; mix lightly but thoroughly. Shape mixture into sixteen ½-in.-thick patties. Brush both sides with olive oil; refrigerate, covered, for 15 minutes to allow the patties to firm up.
2. Grill burgers, covered, over medium heat or broil 3-4 in. from heat 5-6 minutes on each side or until a thermometer reads 165°. Serve on hamburger buns with desired toppings.
1 burger: 371 cal., 19g fat (5g sat. fat), 79mg chol., 498mg sod., 26g carb. (4g sugars, 1g fiber), 24g pro.

🍎
TUNA TERIYAKI KABOBS

I love to barbecue but don't always want a heavy dinner. These are perfect in the spring, and you'll have room for dessert!
—Holly Battiste, Barrington, NJ

Prep: 25 min. + marinating
Grill: 15 min. • **Makes:** 8 kabobs

- 1½ lbs. tuna steaks, cut into 1½-in. chunks
- 2 medium sweet red peppers, cut into 1-in. pieces
- 1 large sweet onion, cut into 1-in. pieces

MARINADE/DRESSING
- ¼ cup minced fresh cilantro
- ¼ cup sesame oil
- 3 Tbsp. lime juice
- 2 Tbsp. soy sauce
- 2 Tbsp. extra virgin olive oil
- 1 Tbsp. minced fresh gingerroot
- 2 garlic cloves, minced

SALAD
- 1 pkg. (5 oz.) fresh baby spinach
- 1 medium sweet yellow pepper, cut into 1-in. pieces
- 8 cherry tomatoes, halved

1. Thread tuna chunks onto 4 metal or soaked wooden skewers. Thread pepper and onion pieces onto 4 more skewers. Place skewers in a 13x9-in. baking dish.
2. Whisk together marinade ingredients. Reserve half the mixture for salad dressing. Pour remaining marinade over skewers; refrigerate, covered, 30 minutes.
3. Grill kabobs, covered, on a greased grill rack over medium heat, turning occasionally, until tuna is slightly pink in center for medium-rare (2-3 minutes per side) and vegetables are crisp-tender (10-12 minutes). Remove tuna kabobs from direct heat and keep warm while vegetables finish grilling.
4. For salad, toss spinach, yellow pepper and cherry tomatoes with the reserved dressing. For each portion, serve a tuna kabob and a vegetable kabob over salad.
2 kabobs: 389 cal., 16g fat (2g sat. fat), 66mg chol., 444mg sod., 15g carb. (9g sugars, 4g fiber), 45g pro. **Diabetic exchanges:** 5 lean meat, 2 vegetable, 2 fat.

⑤ GRILLED MAPLE PORK CHOPS

Pork chops on the grill are hard to beat.
The marinade is simple, and so good.
—Nicholas King, Duluth, MN

Prep: 5 min. + marinating. • **Grill:** 15 min.
Makes: 4 servings

- 6 Tbsp. maple syrup
- 6 Tbsp. balsamic vinegar
- ¾ tsp. salt
- ¾ tsp. coarsely ground pepper
- 4 boneless pork loin chops
  (1½ in. thick and 12 oz. each)

1. In a small bowl, whisk syrup, vinegar, salt and pepper until blended. Pour ½ cup of the marinade into a shallow bowl. Add pork chops and turn to coat. Cover and refrigerate 1 hour. Reserve the remaining marinade for basting.
2. Drain pork chops, discarding marinade. On an oiled grill, cook chops, covered, over medium heat or broil 4 in. from heat for 13-17 minutes or until a thermometer reads 145°, turning occasionally and basting with reserved marinade during the last 5 minutes. Let stand 5 minutes before serving.
1 pork chop: 509 cal., 19g fat (7g sat. fat), 164mg chol., 339mg sod., 15g carb. (14g sugars, 0 fiber), 65g pro.

SOUVLAKI PITA POCKETS

🍎 SOUVLAKI PITA POCKETS

This is a favorite at our house—especially in summer. A quick trip to the market for a few ingredients results in gourmet-style Greek sandwiches we enjoy outdoors by the grill. A simple Greek salad on the side is a nice addition.
—Becky Drees, Pittsfield, MA

Prep: 20 min. + marinating • **Grill:** 10 min.
Makes: 6 servings

- 4 medium lemons, divided
- 4 Tbsp. olive oil
- 4 garlic cloves, minced
- 2 tsp. dried oregano
- ½ tsp. salt
- ¼ tsp. pepper
- 2 lbs. boneless skinless chicken breasts, cut into 1-in. pieces
- 12 pita pocket halves
- 1 carton (8 oz.) refrigerated tzatziki sauce

Optional toppings: Chopped tomatoes, sliced cucumber and sliced red onion

1. Cut 3 of the lemons in half crosswise; squeeze juice from lemons. Transfer to a large bowl or shallow dish. Whisk in oil, garlic, oregano, salt and pepper. Add chicken; turn to coat. Refrigerate 1 hour.
2. Drain chicken, discarding marinade. Thinly slice remaining lemon. On 6 metal or soaked wooden skewers, alternately thread chicken and lemon slices. Grill kabobs, covered, over medium heat or broil 4 in. from heat until chicken is no longer pink, turning occasionally.
3. Remove chicken from kabobs; discard the lemon slices. Serve chicken in pita pockets with tzatziki sauce and toppings of your choice.
2 filled pita halves: 369 cal., 8g fat (2g sat. fat), 90mg chol., 462mg sod., 34g carb. (2g sugars, 1g fiber), 37g pro. **Diabetic exchanges:** 5 lean meat, 2 starch, 1 fat.

JALAPENO POPPER MEXICAN STREET CORN

One of the best things about summer is fresh sweet corn, and this recipe is a definite standout. We love its creamy dressing, crunchy panko coating and spicy jalapeno kick. If you're really feeling wild, sprinkle each serving with a bit of cooked and crumbled bacon!

—Crystal Schlueter, Northglenn, CO

Takes: 30 min. • **Makes:** 4 servings

- 4 ears fresh sweet corn, husked
- 2 jalapeno peppers
- 3 Tbsp. canola oil, divided
- ¾ tsp. salt, divided
- ¼ cup panko bread crumbs
- ½ tsp. smoked paprika
- ½ tsp. dried Mexican oregano
- 4 oz. cream cheese, softened
- ¼ cup media crema table cream or sour cream thinned with 1 tsp. 2% milk
- 2 Tbsp. lime juice
  Ground chipotle pepper or chili powder
  Optional: Chopped fresh cilantro and lime wedges

1. Rub corn and jalapenos with 2 Tbsp. canola oil. Grill, covered, on an oiled grill rack over medium-high direct heat until lightly charred on all sides, 10-12 minutes. Remove from heat. When jalapenos are cool enough to handle, remove skin, seeds and membranes; chop finely. Set aside.

2. Sprinkle corn with ½ tsp. salt. In a small skillet, heat the remaining oil over medium heat. Add panko; cook and stir until starting to brown. Add paprika and oregano; cook until crumbs are toasted and fragrant.

3. Meanwhile, combine cream cheese, crema, lime juice and remaining salt; spread over corn. Sprinkle with crumbs, jalapenos and chipotle. If desired, sprinkle with cilantro and serve with lime wedges.

1 ear of corn: 339 cal., 26g fat (9g sat. fat), 39mg chol., 568mg sod., 25g carb. (8g sugars, 3g fiber), 6g pro.

READER REVIEW

"Wow! What a neat way to jazz up corn on the cob! I have no grill, so used the broiler in my oven to cook the corn."

BEEMA, TASTEOFHOME.COM

JALAPENO POPPER
MEXICAN STREET CORN

CARIBBEAN CHICKEN

SCRUM-DELICIOUS BURGERS

I'm not sure where this recipe originated, but it's one of my family's summertime favorites. I usually serve these juicy burgers when we have company. The guests rave about the flavorful cheesy topping. It's fun to serve a burger that's a little special.
—Wendy Sommers, West Chicago, IL

Takes: 30 min. • **Makes:** 6 servings

- 1½ lbs. ground beef
- 3 Tbsp. finely chopped onion
- ½ tsp. garlic salt
- ½ tsp. pepper
- 1 cup shredded cheddar cheese
- ⅓ cup canned sliced mushrooms
- 6 bacon strips, cooked and crumbled
- ¼ cup mayonnaise
- 6 hamburger buns, split
  Optional: Lettuce leaves and sliced tomato

1. In a large bowl, combine the beef, onion, garlic salt and pepper. Shape into 6 patties, ¾ in. thick.
2. In a small bowl, combine the cheese, mushrooms, bacon and mayonnaise; chill.
3. Grill burgers, covered, over medium heat for 5-7 minutes on each side or until a thermometer reads 160°. During the last 3 minutes, spoon ¼ cup cheese mixture onto each burger. Serve on buns, with lettuce and tomato if desired.
1 burger: 480 cal., 29g fat (12g sat. fat), 86mg chol., 778mg sod., 23g carb. (4g sugars, 2g fiber), 30g pro.

TEST KITCHEN TIP
Using lean ground beef instead of beef that's 80% lean saves 45 calories per 4-oz. serving of beef. Lean ground beef is also 29% lower in saturated fat.

CARIBBEAN CHICKEN

You'd be hard-pressed to find a marinade this flavorful at any store! Add more or fewer jalapenos to suit your crew's taste, and you'll be grilling a new family favorite before you know it.
—Rusty Collins, Orlando, FL

Prep: 15 min. + marinating • **Grill:** 10 min.
Makes: 6 servings

- ½ cup lemon juice
- ⅓ cup honey
- 3 Tbsp. canola oil
- 6 green onions, sliced
- 3 jalapeno peppers, seeded and chopped
- 3 tsp. dried thyme
- ¾ tsp. salt
- ¼ tsp. ground allspice
- ¼ tsp. ground nutmeg
- 6 boneless skinless chicken breast halves (4 oz. each)

1. In a blender, combine the first 9 ingredients; cover and process until smooth. Pour ½ cup into a small bowl for basting; cover and refrigerate. Pour remaining marinade into a bowl or shallow dish. Add the chicken and turn to coat; cover and refrigerate for up to 6 hours.
2. Drain chicken, discarding marinade in the bowl. On a greased grill rack, grill chicken, covered, over medium heat or broil 4 in. from the heat for 4-6 minutes on each side, until a thermometer reads 165°, basting frequently with the reserved marinade.
1 chicken breast half: 186 cal., 6g fat (1g sat. fat), 63mg chol., 204mg sod., 9g carb. (8g sugars, 0 fiber), 23g pro. **Diabetic exchanges:** 3 lean meat, ½ starch, ½ fat.

GRILLED VEGETABLE SALAD WITH POPPY SEED DRESSING

PICTURED ON P. 223

My Italian-style grilled veggies have a wonderful sweet and sour dressing. Best of all, I pick the fresh veggies and herbs from my garden.
—Laura Mast, Defiance, OH

Takes: 25 min. • **Makes:** 2 servings

- 2 Tbsp. canola oil
- 1 Tbsp. cider vinegar
- 2 tsp. sugar
- ½ tsp. grated onion
- ½ tsp. poppy seeds
- ¼ tsp. ground mustard
  Dash salt

SALAD

- 1 small zucchini, cut into ¾-in. pieces
- 1 small sweet yellow pepper, cut into 1-in. pieces
- ⅔ cup cherry tomatoes
- 2 tsp. olive oil
- ¼ tsp. salt
- ⅛ tsp. freshly ground pepper
- 2 tsp. minced fresh basil
- 2 tsp. minced fresh parsley
- 1 tsp. minced fresh thyme

1. In a small bowl, whisk the first 7 ingredients until blended. Refrigerate until ready to serve.

2. In a large bowl, combine the zucchini, yellow pepper and tomatoes. Add oil, salt and pepper; toss to coat. Transfer to a grill wok or an open grill basket; place on grill rack. Grill, covered, over medium-high heat 10-12 minutes or until vegetables are crisp-tender, stirring occasionally.

3. Transfer vegetables to a serving bowl; sprinkle with herbs. Serve with dressing.

1 cup: 219 cal., 19g fat (2g sat. fat), 0 chol., 378mg sod., 11g carb. (8g sugars, 2g fiber), 2g pro.

> **TEST KITCHEN TIP**
> If you do not have a grill wok or basket, use a disposable foil pan. Poke holes in the bottom of the pan with a meat fork to allow the liquid to drain.

GINGER POUND CAKE S'MORES

Kids love this knockoff of the classic campfire dessert, and adults do, too. It's so easy to prepare, and any kind of chocolate can be used. You can also make these in batches in a cast-iron skillet.
—Peter Halferty, Corpus Christi, TX

Takes: 20 min. • **Makes:** 8 servings

- 8 large marshmallows
- 5 oz. bittersweet chocolate candy bars, broken into 8 pieces
- 8 tsp. crystallized ginger
- 16 slices pound cake (¼ in. thick)
- 3 Tbsp. butter, softened

1. Cut each marshmallow lengthwise into 4 slices. Place a chocolate piece, 4 marshmallow slices and 1 tsp. ginger on each of 8 cake slices; top with the remaining cake. Spread the outsides of cake slices with butter.

2. Grill, covered, over medium heat until toasted, 1-2 minutes on each side.

1 s'more: 382 cal., 24g fat (13g sat. fat), 144mg chol., 272mg sod., 44g carb. (10g sugars, 2g fiber), 5g pro.

GINGER POUND CAKE S'MORES

GRILLED LOADED POTATO ROUNDS

My go-to recipe for outdoor potlucks is this awesome grilled potato side dish. I prep everything beforehand, then assemble and grill at the party. Pass with sour cream, cheese, bacon and chives.
—Fay Moreland, Wichita Falls, TX

Takes: 30 min. • **Makes:** 16 appetizers

- 4 large potatoes, baked and cooled
- ¼ cup butter, melted
- ¼ tsp. salt
- ¼ tsp. pepper
- 1 cup sour cream
- 1½ cups shredded cheddar cheese
- 8 bacon strips, cooked and crumbled
- 3 Tbsp. minced chives

Trim ends of potatoes. Slice potatoes into 1-in.-thick rounds. Brush with butter; sprinkle with salt and pepper. Place the potatoes on grill rack, buttered side down. Grill, covered, over medium heat or broil 4 in. from heat until browned, 5-7 minutes. Brush with remaining butter; turn. Grill or broil until browned, 5-7 minutes longer. Top with sour cream, cheddar cheese, bacon and chives.

1 potato round: 188 cal., 11g fat (6g sat. fat), 26mg chol., 212mg sod., 17g carb. (1g sugars, 2g fiber), 6g pro.

BABY BACK RIBS

BABY BACK RIBS

Slow-cook the ribs during the day and they'll be ready to finish off quickly on the grill when you get home.
—Taste of Home *Test Kitchen*

Prep: 5 min. • **Cook:** 6¼ hours
Makes: 4 servings

- 2½ lbs. pork baby back ribs, cut into 8 pieces
- 5 cups water
- 1 medium onion, sliced
- 2 celery ribs, cut in half
- 2 tsp. minced garlic, divided
- 1 tsp. whole peppercorns
- ½ cup barbecue sauce
- ¼ cup plum sauce
- Dash hot pepper sauce

1. Place the ribs in a 5-qt. slow cooker. Add the water, onion, celery, 1 tsp. garlic and peppercorns. Cover and cook on low for 6 hours, until the meat is tender. Remove ribs. Discard the cooking juices and vegetables.
2. In a small saucepan, combine the barbecue sauce, plum sauce, hot pepper sauce and the remaining garlic. Cook and stir over medium heat for 5 minutes or until heated through.
3. Brush ribs with sauce. Grill, covered, on an oiled grill rack over medium-low heat for 8-10 minutes or until browned, turning and basting occasionally with the remaining sauce.
2 pieces: 555 cal., 39g fat (14g sat. fat), 153mg chol., 500mg sod., 15g carb. (11g sugars, 1g fiber), 33g pro.

BANANAS FOSTER ON THE GRILL

Bananas Foster is my husband's favorite dessert, and this is one of the easiest ways to make it that I've ever found. Not only is it delicious, it's a great way to use those bananas that are a little too ripe to just peel and eat.
—Rebecca Clark, Warrior, AL

Takes: 25 min. • **Makes:** 4 servings

- 4 small ripe bananas, unpeeled
  Disposable foil pie pan (9 in.), optional
- 3 Tbsp. butter
- 2 Tbsp. maple syrup
- 2 Tbsp. hot caramel ice cream topping
- 2 cups vanilla ice cream
- 8 vanilla wafers, crushed

1. Trim ends and cut unpeeled bananas lengthwise; place on oiled grill rack over medium heat. Grill, covered, until peel is dark brown and bananas are softened, 3-4 minutes on each side. Cool slightly.
2. Meanwhile, in a small cast-iron skillet or 9-in. disposable foil pie pan, combine butter, syrup and caramel topping; place on grill rack. Cook, uncovered, over medium heat until heated through, 4-5 minutes, stirring frequently. Remove from heat.
3. Remove peel from bananas; cut each half crosswise. To serve, place ice cream in dessert dishes; top with bananas. Drizzle with sauce; sprinkle with crushed wafers.
1 serving: 386 cal., 18g fat (10g sat. fat), 53mg chol., 187mg sod., 56g carb. (41g sugars, 3g fiber), 4g pro.

GRILLED ZUCCHINI & PESTO PIZZA

GRILLED ZUCCHINI & PESTO PIZZA

In the great outdoors, we surprise fellow campers who don't think it's possible to have standout pizza in the backwoods. This one with zucchini proves our point!
—Jesse Arriaga, Reno, NV

Takes: 20 min. • **Makes:** 6 servings

- 4 naan flatbreads
- ½ cup prepared pesto
- 2 cups shredded part-skim mozzarella cheese
- 1 medium zucchini, thinly sliced
- 1 small red onion, thinly sliced
- ¼ lb. thinly sliced hard salami, chopped
- ½ cup fresh basil leaves, thinly sliced
- ¼ cup grated Romano cheese

1. Over each naan, spread 2 Tbsp. pesto; top with ½ cup mozzarella and one-fourth each of the zucchini, onion and salami.
2. Grill, covered, over medium-low heat until the mozzarella has melted and the vegetables are tender, 4-6 minutes. Rotate naan halfway through grilling for evenly browned crust.
3. Remove from heat. Top each naan with basil and Romano cheese; cut into thirds.
2 pieces: 391 cal., 24g fat (9g sat. fat), 51mg chol., 1276mg sod., 25g carb. (4g sugars, 1g fiber), 20g pro.

HAWAIIAN TURKEY BURGERS

My husband and I love to grill, so we have hamburgers on the menu regularly. This recipe uses ground turkey instead of beef. Topped with pineapple slices, the burgers are moist and juicy.

—Babette Watterson, Atglen, PA

Takes: 25 min. • **Makes:** 4 burgers

- 1 can (8 oz.) sliced pineapple
- ½ cup dry bread crumbs
- ½ cup sliced green onions
- ½ cup chopped sweet red pepper
- 1 Tbsp. reduced-sodium soy sauce
- ¼ tsp. salt
- 1 lb. lean ground turkey
- 2 Tbsp. reduced-sodium teriyaki sauce
- 4 sesame hamburger buns

1. Drain pineapple, reserving ¼ cup juice (discard the remaining juice or save for another use); set pineapple aside. In a large bowl, combine the bread crumbs, onions, red pepper, soy sauce, salt and reserved pineapple juice. Crumble the turkey over mixture and mix well. Shape into 4 patties.

2. On a lightly oiled grill rack, grill, covered, over medium heat for 3 minutes on each side. Brush with teriyaki sauce. Grill 4-6 minutes longer on each side or until a thermometer reads 165° and juices run clear.

3. Grill pineapple slices for 2 minutes on each side, basting occasionally with teriyaki sauce. Warm buns on grill; top each with a burger and pineapple slice.

1 burger: 401 cal., 12g fat (3g sat. fat), 78mg chol., 839mg sod., 43g carb. (13g sugars, 3g fiber), 31g pro. **Diabetic exchanges:** 3 starch, 3 lean meat.

LEMON-DILL SALMON PACKETS

PICTURED ON P. 223

Grilling in foil is a technique I use with foods that cook quickly, like fish, shrimp, bite-sized meats and fresh veggies. The options are endless—and the cleanup couldn't be easier.

—A.J. Weinhold, McArthur, CA

Takes: 25 min. • **Makes:** 4 servings

- 1 Tbsp. butter, softened
- 4 salmon fillets (6 oz. each)
- ½ tsp. salt
- ¼ tsp. pepper
- ½ medium onion, sliced
- 4 garlic cloves, sliced
- 4 fresh dill sprigs
- 1 Tbsp. minced fresh basil
- 1 medium lemon, sliced

1. Prepare campfire or grill for medium heat. Spread butter in the center of each of 4 pieces of a double thickness of foil (about 12 in. square). Place a salmon fillet in the center of each piece of foil; sprinkle with salt and pepper. Top with onion slices, garlic, dill sprigs, basil and lemon. Fold foil around fillets; seal.

2. Place packets on a grill grate over a campfire or grill. Cook until fish just begins to flake easily with a fork, 8-10 minutes. Open carefully to allow steam to escape.

1 fillet: 305 cal., 19g fat (5g sat. fat), 93mg chol., 405mg sod., 4g carb. (1g sugars, 1g fiber), 29g pro. **Diabetic exchanges:** 5 lean meat, 1 fat.

> **TEST KITCHEN TIP**
> No grill? No problem! Just place these packets, evenly spaced, on a baking sheet and then pop them into a 350° oven.

HAWAIIAN TURKEY BURGERS

TUNA TACOS WITH MANGO-PINEAPPLE SALSA

TUNA TACOS WITH MANGO-PINEAPPLE SALSA

These tacos taste amazing and they're quick, fresh and heathy.
—Sunee James, Altadena, CA

Prep: 25 min. • **Grill:** 10 min.
Makes: 2 servings

½ cup chopped peeled mango
½ cup cubed avocado
⅓ cup cubed fresh pineapple
4½ tsp. chopped seeded jalapeno pepper
DRESSING
3 Tbsp. sour cream
1 Tbsp. lime juice
1 Tbsp. light coconut milk
¼ tsp. ground ginger
Dash salt
Dash paprika
TUNA
2 tuna steaks (6 oz. each)
1 Tbsp. lime juice
¼ tsp. salt
¼ tsp. pepper
4 corn tortillas (6 in.)

1. In a small bowl, combine the mango, avocado, pineapple and jalapeno. In a second small bowl, combine the dressing ingredients. Chill salsa and dressing until ready to serve.
2. Brush tuna with lime juice; sprinkle with salt and pepper. On a lightly oiled grill rack, grill tuna, covered, over high heat or broil 3-4 in. from the heat. Cook 3-4 minutes on each side or until slightly pink in the center for medium-rare.
3. Cut tuna into bite-sized pieces. Spoon salsa over the tortillas; top with the tuna and dressing.
2 tacos: 456 cal., 13g fat (5g sat. fat), 92mg chol., 528mg sod., 40g carb. (11g sugars, 6g fiber), 45g pro. **Diabetic exchanges:** 5 lean meat, 2 starch, 1½ fat, ½ fruit.

GRILLED SWEET POTATO WEDGES

Because these tasty, healthy fries are pre-boiled and then finished on the grill, they're easy to include as part of a whole-meal cookout.
—Natalie Knowlton, Kamas, UT

Takes: 30 min. • **Makes:** 8 servings

4 large sweet potatoes, cut into ½-in. wedges
½ tsp. garlic salt
¼ tsp. pepper
DIPPING SAUCE
½ cup reduced-fat mayonnaise
½ cup fat-free plain yogurt
1 tsp. ground cumin
½ tsp. seasoned salt
½ tsp. paprika
½ tsp. chili powder

1. Place potatoes in a large saucepan and cover with water. Bring to a boil. Reduce heat; cover and simmer for 4-5 minutes or until crisp-tender. Drain; pat dry with paper towels. Sprinkle potatoes with garlic salt and pepper.
2. Grill, covered, over medium heat for 10-12 minutes or until tender, turning once. In a small bowl, combine the mayonnaise, yogurt and seasonings. Serve with sweet potatoes.
¾ cup with 2 Tbsp. sauce: 166 cal., 5g fat (1g sat. fat), 6mg chol., 349mg sod., 28g carb. (12g sugars, 3g fiber), 3g pro. **Diabetic exchanges:** 1½ starch, 1 fat.

GRILLED LEMON CHICKEN

My grilled chicken gets its subtle bit of pucker from lemonade concentrate. So simple, so sweet!
—Linda Nilsen, Anoka, MN

. . . .

Prep: 5 min. • **Grill:** 40 min.
Makes: 12 servings

- ¾ cup thawed lemonade concentrate
- ⅓ cup soy sauce
- 1 garlic clove, minced
- 1 tsp. seasoned salt
- ½ tsp. celery salt
- ⅛ tsp. garlic powder
- 2 broiler/fryer chickens (3 to 3½ lbs. each), cut up

1. In a bowl, whisk the first 6 ingredients until combined. Pour half into a shallow glass dish. Cover and refrigerate the remaining lemonade mixture.

2. Dip chicken into lemonade mixture, turning to coat; discard lemonade mixture. Grill chicken, covered, over medium heat for 30 minutes, turning occasionally. Brush with the reserved lemonade mixture. Grill 10-20 minutes longer, brushing frequently, until a thermometer reads 165°.

5 oz. cooked chicken: 320 cal., 17g fat (5g sat. fat), 104mg chol., 504mg sod., 6g carb. (5g sugars, 0 fiber), 34g pro.

GRILLED LEMON CHICKEN

GRILLED STONE FRUIT SALAD

PICTURED ON P. 223

Summer is the time we enjoy grilling and adding fresh fruit to our menu, and this smoky-sweet salad is the best of both worlds! I like to marinate the fruits for extra flavor before I grill them.
—Nancy Heishman, Las Vegas, NV

. . . .

Prep: 20 min. + marinating • **Grill:** 10 min.
Makes: 6 servings

- 6 Tbsp. lemon juice, divided
- 3 Tbsp. butter, melted
- 1 Tbsp. minced fresh mint
- 2 peeled peaches, pitted and halved
- 3 medium plums, pitted and halved
- 4 apricots, pitted and halved
- ¼ fresh pineapple, cut into 4 slices
- ¼ cup extra virgin olive oil
- 2 Tbsp. honey
- ¼ tsp. kosher salt
- ⅛ tsp. ground allspice
- 6 oz. fresh baby arugula
- 1 cup crumbled feta cheese

1. In a large shallow bowl, whisk together 3 Tbsp. lemon juice, the melted butter and mint. Add fruit; marinate 30 minutes, turning once. Drain, reserving marinade.

2. Grill fruit, covered, on a greased grill rack over medium-high direct heat for 4-6 minutes. Turn; brush with reserved marinade. Grill, uncovered, brushing again, until the fruit is tender but not mushy, 4-6 more minutes. Remove from heat; cool 5-10 minutes. When cool enough to handle, cut fruit into quarters.

3. Whisk together olive oil, honey, kosher salt, allspice and the remaining lemon juice. Drizzle half the dressing over the arugula, tossing until well coated; place arugula on a large serving platter. Add grilled fruit; drizzle with the remaining dressing. Sprinkle fruit with crumbled feta cheese.

1 serving: 268 cal., 18g fat (7g sat. fat), 25mg chol., 315mg sod., 23g carb. (19g sugars, 3g fiber), 5g pro.

PEACHY PORK RIBS

PEACHY PORK RIBS

These meaty ribs are great picnic fare. Bake them first to make them tender, then simply finish them off on the grill with a fruity basting sauce.
—*Tom Arnold, Milwaukee, WI*

Prep: 20 min. • **Cook:** 2 hours 10 min.
Makes: 4 servings

- 2 racks pork baby back ribs (4 lbs.), cut into serving-size pieces
- ½ cup water
- 3 medium ripe peaches, peeled and cubed
- 2 Tbsp. chopped onion
- 2 Tbsp. butter
- 1 garlic clove, minced
- 3 Tbsp. lemon juice
- 2 Tbsp. orange juice concentrate
- 1 Tbsp. brown sugar
- 2 tsp. soy sauce
- ½ tsp. ground mustard
- ¼ tsp. salt
- ¼ tsp. pepper

1. Place ribs in a shallow roasting pan; add water. Cover and bake at 325° for 2 hours.
2. Meanwhile, for sauce, place peaches in a blender; cover and process until blended. In a small saucepan, saute onion in butter until tender. Add garlic; cook 1 minute longer. Stir in the lemon juice, orange juice concentrate, brown sugar, soy sauce, mustard, salt, pepper and the peach puree; heat through.
3. Drain ribs. Spoon some of the sauce over ribs. Grill ribs on a lightly oiled rack, covered, over medium heat until browned, 8-10 minutes, turning occasionally and brushing with sauce.
1 serving: 884 cal., 67g fat (26g sat. fat), 260mg chol., 553mg sod., 16g carb. (13g sugars, 1g fiber), 52g pro.

BASIL GRILLED CORN ON THE COB

BASIL GRILLED CORN ON THE COB

Corn on the cob is a cherished comfort food here in the Midwest. It's amazing when grilled, and my recipe adds just a few unexpected ingredients to make it taste even better.
—*Caitlin Dawson, Monroe, OH*

Prep: 15 min. + soaking • **Grill:** 20 min.
Makes: 4 servings

- 4 medium ears sweet corn
- 4 tsp. butter, melted
- ¾ tsp. salt
- ¼ tsp. pepper
- 16 fresh basil leaves
- ½ medium lemon
- 2 tsp. minced fresh cilantro
  Additional butter, optional

1. Place corn in a 6-qt. stockpot; cover with cold water. Soak 20 minutes; drain. Carefully peel back corn husks to within 1 in. of bottoms; remove silk. Brush butter over corn; sprinkle with salt and pepper. Press 4 basil leaves onto each cob. Rewrap the corn in husks; secure the husks with kitchen string.
2. Grill corn, covered, over medium heat 20-25 minutes or until tender, turning often. Cut string and peel back husks; discard basil leaves. Squeeze lemon juice over corn; sprinkle with cilantro. If desired, spread with additional butter.
1 ear of corn: 125 cal., 5g fat (3g sat. fat), 10mg chol., 489mg sod., 20g carb. (7g sugars, 2g fiber), 4g pro. **Diabetic exchanges:** 1 starch, 1 fat.

SPIEDIS

This is our favorite cookout dish. The recipe originated here in my hometown in the 1930s. Our meat preference is venison, but we use pork or another meat when it's not available.
—Gertrude Skinner, Binghamton, NY

Prep: 10 min. + marinating • **Grill:** 10 min.
Makes: 8 servings

- 1 cup canola oil
- ⅔ cup cider vinegar
- 2 Tbsp. Worcestershire sauce
- ½ medium onion, finely chopped
- ½ tsp. salt
- ½ tsp. sugar
- ½ tsp. dried basil
- ½ tsp. dried marjoram
- ½ tsp. dried rosemary, crushed
- 2½ lbs. boneless lean pork, beef, lamb, venison, chicken or turkey, cut into 1½- to 2-in. cubes
  Italian rolls or hot dog buns

1. In a glass or plastic bowl, combine the first 9 ingredients. Add meat and toss to coat. Cover and refrigerate for 24 hours, stirring occasionally.
2. Drain and discard marinade. Thread meat onto metal or soaked wooden skewers. Grill, covered, over medium heat until meat reaches desired doneness, 10-15 minutes, turning occasionally. Remove meat from skewers and serve on long Italian rolls or hot dog buns.

4 oz. cooked pork: 205 cal., 12g fat (0 sat. fat), 42mg chol., 104mg sod., 1g carb. (0 sugars, 0 fiber), 22g pro.
Diabetic exchanges: 2 lean meat, 1 fat.

BUFFALO BEEF BURGERS

BUFFALO BEEF BURGERS

Ever-popular Buffalo wings inspired the flavors of this tangy, amped-up burger. The zippy mayonnaise topping gives the sandwiches their kick.
—Michael Cohen, Los Angeles, CA

Takes: 30 min. • **Makes:** 6 servings

- 2 Tbsp. butter, softened
- 2 Tbsp. brown sugar
- ¾ cup mayonnaise
- ¼ cup Louisiana-style hot sauce
- 2 lbs. ground beef
- 1 tsp. salt
- ½ tsp. coarsely ground pepper
- 6 kaiser rolls, split
- 1 celery rib, finely chopped
- 6 Tbsp. crumbled blue cheese

1. In a small bowl, beat the butter and brown sugar until light and fluffy. Add mayonnaise and hot sauce; beat until smooth. Set aside.
2. Crumble beef into a large bowl; sprinkle with salt and pepper and mix well. Shape into 6 patties.
3. Grill burgers, covered, over medium heat for 5-7 minutes on each side or until a thermometer reads 160° and the juices run clear.
4. Place burgers on rolls. Top each with 2 Tbsp. Buffalo mayonnaise and 1 Tbsp. each of celery and cheese.

1 serving: 769 cal., 51g fat (15g sat. fat), 141mg chol., 1109mg sod., 35g carb. (6g sugars, 1g fiber), 40g pro.

TEST KITCHEN TIP
Dark brown sugar contains more molasses than light or golden brown sugar. The two types are generally interchangeable in recipes. If you prefer a bolder flavor, choose dark brown sugar.

CAKE & BERRY CAMPFIRE COBBLER

This warm cobbler is one of our favorite ways to end a busy day of fishing, hiking, swimming or rafting. It's yummy with ice cream—and so easy to make!
—June Dress, Meridian, ID

Prep: 10 min. • **Grill:** 30 min.
Makes: 12 servings

- 2 cans (21 oz. each) raspberry pie filling
- 1 pkg. yellow cake mix (regular size)
- 1¼ cups water
- ½ cup canola oil
  Vanilla ice cream, optional

1. Prepare grill or campfire for low heat, using 16-20 charcoal briquettes or large wood chips.
2. Line an ovenproof Dutch oven with heavy-duty aluminum foil; add pie filling. In a large bowl, combine the cake mix, water and oil. Spread over pie filling.
3. Cover Dutch oven. When briquettes or wood chips are covered with white ash, place Dutch oven directly on top of 8-10 of them. Using long-handled tongs, place remaining briquettes on pot cover.
4. Cook until filling is bubbly and a toothpick inserted in the topping comes out clean, 30-40 minutes. To check for doneness, use the tongs to carefully lift the cover. If desired, serve with ice cream.
1 serving: 342 cal., 12g fat (2g sat. fat), 0 chol., 322mg sod., 57g carb. (34g sugars, 2g fiber), 1g pro.

READER REVIEW

"Nothing better when camping! We serve it with whipped cream."
NO_TIME_TO_COOK, TASTEOFHOME.COM

GRILLED SALMON CAESAR SALAD

Flaky grilled salmon, lettuce, tomatoes and homemade garlic croutons are the stars here. A Caesar-style dressing, seasoned with lemon juice and grated Parmesan cheese, coats this elegant salad.
—Clara Barrett, Madison, FL

Prep: 20 min. • **Grill:** 20 min. + cooling
Makes: 6 servings

- 2 salmon fillets (1 lb. each)
- 3 cups cubed French bread
- 1 Tbsp. olive oil
- ¼ tsp. garlic powder
- 1 bunch romaine, torn
- 2 cups small cherry tomatoes

DRESSING
- 3 Tbsp. olive oil
- 2 Tbsp. lemon juice
- 4½ tsp. mayonnaise
- 2¼ tsp. sugar
- 2 garlic cloves, minced
- ½ tsp. salt
- ⅛ tsp. pepper
- 1 Tbsp. grated Parmesan cheese

1. Place salmon skin side down on a lightly oiled grill rack. Grill, covered, over medium-hot heat or broil 4 in. from the heat for 15-20 minutes or until fish flakes easily with a fork. Cool, then flake salmon into chunks.
2. For croutons, toss the bread cubes, oil and garlic powder in a large bowl. In a nonstick skillet, saute bread cubes for 5-6 minutes or until golden brown, stirring occasionally. Remove from the heat; set aside.
3. In a large bowl, combine romaine and tomatoes. In a small bowl, whisk the oil, lemon juice, mayonnaise, sugar, garlic, salt and pepper. Pour over salad and toss to coat. Add the salmon, croutons and cheese; toss gently.
1 serving: 322 cal., 21g fat (4g sat. fat), 47mg chol., 380mg sod., 15g carb. (4g sugars, 2g fiber), 18g pro.

CAKE & BERRY CAMPFIRE COBBLER

POTLUCKS & PARTIES

If you're hosting a party at your place or looking for the perfect dish to take to a gathering, you've got plenty to choose from here. All the recipes in this chapter—from appetizers to mains to dessert—will feed a dozen or more people!

BROADWAY
BROWNIE BARS

BROADWAY BROWNIE BARS

I named these dessert bars for Broadway because they're a hit every time I serve them. I especially like to make these for the holidays, or to give as hostess gifts. They're always sure to please any sweet tooth!

—Anne Frederick, New Hartford, NY

Prep: 20 min. + chilling • **Bake:** 30 min.
Makes: 2½ dozen

FILLING
- 6 oz. cream cheese, softened
- ½ cup sugar
- ¼ cup butter, softened
- 2 Tbsp. all-purpose flour
- 1 large egg, lightly beaten, room temperature
- ½ tsp. vanilla extract

BROWNIE
- ½ cup butter, cubed
- 1 oz. unsweetened chocolate
- 2 large eggs, lightly beaten, room temperature

- 1 tsp. vanilla extract
- 1 cup sugar
- 1 cup all-purpose flour
- 1 tsp. baking powder
- 1 cup chopped walnuts

TOPPING
- 1 cup semisweet chocolate chips
- ¼ cup chopped walnuts
- 2 cups miniature marshmallows

FROSTING
- ¼ cup butter
- ¼ cup 2% milk
- 2 oz. cream cheese
- 1 oz. unsweetened chocolate
- 3 cups confectioners' sugar
- 1 tsp. vanilla extract

1. Preheat oven to 350°. In a small bowl, combine the first 6 ingredients until smooth; set aside.

2. In a large saucepan over medium heat, melt butter and chocolate. Remove from the heat and let cool. Stir in the eggs and vanilla. Add sugar, flour, baking powder and nuts, stirring until blended.

3. Spread batter in a 13x9-in. baking pan coated with cooking spray. Spread filling over batter. For topping, in small bowl, combine chocolate chips and nuts; sprinkle over filling.

4. Bake 28 minutes or until almost set. Sprinkle with the marshmallows; bake 2 minutes longer.

5. For frosting, in a large saucepan, heat butter, milk, cream cheese and chocolate until melted, stirring until smooth. Remove from heat; stir in confectioners' sugar and vanilla. Immediately drizzle over marshmallows. Chill well; cut into bars.

1 brownie: 271 cal., 15g fat (7g sat. fat), 46mg chol., 108mg sod., 33g carb. (26g sugars, 1g fiber), 4g pro.

TEST KITCHEN TIP
For easy removal of bars, line your pan with foil, letting the ends extend up the sides of the pan. Then use the foil to lift the cooled bars.

RAMEN NOODLE CRANBERRY COLESLAW

The rich red from the cranberries and cabbage makes this a perfect fit for a Christmas spread. Adults and children love this dish, and I'm often asked to bring it to potlucks and other big dinners. Refrigerate any leftovers—it'll still taste great for a day or two, if you can keep people out of it that long!
—Cornelia Cree, Waynesville, NC

Prep: 25 min. + chilling
Makes: 24 servings

- 1 cup peanut or canola oil
- ¾ cup sugar
- ¼ cup cider vinegar
- 1 head Chinese or napa cabbage, thinly sliced
- 1 small head red cabbage, shredded
- 1 small red onion, halved and sliced
- ¾ cup dried cranberries
- 1 pkg. (3 oz.) ramen noodles
- 1 cup salted peanuts or sunflower kernels

1. Whisk together the oil, sugar and vinegar until smooth. In a very large bowl, combine the cabbages, red onion and cranberries. Pour 1 cup dressing over the coleslaw; toss to coat. Refrigerate, covered, several hours or overnight. Cover and refrigerate remaining dressing.
2. Drain coleslaw. Discard seasoning packet from noodles or save for another use. Break noodles into small pieces; add to coleslaw. Stir in peanuts and remaining dressing; toss to coat.

¾ cup: 154 cal., 11g fat (2g sat. fat), 0 chol., 39mg sod., 14g carb. (10g sugars, 1g fiber), 2g pro.

POTLUCK BAKED SPAGHETTI

This casserole is a standby for church suppers and other potluck functions. Keeping the cover on during most of the baking time keeps it moist.
—Doris Heath, Franklin, NC

Prep: 25 min. • **Bake:** 25 min.
Makes: 12 servings

- 2 lbs. ground beef
- 2 medium onions, chopped
- 2 cans (one 15 oz., one 8 oz.) tomato sauce
- 1 can (8 oz.) sliced mushrooms, drained
- 1 tsp. garlic powder
- 1 tsp. dried oregano
- 2 pkg. (7 oz. each) uncooked spaghetti
- 1 pkg. (8 oz.) cream cheese, softened
- 2 cups 4% cottage cheese
- ½ cup sour cream
- 2 Tbsp. minced chives
- ¼ cup dry bread crumbs
- 1½ tsp. butter, melted

1. In a large skillet, cook beef and onions over medium heat until the meat is no longer pink; drain. Add the tomato sauce, mushrooms, garlic powder and oregano. Bring to a boil. Reduce heat; simmer, uncovered, for 15 minutes, stirring occasionally.
2. Meanwhile, cook the spaghetti according to package directions; drain. In a small bowl, combine the cream cheese, cottage cheese, sour cream and chives; beat well. Place half of spaghetti in a greased 4-qt. baking dish. Spoon cream cheese mixture evenly over top. Layer with remaining spaghetti and all of the beef mixture.
3. Toss bread crumbs and butter; sprinkle over the top. Cover and bake at 350° for 20 minutes. Uncover; bake 5-10 minutes longer or until heated through.

1 cup: 378 cal., 20g fat (10g sat. fat), 87mg chol., 586mg sod., 23g carb. (5g sugars, 2g fiber), 25g pro.

RAMEN NOODLE CRANBERRY COLESLAW

CHICKPEA CUCUMBER SALAD

This recipe is a crowd pleaser! My new husband and I take it to parties, barbecues and other gatherings. It's a light but flavorful side dish that brings a little bit of Greek flavor to any meal.
—Kristi Smith, Greenwood, IN

Prep: 10 min. + chilling
Makes: 12 servings

- 3 cans (15 oz. each) chickpeas or garbanzo beans, rinsed and drained
- 4 large cucumbers, seeded and cut into ½-in. pieces
- 2 pkg. (3½ oz. each) crumbled reduced-fat feta cheese (about 1⅓ cups)
- 1 cup finely chopped red onion
- ½ cup reduced-fat ranch salad dressing
- 2 Tbsp. snipped fresh dill
- ¾ tsp. salt
- ¼ tsp. pepper

Combine chickpeas, cucumbers, cheese and onion. In another bowl, mix ranch dressing, dill, salt and pepper. Pour over salad; toss to coat. Refrigerate, covered, 1 hour before serving.

¾ cup: 171 cal., 5g fat (1g sat. fat), 7mg chol.,620mg sod., 23g carb. (5g sugars, 5g fiber), 8g pro. **Diabetic exchanges:** 1½ starch, 1 medium-fat meat.

HONEY WHOLE
WHEAT PAN ROLLS

HONEY WHOLE WHEAT PAN ROLLS

With their pleasant wheat flavor and a honey of a glaze, these rolls impress my guests. Every time I take them to potluck dinners, I come home with an empty pan.
—Nancye Thompson, Paducah, KY

Prep: 35 min. + chilling • **Bake:** 20 min.
Makes: 5 dozen (1¼ cups honey butter)

- 4 to 5 cups bread flour
- ¼ cup sugar
- 2 pkg. (¼ oz. each) active dry yeast
- 1 tsp. salt
- 1 cup 2% milk
- 1 cup butter, cubed
- ½ cup water
- 2 large eggs, room temperature
- 2 cups whole wheat flour

HONEY BUTTER
- 1 cup butter, softened
- 7 Tbsp. honey

HONEY GLAZE
- 2 Tbsp. honey
- 1 Tbsp. butter, melted

1. In a large bowl, combine 2 cups bread flour, sugar, yeast and salt. In a small saucepan, heat the milk, butter and water to 120°-130°. Add to dry ingredients; beat just until moistened. Beat in eggs. Stir in whole wheat flour and enough remaining bread flour to form a soft dough.
2. Turn onto a floured surface; knead until smooth and elastic, about 10 minutes. Cover and let rest 15 minutes.
3. Divide dough into thirds. Roll each portion into a 20-in. rope. Cut each into 20 pieces; shape each into a ball. Grease three 9-in. round baking pans; arrange 20 balls in each pan. Cover the pans and refrigerate overnight.
4. Let rise in a warm place until doubled, about 1¼ hours. Bake at 350° until golden brown, 18-22 minutes. Meanwhile, in a small bowl, cream butter. Add honey; beat until light and fluffy. Remove rolls from pans to wire racks. Combine glaze ingredients; brush over warm rolls. Serve with honey butter.

1 roll with about 1 tsp. honey butter: 114 cal., 7g fat (4g sat. fat), 24mg chol., 107mg sod., 12g carb. (4g sugars, 1g fiber), 2g pro.

CHERRY & FONTINA STUFFED PORTOBELLOS

I developed this hearty appetizer for my mushroom-lovin' kids. They're grown now with families of their own, but they still request these when they come home.
—Wendy Rusch, Cameron, WI

Prep: 30 min. • **Bake:** 15 min.
Makes: 12 servings

- 6 large portobello mushrooms
- ½ cup butter, cubed
- 1 medium onion, chopped
- 1 cup pecan halves, toasted
- 1 pkg. (5 oz.) dried tart cherries, coarsely chopped
- ½ tsp. poultry seasoning
- ½ tsp. dried thyme
- 7 oz. (about 4½ cups) seasoned stuffing cubes
- 1½ to 2 cups chicken broth
- 1½ cups shredded fontina cheese, divided

1. Preheat oven to 375°. Wipe the mushroom caps clean with a damp paper towel; remove stems and gills and discard. Place caps on a foil-lined 15x10x1-in. baking pan.

2. In a large skillet, melt butter over medium heat until it begins to brown and smell nutty. Add onion; saute until translucent, stirring occasionally. Stir in pecans, cherries and seasonings; cook and stir 3 minutes. Remove from heat.

3. Combine onion mixture and stuffing cubes, tossing to coat evenly. Add 1½ cups broth to onion-stuffing mixture, stirring until well mixed. Add remaining broth as needed. Stir in 1 cup cheese.

4. Fill the mushroom caps with stuffing until mounded, about 1 cup each. Sprinkle with the remaining cheese. Bake until the mushrooms are heated through and the cheese is melted, 15-20 minutes. Cut in half; serve warm.

½ stuffed portobello: 301 cal., 19g fat (8g sat. fat), 37mg chol., 531mg sod., 27g carb. (8g sugars, 6g fiber), 8g pro.

PEANUT BUTTER SHEET CAKE

I received the recipe for this simple, classic sheet cake from a minister's wife, and my family loves it. Buttermilk makes it rich, and the chunky peanut butter gives it crunch!
—Brenda Jackson, Garden City, KS

Prep: 15 min. • **Bake:** 20 min.
Makes: 24 servings

- 2 cups all-purpose flour
- 2 cups sugar
- 1 tsp. baking soda
- ½ tsp. salt
- 1 cup water
- ¾ cup butter, cubed
- ½ cup chunky peanut butter
- ¼ cup canola oil
- 2 large eggs, room temperature
- ½ cup buttermilk
- 1 tsp. vanilla extract

GLAZE
- ⅔ cup sugar
- ⅓ cup evaporated milk
- 1 Tbsp. butter
- ⅓ cup chunky peanut butter
- ⅓ cup miniature marshmallows
- ½ tsp. vanilla extract

1. Preheat oven to 350°. Grease a 15x10x1-in. baking pan. In a large bowl, whisk flour, sugar, baking soda and salt. In a small saucepan, combine water and butter; bring just to a boil. Stir in peanut butter and oil until blended. Stir into flour mixture. In a small bowl, whisk the eggs, buttermilk and vanilla until blended; add to flour mixture, whisking constantly.

2. Transfer batter to prepared pan. Bake until a toothpick inserted in center comes out clean, 20-25 minutes.

3. Meanwhile, for glaze, combine sugar, milk and butter in a saucepan. Bring to a boil, stirring constantly; cook and stir 2 minutes. Remove from heat; stir in peanut butter, marshmallows and vanilla until blended. Spoon over warm cake, spreading evenly. Cool on a wire rack.

1 piece: 266 cal., 14g fat (5g sat. fat), 36mg chol., 222mg sod., 33g carb. (23g sugars, 1g fiber), 4g pro.

CHERRY & FONTINA STUFFED PORTOBELLOS

GRUYERE & CRAB PALMIERS

 BUFFALO-STYLE CHICKEN CHILI DIP

Longing for that Buffalo wing thing without the bones? This do-ahead dip freezes well in individual containers, so you can pull them out when you want to spread a little cheer.
—Brenda Calandrillo, Mahwah, NJ

Prep: 30 min. • **Cook:** 30 min.
Makes: 11 cups

- 3 celery ribs, finely chopped
- 1 large onion, chopped
- 1 large carrot, finely chopped
- 5 garlic cloves, minced
- 2 Tbsp. butter
- 2 lbs. ground chicken
- 1 Tbsp. olive oil
- 2 cups chicken broth
- 1 can (16 oz.) kidney beans, rinsed and drained
- 1 can (15 oz.) cannellini beans, rinsed and drained
- 1 can (15 oz.) crushed tomatoes
- 1 can (15 oz.) tomato sauce
- 1 can (6 oz.) tomato paste
- ¼ cup Louisiana-style hot sauce
- 3 tsp. smoked paprika
- 1 bay leaf
- ¾ tsp. salt
- ¼ tsp. pepper
  Crumbled blue cheese, optional
  Celery stalks and tortilla chips

1. In a Dutch oven, saute the celery, onion, carrot and garlic in butter until tender. Remove and set aside. In the same pan, cook chicken in oil until no longer pink; drain.

2. Stir in the broth, beans, tomatoes, tomato sauce, tomato paste, hot sauce, smoked paprika, bay leaf, salt, pepper and vegetable mixture. Bring to a boil; reduce heat. Simmer, uncovered, for 12-15 minutes or until slightly thickened. Discard bay leaf.

3. Sprinkle with blue cheese if desired. Serve with celery and chips.

Freeze option: Transfer cooled dip to freezer containers. Cover and freeze up to 3 months. To use, thaw in the refrigerator. Place in a saucepan; heat through. Sprinkle with cheese. Serve with celery and chips.
¼ cup: 64 cal., 3g fat (1g sat. fat), 15mg chol., 192mg sod., 6g carb. (1g sugars, 1g fiber), 5g pro.

 GRUYERE & CRAB PALMIERS

I keep these little bursts of flavor in my freezer so they can be pulled out and popped into the oven whenever needed. Crab, pancetta and Gruyere make a sophisticated, elegant appetizer. But you can make variations on the filling—try chicken and pesto, or a Mediterranean version with spinach and feta.
—Grace Voltolina, Westport, CT

Prep: 30 min. + chilling • **Bake:** 15 min.
Makes: 3 dozen

- 1 large egg, lightly beaten
- 1 Tbsp. mayonnaise
- 1 tsp. minced fresh thyme or ¼ tsp. dried thyme
- 1 tsp. Dijon mustard
- ½ tsp. pepper
- ½ tsp. smoked paprika
- ½ tsp. prepared horseradish
- ¼ tsp. Worcestershire sauce
- 1 can (6 oz.) lump crabmeat, drained
- 4 oz. sliced pancetta, chopped
- 1 pkg. (17.3 oz.) frozen puff pastry, thawed
- ½ cup shredded Gruyere or Swiss cheese

1. Preheat oven to 400°. In a small bowl, combine the first 8 ingredients; fold in crab. In a small skillet, cook pancetta over medium heat until partially cooked but not crisp; drain on paper towels.

2. Unfold 1 sheet puff pastry. Spread half of the crab mixture to within ½ in. of edges. Sprinkle with half the cheese and half the pancetta.

3. Roll up the left and right sides toward the center, jelly-roll style, until rolls meet in the middle. Repeat with remaining pastry and ingredients. Refrigerate until firm enough to slice, about 30 minutes.

4. Cut each roll crosswise into ½-in. slices. Place 2 in. apart on parchment-lined baking sheets. Bake until golden and crisp, 15-20 minutes. Cool on pans 2 minutes. Remove to wire racks to cool.

Freeze option: Cover and freeze unbaked sliced palmiers on waxed paper-lined baking sheets until firm. Transfer to freezer containers; close tightly and return to freezer. To use, bake palmiers as directed.
1 palmier: 93 cal., 6g fat (2g sat. fat), 14mg chol., 149mg sod., 8g carb. (0 sugars, 1g fiber), 3g pro.

GRUYERE & CRAB PALMIERS

BUFFALO-STYLE
CHICKEN CHILI DIP

Refreshing Infusions

A pitcher of infused water on the table makes a beautiful centerpiece and a delicious refreshment!

* Combine ½ cup each sliced fresh strawberries, fresh raspberries and fresh blackberries with 2 quarts water in a large glass carafe or pitcher. Cover and refrigerate 12-24 hours.

* Combine ½ cup sliced cucumber, ½ medium lemon, sliced, ½ lime sliced, and ½ orange, sliced, with 2 quarts of water. Cover and refrigerate 12-24 hours.

STICKY MAPLE PEPPER GLAZED CHICKEN WINGS

This is one of my favorite party appetizers! Coarse ground pepper adds just the right amount of heat to cut the sweetness of the maple syrup. These are best fresh out of the oven, but are also delicious made ahead and kept warm in a slow cooker.
—Shannon Dobos, Calgary, AB

Prep: 25 min. • **Bake:** 40 min.
Makes: about 40 pieces

- 4 lbs. chicken wings
- ¼ cup all-purpose flour
- ½ Tbsp. baking powder
- 1 tsp. coarsely ground pepper
- 1 tsp. kosher salt
- ½ tsp. garlic powder

GLAZE
- ⅔ cup maple syrup
- 2 tsp. coarsely ground pepper
- 2 tsp. soy sauce
- 1 garlic clove, minced
   Chopped green onions, optional

1. Preheat oven to 425°. Line two 15x10x1-in. baking pans with foil and coat with cooking spray; set aside.
2. Using a sharp knife, cut through the 2 wing joints; discard wing tips. In a shallow bowl, combine the flour, baking powder, pepper, salt and garlic powder. Add wing pieces, a few at a time, and toss to coat; shake off excess.
3. Place wings on prepared baking sheets. Bake until no longer pink, 40-50 minutes, turning once. Meanwhile, in a small saucepan, combine glaze ingredients. Bring to a boil. Reduce heat; simmer until thickened, 5-7 minutes, stirring frequently. Drizzle over wings; toss to coat. If desired, top with chopped green onions.
1 piece: 66 cal., 3g fat (1g sat. fat), 14mg chol., 63mg sod., 4g carb. (3g sugars, 0 fiber), 5g pro.

STICKY MAPLE PEPPER GLAZED CHICKEN WINGS

SUMMER ORZO
PICTURED ON P. 241

I'm always looking for fun ways to use the fresh veggies that come in my Community Supported Agriculture box, and this salad is one of my favorite creations. I like to improvise with whatever I have on hand, so feel free to do the same!
—Shayna Marmar, Philadelphia, PA

Prep: 30 min. + chilling
Makes: 16 servings

- 1 pkg. (16 oz.) orzo pasta
- ¼ cup water
- 1½ cups fresh or frozen corn
- 24 cherry tomatoes, halved
- 2 cups (8 oz.) crumbled feta cheese
- 1 medium cucumber, seeded and chopped
- 1 small red onion, finely chopped
- ¼ cup minced fresh mint
- 2 Tbsp. capers, drained and chopped, optional
- ½ cup olive oil
- ¼ cup lemon juice
- 1 Tbsp. grated lemon zest
- 1½ tsp. salt
- 1 tsp. pepper
- 1 cup sliced almonds, toasted

1. Cook orzo according to the package directions for al dente. Drain orzo; rinse with cold water and drain well. Transfer to a large bowl.
2. In a large nonstick skillet, heat water over medium heat. Add corn; cook and stir until crisp-tender, 3-4 minutes. Add to orzo; stir in tomatoes, feta cheese, cucumber, onion, mint and, if desired, chopped capers.
3. In a small bowl, whisk oil, lemon juice, lemon zest, salt and pepper until blended. Pour over the orzo mixture; toss to coat. Refrigerate 30 minutes. Just before serving, stir in almonds.
¾ cup: 291 cal., 15g fat (4g sat. fat), 15mg chol., 501mg sod., 28g carb. (3g sugars, 3g fiber), 11g pro.

SEAFOOD GUMBO

PICTURED ON P. 241

Gumbo is one of the dishes that makes Louisiana cuisine famous. We live across the border in Texas and can't get enough of this traditional Cajun dish featuring okra, shrimp, spicy seasonings and what is called the holy trinity—onions, green peppers and celery. This recipe calls for seafood, but you could also use chicken, duck or sausage.

—*Ruth Aubey, San Antonio, TX*

....

Prep: 20 min. • **Cook:** 30 min.
Makes: 24 servings (6 qt.)

- 1 **cup all-purpose flour**
- 1 **cup canola oil**
- 4 **cups chopped onion**
- 2 **cups chopped celery**
- 2 **cups chopped green pepper**
- 1 **cup sliced green onions**
- 4 **cups chicken broth**
- 8 **cups water**
- 4 **cups sliced okra**
- 2 **Tbsp. paprika**
- 1 **Tbsp. salt**
- 2 **tsp. oregano**
- 1 **tsp. ground black pepper**
- 6 **cups small shrimp, rinsed and drained, or seafood of your choice**
- 1 **cup minced fresh parsley**
- 2 **Tbsp. Cajun seasoning**

1. In a heavy Dutch oven, combine flour and oil until smooth. Cook over medium-high heat for 5 minutes, stirring constantly. Reduce heat to medium. Cook and stir about 10 minutes more or until mixture is reddish brown.

2. Add onion, celery, green pepper and green onions; cook and stir for 5 minutes. Add the chicken broth, water, okra, paprika, salt, oregano and pepper. Bring to boil; reduce heat and simmer, covered, for 10 minutes.

3. Add shrimp and parsley. Simmer, uncovered, about 5 minutes more or until seafood is done. Remove from heat; stir in Cajun seasoning.

1 cup: 166 cal., 10g fat (1g sat. fat), 96mg chol., 900mg sod., 10g carb. (2g sugars, 2g fiber), 10g pro.

RAWHIDE'S WHISKEY CAKE

For several years, our neighbor shared with us a moist, whiskey-flavored cake. I've since tweaked the recipe, and now my friends want this cake instead of homemade cookie platters. It requires advance planning, as the glaze is added over three days!

—*Cindy Worth, Lapwai, ID*

....

Prep: 15 min. + standing
Bake: 1 hour + cooling • **Makes:** 16 slices

- 1 **pkg. spice cake mix with pudding (regular size)**
- 1 **pkg. (3.4 oz.) instant vanilla pudding mix**
- ¾ **cup 2% milk**
- ¾ **cup whiskey**
- ½ **cup canola oil**
- 4 **large eggs, room temperature**
- 1⅓ **cups coarsely chopped walnuts, divided**

GLAZE
- 1 **cup sugar**
- ½ **cup butter, cubed**
- ½ **cup whiskey**
- 1 **tsp. water**

1. Preheat oven to 300°. Grease and flour a 10-in. tube pan.

2. Combine the first 6 ingredients; beat on low speed 30 seconds. Beat on medium speed 2 minutes; fold in 1 cup nuts. Pour batter into prepared pan; sprinkle with remaining nuts. Bake until a toothpick inserted in center comes out clean, 60-65 minutes. Cool in pan.

3. Mix all glaze ingredients in a small saucepan; bring to a boil over medium-high heat. Reduce heat; simmer mixture for 10 minutes. Cool 3 minutes. Pour one-third of glaze over top of cake; allow some glaze to flow over sides. Let stand for 1 hour. Remove from pan to cool completely; cover.

4. The next day, reheat glaze; brush half the glaze over the cake, letting it cool before covering. Repeat the following day, using the remaining glaze.

1 slice: 400 cal., 23g fat (6g sat. fat), 63mg chol., 298mg sod., 43g carb. (30g sugars, 1g fiber), 5g pro.

RAWHIDE'S
WHISKEY CAKE

SLOW-COOKER CAPONATA

COTTAGE POTATOES

I often make this crunchy and colorful potato dish for our family reunions. It's my cousin's recipe, and we always know we'll never have any leftovers.
—Mary Sholtis, Ashtabula, OH

Prep: 20 min. • **Bake:** 55 min.
Makes: 14 servings

> 12 large potatoes, peeled and diced
> 8 oz. Velveeta, cubed
> 1 large onion, finely chopped
> 1 large green pepper, chopped
> 1 jar (2 oz.) diced pimientos, drained
> 1 slice bread, torn into crumbs
> 3 Tbsp. minced fresh parsley, divided
> ½ tsp. salt
> ½ cup 2% milk
> ½ cup butter, melted
> 1½ cups cornflakes, crushed

1. Place the potatoes in a large saucepan or Dutch oven and cover with water. Bring to a boil; reduce heat to medium. Cover and cook for 5-7 minutes or until tender; drain. In a bowl, combine the cheese, onion, green pepper, pimientos, bread, 2 Tbsp. parsley and salt.
2. In a greased shallow 4-qt. baking dish, layer a third of the potatoes and a third of the cheese mixture. Repeat layers twice. Pour milk and butter over all; sprinkle with cornflake crumbs.
3. Cover and bake at 350° for 45 minutes. Uncover; bake 10-15 minutes longer or until bubbly and top is golden. Sprinkle with remaining parsley.

1 cup: 389 cal., 11g fat (7g sat. fat), 31mg chol., 393mg sod., 64g carb. (8g sugars, 6g fiber), 10g pro.

SLOW-COOKER CAPONATA

This Italian eggplant dip preps quickly and actually gets better as it stands. Serve it warm or at room temperature. Try adding a little leftover caponata to scrambled eggs for a savory breakfast.
—Nancy Beckman, Helena, MT

Prep: 20 min. • **Cook:** 5 hours
Makes: 6 cups

> 2 medium eggplants, cut into ½-in. pieces
> 1 medium onion, chopped
> 1 can (14½ oz.) diced tomatoes, undrained
> 12 garlic cloves, sliced
> ½ cup dry red wine
> 3 Tbsp. extra virgin olive oil
> 2 Tbsp. red wine vinegar
> 4 tsp. capers, undrained
> 5 bay leaves
> 1½ tsp. salt
> ¼ tsp. coarsely ground pepper
>   French bread baguette slices, toasted
>   Optional: Fresh basil leaves, toasted pine nuts and additional olive oil

Place first 11 ingredients in a 6-qt. slow cooker (do not stir). Cook, covered, on high for 3 hours. Stir gently; replace cover. Cook on high 2 hours longer or until vegetables are tender. Cool slightly; discard bay leaves. Serve with toasted baguette slices, adding toppings as desired.

¼ cup: 34 cal., 2g fat (0 sat. fat), 0 chol., 189mg sod., 4g carb. (2g sugars, 2g fiber), 1g pro.

SAUSAGE MUSHROOM APPETIZERS

These stuffed mushrooms are can't-stop-eating-them good. For variations, I sometimes substitute venison or crabmeat for the pork sausage in the stuffing.
—Sheryl Siemonsma, Sioux Falls, SD

Prep: 15 min. • **Bake:** 20 min.
Makes: 4 dozen

- 48 large fresh mushrooms
- 2 large eggs, lightly beaten
- 1 lb. bulk pork sausage, cooked and crumbled
- 1 cup shredded Swiss cheese
- ¼ cup mayonnaise
- 3 Tbsp. butter, melted
- 2 Tbsp. finely chopped onion
- 2 tsp. spicy brown or horseradish mustard
- 1 tsp. garlic salt
- 1 tsp. Cajun seasoning
- 1 tsp. Worcestershire sauce

1. Remove the mushroom stems (discard or save for another use); set caps aside. In a large bowl, combine the remaining ingredients. Stuff into the mushroom caps.
2. Place in 2 greased 13x9-in. baking dishes. Bake, uncovered, at 350° until heated through, 16-20 minutes.
1 stuffed mushroom: 53 cal., 4g fat (2g sat. fat), 17mg chol., 129mg sod., 1g carb. (0 sugars, 0 fiber), 2g pro.

MINI ROSEMARY-ROAST BEEF SANDWICHES

MINI ROSEMARY-ROAST BEEF SANDWICHES

Roast beef sandwiches never last long at a party, especially if you dollop them with mayo, mustard, horseradish and pickled giardiniera relish.
—Susan Hein, Burlington, WI

Prep: 25 min. + chilling
Bake: 50 min. + chilling • **Makes:** 2 dozen

- 1 beef top round roast (3 lbs.)
- 3 tsp. kosher salt
- 2 tsp. crushed dried rosemary
- 2 Tbsp. olive oil, divided
- 2 tsp. pepper
- 2 cups mild giardiniera, drained
- 1 cup reduced-fat mayonnaise
- 2 Tbsp. stone-ground mustard
- 1 to 2 Tbsp. prepared horseradish
- 24 Hawaiian sweet rolls, split

1. Sprinkle roast with salt and rosemary. Cover and refrigerate at least 8 hours or up to 24 hours.
2. Preheat oven to 325°. Uncover roast and pat dry. Rub roast with 1 Tbsp. oil; sprinkle with pepper. In a large cast-iron or other ovenproof skillet, heat remaining oil over medium-high heat. Brown roast on both sides.
3. Transfer to the oven; roast until a thermometer reads 135° for medium-rare, 50-60 minutes. (Temperature of roast will continue to rise about 10° upon standing.) Remove roast from skillet; let stand 1 hour. Refrigerate, covered, at least 2 hours, until cold.
4. Place giardiniera in a food processor; pulse until finely chopped. In a small bowl, mix mayonnaise, mustard and horseradish.
5. To serve, thinly slice cold beef. Serve on rolls with mayonnaise mixture and chopped giardiniera.
1 sandwich with about 2 tsp. mayonnaise mixture and 4 tsp. giardiniera: 220 cal., 9g fat (3g sat. fat), 50mg chol., 466mg sod., 18g carb. (7g sugars, 1g fiber), 17g pro.

APPLE SPICE CAKE WITH BROWN SUGAR FROSTING

I am a healthy eater most of the time, but this cake is worth the splurge! Every year, I treasure the opportunity to make my own birthday cake, and I choose this. You can add a cup of raisins to the batter before baking if you'd like.

—Jennifer Owen, Louisville, KY

Prep: 30 min. • **Bake:** 35 min. + cooling
Makes: 16 servings

- 4 medium Honeycrisp apples, peeled and cut into 1-in. pieces (about 1½ lbs.)
- 2 cups sugar
- ½ cup canola oil
- 2 large eggs, room temperature
- 2 tsp. vanilla extract
- 2 cups all-purpose flour
- 1 Tbsp. pumpkin pie spice
- 2 tsp. baking powder
- 1 tsp. salt
- ½ cup buttermilk
- 1½ cups chopped walnuts, toasted

FROSTING
- 1 pkg. (8 oz.) cream cheese, softened
- ½ cup butter, softened
- 1 cup confectioners' sugar
- 1 cup packed brown sugar
- 1½ tsp. vanilla extract
- 1 tsp. pumpkin pie spice
- 1½ cups chopped walnuts, toasted

1. Preheat oven to 350°. Line bottoms of 2 greased 9-in. round baking pans with parchment; grease parchment.
2. Place apples in a food processor; pulse until finely chopped. In a large bowl, beat the sugar, oil, eggs and vanilla until well blended. In another bowl, whisk flour, pie spice, baking powder and salt; gradually beat into sugar mixture alternately with buttermilk. Stir in apples and walnuts.
3. Transfer batter to prepared pans. Bake until a toothpick inserted in center comes out clean, 35-40 minutes. Cool in pans 10 minutes before removing to wire racks; remove paper. Cool completely.
4. In a large bowl, beat cream cheese, butter, sugars, vanilla and pie spice until smooth. Spread frosting between layers and over top and sides of cake. Gently press walnuts into the frosting on top of the cake. Refrigerate leftovers.

1 piece: 574 cal., 33g fat (9g sat. fat), 53mg chol., 326mg sod., 67g carb. (51g sugars, 2g fiber), 7g pro.

READER REVIEW

"I have been trying to find the recipe to re-create my favorite birthday cake. Here it is, 60 years later. And still special!"

LINDA, TASTEOFHOME.COM

APPLE SPICE CAKE WITH BROWN SUGAR FROSTING

YUMMY CHOCOLATE CAKE

YUMMY CHOCOLATE CAKE

When you're trying to eat better but still crave a sweet treat, this chocolaty cake is the solution! And it's so easy to make.

—LaDonna Reed, Ponca City, OK

Prep: 20 min. • **Bake:** 15 min. + cooling
Makes: 16 servings

- 1 pkg. chocolate cake mix (regular size)
- 1 pkg. (2.1 oz.) sugar-free instant chocolate pudding mix
- 1¾ cups water
- 3 large egg whites, room temperature

FROSTING
- 1¼ cups cold fat-free milk
- ¼ tsp. almond extract
- 1 pkg. (1.4 oz.) sugar-free instant chocolate pudding mix
- 1 carton (8 oz.) frozen reduced-fat whipped topping, thawed
  Chocolate curls, optional

1. Preheat oven to 350°. In a large bowl, combine cake mix, pudding mix, water and egg whites. Beat on low speed for 1 minute, then on medium for 2 minutes. Pour into a greased 15x10x1-in. baking pan. Bake until a toothpick inserted in center comes out clean, 12-18 minutes. Cool on a wire rack.
2. For frosting, place milk and extract in a large bowl. Sprinkle with a third of the pudding mix; let stand for 1 minute. Whisk pudding into the milk. Repeat twice with the remaining pudding mix. Whisk pudding 2 minutes longer. Let stand for 15 minutes. Fold in whipped topping. Frost cake. If desired, garnish with chocolate curls.
1 piece: 184 cal., 3g fat (2g sat. fat), 0 chol., 465mg sod., 34g carb. (17g sugars, 1g fiber), 3g pro. **Diabetic exchanges:** 2 starch, ½ fat.

HOISIN COCKTAIL MEATBALLS

HOISIN COCKTAIL MEATBALLS

These saucy meatballs make a fun and flavorful appetizer for all kinds of get-togethers. Sometimes I prep them a day ahead so I can just pop them in the oven, then serve.

—Deirdre Cox, Kansas City, MO

Prep: 20 min. • **Bake:** 20 min.
Makes: about 2½ dozen

- 2 Tbsp. hoisin sauce
- 1 Tbsp. reduced-sodium soy sauce
- 1 tsp. sesame oil
- ¼ cup dry bread crumbs
- 3 Tbsp. chopped green onions
- 3 Tbsp. minced fresh parsley
- 2 garlic cloves, minced
- 1 tsp. minced fresh gingerroot
- 1½ lbs. lean ground beef

SAUCE
- ¼ cup rice vinegar
- ¼ cup hoisin sauce
- 2 Tbsp. water
- 2 Tbsp. sesame oil
- 2 Tbsp. reduced-sodium soy sauce
- 1 Tbsp. honey
- 2 garlic cloves, minced
- 1 tsp. minced fresh gingerroot

1. Preheat oven to 350°. In a large bowl, combine first 8 ingredients. Crumble beef over mixture; mix lightly but thoroughly.
2. Shape into scant 1-in. balls. Place in a 13x9-in. baking dish coated with cooking spray. Bake, uncovered, until meat is no longer pink, 20-25 minutes.
3. Meanwhile, in a small saucepan, combine the sauce ingredients; heat through. Serve with meatballs.
1 meatball: 56 cal., 3g fat (1g sat. fat), 13mg chol., 121mg sod., 3g carb. (1g sugars, 0 fiber), 4g pro.

HOLIDAY & SEASONAL PLEASERS

Family and friends are the most important part of a holiday gathering, of course—but food is pretty close! Choose from these delicious recipes to set the menu for Easter brunch, a July Fourth cookout, a spooky Halloween party, a Thanksgiving feast with family, and Christmas celebrations!

Strawberry Tarragon Chicken Salad (p. 261) **Apple Butter Pumpkin Pie** (p. 272) **Apricot-Apple Cider** (p. 267)
Mushroom & Smoked Gouda Puff (p. 277) **Sweet Tea Barbecued Chicken** (p. 263)

Easter Brunch

For a perfect Easter celebration, choose light and flavorful dishes that are as pretty as they are tasty. Sweet and savory pancakes and breakfast casseroles, refreshing salads and delectable desserts—every item on the menu is just right for spring.

ORANGE RICOTTA PANCAKES

ORANGE RICOTTA PANCAKES

After you try these pancakes once, you are likely to crave them again and again. They're so soft and sweet, you could even eat them without syrup!
—Brehan Kohl, Anchorage, AK

Takes: 30 min. • **Makes:** 12 pancakes

- 1½ cups all-purpose flour
- 3 Tbsp. sugar
- 1½ tsp. baking powder
- ½ tsp. baking soda
- ¼ tsp. salt
- 1 large egg
- 1 cup part-skim ricotta cheese
- ¾ cup 2% milk
- ½ tsp. grated orange zest
- ½ cup orange juice
- ¼ cup butter, melted
- ½ tsp. vanilla extract
  Maple syrup and confectioners' sugar, optional

1. In a bowl, whisk the first 5 ingredients. In another bowl, whisk egg, cheese, milk, orange zest, orange juice, melted butter and vanilla until blended. Add to the dry ingredients; stir just until moistened.
2. Lightly grease a griddle; heat over medium heat. Pour batter by ¼ cupfuls onto griddle. Cook until bubbles on top begin to pop and bottoms are golden brown. Turn; cook until second side is golden brown. If desired, serve with syrup and confectioners' sugar.

3 pancakes: 449 cal., 19g fat (11g sat. fat), 106mg chol., 654mg sod., 54g carb. (15g sugars, 1g fiber), 15g pro.

EASY CITRUS SEAFOOD SALAD

This super simple, deceptively delicious recipe was inspired by a seafood salad I had in the Bahamas that featured conch. I substitute crab and shrimp and like it even more!
—Cindy Heyd, Edmond, OK

Takes: 15 min. • **Makes:** 4 servings

- 1 medium orange
- 1 medium lemon
- 1 medium lime
- ½ lb. peeled and deveined cooked shrimp (31-40 per lb.), coarsely chopped
- ½ lb. refrigerated fresh or imitation crabmeat, coarsely chopped
- 2 Tbsp. finely chopped sweet onion
- 2 Tbsp. finely chopped sweet red pepper
  Shredded lettuce
  Assorted crackers

Finely grate zest from orange. Cut orange crosswise in half; squeeze juice from orange. Transfer zest and juice to a large bowl. Repeat with lemon and lime. Add shrimp, crab, onion and pepper; toss to coat. Serve on lettuce with crackers.

¾ cup: 128 cal., 2g fat (0 sat. fat), 141mg chol., 309mg sod., 6g carb. (3g sugars, 1g fiber), 22g pro. **Diabetic exchanges:** 3 lean meat.

HAM & CHEESE BREAKFAST STRUDELS

HAM & CHEESE BREAKFAST STRUDELS

These get the morning off to a cheery start! Sometimes I assemble the strudels ahead and freeze them individually, then bake them as we need them.
—Jo Groth, Plainfield, IA

Prep: 25 min. • **Bake:** 10 min.
Makes: 6 servings

- 3 Tbsp. butter, divided
- 2 Tbsp. all-purpose flour
- 1 cup whole milk
- ⅓ cup shredded Swiss cheese
- 2 Tbsp. grated Parmesan cheese
- ¼ tsp. salt
- 5 large eggs, lightly beaten
- ¼ lb. ground fully cooked ham (about ¾ cup)
- 6 sheets phyllo dough (14x9-in. size)
- ½ cup butter, melted
- ¼ cup dry bread crumbs

TOPPING
- 2 Tbsp. grated Parmesan cheese
- 2 Tbsp. minced fresh parsley

1. In a small saucepan, melt 2 Tbsp. butter. Stir in flour until smooth; gradually add milk. Bring to a boil; cook and stir 2 minutes or until thickened. Stir in cheeses and salt.

2. In a large nonstick skillet, melt the remaining 1 Tbsp. butter over medium heat. Add eggs to pan; cook and stir until almost set. Stir in ham and the cheese sauce; heat through. Remove from heat.

3. Preheat oven to 375°. Place 1 sheet of phyllo dough on a work surface. (Keep remaining phyllo covered with a damp towel to prevent it from drying out.) Brush with melted butter; sprinkle with 2 tsp. bread crumbs. Fold phyllo in half lengthwise; brush again with butter. Spoon ½ cup filling onto phyllo about 2 in. from a short side. Fold side and edges over filling and roll up. Brush with butter. Repeat with the remaining phyllo, butter, bread crumbs and filling.

4. Place on a greased baking sheet; sprinkle each with 1 tsp. cheese and 1 tsp. parsley. Bake 10-15 minutes or until golden brown. Serve immediately.

Freeze option: After topping strudels with cheese and parsley, freeze unbaked on a waxed paper-lined baking sheet until firm. Transfer to a freezer container; return to freezer. To use, bake strudels as directed, increasing time to 30-35 minutes or until heated through and golden brown.

1 strudel: 439 cal., 33g fat (18g sat. fat), 255mg chol., 754mg sod., 20g carb. (4g sugars, 1g fiber), 16g pro.

QUICHE PASTRY CUPS

My grandmother used to make egg cup surprises for family brunches on special occasions. The added fillings were always a surprise; she never seemed to use the same combination of ingredients twice. As children, we had a guessing game as to what we'd find in the tender crust, which added an aspect of family fun to our meal.
—Denalee Standart, Rancho Mureta, CA

Prep: 30 min. • **Bake:** 15 min.
Makes: 1½ dozen

- 1 pkg. (17.3 oz.) frozen puff pastry, thawed
- 4 large eggs, divided use
- 1 cup plus 2 Tbsp. half-and-half cream, divided
- 1 Tbsp. minced fresh thyme
- ½ tsp. salt
- ½ tsp. pepper
- ¼ tsp. ground nutmeg
- 1½ cups shredded Gruyere cheese
- 1½ cups chopped fresh spinach
- 1 medium sweet red pepper, chopped
- 8 bacon strips, cooked and crumbled

1. Preheat oven to 400°. On a lightly floured surface, unfold puff pastry. Roll each sheet into a 12-in. square; cut each into 9 squares. Place in ungreased muffin cups, pressing gently onto bottoms and up sides, allowing corners to point up.

2. In a small bowl, whisk 3 eggs, 1 cup cream, thyme and seasonings. In another bowl, combine the cheese, spinach, red pepper and bacon; divide among pastry cups. Pour egg mixture over the cheese mixture.

3. In a small bowl, whisk remaining egg with remaining 2 Tbsp. cream; brush over pastry edges. Bake 15-18 minutes or until golden brown. Remove to wire racks. Serve warm.

Freeze option: Cover and freeze baked pastries on greased baking sheets until firm. Transfer to resealable freezer containers; return to freezer. To use, reheat frozen pastries on ungreased baking sheets in a preheated 375° oven 17-20 minutes or until heated through.

1 pastry cup: 229 cal., 14g fat (5g sat. fat), 63mg chol., 313mg sod., 17g carb. (1g sugars, 2g fiber), 8g pro.

MIXED FRUIT WITH LEMON-BASIL DRESSING

A slightly savory dressing really complements the sweet fruit in this recipe. I also use the dressing on greens.
—Dixie Terry, Goreville, IL

Takes: 15 min. • **Makes:** 8 servings

- 2 Tbsp. lemon juice
- ½ tsp. sugar
- ¼ tsp. salt
- ¼ tsp. ground mustard
- ⅛ tsp. onion powder
  Dash pepper
- 6 Tbsp. olive oil
- 4½ tsp. minced fresh basil
- 1 cup cubed fresh pineapple
- 1 cup sliced fresh strawberries
- 1 cup sliced peeled kiwifruit
- 1 cup seedless watermelon balls
- 1 cup fresh blueberries
- 1 cup fresh raspberries

1. Place lemon juice, sugar, salt, mustard, onion powder and pepper in a blender; cover and pulse until blended. While processing, gradually add oil in a steady stream. Stir in basil.
2. In a large bowl, combine the fruit. Drizzle with dressing and toss to coat. Refrigerate until serving.

¾ cup: 145 cal., 11g fat (1g sat. fat), 0 chol., 76mg sod., 14g carb. (9g sugars, 3g fiber), 1g pro. **Diabetic exchanges:** 2 fat, 1 fruit.

SMOKED GOUDA & SWISS CHARD STRATA

SMOKED GOUDA & SWISS CHARD STRATA

I shared this impressive strata with friends at their new home. For your special occasions, change up the veggies and cheese. I've used tomatoes, spinach and cheddar.
—Kimberly Forni, Laconia, NH

Prep: 30 min. + chilling • **Bake:** 1 hour
Makes: 10 servings

- 10 bacon strips, chopped
- 1 lb. Swiss chard, leaves chopped and stems julienned
- 1 large sweet onion, thinly sliced
- ½ cup chopped roasted sweet red peppers
- 12 slices white bread, toasted and cubed
- 2 cups smoked Gouda or smoked Gruyere cheese, shredded
- 2 cups Swiss cheese, shredded
- 10 large eggs
- 3½ cups 2% milk
- 2 tsp. prepared mustard
- 1 tsp. salt
- ½ tsp. coarsely ground pepper
- ½ tsp. cayenne pepper

1. In a large skillet, cook bacon over medium heat until crisp; drain on paper towels, reserving 1 Tbsp. drippings. Cook chard stems and onion in reserved drippings over medium heat until tender, about 4 minutes. Add chard leaves and red pepper; cook 2 minutes. Drain.
2. Lightly grease a 13x9-in. baking dish. Layer with half the bread cubes, half the vegetable mixture and half the cheeses. Repeat layers.
3. Mix the remaining ingredients until well blended. Pour over layers; press down slightly. Sprinkle bacon over top. Cover and refrigerate several hours or overnight.
4. Preheat oven to 325°. Remove strata from refrigerator while the oven heats. Bake until puffy, lightly browned and set, about 1 hour.

1 piece: 509 cal., 31g fat (14g sat. fat), 257mg chol., 1055mg sod., 28g carb. (10g sugars, 2g fiber), 28g pro.

LEMON DREAM CHEESECAKE

This cheesecake bakes like a dream with no cracks. Plus, it cuts well and everyone loves the light lemon flavor—a refreshing and elegant treat any time of year.
—Bonnie Jost, Manitowoc, WI

Prep: 30 min. • **Bake:** 55 min. + chilling
Makes: 16 servings

- 2 cups graham cracker crumbs
- 6 Tbsp. butter, melted
- ¼ cup sugar

FILLING

- 4 pkg. (8 oz. each) cream cheese, softened
- 1 cup sugar
- ½ cup heavy whipping cream
- ¼ cup lemon juice
- 2 Tbsp. all-purpose flour
- 1 Tbsp. grated lemon zest
- 2½ tsp. vanilla extract
- 1 tsp. lemon extract
- 10 drops yellow food coloring, optional
- 5 large eggs, lightly beaten

1. Preheat oven to 325°. In a small bowl, combine the cracker crumbs, butter and sugar. Press onto bottom and 2 in. up the side of a greased 10-in. springform pan. Place pan on a baking sheet. Bake 10 minutes. Cool on a wire rack.

2. In a large bowl, beat cream cheese and sugar until smooth. Beat in cream, lemon juice, flour, lemon zest, extracts and, if desired, food coloring. Add eggs; beat on low speed just until combined. Pour into crust. Return pan to baking sheet.

3. Bake 55-65 minutes or until center is almost set. Cool on a wire rack 10 minutes. Carefully run a knife around edge of pan to loosen; cool 1 hour. Refrigerate overnight. Remove sides of pan.

1 slice: 396 cal., 29g fat (18g sat. fat), 150mg chol., 286mg sod., 27g carb. (19g sugars, 0 fiber), 7g pro.

STRAWBERRY TARRAGON CHICKEN SALAD
PICTURED ON P. 257

One recent spring, I used my homegrown strawberries and fresh tarragon to do a little experimenting. It didn't take me long to come up with a winner! My husband enjoyed my creation as much as I did. We can't wait for strawberry season to come around again!
—Sue Gronholz, Beaver Dam, WI

Takes: 30 min. • **Makes:** 5 servings

- ½ cup mayonnaise
- 2 tsp. sugar
- 2 tsp. minced fresh tarragon or 1 tsp. dried tarragon
- ¼ tsp. salt
- ⅛ tsp. pepper
- 2½ cups cubed cooked chicken breast
- 2 cups quartered fresh strawberries
- 1 cup fresh shelled peas or frozen peas, thawed
- ½ cup chopped celery
- 2 Tbsp. chopped sweet onion
  Torn mixed salad greens
- ½ cup chopped pecans, toasted

In a large bowl, whisk the first 5 ingredients until blended. Stir in chicken, strawberries, peas, celery and onion. Serve over salad greens; sprinkle with pecans.

1 cup: 378 cal., 26g fat (4g sat. fat), 56mg chol., 285mg sod., 13g carb. (7g sugars, 4g fiber), 23g pro.

TEST KITCHEN TIP
This salad is better when made ahead of time so the flavors can blend. But don't add the strawberries until you're ready to serve, as they tend to turn the salad pink when they sit!

LEMON DREAM CHEESECAKE

Fourth of July Cookout

At the height of the summer, what's better than a holiday cookout? Pull out the stops with deluxe burgers and brats, delicious barbecued chicken, sweet summertime desserts and more!

DAD'S COLA BURGERS

DAD'S COLA BURGERS

Before you hand out the drinks, save a little soda to make these delectable burgers. Cola really sparks the flavor— used in the meat mixture and brushed on during cooking, it takes this favorite to a whole new level.
—*Emily Nelson, Green Bay, WI*

Takes: 25 min. • **Makes:** 6 servings

- ½ cup crushed saltines (about 15 crackers)
- ½ cup (nondiet) cola, divided
- 6 Tbsp. French salad dressing, divided
- 1 large egg
- 2 Tbsp. grated Parmesan cheese
- ½ tsp. salt, divided
- 1½ lbs. lean ground beef (90% lean)
- 6 hamburger buns, split

Optional: Lettuce leaves and tomato and red onion slices

1. Combine saltine crumbs, ¼ cup cola, 3 Tbsp. salad dressing, egg, Parmesan cheese and ¼ tsp. salt. Add beef; mix well. Shape into six ¾-in.-thick patties (the mixture will be moist); sprinkle with the remaining salt. Combine remaining ¼ cup cola and 3 Tbsp. salad dressing.
2. Grill patties, covered, over medium heat 3 minutes per side. Brush with the cola mixture. Grill, brushing and turning occasionally, until a thermometer reads 160°, 3-4 minutes longer. Serve on buns; if desired, top with lettuce, tomato and onion.
1 burger: 419 cal., 20g fat (6g sat. fat), 103mg chol., 698mg sod., 30g carb. (7g sugars, 1g fiber), 28g pro.

EASY BUFFALO CHICKEN DIP

Everyone will simply devour this savory and delicious dip with shredded chicken throughout. The spicy kick makes it perfect summer party food, and the recipe always brings raves.
—*Janice Foltz, Hershey, PA*

Takes: 30 min.
Makes: 21 servings (4 cups dip)

- 1 pkg. (8 oz.) reduced-fat cream cheese
- 1 cup reduced-fat sour cream
- ½ cup Louisiana-style hot sauce
- 3 cups shredded cooked chicken breast
  Assorted crackers

1. Preheat oven to 350°. In a large bowl, beat cream cheese, sour cream and hot sauce until smooth; stir in chicken.
2. Transfer to an 8-in. square baking dish coated with cooking spray. Cover and bake until heated through, 18-22 minutes. Serve warm with crackers.
3 Tbsp.: 77 cal., 4g fat (2g sat. fat), 28mg chol., 71mg sod., 1g carb. (1g sugars, 0 fiber), 8g pro.

**RHUBARB BERRY
UPSIDE-DOWN CAKE**

RHUBARB BERRY UPSIDE-DOWN CAKE

I had leftover rhubarb and wanted to create something fresh. With blueberries, strawberries and dried cranberries on hand, I discovered I had a berry upside-down cake.
—June Paul, Portage, WI

Prep: 30 min. • **Bake:** 35 min. + cooling
Makes: 8 servings

- 2 Tbsp. butter
- 1¾ cups chopped fresh rhubarb
- ½ cup fresh blueberries
- 2 Tbsp. dried cranberries
- 2 Tbsp. brown sugar

CAKE
- 6 Tbsp. butter, softened
- 1 cup sugar
- 1 Tbsp. brown sugar
- 2 large eggs
- 1 Tbsp. seedless strawberry jam
- 1 tsp. vanilla extract
- 1¼ cups all-purpose flour
- 1½ tsp. baking powder
- ½ tsp. salt
- ½ cup 2% milk
- ¼ cup orange juice

1. Preheat oven to 350°. Place 2 Tbsp. butter in an 11x7-in. baking dish. Place in oven for 5-6 minutes or until the butter is melted; carefully swirl to coat evenly.
2. Place the rhubarb, blueberries and cranberries in a bowl; sprinkle with sugar and toss to combine. Transfer to the baking dish.
3. In a large bowl, beat softened butter and sugars until blended. Add eggs, 1 at a time, beating well after each addition. Beat in jam and vanilla. In a small bowl, whisk flour, baking powder and salt. Add to the creamed mixture alternately with milk and orange juice, beating well after each addition. Pour over fruit, spreading evenly.
4. Bake 35-45 minutes or until top is golden brown and a toothpick inserted in center comes out clean. Cool 10 minutes.
5. Loosen edges of cake from pan with a knife; invert onto a serving plate. Serve warm or at room temperature.
1 serving: 344 cal., 13g fat (8g sat. fat), 78mg chol., 343mg sod., 53g carb. (36g sugars, 1g fiber), 5g pro.

SWEET TEA BARBECUED CHICKEN
PICTURED ON P. 257

Marinades sometimes use coffee or espresso—and that inspired me to try tea and apple juice to perk up the sauce for this chicken.
—Kelly Williams, Forked River, NJ

Prep: 15 min. • **Cook:** 1 hour
Makes: 8 servings

- 1 cup unsweetened apple juice
- 1 cup water
- 2 tsp. seafood seasoning
- 1 tsp. paprika
- 1 tsp. garlic powder
- 1 tsp. coarsely ground pepper
- 1 chicken (4 to 5 lbs.), cut up
- 1 cup barbecue sauce
- ½ cup sweet tea

1. Preheat oven to 350°. Pour apple juice and water into a large shallow roasting pan. Mix seafood seasoning, paprika, garlic powder and pepper; rub over chicken. Place in roasting pan.
2. Bake, covered, until juices run clear and a thermometer reads 170°-175°, 50-60 minutes. Transfer chicken to a foil-lined 15x10x1-in. baking pan. Whisk barbecue sauce and sweet tea; brush some of the mixture over chicken.
3. Place chicken on greased grill rack; grill over medium heat 3-4 minutes per side, brushing occasionally with the remaining sauce.
1 piece: 374 cal., 17g fat (5g sat. fat), 104mg chol., 608mg sod., 19g carb. (16g sugars, 1g fiber), 33g pro.

READER REVIEW

"Great BBQ chicken. Slow-baking the chicken first made it juicy and tender. Finished it off on the grill with a North Carolina sauce with the sweet tea. Wonderful Memorial Day dish!"
CBYBEE, TASTEOFHOME.COM

BBQ BRATS

In Wisconsin, brats are a food group! We are always looking for new ways to cook them. This recipe is easy and a hit at any party or cookout, any time of year.
—Jessica Abnet, DePere, WI

Prep: 20 min. • **Cook:** 3 hours
Makes: 10 servings

- 10 uncooked bratwurst links
- 1 bottle (12 oz.) beer or 1½ cups chicken broth
- 1 cup ketchup
- 1 cup honey barbecue sauce
- 10 hot dog buns, split
  Spicy brown mustard

1. Grill bratwursts, covered, on an oiled rack over medium heat or broil 4 in. from heat 10 minutes, turning frequently. Transfer to a 5-qt. slow cooker.
2. In a large bowl, mix beer, ketchup and barbecue sauce; pour over the bratwursts. Cook, covered, on low until cooked through, 3-4 hours. Place bratwursts on buns. Serve with mustard and, if desired, cooking liquid.

1 serving: 480 cal., 27g fat (9g sat. fat), 64mg chol., 1659mg sod., 41g carb. (20g sugars, 1g fiber), 16g pro.

STRAWBERRY-LIME BARS

STRAWBERRY-LIME BARS

Our family loves fresh strawberries so I look for different ways to use them. This tempting, yummy dessert has sweet strawberries, tart lime, pretzels and cream cheese.
—Alexandra Barnett, Forest, VA

Prep: 25 min. + chilling
Bake: 10 min. + cooling • **Makes:** 2 dozen

- 2 cups finely crushed pretzels (about 6 oz.)
- ¾ cup sugar, divided
- ¾ cup butter, melted
- 2 cups boiling water
- 1 pkg. (6 oz.) strawberry gelatin
- 1 lb. fresh strawberries, chopped
- 2 pkg. (8 oz. each) cream cheese, softened
- 1 Tbsp. grated lime zest
- ¼ cup lime juice
- 1 tsp. vanilla extract

1. Preheat oven to 350°. Place crushed pretzels and ¼ cup sugar in a small bowl; stir in the melted butter. Spread out in an ungreased 15x10x1-in. baking pan. To toast, bake until golden brown, 9-11 minutes. Cool completely.
2. Meanwhile, in a bowl, add boiling water to gelatin; stir 2 minutes to completely dissolve. Gently stir in strawberries. Cool slightly. Refrigerate 30 minutes.
3. In a large bowl, beat cream cheese, lime zest, lime juice, vanilla and remaining sugar until blended. Stir in cooled pretzel mixture. Spread into an ungreased 13x9-in. baking pan. Top with strawberry mixture. Refrigerate, covered, 2 hours or until firm.

1 bar: 201 cal., 13g fat (7g sat. fat), 36mg chol., 240mg sod., 21g carb. (14g sugars, 1g fiber), 3g pro.

A Patriotic Cheese Board

Design your cheese board to reflect your holiday theme—right down to the fireworks!

*

Choose ingredients with red, white and blue in mind: white Brie and goat cheese, blue-veined Gorgonzola, bright berries, red grapes and deep red kalamata olives. Provolone cutouts provide the stars, and mozzarella cheese whips mimic fireworks.

Halloween Party Treats

When it comes to Halloween, no one really wants tricks—it's all about the treats! These delightful sweets and appetizers are perfect for the season, ingeniously decorated and just the right size for small party bites.

HALLOWEEN PEANUT SPIDER COOKIES

HALLOWEEN PEANUT SPIDER COOKIES

These adorable spider cookies are so easy to make. They'll be the star at your next Halloween party!
—Rashanda Cobbins, Milwaukee, WI

Prep: 20 min. • **Bake:** 15 min. + cooling
Makes: 2 dozen

- 1 cup creamy peanut butter
- 1 cup sugar
- 1 large egg, room temperature
- 24 Reese's mini peanut butter cups
- ½ cup milk chocolate chips
- 1 tsp. shortening
- 48 candy eyes

1. Preheat oven to 350°. Cream peanut butter and sugar until light and fluffy. Beat in egg.

2. Roll dough into 1-in. balls. Place 2 in. apart on ungreased baking sheets. Flatten slightly with the bottom of a glass. Bake until the tops are slightly cracked, 15-17 minutes. Cool 3 minutes before removing from pans to wire racks. Immediately press 1 mini peanut butter cup into center of each cookie. Let stand until set.

3. In a microwave, melt chocolate chips and shortening; stir until smooth. Place mixture in a resealable plastic bag; cut a small hole in a corner of bag. Adhere candy eyes to peanut butter cups with melted chocolate mixture. Pipe 8 lines alongside each peanut butter cup to resemble spider legs. Let stand until set.

1 cookie: 138 cal., 8g fat (2g sat. fat), 9mg chol., 60mg sod., 15g carb. (13g sugars, 1g fiber), 3g pro.

MUMMY POPPERS

I wrapped these spicy jalapeno poppers in puff pastry to look like a mummy. You can tame the heat by adjusting the amount of chipotle peppers.
—Nick Iverson, Denver, CO

Prep: 30 min. • **Bake:** 30 min.
Makes: 32 appetizers

- 1 pkg. (8 oz.) cream cheese, softened
- 2 cups shredded cheddar cheese
- 2 green onions, finely chopped
- 1 to 2 chipotle peppers in adobo sauce, finely chopped
- 2 Tbsp. lime juice
- 1 Tbsp. honey
- ½ tsp. salt
- ½ tsp. ground cumin
- ¼ tsp. pepper
- 16 jalapeno peppers, halved lengthwise and seeded
- 1 pkg. (17.3 oz.) frozen puff pastry, thawed and cut lengthwise into 32 strips

1. Preheat oven to 400°. Beat the first 9 ingredients until blended. Spoon or pipe cheese mixture into pepper halves.

2. Wrap puff pastry strips around pepper halves. Transfer wrapped peppers to parchment-lined baking sheets. Bake until pastry is golden brown and cheese is melted, 30-40 minutes.

1 popper: 133 cal., 9g fat (4g sat. fat), 14mg chol., 159mg sod., 10g carb. (1g sugars, 1g fiber), 3g pro.

APRICOT-APPLE CIDER
PICTURED ON P. 257
Dried apricots give this comforting cider a delicious twist. Add cranberries, cinnamon, allspice and cloves, and you have the perfect hot drink to sip on cool nights.
—Ginnie Busam, Pewee Valley, KY

Prep: 20 min. • **Cook:** 3 hours
Makes: 13 servings (2½ qt.)

- 8 cups unsweetened apple juice
- 1 can (12 oz.) ginger ale
- ½ cup dried apricots, halved
- ½ cup dried cranberries
- 2 cinnamon sticks (3 in.)
- 1 Tbsp. whole allspice
- 1 Tbsp. whole cloves

In a 5-qt. slow cooker, combine apple juice and ginger ale. Place the apricots, cranberries, cinnamon sticks, allspice and cloves on a double thickness of cheesecloth; bring up corners of cloth and tie with string to form a bag. Place in slow cooker; cover. Cook on high until heated through, 3-4 hours. Discard the spice bag.

¾ cup: 79 cal., 0 fat (0 sat. fat), 0 chol., 8mg sod., 20g carb. (17g sugars, 0 fiber), 0 pro. **Diabetic exchanges:** 2 fruit.

READER REVIEW

"Delicious. Served this for my book club of 10 members, who enjoyed it so much that I had to make another batch on the spot. I left the fruit in the pan to serve with the juice mix and put just the spices in a large tea ball strainer."
RUTH, TASTEOFHOME.COM

PUMPKIN PINWHEELS
Cream cheese, mozzarella and roasted red peppers make these pretty pinwheels devilishly delicious. They were a hit at my last Halloween party.
—Anndrea Bailey, Huntington Beach, CA

Prep: 15 min. + chilling • **Bake:** 20 min.
Makes: 32 pinwheels

- 2 pkg. (8 oz. each) cream cheese, softened
- 1 cup shredded part-skim mozzarella cheese
- ½ cup chopped roasted sweet red peppers, drained
- ¼ tsp. Italian seasoning
- ¼ tsp. garlic salt
- ¼ tsp. onion powder
- 2 tubes (8 oz. each) refrigerated crescent rolls
  Optional: Pretzel sticks and fresh cilantro leaves

1. Preheat oven to 350°. Beat cream cheese until smooth. Beat in mozzarella, red peppers and seasonings until blended. Unroll tubes of crescent dough and separate each into 2 rectangles; press perforations to seal.
2. Spread the cheese mixture over each rectangle. Roll up jelly-roll style, starting with a short side; pinch seam to seal. Wrap and chill at least 1 hour.
3. Cut each roll crosswise into 8 slices; place on ungreased baking sheets, cut side down. Bake until golden brown, 20-22 minutes. If desired, decorate with pretzel sticks and cilantro leaves to look like pumpkins.

1 pinwheel: 112 cal., 8g fat (3g sat. fat), 17mg chol., 204mg sod., 7g carb. (2g sugars, 0 fiber), 3g pro.

WITCHES' FINGERS

You don't need a cauldron to conjure these frightening fingers. They're a sweet-and-salty treat that's spooky easy to make.
—*Beth Tomkiw, Milwaukee, WI*

Takes: 20 min. • **Makes:** 1 dozen

1½ cups vibrant green candy
coating disks
6 pretzel rods, broken in half
6 jelly beans, cut in half lengthwise

In a microwave, melt candy coating; stir until smooth. Dip broken end of pretzel rods in coating; allow excess to drip off. Place on waxed paper; press a jelly bean half onto dipped end of each pretzel to resemble a fingernail. Let stand until almost set. Using a toothpick, make lines on each pretzel to resemble knuckles.

1 pretzel half: 155 cal., 7g fat (7g sat. fat), 1mg chol., 131mg sod., 21g carb. (18g sugars, 0 fiber), 1g pro.

GINGERBREAD SKELETONS

GINGERBREAD SKELETONS

Any small gingerbread-boy cookie cutter takes on new life with these clever cookies. Give the skeletons some cat friends, too. The more the merrier!
—*Dore Merrick Grabski, Utica, NY*

Prep: 15 min. + chilling • **Bake:** 10 min./ batch • **Makes:** about 2 dozen

⅔ cup shortening
½ cup sugar
½ cup molasses
1 large egg, room temperature
3 cups all-purpose flour
1 tsp. baking soda
1 tsp. each ground cinnamon, ginger and cloves
½ tsp. salt
½ tsp. ground nutmeg
Confectioners' sugar icing

1. In a bowl, cream shortening and sugar. Add molasses and egg; mix well. Combine flour, baking soda, cinnamon, ginger, cloves, salt and nutmeg; gradually add to creamed mixture and mix well. Divide dough in half. Refrigerate at least 2 hours.
2. Preheat oven to 350°. On a lightly floured surface, roll out each portion of dough to ⅛-in. thickness. Cut with a floured 2-in. cookie cutter. Place 2 in. apart on greased baking sheets.
3. Bake 9 minutes or until edges are firm. Remove to wire racks to cool. Decorate with icing to resemble bones of skeletons.

1 cookie: 145 cal., 6g fat (1g sat. fat), 8mg chol., 108mg sod., 21g carb. (9g sugars, 1g fiber), 2g pro.

MAKE-A-MONSTER PIZZA

Creepy creatures have completely taken over this Halloween meal! Once you make a grid with ham strips, you can place a different spooky face or creature, such as a black olive spider, in each section.
—Marie Louise Ludwig, Phoenixville, PA

Prep: 30 min. • **Bake:** 20 min.
Makes: 6 servings

- 1 tube (13.8 oz.) refrigerated pizza crust
- 1 can (8 oz.) pizza sauce
- 4 cups shredded part-skim mozzarella cheese
- 2 oz. sliced deli ham, cut into ½-in. strips

    Optional: Asparagus, sweet peppers, tomatoes, mushrooms, ripe olives, pineapple, pepperoni and red onion

1. Preheat oven to 425°. Unroll pizza crust and press to fit into a greased 15x10x1-in. baking pan, pinching edges to form a rim. Bake until edges are lightly browned, 8-10 minutes.
2. Spread crust with pizza sauce; top with mozzarella cheese. Using ham strips, outline 12 sections. Arrange toppings of your choice in each section to create individual monster faces or other designs. Bake until crust is golden brown and cheese is melted, 10-15 minutes.
2 pieces: 413 cal., 18g fat (9g sat. fat), 52mg chol., 1193mg sod., 39g carb. (7g sugars, 2g fiber), 25g pro.

> **TEST KITCHEN TIP**
> Look to salad and olive bars for tiny treasures to boost the cuteness factor of faces or scenes.

BLACK-HEARTED CANDY APPLES

Color these old-fashioned candy apples whatever shade you like—black and red set an eerie scene on Halloween. The glossy coating on these apples is hard, not soft like the caramel variety, so it's best to lick them like a lollipop.
—Agnes Ward, Stratford, ON

Prep: 10 min. • **Cook:** 30 min. + standing
Makes: 4 apples

- 4 medium red apples
- 4 wooden or decorative pop sticks
- 2 cups sugar
- 1 cup water
- ⅔ cup light corn syrup
- ½ tsp. ground cinnamon, divided
    Red and black food coloring

1. Wash and thoroughly dry apples; remove stems. Insert wooden pop sticks into apples. Place on a waxed paper-lined baking sheet; set aside.
2. In a large heavy saucepan, combine the sugar, water and corn syrup. Cook and stir over medium heat until sugar is dissolved. Bring to a boil. Cook, without stirring, until a candy thermometer reads 290° (soft-crack stage).
3. Remove from heat and pour sugar mixture into 2 small bowls; stir ¼ tsp. cinnamon and red food coloring into 1 bowl. Stir black food coloring and remaining cinnamon into other bowl.
4. Working quickly, dip apples into hot sugar mixtures to completely coat. Place on the prepared baking sheet; let stand until set.
1 candy apple: 614 cal., 0 fat (0 sat. fat), 0 chol., 35mg sod., 161g carb. (129g sugars, 3g fiber), 0 pro.

BLACK-HEARTED CANDY APPLES

Giving Thanks

When your loved ones gather at Thanksgiving, treat them to a jaw-dropping spread with this array of traditional holiday dishes. From the turkey to the sides to the pie (and more pie!), these are recipes to please the whole family—and will guarantee a post-feast siesta!

CREAM CHEESE MASHED POTATOES

CREAM CHEESE MASHED POTATOES

Whenever I serve this easy mash, the bowl is always scraped clean. Before a big feast, I make it early and keep it warm in a slow cooker so I can focus on the last-minute details.
—Jill Thomas, Washington, IN

Prep: 20 min. • **Cook:** 15 min.
Makes: 20 servings

- 8 lbs. russet potatoes
- 1 pkg. (8 oz.) cream cheese, softened
- ½ cup butter, melted
- 2 tsp. salt
- ¾ tsp. pepper
  Additional melted butter, optional
- ¼ cup finely chopped green onions

1. Peel and cube potatoes. Place in a large stockpot; add water to cover. Bring to a boil. Reduce heat; cook, uncovered, until tender, 12-15 minutes. Drain.
2. With a mixer, beat cream cheese, ½ cup melted butter, salt and the pepper until smooth. Add potatoes; beat until light and fluffy. If desired, top with additional melted butter. Sprinkle with green onions.
¾ cup: 185 cal., 9g fat (5g sat. fat), 25mg chol., 318mg sod., 25g carb. (2g sugars, 2g fiber), 3g pro.

HOLIDAY RICE SALAD

It's nice to prepare a cold salad like this when you're entertaining because you can make it ahead and it doesn't take up valuable oven space.
—Debra Walter, Huntington Woods, MI

Prep: 10 min. + chilling
Makes: 14 servings

- 7 cups cooked wild rice, cooled
- 1 cup chopped pecans, toasted
- 1 cup thinly sliced green onions
- ½ cup dried cranberries
- ½ cup dried cherries or additional dried cranberries
- ½ cup golden raisins
- ½ cup minced fresh parsley
- ¼ cup slivered almonds, toasted
- 1 Tbsp. chopped fresh mint or 1 tsp. dried mint flakes

DRESSING
- ½ cup orange juice
- ⅓ cup cider vinegar
- ¼ cup olive oil
- 1 Tbsp. lime juice
- 2 tsp. sugar
- 1 tsp. salt
- ⅛ tsp. pepper

Combine the first 9 ingredients. In a jar with a tight-fitting lid, combine dressing ingredients; shake well. Pour over the rice mixture and toss to coat. Refrigerate, covered, for 2 hours or until serving.
¾ cup: 245 cal., 11g fat (1g sat. fat), 0 chol., 175mg sod., 35g carb. (14g sugars, 3g fiber), 5g pro. **Diabetic exchanges:** 2 starch, 2 fat.

APPLE & HERB ROASTED TURKEY

ELEGANT GREEN BEANS

Mushrooms and water chestnuts give new life to ordinary green bean casserole. Every time I make it for friends, I'm asked to share the recipe.
—Linda Poe, Sandstone, MN

Prep: 20 min. • **Bake:** 50 min.
Makes: 8 servings

- 1 can (8 oz.) sliced water chestnuts, drained
- 1 small onion, chopped
- 1 jar (4½ oz.) sliced mushrooms, drained
- 6 Tbsp. butter, divided
- ¼ cup all-purpose flour
- 1 cup 2% milk
- ½ cup chicken broth
- 1 tsp. reduced-sodium soy sauce
- ⅛ tsp. hot pepper sauce
  Dash salt
- 1 pkg. (16 oz.) frozen French-style green beans, thawed
- ½ cup shredded cheddar cheese
- 1 cup crushed french-fried onions

1. Preheat oven to 350°. In a small skillet, saute water chestnuts, onion and mushrooms in 2 Tbsp. butter until the onion is crisp-tender, 4-5 minutes; set aside.
2. In large skillet, melt the remaining 4 Tbsp. butter; stir in flour until smooth. Stir in milk, broth, soy sauce, pepper sauce and salt. Bring to a boil; cook and stir until thickened, about 2 minutes. Remove from heat; stir in green beans and cheese.
3. Spoon half of the bean mixture into a greased 1½-qt. baking dish. Layer with the water chestnut mixture and the remaining bean mixture.
4. Bake, uncovered, 45 minutes. Top with French-fried onions. Bake until heated through, about 5 minutes longer.
¾ cup: 218 cal., 15g fat (8g sat. fat), 35mg chol., 392mg sod., 17g carb. (5g sugars, 3g fiber), 5g pro.

APPLE & HERB ROASTED TURKEY

My daughter loves to help me make this moist roasted turkey with herbs. Her job is to hand Mommy the ingredients— if she doesn't eat the apples first!
—Kimberly Jackson, Gay, GA

Prep: 20 min. • **Bake:** 3 hours + standing
Makes: 14 servings

- ¼ cup minced fresh sage
- ¼ cup minced fresh rosemary
- 1 turkey (14 lbs.)
- 1 medium apple, quartered
- 1 medium onion, halved
- 1 celery rib, halved
- ½ cup butter, melted
- ½ cup apple jelly, warmed

1. Preheat oven to 325°. Combine sage and rosemary. With fingers, carefully loosen skin from the turkey breast; rub herbs under the skin. Secure skin to underside of breast with toothpicks.
2. Place turkey breast side up on a rack in a roasting pan. Stuff with apple, onion and celery. Brush with butter.
3. Roast, uncovered, until a thermometer inserted in thickest part of thigh reads 170°-175°, 3-3½ hours. (Cover loosely with foil if turkey browns too quickly.) Remove turkey from oven; brush with apple jelly. Tent with foil and let stand for 15 minutes before removing toothpicks and carving.
8 oz. cooked turkey: 626 cal., 31g fat (11g sat. fat), 262mg chol., 222mg sod., 10g carb. (9g sugars, 0 fiber), 72g pro.

BUTTERNUT & CHARD PASTA BAKE

BUTTERNUT & CHARD PASTA BAKE

This is a veggie hybrid of ever-popular holiday sides. With pureed squash in the creamy sauce and squash pieces in the casserole, it's made for butternut squash lovers! Swiss chard makes an ideal companion to the squash.
—Arlene Erlbach, Morton Grove, IL

Prep: 25 min. • **Bake:** 30 min.
Makes: 9 servings

- 3 cups uncooked bow tie pasta
- 2 cups fat-free ricotta cheese
- 4 large eggs
- 3 cups frozen cubed butternut squash, thawed and divided
- 1 tsp. dried thyme
- ½ tsp. salt, divided
- ¼ tsp. ground nutmeg
- 1 cup coarsely chopped shallots
- 1½ cups chopped Swiss chard, stems removed
- 2 Tbsp. olive oil
- 1½ cups panko bread crumbs
- ⅓ cup coarsely chopped fresh parsley
- ¼ tsp. garlic powder

1. Preheat oven to 375°. Cook pasta according to package directions for al dente; drain. Meanwhile, place the ricotta, eggs, 1½ cups squash, thyme, ¼ tsp. salt and nutmeg in a food processor; process until smooth. Pour into a large bowl. Stir in pasta, shallots, Swiss chard and remaining squash. Transfer to a greased 13x9-in. baking dish.
2. In a large skillet, heat oil over medium-high heat. Add bread crumbs; cook and stir until golden brown, 2-3 minutes. Stir in the parsley, garlic powder and remaining ¼ tsp. salt. Sprinkle over the pasta mixture.
3. Bake, uncovered, until set and topping is golden brown, 30-35 minutes.

1 cup: 223 cal., 6g fat (1g sat. fat), 83mg chol., 209mg sod., 33g carb. (4g sugars, 2g fiber), 9g pro.

APPLE BUTTER PUMPKIN PIE
PICTURED ON P. 257

The addition of apple butter gives this pumpkin pie a slightly fruity flavor that sets it apart from the ordinary. I'm always happy to share reliable recipes like this.
—Edna Hoffman, Hebron, IN

Prep: 25 min. • **Bake:** 50 min. + cooling
Makes: 8 servings

- Dough for single-crust pie
- 3 large eggs, lightly beaten
- 1 cup canned pumpkin
- 1 cup apple butter
- ¾ cup packed brown sugar
- 1 can (5 oz.) evaporated milk
- ⅓ cup 2% milk
- 1 tsp. vanilla extract
- ½ tsp. salt
- ½ tsp. ground cinnamon
- ⅛ tsp. each ground ginger, cloves and nutmeg
- Whipped cream, optional

1. Preheat oven to 400°. On a lightly floured surface, roll dough to a ⅛-in.-thick circle; transfer to a 9-in. pie plate. Trim crust to ½ in. beyond rim of plate; flute edge. In a large bowl, combine the next 7 ingredients. Whisk in salt and spices until well blended. Pour into crust.
2. Bake until a knife inserted in the center comes out clean, 50-55 minutes; cover edge loosely with foil during the last 20 minutes if necessary. Cool on a wire rack. If desired, garnish with whipped cream. Refrigerate leftovers.

1 piece: 328 cal., 10g fat (5g sat. fat), 92mg chol., 304mg sod., 53g carb. (37g sugars, 2g fiber), 5g pro.

MAPLE-PUMPKIN DINNER ROLLS

Every year my family and I visit our local pumpkin patch. Afterward, we come home and enjoy our first autumn meal at which these dinner rolls appear, along with corn chowder and apple pie.
—Sabrina Fraley, Georgetown, KY

Prep: 30 min. + rising • **Bake:** 15 min.
Makes: 16 rolls

- ½ cup cornmeal
- ¼ cup packed brown sugar
- 1 pkg. (¼ oz.) quick-rise yeast
- ½ tsp. salt
- ¼ tsp. pumpkin pie spice
- 2½ to 3 cups all-purpose flour
- ¾ cup plus 2 Tbsp. 2% milk, divided
- ¼ cup maple syrup
- 4 Tbsp. butter, divided
- ¾ cup canned pumpkin

1. In a large bowl, mix cornmeal, brown sugar, yeast, salt, pie spice and 2 cups flour. In a small saucepan, heat ¾ cup milk, syrup and 2 Tbsp. butter to 120°-130°; stir into the dry ingredients. Stir in the pumpkin and enough remaining flour to form a soft dough (dough will be sticky).
2. Turn dough onto a floured surface; knead until dough is smooth and elastic, 6-8 minutes. Cover; let rest 10 minutes.
3. Divide and shape dough into 16 balls. Place in 2 greased 9-in. round baking pans or cast-iron skillets. Cover with kitchen towels; let rise until doubled, about 1 hour. Preheat oven to 375°.
4. Brush remaining milk over dough. Bake 12-15 minutes or until golden brown.
5. Melt remaining butter; brush over hot rolls. Remove from pans to wire racks; serve warm.

1 roll: 151 cal., 4g fat (2g sat. fat), 9mg chol., 102mg sod., 27g carb. (8g sugars, 1g fiber), 3g pro. **Diabetic exchanges:** 2 starch, 1 fat.

CREAMY MUSHROOM BRUSCHETTA

Mushrooms—button, portobello and shiitake—plus a lovely blend of herbs make a hearty, flavorful topping for bruschetta.
—Amy Chase, Vanderhoof, BC

Prep: 15 min. • **Cook:** 30 min.
Makes: 28 appetizers

- 1½ cups sliced fresh mushrooms
- 1½ cups sliced baby portobello mushrooms
- 1 cup sliced fresh shiitake mushrooms
- ¾ cup chopped onion
- 2 Tbsp. olive oil
- 1 cup heavy whipping cream
- 2 Tbsp. Worcestershire sauce
- ¼ tsp. kosher salt
- ¼ tsp. coarsely ground pepper
- 28 slices French bread baguette (½ in. thick)
- 1 garlic clove, peeled and halved
- 1 Tbsp. each minced fresh basil, parsley and thyme

1. In a large skillet, saute mushrooms and onion in oil for 6-7 minutes or until the mushrooms are browned.
2. Stir in the cream, Worcestershire sauce, salt and pepper. Bring to a boil. Reduce heat; simmer, uncovered, for 20-25 minutes or until thickened, stirring occasionally.
3. Meanwhile, place baguette slices on ungreased baking sheets. Broil 4-6 in. from the heat for 1-1½ minutes on each side or until toasted. Rub garlic over toasts; discard garlic.
4. Stir the basil, parsley and thyme into the mushroom mixture; heat through. Spoon about 1 Tbsp. onto each toast. Serve immediately.

1 appetizer: 94 cal., 5g fat (2g sat. fat), 12mg chol., 104mg sod., 10g carb. (0 sugars, 1g fiber), 2g pro. **Diabetic exchanges:** 1 fat, ½ starch.

MAPLE-PUMPKIN DINNER ROLLS

PECAN-CORNBREAD DRESSING

Plenty of pecans and bacon give this stuffing a unique flavor—while using a packaged mix cuts down on the preparation time.
—Taste of Home *Test Kitchen*

Prep: 25 min. • **Bake:** 45 min.
Makes: 10 servings

- 3 cups water
- ½ cup butter
- 1 pkg. (16 oz.) cornbread stuffing mix
- 10 bacon strips, diced
- 1 cup chopped celery
- 1½ cups chopped green onions
- ½ cup coarsely chopped pecans
- ½ tsp. salt
- ¼ tsp. pepper

1. In a large saucepan, bring water and butter to a boil. Remove from the heat and stir in the stuffing mix; cover and set aside.
2. In a large skillet, cook the bacon until crisp; remove with a slotted spoon to drain on paper towels. Discard all but 3 Tbsp. of drippings.
3. Cook celery in drippings over medium heat for 5 minutes. Add onions and cook 5 minutes or until celery is tender, stirring constantly. Add to the cornbread mixture along with pecans, salt, pepper and bacon; mix well.
4. Transfer to a greased 2-qt. casserole. Cover and bake at 325° for 45 minutes or until heated through.
¾ cup: 404 cal., 26g fat (10g sat. fat), 43mg chol., 1035mg sod., 14g carb. (4g sugars, 3g fiber), 9g pro.

HAZELNUT PECAN PIE

With a blend of chocolate, pecans and hazelnuts, this pie is top-level tasty. But because so it's easy to make, you can enjoy it often. Your family and friends will think you worked for hours in the kitchen. It's incredible served plain, but a dollop of whipped cream takes it over the top.
—Brenda Melancon, McComb, MS

Prep: 25 min. • **Bake:** 50 min. + cooling
Makes: 8 servings

- 1 sheet refrigerated pie crust
- 3 large eggs
- 1 cup sugar
- ½ cup hazelnut flavoring syrup
- ½ cup dark corn syrup
- 3 Tbsp. all-purpose flour
- 2 Tbsp. butter, softened
- 1 tsp. vanilla extract
- 1½ cups coarsely chopped pecans
- ½ cup chopped hazelnuts
- ½ cup semisweet chocolate chips
  Whipped cream, optional

1. Preheat oven to 350°. Unroll crust into a 9-in. pie plate; flute the edge. In a large bowl, whisk the eggs, sugar, syrups, flour, butter and vanilla. Stir in the pecans, hazelnuts and chocolate chips. Transfer to crust.
2. Bake for 50-55 minutes or until set. Cool on a wire rack. Serve with whipped cream if desired. Refrigerate leftovers.
1 piece: 629 cal., 35g fat (9g sat. fat), 92mg chol., 179mg sod., 77g carb. (48g sugars, 4g fiber), 7g pro.

HAZELNUT PECAN PIE

CORN PUDDING

HOT CIDER

I dress up apple cider using lemonade, orange juice, honey and spices for a new version of a classic fall beverage.

—Glenna Tooman, Boise, ID

Prep: 5 min. • **Cook:** 45 min.
Makes: 18 servings (4½ qt.)

4 cups water
2 tsp. ground allspice
1 cinnamon stick (3 in.)
  Dash ground cloves
1 gallon apple cider or unsweetened apple juice
1 can (12 oz.) frozen lemonade concentrate, thawed
¾ cup orange juice
⅓ cup honey
1 tea bag

1. In a large stockpot, combine the water, allspice, cinnamon stick and cloves. Bring to a boil. Reduce heat; simmer, uncovered, for 30 minutes.
2. Add the remaining ingredients. Return just to a boil. Discard cinnamon stick and tea bag. Stir and serve warm.
1 cup: 168 cal., 0 fat (0 sat. fat), 0 chol., 24mg sod., 42g carb. (38g sugars, 0 fiber), 0 pro.

CORN PUDDING

The pleasing flavor of this golden corn pudding side dish makes it real comfort food. And because the recipe calls for a packaged cornbread mix, it's easy to prepare.

—P. Lauren Fay-Neri, Syracuse, NY

Prep: 20 min. • **Bake:** 45 min.
Makes: 8 servings

½ cup butter, softened
½ cup sugar
2 large eggs, room temperature
1 cup sour cream
1 pkg. (8½ oz.) cornbread/muffin mix
½ cup 2% milk
1 can (15¼ oz.) whole kernel corn, drained
1 can (14¾ oz.) cream-style corn

1. Preheat oven to 325°. In a large bowl, cream butter and sugar until light and fluffy, 5-7 minutes. Add eggs, 1 at a time, beating well after each addition. Beat in sour cream. Gradually add the muffin mix alternately with milk. Fold in corn.
2. Pour into a greased 3-qt. baking dish or 13x9-in. baking pan. Bake, uncovered, until set and lightly browned, 45-50 minutes.
¾ cup: 435 cal., 22g fat (12g sat. fat), 112mg chol., 700mg sod., 52g carb. (24g sugars, 2g fiber), 7g pro.

TEST KITCHEN TIP
To give this dish a Tex-Mex spin, add a can of diced green chiles to the batter and top with 1 cup shredded Monterey Jack cheese before baking.

'Tis the Season

Pull out the stops this Christmas with an elegant, amazing menu. Rich and luscious appetizers, spiced mulled wine, home-baked bread, delicious sides, a gorgeous holiday cake and a showstopping centerpiece of tender prime rib—this is the kind of meal that makes memories.

CRANBERRY-PECAN WHEAT BERRY SALAD

CRANBERRY-PECAN WHEAT BERRY SALAD

I love to experiment with different grains, and I wanted to give wheat berries a try. My whole family goes nuts for this salad, especially my mom.
—Kristen Heigl, Staten Island, NY

Prep: 20 min. • **Cook:** 70 min. + cooling
Makes: 8 servings

- 1 cup uncooked wheat berries, rinsed
- 2 celery ribs, finely chopped
- 1 medium tart apple, diced
- 4 green onions, sliced
- 1 cup dried cranberries
- 1 cup chopped pecans

DRESSING
- 3 Tbsp. walnut oil
- 2 Tbsp. cider vinegar
- 1 Tbsp. minced fresh sage or 1 tsp. rubbed sage
- 2 tsp. minced fresh thyme or ¾ tsp. dried thyme
- 2 tsp. Worcestershire sauce
- 1 tsp. Dijon mustard
- ¾ tsp. salt
- ½ tsp. pepper

Cook wheat berries according to package directions; drain and cool. Meanwhile, combine the next 5 ingredients; add the wheat berries. Whisk together dressing ingredients. Pour over salad; toss to coat. Serve at room temperature or chilled.
¾ cup: 298 cal., 15g fat (1g sat. fat), 0 chol., 261mg sod., 39g carb. (17g sugars, 6g fiber), 5g pro.

BRANDIED BLUE CHEESE SPREAD

Pour on the holiday spirit with a splash of brandy and three kinds of cheese. Pumpkin seeds, or pepitas, are a crunchy topping for the smooth spread.
—T.B. England, San Antonio, TX

Prep: 15 min. + chilling
Makes: about 2 cups

- 1 pkg. (8 oz.) cream cheese, softened
- 1 pkg. (4 oz.) garlic-herb spreadable cheese
- ¾ cup crumbled blue cheese
- 2 Tbsp. brandy
- 1 shallot, finely chopped
- 1 Tbsp. minced fresh parsley
- 1 Tbsp. honey
- ⅛ tsp. salt
  Dash pepper
- ¼ cup salted pumpkin seeds or pepitas
  Assorted crackers

In a small bowl, mix the first 9 ingredients until blended. Transfer to a serving dish; sprinkle with pumpkin seeds. Refrigerate, covered, 2 hours before serving. Serve with crackers.
2 Tbsp.: 121 cal., 11g fat (6g sat. fat), 27mg chol., 183mg sod., 3g carb. (2g sugars, 0 fiber), 3g pro.

HERB-CRUSTED PRIME RIB

MUSHROOM & SMOKED GOUDA PUFF

PICTURED ON P. 257

It's so very easy, but it looks and tastes gourmet. Dinner party guests will be impressed with this perfect starter course. Serve with a spicy mustard for dipping if desired.
—*Christina Singer, Bellefontaine, OH*

Prep: 30 min. • **Bake:** 30 min. + standing
Makes: 8 servings

4½ tsp. butter
½ cup sliced fresh mushrooms
½ cup sliced baby portobello mushrooms
¼ cup chopped fresh shiitake mushrooms
1 shallot, minced
2 tsp. minced fresh thyme
¼ tsp. salt
⅛ tsp. pepper
1 sheet frozen puff pastry, thawed
½ cup shredded smoked Gouda cheese
1 large egg
2 Tbsp. water

1. Preheat oven to 350°. In a large skillet, heat butter over medium-high heat. Add mushrooms and shallot; cook and stir until tender, about 5 minutes. Stir in thyme, salt and pepper.
2. Unfold puff pastry. Spread mushroom mixture to within 1 in. of edges. Sprinkle with cheese. Roll up jelly-roll style; pinch seam and ends to seal. Place on a parchment-lined baking sheet, seam side down. In a small bowl, whisk egg and water; brush over pastry. Cut slits in top.
3. Bake until golden brown, about 30 minutes. Let stand for 10 minutes before cutting.
1 slice: 210 cal., 13g fat (5g sat. fat), 37mg chol., 260mg sod., 19g carb. (1g sugars, 2g fiber), 5g pro.

TEST KITCHEN TIP
Feel free to swap in your favorite mushrooms, or some of the freshest you can find at your local market. You can also experiment with the cheese here—try a sharp cheddar, a creamy provolone or a blend of different cheeses.

HERB-CRUSTED PRIME RIB

Prime rib always makes an impression on a holiday dinner table, but it's actually easy to prepare. This roast is wonderfully flavored with lots of fresh herbs.
—*Jennifer Dennis, Alhambra, CA*

Prep: 20 min. • **Bake:** 1¾ hours + standing
Makes: 8 servings

1 large shallot, coarsely chopped
6 garlic cloves, quartered
3 Tbsp. minced fresh rosemary or 1 Tbsp. dried rosemary
2 Tbsp. minced fresh oregano or 2 tsp. dried oregano
2 Tbsp. minced fresh thyme or 2 tsp. dried thyme
2 Tbsp. minced fresh sage or 2 tsp. rubbed sage
2 Tbsp. olive oil
3 tsp. pepper
1 tsp. salt
1 bone-in beef rib roast (4 lbs.)
SAUCE
1½ cups reduced-sodium beef broth
1 cup dry red wine or additional reduced-sodium beef broth
1 tsp. butter
½ tsp. salt

1. Preheat oven to 350°. Place the first 6 ingredients in a food processor; cover and pulse until finely chopped. Add oil, pepper and salt; cover and process until blended. Rub over roast. Place on a rack in a large roasting pan.
2. Bake, uncovered, 1¾-2¼ hours or until meat reaches desired doneness (for medium-rare, a thermometer should read 135°; medium, 140°; medium-well, 145°). Remove roast to a serving platter and keep warm; let stand 15 minutes before slicing.
3. Meanwhile, in a small saucepan, bring broth and wine to a boil; cook until liquid is reduced to 1 cup. Remove from heat; stir in butter and salt. Slice roast; serve with sauce.
½ pound cooked beef: 338 cal., 19g fat (7g sat. fat), 92mg chol., 612mg sod., 4g carb. (1g sugars, 0 fiber), 31g pro.

ROAST BEETS WITH ORANGE GREMOLATA & GOAT CHEESE

Both golden and red beets, roasted and sliced and topped with herbs and goat cheese, make a gorgeous holiday side!
—Courtney Archibeque, Greeley, CO

Prep: 25 min. • **Bake:** 55 min. + cooling
Makes: 12 servings

- 3 medium fresh golden beets (about 1 lb.)
- 3 medium fresh beets (about 1 lb.)
- 2 Tbsp. lime juice
- 2 Tbsp. orange juice
- ½ tsp. fine sea salt
- 1 Tbsp. minced fresh parsley
- 1 Tbsp. minced fresh sage
- 1 garlic clove, minced
- 1 tsp. grated orange zest
- 3 Tbsp. crumbled goat cheese
- 2 Tbsp. sunflower kernels

1. Preheat oven to 400°. Scrub beets and trim tops by 1 in. Place beets on a double thickness of heavy-duty foil (about 24x12 in.). Fold foil around beets, sealing tightly. Place on a baking sheet. Roast until tender, 55-65 minutes. Open foil carefully to allow steam to escape.
2. When cool enough to handle, peel, halve and slice beets; place in a serving bowl. Add lime juice, orange juice and salt; toss to coat. Combine parsley, sage, garlic and orange zest; sprinkle over beets. Top with goat cheese and sunflower kernels. Serve warm or chilled.

¾ cup: 49 cal., 1g fat (0 sat. fat), 2mg chol., 157mg sod., 9g carb. (6g sugars, 2g fiber), 2g pro. **Diabetic exchanges:** 1 vegetable.

GREEN BEANS WITH CREAMY PISTACHIO SAUCE

I was asked to bring vegetables for a party and wasn't feeling inspired until I remembered that Mom served beans with butter and evaporated milk. I love pistachios, so I added those instead of almonds. Everybody wanted the recipe, and I was really pleased—very little work and lots of happy family and friends!
—Loretta Ouellette, Pompano Beach, FL

Takes: 30 min. • **Makes:** 10 servings

- 2 lbs. fresh green beans, trimmed
- 1 tsp. salt
- ½ cup butter, cubed
- ½ cup pistachios, coarsely chopped
- 1 cup evaporated milk
  Salt and pepper to taste

1. Place green beans and salt in a Dutch oven; add water to cover. Bring to a boil. Cook, uncovered, until tender, stirring occasionally, 5-8 minutes. Drain and remove from pan.
2. In same pan, melt butter over medium heat. Add pistachios; cook and stir until pistachios begin to brown, 1-2 minutes. Stir in evaporated milk; bring to a boil. Cook until sauce is slightly thickened, 2-4 minutes. Add green beans; heat through, stirring to coat with sauce. Season with salt and pepper to taste.

¾ cup: 177 cal., 14g fat (7g sat. fat), 32mg chol., 365mg sod., 11g carb. (5g sugars, 4g fiber), 5g pro.

GREEN BEANS WITH CREAMY PISTACHIO SAUCE

GARLIC-HERB PARMESAN ROLLS

Fresh-baked yeast rolls are always a hit at dinners. To make it easy, I start these in the bread machine. I arrange them in a tree shape for the Yuletide season, but you can just as easily make them in a 13x9-inch baking pan.

—Lorri Reinhardt, Big Bend, WI

....

Prep: 20 min. • **Bake:** 20 min. + cooling
Makes: 16 servings

- 1 cup water (70° to 80°)
- 2 Tbsp. butter, softened
- 1 large egg, lightly beaten
- 3 Tbsp. sugar
- 2 tsp. dried minced garlic
- 1 tsp. Italian seasoning
- 1 tsp. salt
- 2¼ cups bread flour
- 1 cup whole wheat flour
- 1 pkg. (¼ oz.) active dry yeast

TOPPING
- 1 Tbsp. butter, melted
- 1 Tbsp. grated Parmesan cheese
- 1 tsp. Italian seasoning
- ½ tsp. coarse salt

1. In bread machine pan, place the first 10 ingredients in order suggested by manufacturer. Select dough setting (check dough after 5 minutes of mixing; add 1-2 Tbsp. water or flour if needed).

2. When cycle is completed, turn dough onto a lightly floured surface; divide into 16 balls. Line a baking sheet with foil and grease the foil. Center 1 roll near the top of prepared baking sheet. Arrange rolls snugly into 4 additional rows, adding 1 more roll for each row, forming a tree. Center remaining ball under tree for trunk. Cover and let rise until doubled, about 1 hour.

3. Brush rolls with butter. Combine cheese and Italian seasoning and sprinkle over rolls. Sprinkle with salt. Bake at 350° for 20-25 minutes or until golden brown. Serve warm.

1 roll: 132 cal., 3g fat (2g sat. fat), 18mg chol., 236mg sod., 22g carb. (2g sugars, 1g fiber), 4g pro.

GARLIC-HERB PARMESAN ROLLS

LAYERED CHRISTMAS GELATIN

My jewel-toned gelatin always makes an appearance during our Christmas feast. Filled with cranberries and pineapple, the sweet-tart salad could even serve as a light dessert.
—Diane Schefelker, Ireton, IA

Prep: 30 min. + chilling
Makes: 10 servings

- 1 pkg. (3 oz.) lime gelatin
- 1 cup boiling water
- ⅓ cup unsweetened pineapple juice
- 1 cup crushed pineapple, drained

CREAM CHEESE LAYER
- 1 tsp. unflavored gelatin
- 2 Tbsp. cold water
- 1 pkg. (8 oz.) cream cheese, softened
- ⅓ cup whole milk

BERRY LAYER
- 2 pkg. (3 oz. each) strawberry gelatin
- 2 cups boiling water
- 1 can (14 oz.) whole-berry cranberry sauce
- Optional: thawed whipped topping, lime wedges and fresh strawberries

1. Dissolve lime gelatin in boiling water; stir in pineapple juice. Stir in pineapple. Pour into an 11x7-in. dish; refrigerate until set.

2. In a small saucepan, sprinkle unflavored gelatin over cold water; let stand for 1 minute. Heat over low heat, stirring until gelatin is completely dissolved. Transfer to a small bowl. Beat in cream cheese and milk until smooth. Spread over the lime layer; refrigerate until set.

3. Dissolve strawberry gelatin in boiling water; stir in cranberry sauce. Cool for 10 minutes. Carefully spoon over cream cheese layer. Refrigerate until set.

4. Cut into squares. If desired, serve with whipped topping, lime wedges and fresh strawberries.

1 piece: 267 cal., 8g fat (5g sat. fat), 26mg chol., 139mg sod., 46g carb. (39g sugars, 1g fiber), 5g pro.

SPICY CRANBERRY SALSA

This beautiful holiday dish is a big hit at our house. We serve it with wheat or other crispy crackers. Cranberries and various forms of chile peppers combine to make a very nice sweet-heat treat.
—Diane Atherton, Pine Mountain, GA

Prep: 25 min. + chilling
Makes: 24 servings

- 1 pkg. (12 oz.) fresh or frozen cranberries
- ¼ cup coarsely chopped green onions
- ¼ cup fresh cilantro leaves
- ¼ cup coarsely chopped green pepper
- 1 Tbsp. minced fresh gingerroot
- 2 to 3 tsp. ground chipotle pepper
- 1 medium lime
- 1 can (10 oz.) diced tomatoes and green chiles, drained
- ¾ cup sugar
- ½ tsp. kosher salt
- ⅛ tsp. cayenne pepper
- 3 pkg. (8 oz. each) cream cheese, softened
- Assorted crackers

1. Place the first 6 ingredients in a food processor. Finely grate enough zest from lime to measure 2 tsp. Cut lime crosswise in half; squeeze juice from lime. Add zest and juice to food processor. Process until coarsely chopped. Transfer to a bowl. Stir in diced tomatoes and green chiles, sugar, salt and cayenne. Refrigerate, covered, at least 4 hours.

2. Arrange cream cheese on a serving platter; top with cranberry salsa. Serve with crackers.

1 serving: 134 cal., 10g fat (6g sat. fat), 29mg chol., 184mg sod., 11g carb. (8g sugars, 1g fiber), 2g pro.

SPICY CRANBERRY SALSA

GINGER-GLAZED LEMON BUNDT

MULLED MERLOT

Our delightful recipe is sure to warm up your holiday guests! Keeping it ready to serve in the slow cooker means you can enjoy the party.
—Taste of Home *Test Kitchen*

Prep: 10 min. • **Cook:** 1 hour
Makes: 9 servings

- 4 cinnamon sticks (3 in. each)
- 4 whole cloves
- 2 bottles (750 ml each) merlot
- ½ cup sugar
- ½ cup orange juice
- ½ cup brandy
- 1 medium orange, thinly sliced
  Optional: Orange wedges and additional cinnamon sticks

1. Place cinnamon sticks and cloves on a double thickness of cheesecloth; bring up corners of cloth and tie with string to form a bag.
2. In a 3-qt. slow cooker, combine the wine, sugar, orange juice, brandy and orange slices. Add spice bag. Cover and cook on high for 1 hour or until heated through. Discard spice bag and orange slices. Serve warm; if desired, garnish with orange wedges and additional cinnamon sticks.

¾ cup: 143 cal., 0 fat (0 sat. fat), 0 chol., 4mg sod., 15g carb. (13g sugars, 0 fiber), 0 pro.

GINGER-GLAZED LEMON BUNDT

Tangy ginger, tart lemon and puckery cranberries make this melt-in-your-mouth cake a crisp and gorgeous holiday treat.
—Taste of Home *Test Kitchen*

Prep: 20 min. • **Bake:** 1 hour + cooling
Makes: 12 servings

SUGARED CRANBERRIES
- 3 Tbsp. light corn syrup
- 1 cup fresh or frozen, thawed cranberries
- ⅓ cup sugar

CAKE
- 1 cup butter, softened
- 2 cups sugar
- 4 large eggs, room temperature
- 2 Tbsp. grated lemon zest
- 1 tsp. lemon extract
- 2½ cups all-purpose flour
- 2 tsp. baking powder
- ½ tsp. salt
- 1 cup fat-free vanilla Greek yogurt

GLAZE
- ⅔ cup confectioners' sugar
- 2 Tbsp. butter, melted
- 1 to 3 tsp. lemon juice
- ½ tsp. ground ginger

1. For sugared cranberries, heat corn syrup in a microwave until warm; gently toss cranberries in syrup, allowing excess to drip off. Toss in sugar to coat. Place on waxed paper; let stand until set, about 1 hour.
2. Preheat oven to 325°. Grease and flour a 10-in. fluted tube pan. In a large bowl, cream butter and sugar until light and fluffy, 5-7 minutes. Add eggs, 1 at a time, beating well after each addition. Beat in lemon zest and extract.
3. In another bowl, whisk flour, baking powder and salt; add to creamed mixture alternately with yogurt, beating well after each addition.
4. Transfer to prepared pan. Bake for 60-70 minutes or until a toothpick inserted in center comes out clean. Cool in pan 10 minutes before removing to a wire rack to cool completely.
5. Mix confectioners' sugar, butter, lemon juice and ginger until smooth. Drizzle over cake. Top with sugared cranberries.

1 slice: 468 cal., 19g fat (12g sat. fat), 108mg chol., 350mg sod., 69g carb. (48g sugars, 1g fiber), 7g pro.

Cookies for Santa

Sure, you set out a plate on Christmas Eve, but jolly old Saint Nick isn't the only one to benefit from this array of scrumptious cookies. Create platters for co-workers, friends and neighbors, box up tins for teachers, and send care packages to loved ones when you can't be with them at the holiday.

CHOCOLATE AMARETTI

⑤ⁱ
CHOCOLATE AMARETTI

These classic almond paste cookies are like ones you'd find in an Italian bakery. My husband and children are always excited when I include these goodies in my holiday baking lineup.
—Kathy Long, Whitefish Bay, WI

Prep: 15 min. • **Bake:** 20 min./batch
Makes: 2 dozen

1¼ cups almond paste
¾ cup sugar
2 large egg whites, room temperature
½ cup confectioners' sugar
¼ cup baking cocoa

1. Preheat oven to 350°. Crumble almond paste into a food processor; add sugar and pulse until evenly combined. Add the egg whites and process until incorporated. Transfer to a bowl. Sift together confectioners' sugar and cocoa; gradually add to the almond mixture and mix well.
2. Drop by tablespoonfuls 2 in. apart onto parchment-lined baking sheets. Bake until tops are cracked, 17-20 minutes. Cool 1 minute before removing to wire racks. Store in an airtight container.
1 cookie: 92 cal., 3g fat (0 sat. fat), 0 chol., 6mg sod., 15g carb. (13g sugars, 1g fiber), 2g pro. **Diabetic exchanges:** 1 starch, ½ fat.

⑤ⁱ
HOLIDAY BUTTER MINT COOKIES

My mom gave me this recipe in a special recipe collection when I got married. I make goodie boxes of them for holiday gifts for friends and neighbors—and everyone loves them!
—Sherry Flaquel, Cutler Bay, FL

Prep: 15 min.
Bake: 15 min./batch + cooling
Makes: 4½ dozen

1 cup butter, softened
¼ cup confectioners' sugar
1 Tbsp. water
2 tsp. mint extract
2 cups all-purpose flour
¾ cup crushed butter mints, divided

1. Preheat oven to 325°. In a large bowl, cream butter and confectioners' sugar until light and fluffy. Beat in water and extract. Gradually beat flour into creamed mixture. Stir in ¼ cup crushed mints.
2. Shape dough into 1-in. balls. Place 2 in. apart on ungreased baking sheets; flatten slightly. Bake until bottoms are lightly browned, 12-15 minutes.
3. Coat warm cookies with the remaining crushed mints. Cool on wire racks.
1 cookie: 56 cal., 3g fat (2g sat. fat), 9mg chol., 30mg sod., 6g carb. (2g sugars, 0 fiber), 1g pro.

EASY PECAN PIE BARS

MOLE NEW MEXICAN WEDDING COOKIES

Heat and sweet is such an amazing combination. I added chili powder and chocolate chips to give a new twist to traditional Mexican cookies. They melt in your mouth, and then the spice hits you. I just love them.

—*Marla Clark, Albuquerque, NM*

Prep: 30 min.
Bake: 15 min./batch + cooling
Makes: 2½ dozen

- ½ cup butter, softened
- ¾ cup confectioners' sugar, divided
- 1 tsp. vanilla extract
- 1 cup all-purpose flour
- ½ cup ground pecans
- 1 tsp. chili powder
- ¼ tsp. ground cinnamon
- ¼ tsp. ground cloves
- ¼ tsp. ground allspice
- ½ cup miniature semisweet chocolate chips

1. Preheat oven to 350°. Cream butter and ⅓ cup confectioners' sugar until light and fluffy; beat in vanilla. In another bowl, whisk together the next 6 ingredients. Gradually beat into the creamed mixture. Fold in chocolate chips.
2. Shape dough into 1-in. balls. Place 1 in. apart on ungreased baking sheets. Bake until bottoms are lightly browned, 12-15 minutes. Remove from pans to wire racks to cool 5 minutes.
3. Roll in remaining confectioners' sugar. Let cool completely.
1 cookie: 81 cal., 5g fat (3g sat. fat), 8mg chol., 27mg sod., 8g carb. (5g sugars, 1g fiber), 1g pro.

EASY PECAN PIE BARS

I am always searching for fast and easy recipes to take to the teachers lounge. The staff goes nuts for these shortcut pecan pie bars.
—*Kathro Yoder, Defiance, OH*

Prep: 10 min. • **Bake:** 40 min. + cooling
Makes: 2 dozen

- 1 pkg. yellow cake mix (regular size)
- ⅓ cup butter, softened
- 1 large egg, room temperature

FILLING
- 1½ cups corn syrup
- ½ cup packed brown sugar
- 1 tsp. vanilla extract
- 3 large eggs, room temperature
- 1 cup chopped pecans

1. Preheat oven to 350°. Line a 13x9-in. baking pan with foil; grease foil.
2. Reserve ⅔ cup cake mix; set aside. Combine remaining cake mix, butter and 1 egg; beat on low speed until blended. Press onto bottom of prepared pan. Bake 15 minutes. Cool on a wire rack.
3. For filling, beat corn syrup, brown sugar, vanilla and the reserved cake mix until blended. Add eggs; beat on low speed just until combined. Pour over warm crust; sprinkle with pecans.
4. Bake until center is set, 25-30 minutes longer. Cool completely in pan on a wire rack. To serve, refrigerate at least 15 minutes. Lift out of pan; discard foil, then cut into bars.
1 bar: 223 cal., 8g fat (3g sat. fat), 38mg chol., 174mg sod., 38g carb. (30g sugars, 0 fiber), 2g pro.

TEST KITCHEN TIP
Spritz the inside of the measuring cup with cooking spray when you're measuring honey. The honey will slide right out, ensuring you get every last drop in the recipe.

RASPBERRY WHITE CHOCOLATE BARS

A co-worker's mother gave me this gem of a recipe a few years back. I can never decide what's more appealing—the attractive look of the bars or their incredible aroma while they're baking! Everyone who tries these asks for the recipe.
—Mimi Priesman, Pace, FL

Prep: 20 min. • **Bake:** 45 min.
Makes: 2 dozen

- ½ cup butter, cubed
- 1 pkg. (10 to 12 oz.) white baking chips, divided
- 2 large eggs
- ½ cup sugar
- 1 tsp. almond extract
- 1 cup all-purpose flour
- ½ tsp. salt
- ½ cup seedless raspberry jam
- ¼ cup sliced almonds

1. Preheat oven to 325°. In a small saucepan, melt butter. Remove from the heat; add 1 cup chips (do not stir). In a small bowl, beat eggs until foamy; gradually add sugar. Stir in chip mixture and almond extract. Combine flour and salt; gradually add to the egg mixture just until combined.
2. Spread half of the batter into a greased 9-in. square baking pan. Bake for 15-20 minutes or until golden brown.
3. In a small saucepan, melt jam over low heat; spread over warm crust. Stir the remaining chips into the remaining batter; drop by spoonfuls over the jam layer. Sprinkle with almonds.
4. Bake 30-35 minutes longer or until a toothpick inserted in the center comes out clean. Cool on a wire rack. Cut into bars.

1 bar: 162 cal., 9g fat (5g sat. fat), 30mg chol., 104mg sod., 20g carb. (8g sugars, 0 fiber), 2g pro.

SPICED EGGNOG RUM COOKIES

One year, when I had a lot of eggnog on hand, I created a new holiday cookie recipe. The flavor is subtle, but somehow it transforms regular sugar cookies into something special for the holidays.
—Mark Banick, Turner, OR

Prep: 25 min. + chilling
Bake: 10 min./batch + cooling
Makes: 4 dozen

- ¾ cup butter, softened
- 1¼ cups sugar
- 1 large egg, room temperature
- 1 cup eggnog, divided
- 1¾ tsp. rum extract, divided
- 3½ cups all-purpose flour
- 1 tsp. baking powder
- ½ tsp. ground cinnamon
- ½ tsp. ground nutmeg
- ¼ tsp. salt
- ¼ tsp. ground ginger
- ¼ tsp. ground allspice
- 3 cups confectioners' sugar
  Colored sugar or sprinkles

1. In a large bowl, cream butter and sugar until light and fluffy, 5-7 minutes. Beat in the egg, ⅓ cup eggnog and 1 tsp. extract. In another bowl, whisk the flour, baking powder, cinnamon, nutmeg, salt, ginger and allspice; gradually beat into the creamed mixture.
2. Divide dough in half and shape each half into a disk; cover and refrigerate until firm enough to roll, about 30 minutes.
3. Preheat oven to 375°. On a lightly floured surface, roll each portion of dough to ¼-in. thickness. Cut with a floured 3¼-in. star-shaped cookie cutter. Place stars 1 in. apart on parchment-lined baking sheets.
4. Bake until the edges begin to brown, 8-10 minutes. Cool on pans 1 minute. Remove to wire racks to cool completely.
5. For glaze, mix confectioners' sugar, the remaining ¾ tsp. extract and enough of the remaining eggnog to achieve a drizzling consistency; drizzle over cookies. Decorate as desired.

1 cookie: 114 cal., 3g fat (2g sat. fat), 14mg chol., 50mg sod., 20g carb. (13g sugars, 0 fiber), 1g pro.

SPICED EGGNOG RUM COOKIES

CHIPOTLE CRACKLE COOKIES

MINI BAKLAVA

Baklava has amazing memories for me: My best friend made it for my bridal and baby showers. And then she taught me how to make it! These delicious little miniatures give you the taste of baklava in a bite-sized package.
—*Margaret Guillory, Eunice, LA*

Prep: 20 min. • **Bake:** 10 min. + cooling
Makes: about 2½ dozen

- ½ cup butter
- ¼ cup sugar
- 1 tsp. ground cinnamon
- 1 cup finely chopped pecans
- 1 cup finely chopped walnuts
- 2 pkg. (1.9 oz. each) frozen miniature phyllo tart shells
  Honey

1. Preheat oven to 350°. In a small saucepan over medium heat, melt butter. Stir in sugar and cinnamon. Bring to a boil. Reduce heat; add pecans and walnuts, tossing to coat. Simmer, uncovered, until nuts are lightly toasted, 5-10 minutes.
2. Place phyllo shells on a parchment-lined baking sheet. Spoon nut mixture and butter sauce evenly into shells. Bake until golden brown, 9-11 minutes. Cool completely on pan on a wire rack.
3. Drizzle a drop of honey into each shell; let stand, covered, until serving. Serve with additional honey if desired.

1 filled phyllo cup: 105 cal., 9g fat (2g sat. fat), 8mg chol., 33mg sod., 5g carb. (2g sugars, 1g fiber), 1g pro.

CHIPOTLE CRACKLE COOKIES

I bake these special cookies for the holidays, birthdays and more! The addition of ground chipotle chile pepper gives them a little zing. The dough is sometimes sticky so I dip my hands in confectioners' sugar for easier handling.
—*Gloria Bradley, Naperville, IL*

Prep: 25 min. + chilling
Bake: 10 min./batch • **Makes:** 2½ dozen

- 2 large eggs, room temperature
- 1 cup sugar
- ¼ cup canola oil
- 2 tsp. vanilla extract
- 2 oz. unsweetened chocolate, melted and cooled
- 1 cup all-purpose flour
- 1 Tbsp. toasted wheat germ
- ¾ tsp. baking powder
- ¼ tsp. salt
- ⅛ tsp. ground chipotle pepper
- ¼ cup miniature semisweet chocolate chips
- ⅓ cup confectioners' sugar

1. In a large bowl, beat eggs, sugar, oil and vanilla until combined. Add melted chocolate. Combine flour, wheat germ, baking powder, salt and chipotle pepper. Gradually add to the egg mixture and mix well. Fold in chocolate chips. Cover and refrigerate for 2 hours.
2. Preheat oven to 350°. Place the confectioners' sugar in a small bowl. Shape dough into 1-in. balls; roll in confectioners' sugar. Place balls 2 in. apart on baking sheets coated with cooking spray. Bake 8-10 minutes or until set. Remove to wire racks to cool.

1 cookie: 85 cal., 4g fat (1g sat. fat), 14mg chol., 35mg sod., 13g carb. (9g sugars, 1g fiber), 1g pro. **Diabetic exchanges:** 1 starch, ½ fat.

DELECTABLE
DESSERTS

Finish your meal in style with a scrumptiously sweet dessert! There's no need to wait for a special occasion or a free day for baking—with these timesaving recipes, you can indulge your sweet tooth any night of the week.

DEVIL'S FOOD SANDWICH COOKIES

These cookies freeze well, so it's easy to keep some on hand for last-minute munching. In summer, I often make them larger to use for ice cream sandwiches.
—Mary Rempel, Altona, MB

Prep: 15 min.
Bake: 10 min./batch + cooling
Makes: about 6 dozen

- 2 pkg. devil's food cake mix (regular size)
- 1 cup canola oil
- 4 large eggs, room temperature

FILLING
- 8 oz. cream cheese, softened
- ¼ cup butter, softened
- 2½ cups confectioners' sugar
- 1 tsp. vanilla extract

1. Preheat oven to 350°. In a large bowl, combine the cake mixes, oil and eggs until well blended. Roll into 1-in. balls. Place 2 in. apart on ungreased baking sheets. Do not flatten.
2. Bake until set, 8-10 minutes. Cool for 5 minutes before removing to wire racks (cookies will flatten as they cool).
3. In a small bowl, beat cream cheese and butter until fluffy. Beat in sugar and vanilla until smooth. Spread or pipe filling on the bottoms of half of the cookies; top with the remaining cookies. Store cookies in the refrigerator.

2 cookies: 188 cal., 11g fat (4g sat. fat), 34mg chol., 149mg sod., 20g carb. (14g sugars, 0 fiber), 2g pro.

CLASSIC CARROT CAKE

CLASSIC CARROT CAKE

I entered this moist cake in a Colorado Outfitters Association dessert contest, and it took first place.
—Cheri Eby, Gunnison, CO

Prep: 30 min. • **Bake:** 35 min. + cooling
Makes: 15 servings

- 1 can (8 oz.) unsweetened crushed pineapple
- 4 large eggs, room temperature
- 2 cups shredded carrots (about 4 medium)
- 1 cup sugar
- 1 cup packed brown sugar
- 1 cup canola oil
- 2 cups all-purpose flour
- 2 tsp. baking soda
- 2 tsp. ground cinnamon
- ¼ tsp. salt
- ¾ cup chopped walnuts

FROSTING
- 2 pkg. (8 oz. each) cream cheese, softened
- ¼ cup butter, softened
- 2 tsp. vanilla extract
- 1½ cups confectioners' sugar

1. Preheat oven to 350°. Grease a 13x9-in. baking dish; set aside.
2. Drain pineapple, reserving 2 Tbsp. juice (discard the remaining juice or save for another use). In a large bowl, beat eggs, carrots, sugars, oil, drained pineapple and reserved juice until well blended.
3. In another bowl, whisk together flour, baking soda, cinnamon and salt; gradually beat into carrot mixture until blended. Stir in walnuts. Transfer to prepared dish.
4. Bake until a toothpick inserted in center comes out clean, 35-40 minutes. Cool completely on a wire rack.
5. For frosting, in a large bowl, beat cream cheese and butter until smooth. Beat in vanilla. Gradually beat in confectioners' sugar. Spread over cake.

1 piece: 555 cal., 34g fat (10g sat. fat), 88mg chol., 361mg sod., 59g carb. (44g sugars, 2g fiber), 6g pro.
Coconut Carrot Cake: Omit walnuts. Fold 1 cup flaked coconut into batter.
Cranberry Carrot Cake: Omit walnuts. Fold 1 cup dried cranberries into batter.

PEAR-PECAN CRISP WITH LEMON SAUCE

Pear-adise on a plate is a great way to describe this fruity crisp. A lovely lemon custard sauce tastefully complements the tender pears and crunchy topping.
—Lisa Varner, El Paso, TX

Prep: 30 min. • **Bake:** 30 min.
Makes: 6 servings

- 5 cups sliced peeled ripe pears (about 5 medium)
- 1 Tbsp. sugar
- ⅔ cup old-fashioned oats
- ⅓ cup all-purpose flour
- ⅓ cup packed brown sugar
- ¼ tsp. ground cinnamon
- ¼ cup cold butter
- ⅓ cup chopped pecans

SAUCE
- ¼ cup sugar
- 2 tsp. cornstarch
- ½ cup water
- 1 large egg yolk, beaten
- 1 Tbsp. butter
- 1 Tbsp. lemon juice
- ¼ tsp. grated lemon zest

1. Preheat oven to 350°. Place pears in a greased 8-in. cast-iron skillet or 8-in. square baking dish; sprinkle with sugar. In a small bowl, combine the oats, flour, brown sugar and cinnamon. Cut in butter until mixture resembles coarse crumbs; stir in pecans. Sprinkle over pears. Bake for 30-35 minutes or until bubbly.
2. Meanwhile, in a small saucepan, combine the sugar, cornstarch and water. Cook and stir over medium-high heat until thickened and bubbly. Reduce heat; cook and stir 2 minutes longer.
3. Remove from the heat. Stir a small amount of hot mixture into egg yolk; return all to the pan, stirring constantly. Bring to a gentle boil; cook and stir 2 minutes longer. Remove from the heat; stir in the butter, lemon juice and zest. Serve with warm pear crisp.

1 serving: 288 cal., 16g fat (7g sat. fat), 61mg chol., 103mg sod., 36g carb. (22g sugars, 2g fiber), 3g pro.

PEPPERMINT CHIP CHEESECAKE
PICTURED ON P. 287

I love to make cheesecakes and frequently give them as gifts or donate them to fundraisers. This one is always popular with whoever receives it!
—Gretchen Ely, West Lafayette, IN

Prep: 20 min. • **Bake:** 50 min. + chilling
Makes: 12 servings

- 1 pkg. (10 oz.) chocolate-covered mint cookies, crushed
- 3 Tbsp. butter, melted

FILLING
- 3 pkg. (8 oz. each) cream cheese, softened
- ¾ cup sugar
- 5 tsp. cornstarch
- 3 large eggs, room temperature, lightly beaten
- 1 large egg yolk, room temperature, lightly beaten
- ½ cup heavy whipping cream
- 2 tsp. peppermint extract
- 1¼ tsp. vanilla extract
- 3 to 4 drops green food coloring, optional
- 1 cup miniature semisweet chocolate chips
- ½ cup chocolate-covered mint cookies, crushed, optional

1. Preheat oven to 325°. In a small bowl, combine cookie crumbs and butter. Press onto the bottom and 1 in. up the sides of a greased 9-in. springform pan.
2. In a large bowl, beat the cream cheese, sugar and cornstarch until smooth. Add eggs and egg yolk; beat on low speed just until combined. Stir in the cream, extracts and, if desired, food coloring. Fold in the chocolate chips. Pour into crust. Place pan on a baking sheet.
3. Bake until center is almost set, 50-60 minutes. Cool on a wire rack for 10 minutes. Carefully run a knife around edge of pan to loosen; cool 1 hour longer. Refrigerate overnight, covering when completely cooled. Top with additional crushed cookies if desired. Refrigerate any leftovers.

1 slice: 391 cal., 25g fat (15g sat. fat), 113mg chol., 166mg sod., 39g carb. (30g sugars, 2g fiber), 5g pro.

PEAR-PECAN CRISP WITH LEMON SAUCE

SHORTBREAD LEMON BARS

SHORTBREAD LEMON BARS

I've put together two family cookbooks over the years, and this recipe ranks among my favorites. The special lemon bars have a yummy shortbread crust and refreshing flavor. I'm never afraid to make this dessert for guests because I know everyone will love it.
—Margaret Peterson, Forest City, IA

Prep: 25 min. • **Bake:** 15 min. + chilling
Makes: 3 dozen

1½ cups all-purpose flour
½ cup confectioners' sugar
1 tsp. grated lemon zest
1 tsp. grated orange zest
¾ cup cold butter, cubed

FILLING
4 large eggs, room temperature
2 cups sugar
⅓ cup lemon juice
¼ cup all-purpose flour
2 tsp. grated lemon zest
2 tsp. grated orange zest
1 tsp. baking powder

TOPPING
2 cups sour cream
⅓ cup sugar
½ tsp. vanilla extract

1. Preheat oven to 350°. In a food processor, combine flour, confectioners' sugar, and lemon and orange zest. Add butter; cover and process until the mixture forms a ball.
2. Pat into a greased 13x9-in. baking pan. Bake until set and the edges are lightly browned, 12-14 minutes.
3. In a large bowl, combine all the filling ingredients. Pour over hot crust. Bake until set and lightly browned, 14-16 minutes. In a small bowl, combine topping ingredients. Spread over filling.
4. Bake until topping is set, 7-9 minutes longer. Cool on a wire rack. Refrigerate overnight. Cut into bars just before serving. Store in the refrigerator.

1 bar: 172 cal., 9g fat (5g sat. fat), 51mg chol., 70mg sod., 20g carb. (15g sugars, 0 fiber), 2g pro.

MAPLE SUGAR PUMPKIN PIE

We make our own maple syrup and use it for this distinctive spin on pumpkin pie. Go ahead and bake this for Thanksgiving!
—Martha Boudah, Essex Center, VT

Prep: 10 min. + chilling
Bake: 1 hour + cooling
Makes: 8 servings

1 can (15 oz.) solid-pack pumpkin
2 Tbsp. all-purpose flour
½ tsp. ground cinnamon
½ tsp. ground nutmeg
½ tsp. ground ginger
1 Tbsp. butter, softened
1 cup sugar
1 cup 2% milk
2 Tbsp. maple syrup
2 large eggs, room temperature
1 pastry shell (9 in.), unbaked
   Whipped cream, optional

Preheat oven to 425°. In a bowl, combine the first 10 ingredients. Pour into the pie shell. Bake for 15 minutes. Reduce heat to 350° and continue baking for about 45 minutes or until a knife inserted in the center comes out clean. Cool to room temperature. Refrigerate. Garnish with whipped cream if desired.

1 piece: 308 cal., 11g fat (5g sat. fat), 66mg chol., 148mg sod., 49g carb. (32g sugars, 3g fiber), 5g pro.

5i
PEACH BAVARIAN

Fruit molds are my specialty. This one, with its refreshing peach taste, makes a colorful salad or dessert.
—Adeline Piscitelli, Sayreville, NJ

....

Prep: 15 min. + chilling
Makes: 8 servings

- 1 can (15¼ oz.) sliced peaches
- 2 pkg. (3 oz. each) peach or apricot gelatin
- ½ cup sugar
- 2 cups boiling water
- 1 tsp. almond extract
- 1 carton (8 oz.) frozen whipped topping, thawed
   Sliced fresh peaches, optional

1. Drain peaches, reserving ⅔ cup juice. Chop peaches into small pieces; set aside.
2. In a large bowl, dissolve gelatin and sugar in boiling water. Stir in reserved syrup. Chill until slightly thickened. Stir extract into whipped topping; gently fold in gelatin mixture. Fold in peaches.
3. Pour into an oiled 6-cup mold. Chill overnight. Unmold onto a serving platter; garnish with fresh peach slices if desired.
1 slice: 249 cal., 5g fat (5g sat. fat), 0 chol., 53mg sod., 47g carb. (47g sugars, 0 fiber), 2g pro.

CHOCOLATE CANNOLI CAKE
PICTURED ON P. 287

Hints of orange and coffee lend standout flavor to my tasty cannoli-inspired cake. A variation of this cake was a finalist in the Best Cake in Michigan contest.
—Mary Bilyeu, Ann Arbor, MI

....

Prep: 25 min. • **Bake:** 25 min. + cooling
Makes: 15 servings

- 1 large egg white, lightly beaten
- 1 cup reduced-fat ricotta cheese
- ¼ cup sugar
- 1 Tbsp. cold brewed coffee
- 2 tsp. grated orange zest
- ½ cup miniature semisweet chocolate chips

BATTER
- 1 cup sugar
- ½ cup cold brewed coffee
- ⅓ cup canola oil
- ⅓ cup orange juice
- 1 large egg, room temperature
- 1 large egg white, room temperature
- 1 Tbsp. cider vinegar
- 1 Tbsp. vanilla extract
- 1 cup all-purpose flour
- ½ cup whole wheat flour
- ⅓ cup baking cocoa
- 2 tsp. baking powder
- ½ tsp. salt

1. Preheat oven to 350°. In a small bowl, combine the egg white, ricotta cheese, sugar, coffee and orange zest. Stir in chocolate chips; set aside.
2. In a large bowl, combine first 8 batter ingredients; beat until well blended. Combine the flours, cocoa, baking powder and salt; gradually beat into the sugar mixture until blended.
3. Transfer to a 13x9-in. baking dish coated with cooking spray. Top with heaping tablespoonfuls of ricotta mixture; cut through batter with a knife to swirl.
4. Bake for 25-30 minutes or until a toothpick inserted in the center comes out clean. Cool on a wire rack. Refrigerate any leftovers.
1 piece: 213 cal., 8g fat (2g sat. fat), 18mg chol., 160mg sod., 32g carb. (21g sugars, 1g fiber), 4g pro. **Diabetic exchanges:** 2 starch, 1½ fat.

PEACH BAVARIAN

CARAMEL APPLE BARS

MAMAW EMILY'S STRAWBERRY CAKE

My husband loved his mamaw's strawberry cake. He thought no one could duplicate it. I made it, and it's just as scrumptious as he remembers.
—Jennifer Bruce, Manitou, KY

Prep: 15 min. • **Bake:** 25 min. + cooling
Makes: 12 servings

- 1 pkg. white cake mix (regular size)
- 1 pkg. (3 oz.) strawberry gelatin
- 3 Tbsp. sugar
- 3 Tbsp. all-purpose flour
- 1 cup water
- ½ cup canola oil
- 2 large eggs, room temperature
- 1 cup finely chopped strawberries

FROSTING
- ½ cup butter, softened
- ½ cup crushed strawberries
- 4½ to 5 cups confectioners' sugar

1. Preheat oven to 350°. Line the bottoms of 2 greased 8-in. round baking pans with parchment; grease parchment.
2. In a large bowl, combine the cake mix, gelatin, sugar and flour. Add water, oil and eggs; beat on low speed 30 seconds. Beat on medium 2 minutes. Fold in chopped strawberries. Transfer to prepared pans.
3. Bake until a toothpick inserted in center comes out clean, 25-30 minutes. Cool in pans 10 minutes before removing to wire racks; remove parchment. Let cake cool completely.
4. For frosting, in a small bowl, beat butter until creamy. Beat in crushed strawberries. Gradually beat in enough confectioners' sugar to reach desired consistency. Spread frosting between layers and over top and sides of cake.

1 slice: 532 cal., 21g fat (7g sat. fat), 51mg chol., 340mg sod., 85g carb. (69g sugars, 1g fiber), 4g pro.

> **TEST KITCHEN TIP**
> You'll be smitten with the nostalgic charm of this rich pink buttercream frosting, but for a change of pace, try icing the cake with whipped cream or whipped topping and serve with fresh berries. Save your prettiest strawberries for garnishing. Use second-tier berries for the cake interior and frosting.

CARAMEL APPLE BARS

These bars make an excellent fall dessert. We like to warm individual servings in the microwave and serve with a scoop of vanilla ice cream. It quickly became a family favorite; maybe it'll become one of your family's, too.
—Carol Stuber, Osawatomie, KS

Prep: 25 min. • **Bake:** 25 min. + cooling
Makes: 20 servings

- ½ cup butter, softened
- ¼ cup shortening
- 1 cup packed brown sugar
- 1¾ cups all-purpose flour
- 1 cup old-fashioned or quick-cooking oats
- 1 tsp. salt
- ½ tsp. baking soda
- ½ cup chopped pecans, optional

FILLING
- 4½ cups coarsely chopped peeled tart apples
- 3 Tbsp. all-purpose flour
- 1 pkg. (11 oz.) caramels
- 3 Tbsp. butter

1. Preheat oven to 400°. In a large bowl, cream the butter, shortening and brown sugar until light and fluffy, 5-7 minutes. Add flour, oats, salt and baking soda; mix well. If desired, stir in pecans. Set aside 2 cups. Press remaining oat mixture into an ungreased 13x9-in. baking pan.
2. For filling, toss the apples with flour; spoon over the crust. In a saucepan, melt the caramels and butter over low heat; drizzle over apples. Top with the reserved oat mixture.
3. Bake until topping is lightly browned, 25-30 minutes. Cool before slicing.

1 bar: 250 cal., 10g fat (5g sat. fat), 18mg chol., 241mg sod., 38g carb. (24g sugars, 1g fiber), 3g pro.

MAMAW EMILY'S STRAWBERRY CAKE

LEMON-MISU

I created this recipe to please everyone in my family. It's a cross between cheesecake and tiramisu with a refreshing lemony flavor. Garnish with fresh blueberries if you have them on hand!
—Monica Marolt, Willowick, OH

Prep: 30 min. + chilling
Makes: 9 servings

- 1 carton (8 oz.) mascarpone cheese
- 1 pkg. (8 oz.) cream cheese, softened
- 1 pkg. (3.4 oz.) instant lemon pudding mix
- 1 cup 2% milk
- 1 tsp. lemon extract
- ⅔ cup lemon juice
- 3 Tbsp. sugar
- 24 crisp ladyfinger cookies
- 2 tsp. grated lemon zest

1. Beat the first 5 ingredients on medium speed until blended, 2-3 minutes (do not overbeat).
2. Whisk lemon juice and sugar in a shallow bowl until the sugar is dissolved. Quickly dip 8 ladyfingers into the lemon juice, allowing excess to drip off; place in a single layer in an 8-in. square dish. Spread a third of the mascarpone mixture over top. Repeat layers twice.
3. Sprinkle with lemon zest. Refrigerate, covered, at least 2 hours before serving.
1 piece: 350 cal., 22g fat (12g sat. fat), 82mg chol., 272mg sod., 33g carb. (24g sugars, 0 fiber), 6g pro.

CUPPA JOE CARAMEL CAKE

CUPPA JOE CARAMEL CAKE

I get compliments on this wherever I take it. Adults especially really love the hint of coffee that goes perfectly with the brown sugar and caramel flavors.
—Leigh Doutt, Pueblo West, CO

Prep: 30 min. • **Bake:** 20 min. + cooling
Makes: 15 servings

- 1 cup buttermilk
- 4 tsp. instant coffee granules
- ½ cup butter, softened
- 1 cup packed brown sugar
- 2 large eggs, room temperature
- 1 tsp. vanilla extract
- 2 cups all-purpose flour
- 2 Tbsp. cornstarch
- 1½ tsp. baking powder
- ½ tsp. baking soda
- ½ tsp. salt
- ¼ tsp. ground nutmeg
- ¾ cup caramel ice cream topping, divided

FROSTING

- 1 Tbsp. baking cocoa
- 2 tsp. instant coffee granules
- ¼ cup boiling water
- ½ cup butter, softened
- ¼ cup confectioners' sugar
- ¾ cup semisweet chocolate chips, melted

1. Preheat oven to 350°. Microwave buttermilk for 30-45 seconds or just until warmed. Stir in coffee granules until dissolved.
2. In a large bowl, cream the butter and brown sugar until light and fluffy, 5-7 minutes. Add eggs, 1 at a time, beating well after each addition. Beat in vanilla. Combine the flour, cornstarch, baking powder, baking soda, salt and nutmeg; add to creamed mixture alternately with buttermilk mixture, beating well after each addition.
3. Transfer to a greased 13x9-in. baking pan. Bake until a toothpick inserted in the center comes out clean, 20-25 minutes. Cool on a wire rack 5 minutes.
4. Using end of a wooden spoon handle, poke holes in cake 2 in. apart. Pour ½ cup caramel topping into holes. Spoon the remaining caramel topping over cake. Cool completely.
5. In a small bowl, stir cocoa and coffee granules into boiling water until dissolved; cool to room temperature. In another bowl, cream butter and confectioners' sugar until light and fluffy. Stir in melted chocolate and cocoa mixture until well combined. Frost cake.
1 piece: 335 cal., 16g fat (10g sat. fat), 61mg chol., 338mg sod., 47g carb. (22g sugars, 1g fiber), 4g pro.

FAVORITE BANANA CREAM PIE

Homemade banana cream pie is my mom's specialty, and this dreamy dessert has a wonderful banana flavor. It looks so pretty, and it cuts easily, too.
—Jodi Grable, Springfield, MO

Prep: 10 min. • **Cook:** 15 min. + chilling
Makes: 8 servings

     Pastry for single-crust pie
  1 cup sugar
  ¼ cup cornstarch
  ½ tsp. salt
  3 cups 2% milk
  2 large eggs, room temperature, lightly beaten
  3 Tbsp. butter
  1½ tsp. vanilla extract
  2 large firm bananas
  1 cup heavy whipping cream, whipped

1. On a lightly floured surface, roll dough to a ⅛-in.-thick circle; transfer to a 9-in. pie plate. Trim to ½ in. beyond the rim of plate; flute edge. Refrigerate 30 minutes.

2. Preheat oven to 425°. Line crust with a double thickness of foil. Fill with pie weights, dried beans or uncooked rice. Bake on a lower oven rack until edges are golden brown, 20-25 minutes. Remove foil and weights; bake until bottom is golden brown, 3-6 minutes. Cool on a wire rack.

3. In a large saucepan, combine sugar, cornstarch, salt and milk until smooth. Cook and stir over medium-high heat until thickened and bubbly. Reduce heat; cook and stir 2 minutes longer. Remove from heat. Stir a small amount of hot filling into eggs; return all to pan. Bring to a gentle boil; cook and stir 2 minutes longer.

4. Remove from heat. Gently stir in butter and vanilla extract. Press plastic wrap onto surface of custard; refrigerate, covered, for 30 minutes.

5. Spread half of the custard into crust. Slice bananas; arrange over filling. Pour the remaining custard over bananas. Spread with whipped cream. Refrigerate 6 hours or overnight.

1 piece: 521 cal., 30g fat (18g sat. fat), 129mg chol., 406mg sod., 57g carb. (35g sugars, 1g fiber), 8g pro.

FAVORITE BANANA CREAM PIE

BING CHERRY-AMARETTI FOOL

PICTURED ON P. 287

When Bing cherries are in season, I make this fruity custard-style fool. The sweet cherries and whipped cream balance perfectly with the sour cream.
—Mary Ann Lee, Clifton Park, NY

Prep: 30 min. + chilling
Makes: 8 servings

  1 envelope unflavored gelatin
  ⅓ cup cold water
  1 cup sour cream
  ½ cup sugar
  1 Tbsp. lemon juice
  ½ tsp. almond extract
  ½ tsp. vanilla extract
  2 cups coarsely chopped fresh Bing or other dark sweet cherries, divided
  1 cup heavy whipping cream
  1 cup coarsely crushed amaretti cookies (about 16 cookies)
     Optional: Fresh mint leaves, additional Bing cherries and crushed amaretti cookies

1. In a small saucepan, sprinkle gelatin over cold water; let stand 1 minute. Heat and stir over low heat until the gelatin is completely dissolved. Let stand 5 minutes.

2. Place sour cream, sugar, lemon juice, extracts, 1 cup cherries and the gelatin mixture in a blender; cover and process until the cherries are pureed. Transfer to a large bowl.

3. In a small bowl, beat cream until soft peaks form. Remove ½ cup whipped cream; reserve for topping. Gently fold remaining whipped cream into cherry mixture. Fold in crushed cookies and remaining chopped cherries. Divide the mixture among 8 dessert dishes. Refrigerate at least 2 hours.

4. Serve with reserved whipped cream and optional toppings as desired.

1 serving: 323 cal., 19g fat (10g sat. fat), 41mg chol., 26mg sod., 36g carb. (32g sugars, 1g fiber), 4g pro.

CHOCOLATE CHIP
BROWNIES

CHOCOLATE CHIP BROWNIES

People love these rich brownies so much that I never take them anywhere without also taking along several copies of the recipe. The treats are a no-brainer to take on a picnic because you don't have to worry about melting frosting.
—Brenda Kelly, Ashburn, VA

Prep: 10 min. • **Bake:** 30 min. + cooling
Makes: 4 dozen

- 1 cup butter, softened
- 3 cups sugar
- 6 large eggs, room temperature
- 1 Tbsp. vanilla extract
- 2¼ cups all-purpose flour
- ½ cup baking cocoa
- 1 tsp. baking powder
- ½ tsp. salt
- 1 cup semisweet chocolate chips
- 1 cup vanilla or white chips
- 1 cup chopped walnuts

1. Preheat oven to 350°. In a large bowl, cream butter and sugar until light and fluffy, 5-7 minutes. Add eggs and vanilla; mix well. Combine the flour, baking cocoa, baking powder and salt; gradually add to creamed mixture just until blended (do not overmix).

2. Pour into 2 greased 9-in. square baking pans. Sprinkle with chips and nuts. Bake until a toothpick inserted in the center comes out clean, 30-35 minutes. Cool.

1 brownie: 167 cal., 8g fat (4g sat. fat), 38mg chol., 83mg sod., 22g carb. (14g sugars, 1g fiber), 3g pro.

BERRY COOL CREAM & PRETZEL PIE

This cool no-bake strawberry pie is the perfect antidote for your sweet tooth this summer. Made with pantry staples and as easy as pie to make, it's become one of my family's most requested warm-weather treats.
—Shauna Havey, Roy, UT

Prep: 45 min. + chilling
Makes: 16 servings

- 4 cups miniature pretzels
- 6 Tbsp. butter, melted
- ¼ cup sugar
- ¾ cup boiling water
- 1 pkg. (6 oz.) strawberry gelatin
- ¼ cup lemon juice

BERRY COOL CREAM & PRETZEL PIE

- 1 lb. fresh strawberries, hulled, divided
- 2 cups heavy whipping cream, divided
- 1 jar (7 oz.) marshmallow creme
- ⅔ cup whipped cream cheese
- ⅔ cup sweetened condensed milk

1. Place the pretzels in a food processor; pulse until chopped. Add butter and sugar; pulse until combined. Reserve ⅓ cup of the pretzel mixture for topping. Press the remaining mixture onto the bottom of a greased 9-in. springform pan. Refrigerate for 30 minutes.

2. Meanwhile, in a bowl, add boiling water to gelatin; stir 2 minutes to completely dissolve. Stir in lemon juice. Refrigerate for 30 minutes, stirring occasionally.

3. Chop half the strawberries; slice the remaining berries and reserve for topping. In a large bowl, beat 1 cup heavy cream until stiff peaks form. Beat marshmallow creme, cream cheese and sweetened condensed milk into cooled gelatin mixture until blended. Gently fold in the chopped strawberries and whipped cream. Pour into crust.

4. Refrigerate, covered, until firm, 4-6 hours. Beat the remaining 1 cup heavy cream until stiff peaks form; spread over pie. Top with reserved strawberries and pretzel mixture.

1 piece: 350 cal., 19g fat (12g sat. fat), 56mg chol., 284mg sod., 39g carb. (30g sugars, 1g fiber), 4g pro.

HOT MILK CAKE

When I think back on my mom's delicious meals, her milk cake always comes to mind as the perfect dessert. The simple, old-fashioned treat tastes so good, it will surprise you!
—Rosemary Pryor, Pasadena, MD

Prep: 20 min. • **Bake:** 30 min. + cooling
Makes: 16 servings

- 4 large eggs, room temperature
- 2 cups sugar
- 1 tsp. vanilla extract
- 2¼ cups all-purpose flour
- 2¼ tsp. baking powder
- 1¼ cups 2% milk
- 10 Tbsp. butter, cubed

1. Preheat oven to 350°. In a large bowl, beat eggs on high speed for 5 minutes or until thick and lemon-colored. Gradually add sugar, beating until mixture is light and fluffy. Beat in vanilla. Combine flour and baking powder; gradually add to batter, beating on low speed until smooth.
2. In a small saucepan, heat the milk and butter just until butter is melted. Gradually add to batter; beat just until combined.
3. Pour into a greased 13x9-in. baking pan. Bake until a toothpick inserted in the center comes out clean, 30-35 minutes. Cool on a wire rack.

1 piece: 254 cal., 9g fat (5g sat. fat), 75mg chol., 154mg sod., 39g carb. (26g sugars, 0 fiber), 4g pro.

GANACHE-TOPPED CHOCOLATE CAKE

GANACHE-TOPPED CHOCOLATE CAKE

To say this cake is elegant would be an understatement. It's worthy of special occasions, but it's so easy to whip up that you can enjoy it whenever you like.
—Taste of Home *Test Kitchen*

Prep: 20 min. • **Bake:** 20 min. + cooling
Makes: 12 servings

- ¾ cup boiling water
- 2 oz. 53% cacao dark baking chocolate, coarsely chopped
- 2 Tbsp. butter
- ¾ cup sugar
- ¼ cup buttermilk
- 1 large egg, room temperature
- 1 tsp. vanilla extract
- ½ tsp. orange extract
- 1 cup all-purpose flour
- 1 tsp. baking soda
- ½ tsp. salt

GANACHE
- 3 oz. 53% cacao dark baking chocolate, coarsely chopped
- ¼ cup half-and-half cream
  Optional: Fresh raspberries, confectioners' sugar and baking cocoa

1. Preheat oven to 350°. Pour boiling water over chocolate and butter; stir until smooth. Cool slightly. Whisk in sugar, buttermilk, egg and extracts. Combine flour, baking soda and salt; whisk into chocolate mixture just until blended.
2. Transfer to a 9-in. round baking pan coated with cooking spray. Bake until a toothpick inserted in the center comes out clean, 18-22 minutes. Cool for 10 minutes before removing from pan to a wire rack to cool completely. Place rack on a waxed paper-lined baking sheet.
3. For ganache, place chopped chocolate in a small bowl. Bring cream just to a boil in a small saucepan. Pour over chocolate; whisk until smooth. Cool until slightly thickened, about 10 minutes. Slowly pour the ganache over cake, allowing some to drape over sides.
4. Refrigerate until serving. If desired, sprinkle with raspberries, confectioners' sugar and cocoa. Cut into wedges.

1 piece: 179 cal., 7g fat (4g sat. fat), 26mg chol., 236mg sod., 28g carb. (18g sugars, 1g fiber), 3g pro. **Diabetic exchanges:** 2 starch, 1 fat.

CRANBERRY AMARETTO BREAD PUDDING

This is an update to a recipe that has been in our family for three generations. The delicous combination of white chocolate and amaretto mingled with cranberry is my favorite way to end any celebratory meal.

—Jennifer Evans DaCastello, Virginia Beach, VA

....

Prep: 15 min. + standing • **Bake:** 50 min.
Makes: 12 servings (1 cup sauce)

- 3 large eggs, room temperature
- 4 cups 2% milk
- 1 cup packed brown sugar
- ¼ cup butter, melted
- 3 tsp. vanilla extract
- 2 Tbsp. ground cinnamon
- 3 tsp. ground nutmeg
- 1 tsp. ground cloves
- ½ cup dried cranberries
- ½ cup toasted chopped pecans, optional
- 6 cups cubed day-old French bread

SAUCE
- 1 cup white baking chips
- ¼ cup butter, cubed
- ¼ cup amaretto

1. Preheat oven to 350°. Whisk together eggs, milk, brown sugar, melted butter, vanilla and spices. Stir in cranberries and, if desired, pecans. Gently stir in bread; let stand until bread is softened, about 15 minutes.

2. Transfer to a greased 13x9-in. baking dish. Bake until pudding is puffed and golden, and a knife inserted in the center comes out clean, 50-55 minutes.

3. In a small heavy saucepan, heat chips and butter over low heat until melted and smooth, stirring constantly. Remove from the heat; stir in amaretto. Serve with warm bread pudding.

½ cup pudding with about 1 Tbsp. sauce: 367 cal., 16g fat (9g sat. fat), 76mg chol., 222mg sod., 48g carb. (38g sugars, 2g fiber), 7g pro.

CREAMY PINEAPPLE PIE
PICTURED ON P. 287

This light and refreshing dessert is the best of both worlds—quick to make and impressive to serve! This pie makes a great finishing touch to a summer meal.

—Sharon Bickett, Chester, SC

....

Takes: 10 min. • **Makes:** 8 servings

- 1 can (14 oz.) sweetened condensed milk
- 1 can (8 oz.) crushed pineapple, undrained
- ¼ cup lemon juice
- 1 carton (8 oz.) frozen whipped topping, thawed
- 1 prepared graham cracker crust
  Optional: Chopped toasted macadamia nuts and additional crushed pineapple

Combine milk, pineapple and lemon juice; fold in whipped topping. Pour into the prepared crust. Refrigerate until serving. If desired, serve with toasted macadamia nuts and additional crushed pineapple.

1 piece: 367 cal., 14g fat (9g sat. fat), 17mg chol., 185mg sod., 54g carb. (46g sugars, 1g fiber), 5g pro.

READER REVIEW

"This is one of my favorite recipes! I do drain off a bit of the pineapple juice if the can seems too juicy before adding to the recipe."

KATHLEEN, TASTEOFHOME.COM

CRANBERRY AMARETTO BREAD PUDDING

PUMPKIN PIE SQUARES

POACHED PEARS WITH ORANGE CREAM

End the meal with a flourish with this easy and elegant dessert. A hint of orange lends just enough sweetness to temper the wine's bold taste.
—Julianne Schnuck, Milwaukee, WI

Prep: 10 min. • **Cook:** 45 min. + cooling
Makes: 2 servings

- 2 firm medium pears
- 1½ cups water
- 1 cup dry red wine or red grape juice
- ½ cup sugar
- 2 tsp. vanilla extract
- ¼ cup reduced-fat sour cream
- 2 tsp. confectioners' sugar
- ½ tsp. grated orange zest
- ⅛ tsp. orange extract
  Additional grated orange zest, optional

1. Core pears from bottom, leaving stems intact. Peel pears; cut ¼ in. from bottom to level if necessary. Place pears on their sides in a large saucepan. Add water, wine, sugar and vanilla. Bring to a boil. Reduce heat; simmer, covered, turning once, until pears are almost tender, 35-40 minutes. (For more intense flavor and color, leave fruit in cooking liquid and refrigerate overnight.)
2. Meanwhile, combine sour cream, confectioners' sugar, orange zest and extract. Refrigerate until serving.
3. Remove pears with a slotted spoon; pat dry and, if warm, cool to room temperature. Discard cooking liquid. Place pears on dessert plates. Serve with orange cream; if desired, top with additional grated orange zest.
1 serving: 239 cal., 3g fat (2g sat. fat), 10mg chol., 23mg sod., 46g carb. (36g sugars, 5g fiber), 3g pro.

TEST KITCHEN TIP
Using red wine in the poaching liquid will give you an intensely flavored pear with a beautiful rosy red color but you can also use a fruity white wine for a pear that is natural looking.

PUMPKIN PIE SQUARES

The first time my husband and daughters tried this dessert, they thought it was delicious. It has all the spicy pumpkin goodness of the traditional pie without the fuss of a pastry crust.
—Denise Goedeken, Platte Center, NE

Prep: 15 min.
Bake: 1 hour 20 min. + cooling
Makes: 20 servings

- 1 cup all-purpose flour
- ½ cup quick-cooking oats
- ½ cup packed brown sugar
- ½ cup cold butter
  FILLING
- 2 cans (15 oz. each) solid-pack pumpkin
- 2 cans (12 oz. each) evaporated milk
- 4 large eggs
- 1½ cups sugar
- 2 tsp. ground cinnamon
- 1 tsp. ground ginger
- ½ tsp. ground cloves
- 1 tsp. salt

TOPPING
- ½ cup packed brown sugar
- ½ cup chopped pecans
- 2 Tbsp. butter, softened
  Sweetened whipped cream, optional

1. Preheat oven to 350°. Combine flour, oats and brown sugar. Cut in butter until mixture is crumbly. Press into a greased 13x9-in. pan. Bake until golden brown, about 20 minutes.
2. Meanwhile, beat filling ingredients until smooth; pour over crust. Bake 45 minutes.
3. Combine topping ingredients; sprinkle over filling. Bake until a knife inserted in center comes out clean, 15-20 minutes longer. Cool, then refrigerate until serving. If desired, serve with whipped cream.
1 piece: 248 cal., 10g fat (5g sat. fat), 64mg chol., 212mg sod., 36g carb. (28g sugars, 2g fiber), 4g pro.

Whip Up Something Special

Top off dessert with your own flavored whipped cream! Start with the basic recipe, and go from there.

Basic Whipped Cream

In a chilled glass bowl and with chilled beaters, beat 1 cup heavy whipping cream until it begins to thicken. Add 3 Tbsp. confectioners' sugar and ½ tsp. vanilla; beat until soft peaks form.

Mocha
Use basic recipe; with sugar, add 1 Tbsp. baking cocoa and 1 tsp. instant coffee granules.

MOCHA

MOJITO

PEANUT BUTTER &BANANA

Mojito
Microwave 1 cup heavy whipping cream until hot (not boiling), about 1 minute. Add mint leaves and refrigerate 1 hour. Strain, then beat. Add 3 Tbsp. confectioners' sugar, 1 tsp. lime zest and ½ tsp. rum extract.

Peanut Butter & Banana
Use basic recipe; with sugar, add 1-2 Tbsp. creamy peanut butter and ½ tsp. banana extract.

Hazelnut
Use basic recipe; with sugar and vanilla, add 1-2 Tbsp. hazelnut liqueur.

HAZELNUT

5i

HAZELNUT CAKE SQUARES

Whenever one of my daughters is asked to bring a dish to a church function, a birthday party or any special occasion, they ask me for this recipe. It is so easy to prepare because it starts with a cake mix. It doesn't need icing, so it is great for bake sales, too.
—Brenda Melancon, McComb, MS

Prep: 10 min. • **Bake:** 25 min. + cooling
Makes: 15 servings

- 1 pkg. yellow cake mix (regular size)
- 3 large eggs, room temperature
- ⅔ cup water
- ⅔ cup Nutella
- ¼ cup canola oil
- ½ cup semisweet chocolate chips
- ½ cup chopped hazelnuts, toasted
- ½ cup brickle toffee bits, optional
- Confectioners' sugar, optional

1. Preheat oven to 350°. Grease a 13x9-in. baking pan.
2. In a large bowl, combine cake mix, eggs, water, Nutella and oil; beat on low speed 30 seconds. Beat on medium speed for 2 minutes. Fold in the chocolate chips, hazelnuts and, if desired, brickle toffee bits. Transfer to prepared pan. Bake until a toothpick inserted in center comes out clean, 25-30 minutes.
3. Cool completely in pan on a wire rack. Dust with confectioners' sugar if desired.
1 piece: 280 cal., 14g fat (3g sat. fat), 37mg chol., 245mg sod., 38g carb. (24g sugars, 2g fiber), 4g pro.

STRAWBERRY CHEESECAKE

STRAWBERRY CHEESECAKE

The creamy texture and lovely look of this cheesecake always get compliments.
—L.C. Herschap, Luling, TX

Prep: 30 min. • **Bake:** 50 min. + chilling
Makes: 16 servings

CRUST
- ¾ cup ground pecans
- ¾ cup graham cracker crumbs
- 3 Tbsp. butter, melted

FILLING
- 4 pkg. (8 oz. each) cream cheese, softened
- 1¼ cups sugar
- 1 Tbsp. lemon juice
- 2 tsp. vanilla extract
- 4 large eggs, room temperature, lightly beaten

TOPPING
- 2 cups sour cream
- ¼ cup sugar
- 1 tsp. vanilla extract

STRAWBERRY GLAZE
- 2 Tbsp. cornstarch
- ¼ cup water
- 1 jar (12 oz.) strawberry jelly
- 3 Tbsp. orange-flavored liqueur or lemon juice
- Red food coloring, optional
- 1 qt. whole fresh strawberries, halved

1. Preheat oven to 350°. Combine the pecans, crumbs and butter. Press onto the bottom of a 10-in. springform pan. Set aside.
2. In a large bowl, beat cream cheese and sugar until smooth. Beat in lemon juice and vanilla. Add eggs; beat on low speed just until blended. Spoon over crust.
3. Bake until filling is almost set, 45-50 minutes. Cool on a wire rack 15 minutes. Meanwhile, for topping, combine sour cream, sugar and vanilla. Spread over cheesecake; return to oven for 5 minutes. Cool on a wire rack for 1 hour. Refrigerate overnight, covering when cheesecake is completely cooled.
4. Several hours before serving, prepare glaze. In a saucepan, combine cornstarch and water until smooth. Add strawberry jelly and cook over medium-high heat, stirring constantly, until jelly is melted and the mixture has thickened. Remove from heat; stir in liqueur and, if desired, food coloring. Cool to room temperature.
5. Just before serving, loosen and remove the sides of springform pan. Arrange the strawberries on top with pointed ends up. Spoon glaze over berries, allowing some to drip down the sides of cake. Serve immediately.
1 piece: 453 cal., 22g fat (11g sat. fat), 126mg chol., 159mg sod., 56g carb. (48g sugars, 2g fiber), 6g pro.

NOT YOUR MAMA'S SEVEN-LAYER BARS

The addition of dulce de leche makes this a decadent new take on traditional seven-layer bars. You can cut this recipe in half and make it in an 8x8-inch pan.
—Andrea Barlow, Hot Springs, AR

Prep: 10 min. • **Bake:** 30 min. + cooling
Makes: 2 dozen

- 24 Oreo cookies
- ½ cup butter, melted
- 1 cup flaked coconut
- 1½ cups crisp brown rice cereal
- 1 can (13.4 oz.) dulce de leche
- 6 Tbsp. warm water (110° to 115°)
- 1½ cups coarsely chopped pecans
- ¼ tsp. sea salt

1. Preheat oven to 350°. Pulse cookies in food processor until finely chopped. Combine crumbs and melted butter; press onto bottom of greased, foil-lined 13x9-in. baking pan. Spread coconut over crust; sprinkle with crisp rice cereal.
2. Combine dulce de leche and water until smooth. Pour over cereal. Sprinkle pecans over dulce de leche; press down lightly.
3. Bake until edges are set but center is still soft, about 30 minutes. (Do not overbake.) Remove bars from oven; immediately sprinkle with sea salt. Cool completely on a wire rack before cutting into 24 squares.

1 bar: 228 cal., 14g fat (6g sat. fat), 16mg chol., 156mg sod., 24g carb. (18g sugars, 1g fiber), 2g pro.

SLOW-COOKER APPLE PUDDING CAKE
PICTURED ON P. 287

A satisfying dessert like this is a superb treat on a chilly night. It has three separate layers—apples, cake and sauce. I like to serve it in a bowl.
—Ellen Schroeder, Reedsburg, WI

Prep: 15 min. • **Cook:** 2 hours
Makes: 10 servings

- 2 cups all-purpose flour
- ⅔ cup plus ¼ cup sugar, divided
- 3 tsp. baking powder
- 1 tsp. salt
- ½ cup cold butter
- 1 cup 2% milk
- 2 medium tart apples, peeled and chopped
- 1½ cups orange juice
- ½ cup honey
- 2 Tbsp. butter, melted
- 1 tsp. ground cinnamon
- 1⅓ cups sour cream
- ¼ cup confectioners' sugar

1. In a small bowl, combine the flour, ⅔ cup sugar, baking powder and salt. Cut in butter until mixture resembles coarse crumbs. Stir in milk just until moistened. Spread into the bottom of a greased 4- or 5-qt. slow cooker; sprinkle chopped apples over batter.
2. In a small bowl, combine orange juice, honey, melted butter, cinnamon and the remaining ¼ cup sugar; pour over apples. Cover and cook on high 2-3 hours, until apples are tender.
3. In a small bowl, combine sour cream and confectioners' sugar. Serve with warm pudding cake.

1 cup with 2 Tbsp. sour cream mixture: 431 cal., 17g fat (11g sat. fat), 53mg chol., 461mg sod., 64g carb. (44g sugars, 1g fiber), 5g pro.

NOT YOUR MAMA'S SEVEN-LAYER BARS

EASY
ODDS & ENDS

Make the most of your favorite kitchen gadgets with the quick, simple and oh-so-satisfying recipes in this chapter. Start with small-plate specials crisped up in an air fryer, move on to main courses created in the Instant Pot, and finish with delectable desserts served up in classic cast iron!

Air-Fryer Appetizers

Delivering all the crispiness but without the fat of deep-fried foods, air fryers are the new favorite gadget in kitchens across the country. If you're looking for a tasty hot appetizer that doesn't load up on the grease, check out these air-fryer recipes!

QUINOA ARANCINI

QUINOA ARANCINI

We love arancini, but they're not the healthiest thing going. I wanted to make a version that we could enjoy guilt-free. I substituted quinoa for rice and tried baking instead of frying. Now we can have them anytime.
—Sabrina Ovadia, New York, NY

Takes: 25 min. • **Makes:** 3 servings

- 1 pkg. (9 oz.) ready-to-serve quinoa or 1¾ cups cooked quinoa
- 2 large eggs, lightly beaten, divided use
- 1 cup seasoned bread crumbs, divided
- ¼ cup shredded Parmesan cheese
- 1 Tbsp. olive oil
- 2 Tbsp. minced fresh basil or 2 tsp. dried basil
- ½ tsp. garlic powder
- ½ tsp. salt
- ⅛ tsp. pepper
- 6 cubes part-skim mozzarella cheese (¾ in. each)
   Cooking spray
   Warmed pasta sauce, optional

1. Preheat air fryer to 375°. Prepare quinoa according to package directions. Stir in 1 egg, ½ cup bread crumbs, the Parmesan cheese, oil, basil and seasonings.
2. Divide mixture into 6 portions. Shape each portion around a cheese cube to cover completely, forming a ball.
3. Place the remaining egg and ½ cup bread crumbs in separate shallow bowls. Dip quinoa balls in egg, then roll in bread crumbs. Place on greased tray in air-fryer basket; spritz with cooking spray. Cook until golden brown, 6-8 minutes. If desired, serve with pasta sauce.
2 arancini: 423 cal., 19g fat (6g sat. fat), 142mg chol., 1283mg sod., 40g carb. (4g sugars, 5g fiber), 21g pro.

ROSEMARY SAUSAGE MEATBALLS

These air-fryer meatballs were created as hors d'oeuvres for a friend's wedding and became an instant hit. Now we enjoy them often at our house.
—Steve Hansen, Redmond, WA

Prep: 20 min. • **Cook:** 10 min./batch
Makes: about 2 dozen

- 2 Tbsp. olive oil
- 4 garlic cloves, minced
- 1 tsp. curry powder
- 1 large egg, lightly beaten
- 1 jar (4 oz.) diced pimientos, drained
- ¼ cup dry bread crumbs
- ¼ cup minced fresh parsley
- 1 Tbsp. minced fresh rosemary
- 2 lbs. bulk pork sausage
   Pretzel sticks, optional

1. Preheat air fryer to 400°. In a small skillet, heat oil over medium heat; saute garlic with curry powder until tender, 1-2 minutes. Cool slightly.
2. Combine egg, pimientos, bread crumbs, parsley, rosemary and garlic mixture. Add sausage; mix lightly but thoroughly.
3. Shape into 1¼-in. balls. Place in a single layer on tray in air-fryer basket; cook until lightly browned and cooked through, 7-10 minutes. If desired, serve with pretzels.
1 meatball: 96 cal., 8g fat (2g sat. fat), 24mg chol., 208mg sod., 2g carb. (0 sugars, 0 fiber), 4g pro.

**CARIBBEAN
WONTONS**

CARIBBEAN WONTONS

*I first served these fresh and fruity treats
as an appetizer at a summer luau. My
family and friends now enjoy them as a
dessert for special occasions throughout
the year.*
—Melissa Pelkey Hass, Waleska, GA

Prep: 30 min. • **Cook:** 10 min./batch
Makes: 2 dozen (1¼ cups sauce)

- 4 oz. cream cheese, softened
- ¼ cup sweetened shredded coconut
- ¼ cup mashed ripe banana
- 2 Tbsp. chopped walnuts
- 2 Tbsp. canned crushed pineapple
- 1 cup marshmallow creme
- 24 wonton wrappers
  Cooking spray

SAUCE
- 1 lb. fresh strawberries, hulled
- ¼ cup sugar
- 1 tsp. cornstarch
  Confectioners' sugar and
    ground cinnamon

1. Preheat air fryer to 350°. In a small
bowl, beat cream cheese until smooth.
Stir in coconut, banana, walnuts and
pineapple. Fold in marshmallow creme.
2. Position a wonton wrapper with
1 point toward you. Keep the remaining
wrappers covered with a damp paper
towel until ready to use. Place 2 tsp. filling
in the center of wrapper. Moisten edges
with water; fold opposite corners together
over filling and press to seal. Repeat with
the remaining wrappers and filling.
3. In batches, arrange wontons in a single
layer on greased tray in air-fryer basket;
spritz with cooking spray. Cook until
golden brown and crisp, 10-12 minutes.
4. Meanwhile, place strawberries in a
food processor; cover and process until
pureed. In a small saucepan, combine
sugar and cornstarch. Stir in pureed
strawberries. Bring to a boil; cook and
stir until thickened, 2 minutes. If desired,
strain mixture, reserving sauce and
discarding seeds.
5. Sprinkle wontons with confectioners'
sugar and cinnamon. Serve with sauce.
1 wonton with 1½ tsp. sauce: 83 cal.,
3g fat (1g sat. fat), 5mg chol., 67mg sod.,
13g carb. (7g sugars, 1g fiber), 1g pro.

GREEK BREADSTICKS
PICTURED ON P. 305

*These crisp breadsticks
are twisted with Greek-
inspired goodness and
are best served fresh
and hot. Get ready for
lots of rave reviews!*
—Jane Whittaker, Pensacola, FL

Prep: 20 min. • **Cook:** 15 min./batch
Makes: 32 breadsticks

- ¼ cup marinated quartered artichoke
    hearts, drained
- 2 Tbsp. pitted Greek olives
- 1 pkg. (17.3 oz.) frozen puff pastry,
    thawed
- 1 carton (6½ oz.) spreadable spinach
    and artichoke cream cheese
- 2 Tbsp. grated Parmesan cheese
- 1 large egg
- 1 Tbsp. water
- 2 tsp. sesame seeds
  Refrigerated tzatziki sauce, optional

1. Preheat air fryer to 325°. Place
artichokes and olives in a food processor;
cover and pulse until finely chopped.
Unfold 1 pastry sheet on a lightly floured
surface; spread half the cream cheese
over half of the pastry. Top with half the
artichoke mixture. Sprinkle with half the
Parmesan cheese. Fold plain half over
filling; press gently to seal.
2. Repeat with remaining pastry, cream
cheese, artichoke mixture and Parmesan
cheese. Whisk egg and water; brush over
tops. Sprinkle with sesame seeds. Cut
each rectangle into sixteen ¾-in.-wide
strips. Twist strips several times.
3. In batches, arrange strips in a single
layer on greased tray in air-fryer basket.
Cook until breadsticks are golden brown,
12-15 minutes. Serve warm, with tzatziki
sauce if desired.
1 breadstick: 99 cal., 6g fat (2g sat. fat),
11mg chol., 108mg sod., 9g carb.
(0 sugars, 1g fiber), 2g pro.

TEST KITCHEN TIP
If you don't have an air fryer, you
can make this recipe in an oven.

PUMPKIN FRIES
PICTURED ON P. 305

Move over, french fries—these homemade pumpkin fries are divine! Not only are they healthier than traditional fries, but they're simple to make and they crisp up beautifully in the air fryer. The maple-chipotle dipping sauce is the perfect accompaniment.
—Julie Peterson, Crofton, MD

Prep: 25 min. • **Cook:** 15 min./batch
Makes: 4 servings

- ½ cup plain Greek yogurt
- 2 Tbsp. maple syrup
- 2 to 3 tsp. minced chipotle peppers in adobo sauce
- ⅛ tsp. plus ½ tsp. salt, divided
- 1 medium pie pumpkin
- ¼ tsp. garlic powder
- ¼ tsp. ground cumin
- ¼ tsp. chili powder
- ¼ tsp. pepper

1. In a small bowl, combine yogurt, maple syrup, chipotle peppers and ⅛ tsp. salt. Refrigerate, covered, until serving.
2. Preheat air fryer to 400°. Peel pumpkin; cut in half lengthwise. Discard seeds or save for toasting. Cut into ½-in. strips. Transfer to a large bowl. Sprinkle with remaining ½ tsp. salt, garlic powder, cumin, chili powder and pepper; toss to coat.
3. In batches, arrange pumpkin on greased tray in air-fryer basket. Cook until just tender, 6-8 minutes. Toss to redistribute; cook until browned and crisp, 3-5 minutes longer. Serve with sauce.

½ cup pumpkin fries with 2 Tbsp. sauce: 151 cal., 3g fat (2g sat. fat), 8mg chol., 413mg sod., 31g carb. (12g sugars, 2g fiber), 5g pro.

TEST KITCHEN TIP
If you don't have pumpkin on hand, butternut squash makes an excellent substitute. And don't forget to save the seeds for roasting!

HAM & CHEESE TURNOVERS

HAM & CHEESE TURNOVERS

I adore the combo of pears, blue cheese and walnuts in a salad, so I turned them into this turnover recipe. I added black forest ham, so you could pair it with a salad and have a complete dinner.
—Trisha Kruse, Eagle, ID

Prep: 20 min. • **Cook:** 10 min./batch
Makes: 4 servings

- 1 tube (13.8 oz.) refrigerated pizza crust
- ¼ lb. thinly sliced black forest deli ham
- 1 medium pear, thinly sliced and divided
- ¼ cup chopped walnuts, toasted
- 2 Tbsp. crumbled blue cheese

1. Preheat air fryer to 400°. On a lightly floured surface, unroll pizza crust into a 12-in. square. Cut into 4 squares. Layer ham, half of pear slices, walnuts and blue cheese diagonally over half of each square to within ½ in. of edges. Fold 1 corner over filling to the opposite corner, forming a triangle; press edges with a fork to seal.
2. In batches, arrange turnovers in a single layer on greased tray in air-fryer basket; spritz with cooking spray. Cook until golden brown, 4-6 minutes on each side. Garnish with remaining pear slices.

1 turnover: 357 cal., 10g fat (2g sat. fat), 16mg chol., 885mg sod., 55g carb. (11g sugars, 3g fiber), 15g pro.

COCONUT SHRIMP WITH APRICOT SAUCE

Coconut and panko crumbs give this spicy shrimp appetizer its crunch. You could make a whole meal by pairing them with a salad or using them for shrimp tacos.
—Debi Mitchell, Flower Mound, TX

Takes: 30 min. • **Makes:** 2 servings

- ½ lb. uncooked large shrimp
- ½ cup sweetened shredded coconut
- 3 Tbsp. panko bread crumbs
- 2 large egg whites
- ⅛ tsp. salt
  Dash pepper
  Dash Louisiana-style hot sauce
- 3 Tbsp. all-purpose flour

SAUCE
- ⅓ cup apricot preserves
- ½ tsp. cider vinegar
  Dash crushed red pepper flakes

1. Preheat air fryer to 375°. Peel and devein shrimp, leaving tails on if desired.
2. In a shallow bowl, toss coconut with bread crumbs. In another shallow bowl, whisk egg whites, salt, pepper and hot sauce. Place flour in a third shallow bowl.
3. Dip shrimp in flour to coat lightly; shake off excess. Dip in egg white mixture, then in coconut mixture, patting to help coating adhere.
4. Place shrimp in a single layer on greased tray in air-fryer basket. Cook 4 minutes; turn shrimp and continue cooking until coconut is lightly browned and shrimp turn pink, another 4 minutes.
5. Meanwhile, combine sauce ingredients in a small saucepan; cook and stir over medium-low heat until preserves are melted. Serve shrimp immediately with sauce.

6 shrimp with 2 Tbsp. sauce: 423 cal., 10g fat (8g sat. fat), 138mg chol., 440mg sod., 59g carb. (34g sugars, 2g fiber), 25g pro.

COCONUT SHRIMP WITH APRICOT SAUCE

AIR-FRYER RAVIOLI

While visiting a friend who'd just moved to St. Louis, Missouri, I tried these toasted ravioli at almost every restaurant we visited! When I got home, I had to try to replicate them, and I do think this recipe comes pretty close.
—Cristina Carrera, Kenosha, WI

Prep: 20 min. • **Cook:** 10 min./batch
Makes: about 1½ dozen

- 1 cup seasoned bread crumbs
- ¼ cup shredded Parmesan cheese
- 2 tsp. dried basil
- ½ cup all-purpose flour
- 2 large eggs, lightly beaten
- 1 pkg. (9 oz.) frozen beef ravioli, thawed
  Cooking spray
  Fresh minced basil, optional
- 1 cup marinara sauce, warmed

1. Preheat air fryer to 350°. In a shallow bowl, mix bread crumbs, Parmesan cheese and basil. Place flour and eggs in separate shallow bowls. Dip ravioli in flour to coat both sides; shake off excess. Dip in eggs, then in crumb mixture, patting to help coating adhere.
2. In batches, arrange ravioli in a single layer on greased tray in air-fryer basket; spritz with cooking spray. Cook until golden brown, 3-4 minutes. Turn; spritz with cooking spray. Cook until golden brown, 3-4 minutes longer. If desired, immediately sprinkle with basil and additional Parmesan cheese. Serve warm with marinara sauce.

1 piece: 40 cal., 1g fat (0 sat. fat), 6mg chol., 117mg sod., 6g carb. (1g sugars, 1g fiber), 2g pro.

Instant Pot™ Inventions

The busy cook's best friend, the Instant Pot is perfect for creating comforting, satisfying main courses that taste as if they've taken hours. From stews to pasta to hot sandwiches and everything between, this miraculous gadget makes quick cooking a breeze.

SMOKED SALMON & DILL PENNE

TEQUILA SALSA CHICKEN

I had this dish at a local Mexican restaurant when celebrating a friend's birthday. I fell in love with the spicy, smoky flavor from the tequila and decided to try it at home in my Instant Pot. Boy, was it a success! It's also fabulous stuffed into flour tortillas or for making nachos. This can be made with frozen chicken breasts; just increase the cooking time to 15 minutes.
—Trisha Kruse, Eagle, ID

Takes: 15 minutes • **Makes:** 3 cups

- 1 envelope taco seasoning
- 1 lb. boneless skinless chicken breasts
- 1 cup chunky salsa
- ¼ cup tequila
  Hot cooked rice
  Optional: Avocado slices, chopped fresh cilantro and lime wedges

1. Sprinkle taco seasoning over chicken breasts; place in a 6-qt. electric pressure cooker. Combine salsa and tequila; pour over chicken. Lock lid; close pressure-release valve. Adjust to pressure-cook on high for 6 minutes. Quick-release pressure. A thermometer inserted in chicken should read at least 165°.
2. Remove chicken. When cool enough to handle, shred meat with 2 forks; return to pressure cooker. Serve with hot cooked rice and desired toppings.
¾ cup: 187 cal., 3g fat (1g sat. fat), 63mg chol., 1107mg sod., 11g carb. (2g sugars, 0 fiber), 23g pro.

SMOKED SALMON & DILL PENNE

I love making one-pot pastas in my pressure cooker. Every noodle soaks up the flavors of the ingredients. I experimented with some leftover smoked fish and fresh dill, and boom— this recipe was born! It's now a staple in our house because it's on the table in half an hour and the kids love it!
—Shannon Dobos, Calgary, AB

Takes: 20 min.
Makes: 6 servings

- 2¼ cups chicken broth
- ½ lb. smoked salmon fillets, flaked
- ½ cup heavy whipping cream
- 2 Tbsp. snipped fresh dill
- ½ tsp. pepper
- 12 oz. uncooked penne pasta
  Additional fresh dill
  Lemon slices, optional

Place broth, salmon, cream, dill and pepper in a 6-qt. electric pressure cooker; top with penne (do not stir). Lock lid; close pressure-release valve. Adjust to pressure-cook on high for 8 minutes. Quick-release pressure. Gently stir before serving; top with additional dill and, if desired, lemon slices.
1¼ cups: 322 cal., 10g fat (5g sat. fat), 33mg chol., 672mg sod., 42g carb. (3g sugars, 2g fiber), 15g pro.

SPICY PORK ROAST WITH APRICOTS

SESAME CHICKEN
PICTURED ON P. 305

Your family will love the flavorful sauce that coats this chicken, and you'll love how quick and easy it is for a weeknight dinner! If you serve gluten-free meals, use tamari instead of soy sauce.
—Karen Kelly, Germantown, MD

....

Takes: 20 min. • **Makes:** 4 servings

- 1 Tbsp. sesame oil
- 1½ lbs. boneless skinless chicken breasts, cut into 1-in. pieces
- ¼ cup honey
- ¼ cup soy sauce or gluten-free tamari soy sauce
- ¼ cup water
- 3 garlic cloves, minced
- ¼ tsp. crushed red pepper flakes
- 3 tsp. cornstarch
- 2 Tbsp. cold water
   Hot cooked rice
- 1 Tbsp. sesame seeds
   Thinly sliced green onions, optional

1. Select saute or browning setting on a 6-qt. electric pressure cooker. Adjust for medium heat; add sesame oil. When oil is hot, brown chicken in batches. Press cancel. Return chicken to pressure cooker. In a small bowl, whisk honey, soy sauce, water, garlic and pepper flakes; stir into pressure cooker. Lock lid; close pressure-release valve. Adjust to pressure-cook on high for 4 minutes.

2. Quick-release pressure. In a small bowl, mix cornstarch and water until smooth; stir into pressure cooker. Select saute setting and adjust for low heat. Simmer, stirring constantly, until thickened, 1-2 minutes. Serve with rice. Sprinkle with sesame seeds and, if desired, green onions.

1 serving: 311 cal., 9g fat (2g sat. fat), 94mg chol., 1004mg sod., 20g carb. (17g sugars, 0 fiber), 37g pro.

SPICY PORK ROAST WITH APRICOTS

I wanted to create a roast all in one pot that had a slightly sweet taste and was good both for dinner one night and sliced for sandwiches the next day. I serve it with a country gravy made with some of the juices and pieces of apricots from the roast mixed in.
—Paulina Parker, Livingston, TX

....

Prep: 15 min. + marinating
Cook: 25 min. • **Makes:** 8 servings

- 2 tsp. garlic powder
- 1½ tsp. lemon-pepper seasoning
- 1 to 2 tsp. Caribbean jerk seasoning
- 1 tsp. paprika
- ½ tsp. salt
- ½ tsp. crushed red pepper flakes
- ½ tsp. pepper
- 1 boneless pork loin roast (2 lbs.)
- 1 Tbsp. olive oil
- 1 cup dried apricots, finely chopped
- ⅓ cup honey
- 1 envelope country gravy mix

1. Combine the first 7 ingredients; rub over roast. Refrigerate, covered, overnight.

2. Place 1 cup water in a 6-qt. electric pressure cooker. Add roast; drizzle with oil. Combine apricots and honey; pour over roast. Lock lid; close pressure-release valve. Adjust to pressure cook on high for 20 minutes. Quick-release pressure. Remove roast and keep warm.

3. Strain cooking juices into a 4-cup measuring cup; add enough water to measure 3 cups. Return juices to the pressure cooker. Select saute setting and adjust for low heat; bring liquid to a boil. Gradually stir gravy mix into cooking juices. Simmer, stirring constantly, until thickened, 1-2 minutes. Slice pork and serve with gravy.

1 serving: 288 cal., 10g fat (2g sat. fat), 57mg chol., 591mg sod., 27g carb. (20g sugars, 1g fiber), 23g pro.

RED PEPPER CHICKEN

Chicken breasts are treated to black beans, red peppers and juicy tomatoes in this southwestern supper. We love it served with rice cooked in chicken broth—but it would also make a great filling for tacos or burritos.
—Piper Spiwak, Vienna, VA

Takes: 30 min. • **Makes:** 4 servings

- 4 boneless skinless chicken breast halves (4 oz. each)
- 1 can (15 oz.) no-salt-added black beans, rinsed and drained
- 1 can (14½ oz.) Mexican stewed tomatoes, undrained
- 1 jar (12 oz.) roasted sweet red peppers, drained and cut into strips
- 1 large onion, chopped
- ½ cup water
  Pepper to taste
  Hot cooked rice

1. Place chicken in a 6-qt. electric pressure cooker. In a bowl, combine beans, tomatoes, red peppers, onion, water and pepper; pour over chicken. Lock lid; close pressure-release valve. Adjust to pressure-cook on high for 5 minutes. Quick-release pressure. A thermometer inserted in chicken should read at least 165°. Remove chicken and keep warm.
2. Select saute setting; adjust for low heat. Simmer cooking juices until thickened, 8-10 minutes. Serve juices with rice and chicken.
Freeze option: Place chicken and bean mixture in freezer containers; top with cooking juices. Cool and freeze. To use, partially thaw in refrigerator overnight. Microwave, covered, on high in a microwave-safe dish until heated through, stirring gently; add a little broth or water if necessary.
1 chicken breast half with 1 cup bean mixture: 288 cal., 3g fat (1g sat. fat), 63mg chol., 657mg sod., 28g carb. (8g sugars, 7g fiber), 30g pro. **Diabetic exchanges:** 3 lean meat, 1½ starch, 1 vegetable.

PHILLY CHEESESTEAK SANDWICHES

These sandwiches are melt-in-your-mouth delicious! Everybody loves a good cheesesteak smothered with onions and peppers, then topped with ready-to-melt cheese.
—Kimberly Wallace, Dennison, OH

Prep: 15 min. • **Cook:** 15 min. + releasing
Makes: 8 servings

- 1 beef top sirloin steak (3 lbs.), thinly sliced
- 2 large onions, cut into ½-in. strips
- 1 can (10½ oz.) condensed French onion soup, undiluted
- 2 garlic cloves, minced
- 1 pkg. Italian salad dressing mix
- 2 tsp. beef base
- ½ tsp. pepper
- 2 large red or green peppers, cut into ½-in. strips
- ½ cup pickled pepper rings
- 8 hoagie buns or French rolls, split
- 8 slices provolone cheese

1. Combine the first 7 ingredients in a 6-qt. electric pressure cooker. Lock lid; close pressure-release valve. Adjust to pressure-cook on high for 10 minutes. Quick-release pressure. Add peppers and pepper rings. Lock lid; close pressure-release valve. Adjust to pressure-cook on high for an additional 5 minutes. Let pressure release naturally for 10 minutes; quick-release any remaining pressure.
2. Place buns on ungreased baking sheets, cut sides up. Using tongs, place beef and vegetables on bun bottoms. Place cheese on bun tops. Broil 3-4 in. from heat until cheese is melted, 1-2 minutes. Close sandwiches; serve with cooking juices.
1 sandwich: 547 cal., 18g fat (7g sat. fat), 85mg chol., 1381mg sod., 45g carb. (10g sugars, 3g fiber), 51g pro.
Slow-cooker option: Combine the first 7 ingredients in a 4- or 5-qt. slow cooker. Cook, covered, on low 6 hours. Stir in peppers and pepper rings; cook, covered, 1-2 hours longer or until meat is tender. Place buns on ungreased baking sheets, cut sides up. Using tongs, place beef and vegetables on bun bottoms. Place cheese on bun tops. Broil 3-4 in. from heat until cheese is melted, 1-2 minutes. Close sandwiches; serve with cooking juices.

PHILLY CHEESESTEAK SANDWICHES

CHICKPEA & POTATO CURRY

TACO PASTA

This dish makes a welcome refresher to our normal Taco Tuesdays. I've taken all the flavors of tacos and created an easy pasta dish. Kids love the taste, and Mom loves how quick and easy it comes together in the Instant Pot. To lighten things up, use ground turkey.
—Christine Hadden, Whitman, MA

Takes: 25 min.
Makes: 4 servings

- 1 lb. lean ground beef (90% lean)
- 1 envelope taco seasoning
- 2 cups beef broth
- 1 can (8 oz.) tomato sauce
- 8 oz. uncooked medium pasta shells
- 1½ cups shredded Mexican cheese blend
  Optional: Sour cream, cilantro, chopped tomatoes, black olives

1. Select saute setting on a 6-qt. electric pressure cooker and adjust for high heat; cook beef until no longer pink, 6-8 minutes, breaking into crumbles. Press cancel; drain beef. Add the taco seasoning; stir to combine. Add beef broth, tomato sauce and pasta.
2. Lock lid; close pressure-release valve. Adjust pressure to high and set time for 5 minutes. When finished cooking, quick-release pressure. Stir; top with cheese. Let stand until cheese melts, 1 minute. If desired, serve with toppings.
2 cups: 598 cal., 25g fat (11g sat. fat), 108mg chol., 1845mg sod., 53g carb. (3g sugars, 3g fiber), 40g pro.

CHICKPEA & POTATO CURRY

Classic Indian cooking is famous for taking hours, even days, to layer on the flavor. Here's a version of a classic Indian dish made quick in the pressure cooker.
—Anjana Devasahayam, San Antonio, TX

Prep: 25 min. • **Cook:** 5 min. + releasing
Makes: 6 servings

- 1 Tbsp. canola oil
- 1 medium onion, chopped
- 2 garlic cloves, minced
- 2 tsp. minced fresh gingerroot
- 2 tsp. ground coriander
- 1 tsp. garam masala
- 1 tsp. chili powder
- ½ tsp. salt
- ½ tsp. ground cumin
- ¼ tsp. ground turmeric
- 2½ cups vegetable stock
- 2 cans (15 oz. each) chickpeas or garbanzo beans, rinsed and drained
- 1 can (15 oz.) crushed tomatoes
- 1 large baking potato, peeled and cut into ¾-in. cubes
- 1 Tbsp. lime juice
  Chopped fresh cilantro
  Hot cooked rice
  Optional: Sliced red onion and lime wedges

1. Select saute setting on a 6-qt. electric pressure cooker. Adjust for medium heat; add oil. When oil is hot, cook and stir onion until crisp-tender, 2-4 minutes. Add garlic, ginger and dry seasonings; cook and stir 1 minute. Add stock to pressure cooker. Cook 30 seconds, stirring to loosen browned bits from pan. Press cancel. Stir in the chickpeas, tomatoes and potato.
2. Lock lid; close pressure-release valve. Adjust to pressure-cook on high for 3 minutes. Let pressure release naturally for 10 minutes; quick-release any remaining pressure.
3. Stir in lime juice; sprinkle with cilantro. Serve with rice and, if desired, red onion slices and lime wedges.
1¼ cups: 240 cal., 6g fat (0 sat. fat), 0 chol., 767mg sod., 42g carb. (8g sugars, 9g fiber), 8g pro.

JAMBALAYA RISOTTO

STEAK FAJITAS

I've enjoyed cooking since I was a girl growing up in the Southwest, and fajitas are one of my favorite dishes—they're an easy way to add wallop to ho-hum dinner lineups. This simply delicious main dish is an excellent option if you're looking for something new to serve.
—Janie Reitz, Rochester, MN

Takes: 25 min.
Makes: 6 servings

- 2 Tbsp. canola oil
- 1½ lbs. beef top sirloin steak, cut into thin strips
- 1 large onion, julienned
- 1 large sweet red pepper, julienned
- 1 garlic clove, minced
- ½ cup reduced-sodium beef broth
- 2 Tbsp. lemon juice
- 1½ tsp. ground cumin
- 1 tsp. seasoned salt
- ½ tsp. chili powder
- ¼ to ½ tsp. crushed red pepper flakes
- 12 mini flour tortillas (5 in.), warmed
     Optional: Shredded cheddar cheese, fresh cilantro leaves, sliced jalapeno pepper and avocado

1. Select saute or browning setting on a 6-qt. electric pressure cooker. Adjust for medium heat; add oil. When oil is hot, brown beef. Press cancel. Place onion, pepper and garlic on meat. Top with broth, lemon juice and seasonings.
2. Lock lid; close pressure-release valve. Adjust to pressure-cook on high for 3 minutes. Quick-release pressure. A thermometer inserted in beef should read at least 160°. Using tongs, serve meat with tortillas and your choice of toppings.

2 fajitas: 337 cal., 14g fat (4g sat. fat), 46mg chol., 554mg sod., 21g carb. (2g sugars, 3g fiber), 28g pro. **Diabetic exchanges:** 4 lean meat, 1½ starch, 1 fat.

JAMBALAYA RISOTTO

This pressure-cooker jambalaya is delicious any night, but I especially like making it when I'm entertaining. The risotto makes it creamy and delicious.
—Janice Elder, Charlotte, NC

Takes: 25 min.
Makes: 8 servings

- 2 Tbsp. canola oil, divided
- 1 lb. fully cooked andouille sausage links, cut into ¼-in. slices
- ½ lb. boneless skinless chicken breasts, cut into 1-in. pieces
- 1 Tbsp. Cajun seasoning
- 1 large onion, chopped
- 1 large green pepper, chopped
- ½ cup chopped celery
- 2 garlic cloves, minced
- 1½ cups uncooked arborio rice
- 2 cans (14 oz. each) reduced-sodium chicken broth
- ½ cup dry white wine
- ¾ cup shredded Parmesan cheese
- 2 plum tomatoes, seeded and chopped
- ⅓ cup chopped flat-leaf parsley
- ¼ tsp. pepper
     Optional: Additional parsley and shredded Parmesan cheese

1. Select saute setting on a 6-qt. electric pressure cooker and adjust for medium heat; add 1 Tbsp. oil. When oil is hot, cook and stir sausage until lightly browned, 5-7 minutes; remove and keep warm. Sprinkle chicken with Cajun seasoning; add to pressure cooker; cook and stir until no longer pink, 5-7 minutes. Remove and keep warm. Add remaining 1 Tbsp. oil, the onion, green pepper, celery and garlic. Cook and stir until vegetables are crisp-tender, 2-3 minutes. Stir in rice. Add broth and wine, stirring to loosen browned bits from pan. Press cancel.
2. Lock lid; close pressure-release valve. Adjust to pressure-cook on high for 4 minutes. Let pressure release naturally.
3. Select saute setting and adjust for medium heat. Add sausage, chicken, cheese, tomatoes, parsley and pepper. Cook and stir until heated through. If desired, garnish with additional parsley and Parmesan cheese.

1¼ cups: 396 cal., 18g fat (6g sat. fat), 95mg chol., 1050mg sod., 36g carb. (3g sugars, 2g fiber), 24g pro.

STEAK FAJITAS

PORK & APPLE CURRY

Here's a gentle curry dish that won't overwhelm more delicate palates. For fun, try varying the garnish—add a few chopped peanuts or a little chutney.
—Nancy Reck, Mill Valley, CA

Takes: 25 min.
Makes: 8 servings

- 2 lbs. boneless pork loin roast, cut into 1-in. cubes
- 1 small onion, chopped
- ½ cup orange juice
- 1 Tbsp. curry powder
- 1 tsp. chicken bouillon granules
- 1 garlic clove, minced
- ½ tsp. salt
- ½ tsp. ground ginger
- ¼ tsp. ground cinnamon
- 1 medium apple, peeled and chopped
- 2 Tbsp. cornstarch
- 2 Tbsp. cold water
  Hot cooked rice, optional
- ¼ cup raisins
- ¼ cup sweetened shredded coconut, toasted

1. In a 6-qt. electric pressure cooker, combine the first 9 ingredients. Lock lid; close pressure-release valve. Adjust to pressure-cook on high for 3 minutes. Quick-release pressure. A thermometer inserted in pork should read at least 145°.
2. Add apple to pressure cooker. In a small bowl, combine the cornstarch and water until smooth; stir into pressure cooker. Select saute setting and adjust for low heat. Simmer, stirring constantly, until thickened and apple is tender, 3-5 minutes.
3. If desired, serve with rice. Sprinkle with raisins and coconut.
⅔ cup: 174 cal., 6g fat (2g sat. fat), 57mg chol., 287mg sod., 8g carb. (4g sugars, 1g fiber), 22g pro. **Diabetic exchanges:** 3 lean meat, ½ starch.

CHICKEN PAPRIKA

CHICKEN PAPRIKA

I truly appreciate the speed of the pressure cooker. We use it often to make these tender chicken breasts with a paprika-seasoned sauce that gets its richness from sour cream.
—Holly Ottum, Racine, WI

Prep: 15 min. • **Cook:** 15 min. + releasing
Makes: 2 servings

- 2 bone-in chicken breast halves (about 2 lbs.)
- 1 small onion, chopped
- 1 cup chicken broth, divided
- 2 tsp. paprika
- 2 tsp. tomato paste
- 1 garlic clove, minced
- ¼ tsp. salt
- ¼ tsp. dried thyme
  Dash hot pepper sauce
- 1 Tbsp. all-purpose flour
- ½ cup sour cream

1. Place chicken in a 3- or 6-qt. electric pressure cooker; top with onion. In a small bowl, whisk ¾ cup broth, the paprika, tomato paste, garlic, salt, thyme and hot pepper sauce; pour over chicken.
2. Lock lid; close the pressure-release valve. Adjust to pressure-cook on high for 15 minutes. Let pressure release naturally for 10 minutes; quick-release any remaining pressure. A thermometer inserted into chicken should read at least 165°.
3. Remove chicken; keep warm. In a small bowl, whisk flour and remaining ¼ cup broth until smooth; stir into pressure cooker. Select saute setting and adjust for low heat. Simmer, stirring constantly, until thickened and sauce is slightly reduced, 8-10 minutes. Press cancel; stir in sour cream. Serve with chicken.
1 serving: 688 cal., 33g fat (13g sat. fat), 238mg chol., 999mg sod., 12g carb. (5g sugars, 2g fiber), 82g pro.

BEEF & BLACK BEAN SPAGHETTI SQUASH

I've been working on developing healthier recipes that still taste delicious—and keep me satisfied. This squash tossed with beef, beans and kale has so much flavor, it's easy to forget it's good for you!
—Charlotte Cravins, Opelousas, LA

Takes: 30 min. • **Makes:** 4 servings

- 1 medium spaghetti squash
- ¾ lb. lean ground beef (90% lean)
- ½ cup chopped red onion
- 2 Tbsp. yellow mustard
- 2 to 3 tsp. Louisiana-style hot sauce
- 4 small garlic cloves, minced
- 1 can (15 oz.) no-salt-added black beans, rinsed and drained
- 2 cups chopped fresh kale
- ¼ cup plain Greek yogurt

1. Trim ends of squash and halve lengthwise; discard seeds. Place squash, cut side down, on a trivet insert in a 6-qt. electric pressure cooker. Add 1 cup water to cooker. Lock lid; close pressure-release valve. Adjust to pressure-cook on high for 7 minutes. Quick-release pressure. Set squash aside.

2. In a large skillet, crumble beef and cook with onion over medium heat until no longer pink, 4-6 minutes; drain. Add mustard, hot sauce and garlic; cook 1 minute more. Stir in black beans and kale; cook just until kale wilts, 2-3 minutes.

3. Using a fork, separate strands of spaghetti squash; combine with meat mixture. Dollop individual servings with Greek yogurt.

1½ cups: 401 cal., 12g fat (4g sat. fat), 57mg chol., 314mg sod., 51g carb. (2g sugars, 13g fiber), 26g pro.

TEST KITCHEN TIP
If you don't have a pressure cooker, pop the squash halves in the microwave on high for 15-20 minutes or roast them in the oven upside down until tender.

BEEF & BLACK BEAN SPAGHETTI SQUASH

LAMB PITAS WITH YOGURT SAUCE
PICTURED ON P. 305

The spiced lamb in these stuffed pita pockets goes perfectly with cool cucumber and yogurt. It's like having your own Greek gyro stand in the kitchen!
—Angela Leinenbach, Mechanicsville, VA

Prep: 25 min. • **Cook:** 15 min. + releasing
Makes: 8 servings

- 2 Tbsp. olive oil
- 2 lbs. lamb stew meat (¾-in. pieces)
- ½ cup dry red wine
- 1 large onion, chopped
- 1 garlic clove, minced
- 1¼ tsp. salt, divided
- 1 tsp. dried oregano
- ½ tsp. dried basil
- ⅓ cup tomato paste
- 1 medium cucumber
- 1 cup plain yogurt
- 16 pita pocket halves, warmed
- 4 plum tomatoes, sliced

1. Select the saute or browning setting on a 6-qt. electric pressure cooker. Adjust for medium heat; add oil. When oil is hot, brown lamb in batches; set lamb aside. Add wine to pressure cooker. Cook 30 seconds, stirring to loosen browned bits from pan. Press cancel. Add onion, garlic, 1 tsp. salt, oregano and basil. Return lamb to pressure cooker.

2. Lock lid; close pressure-release valve. Adjust to pressure-cook on high for 15 minutes. Let pressure release naturally for 10 minutes; quick-release any remaining pressure.

3. Select saute setting; adjust for low heat. Add tomato paste; simmer, uncovered, until mixture is slightly thickened, 8-10 minutes, stirring occasionally.

4. To serve, dice enough cucumber to measure 1 cup; thinly slice remaining cucumber. Combine diced cucumber with yogurt and remaining salt. Fill pitas with lamb mixture, tomatoes, sliced cucumbers and the yogurt mixture.

2 filled pita halves: 383 cal., 11g fat (3g sat. fat), 78mg chol., 766mg sod., 39g carb. (5g sugars, 3g fiber), 31g pro.
Diabetic exchanges: 3 lean meat, 2½ starch, 1 fat.

Cast-Iron Confections

The old, reliable skillet like the one Great-Grandma used is back in style! This beautiful, naturally nonstick tool goes from stovetop to oven and can even double as a pie plate—making it just right for turning out picture-perfect desserts with a minimum of fuss and cleanup.

CARAMEL-PECAN CHEESECAKE PIE

CARAMEL-PECAN CHEESECAKE PIE

In fall or any time of year, this nutty, rich and delicious pecan pie recipe is one I'm proud to serve. While it's undeniably special, the cheesecake is a snap to make.
—Becky Ruff, McGregor, IA

Prep: 15 min. • **Bake:** 35 min. + chilling
Makes: 8 servings

- 1 sheet refrigerated pie crust
- 1 pkg. (8 oz.) cream cheese, softened
- ½ cup sugar
- 4 large eggs, room temperature, divided use
- 1 tsp. vanilla extract
- 1¼ cups chopped pecans
- 1 jar (12¼ oz.) fat-free caramel ice cream topping

Additional fat-free caramel ice cream topping, optional

1. Preheat oven to 375°. Line a 9-in. cast-iron skillet or deep-dish pie plate with crust. Trim and flute edges. In a small bowl, beat cream cheese, sugar, 1 egg and vanilla until smooth. Spread into crust; sprinkle with pecans.
2. In a small bowl, whisk the remaining 3 eggs; gradually whisk in caramel topping until blended. Pour slowly over pecans.
3. Bake for 35-40 minutes or until lightly browned (loosely cover edges with foil after 20 minutes if the pie browns too quickly). Cool on a wire rack 1 hour. Refrigerate 4 hours or overnight before slicing. If desired, garnish with additional caramel ice cream topping.
1 piece: 502 cal., 33g fat (11g sat. fat), 142mg chol., 277mg sod., 45g carb. (26g sugars, 2g fiber), 8g pro.

CHOCOLATE-STUFFED PEANUT BUTTER SKILLET COOKIE

A surprise chocolate filling makes this dessert extra delicious! Serve it warm from the oven with a scoop of your favorite ice cream.
—Andrea Price, Grafton, WI

Prep: 20 min. • **Bake:** 35 min. + cooling
Makes: 12 servings

- 1 cup creamy peanut butter
- ¾ cup butter, softened
- 1¼ cups plus 1 Tbsp. sugar, divided
- 1 large egg, room temperature
- 1 tsp. vanilla extract
- 1½ cups all-purpose flour
- ½ tsp. baking soda
- ½ tsp. salt
- 1 cup milk chocolate chips
  Vanilla ice cream, optional

1. Preheat oven to 350°. In a large bowl, cream peanut butter, butter and 1¼ cups sugar until blended. Beat in egg and vanilla. In another bowl, whisk the flour, baking soda and salt; gradually beat into the creamed mixture.
2. Press half the dough into a well-greased 10-in. cast-iron or other ovenproof skillet. Sprinkle chocolate chips over dough in skillet to within ½ in. of edges. Drop remaining dough over chocolate chips; spread until even. Sprinkle remaining 1 Tbsp. sugar over top.
3. Bake until a toothpick inserted in center comes out with moist crumbs, 35-40 minutes. Cool on a wire rack. If desired, serve with vanilla ice cream.
1 piece: 453 cal., 27g fat (12g sat. fat), 49mg chol., 351mg sod., 47g carb. (32g sugars, 2g fiber), 8g pro.

**STRAWBERRY BUTTERMILK
SKILLET SHORTCAKE**

GIANT BUCKEYE COOKIE

PICTURED ON P. 305

Buckeye candies are a delicious combination of peanut butter and chocolate, which is exactly what this cookie is. All you need is a box of cake mix and a few pantry ingredients. Voila—you have a tasty dessert ready for family and friends in under an hour. You can customize it, too, by substituting other mix-ins for the chocolate chips. We serve it warm with ice cream or whipped cream.
—*Arianna Joy Harding, Cincinnati, OH*

Prep: 15 min. • **Bake:** 20 min. + cooling
Makes: 12 servings

- 1 pkg. chocolate cake mix (regular size)
- 2 large eggs, room temperature
- ½ cup canola oil
- 1 cup semisweet chocolate chips
- 1 cup creamy peanut butter
- ½ cup confectioners' sugar
  Optional: Hot fudge ice cream topping, vanilla ice cream, whipped cream and melted creamy peanut butter

1. Preheat oven to 350°. In a large bowl, combine cake mix, eggs and oil until blended. Stir in chocolate chips. Press half the dough into a 10-in. cast-iron or other ovenproof skillet.
2. Combine the peanut butter and confectioners' sugar; spread over dough in skillet. Press the remaining dough between sheets of parchment into a 10-in. circle; place over filling.
3. Bake until a toothpick inserted in center comes out with moist crumbs, 20-25 minutes. Serve warm, with optional toppings as desired.
1 piece: 443 cal., 27g fat (6g sat. fat), 31mg chol., 372mg sod., 48g carb. (31g sugars, 3g fiber), 8g pro.

STRAWBERRY BUTTERMILK SKILLET SHORTCAKE

This scratch-made buttermilk shortcake is a family favorite. The recipe for the old-fashioned summer tradition goes back more than 100 years.
—*Claudia Lamascolo, Melbourne, FL*

Prep: 25 min. • **Bake:** 50 min.
Makes: 10 servings

- 10 Tbsp. shortening
- ¼ cup butter, softened
- 1 cup sugar
- 2 large eggs, room temperature
- 2½ cups all-purpose flour
- 3 tsp. baking powder
- ½ tsp. salt
- ⅔ cup buttermilk
  STREUSEL TOPPING
- ⅔ cup all-purpose flour
- ½ cup sugar
- 1 tsp. ground cinnamon
- ¼ tsp. ground allspice
- ½ cup butter, softened
- 2 cups sliced fresh strawberries
  Whipped cream

1. Preheat oven to 350°. In a large bowl, cream shortening, butter and sugar until light and fluffy, 5-7 minutes. Add eggs, 1 at a time, beating well after each addition. In another bowl, whisk flour, baking powder and salt; add to the creamed mixture alternately with buttermilk, beating well after each addition. Transfer to a 12-in. cast-iron or other ovenproof skillet.
2. For streusel topping, in a small bowl, mix flour, sugar, cinnamon and allspice; cut in butter until crumbly. Sprinkle over batter. Top with strawberries. Bake until center is puffed and edges are golden brown, 50-60 minutes. Serve warm with whipped cream.
1 slice: 526 cal., 27g fat (12g sat. fat), 74mg chol., 418mg sod., 64g carb. (33g sugars, 2g fiber), 6g pro.

TEST KITCHEN TIP
Blot the strawberries dry after washing and slicing; use only the firm ones. Try sprinkling cinnamon and sugar on top for a glistening top during the baking.

TILLIE'S GINGER CRUMB CAKE

This recipe goes back at least as far as my grandmother, who was born in the early 1900s. Our sons and I enjoy eating it in a bowl with milk poured over top—much to the dismay of my husband, who prefers it plain!
—Kathy Nienow Clark, Byron, MI

Prep: 20 min. • **Bake:** 35 min.
Makes: 16 servings

    4 cups all-purpose flour
    2 cups sugar
    1 cup cold butter
    ½ tsp. ground ginger
    ¼ tsp. ground cloves
    ½ tsp. ground cinnamon
    ½ tsp. ground nutmeg
    1 cup plus 2 Tbsp. buttermilk
    1¼ tsp. baking soda
    2 large eggs, room temperature
       Confectioners' sugar, optional

1. In a large bowl, combine flour and sugar; cut in butter until crumbly. Set aside 2 cups. Combine remaining crumb mixture with the next 7 ingredients.
2. Sprinkle 1 cup of the reserved crumbs into a greased 12-in. cast-iron skillet or 13x9-in. baking dish. Pour batter over crumbs and sprinkle with remaining crumbs. Bake at 350° until a toothpick inserted in the center comes out clean, about 35 minutes. If desired, sprinkle with confectioners' sugar before serving.
1 piece: 330 cal., 13g fat (8g sat. fat), 54mg chol., 232mg sod., 50g carb. (26g sugars, 1g fiber), 5g pro.

SKILLET CHOCOLATE DUMPLINGS

Why bake when you can make an entire dessert on the stovetop? These dumplings are often requested by my family for special events like birthdays.
—Becky Magee, Chandler, AZ

Prep: 20 min. • **Cook:** 20 min.
Makes: 8 servings

    ¾ cup packed brown sugar
    ¼ cup baking cocoa
    1 Tbsp. cornstarch
       Dash salt
    2 cups water
    2 Tbsp. butter
DUMPLINGS
    1¼ cups all-purpose flour
    2 tsp. baking powder
    ½ tsp. salt
    ½ cup sugar
    2 Tbsp. baking cocoa
    3 Tbsp. butter
    1 large egg, lightly beaten
    ⅓ cup 2% milk
    1 tsp. vanilla extract
       Whipped cream or ice cream

1. For sauce, combine brown sugar, cocoa, cornstarch and salt in a large, heavy cast-iron or other ovenproof skillet. Stir in water; cook, stirring constantly, until mixture begins to boil and thicken slightly. Add butter; mix well. Remove sauce from heat.
2. For dumplings, sift together flour, baking powder, salt, sugar and cocoa. Cut in butter until mixture resembles a fine meal. Combine egg, milk and vanilla; blend gradually into the flour mixture.
3. Return skillet to heat; bring chocolate sauce to a boil. Drop dumplings by tablespoonfuls into the hot sauce. Reduce heat to low; cover and simmer until just set, about 20 minutes. Serve warm with whipped cream or ice cream.
1 serving: 294 cal., 9g fat (5g sat. fat), 43mg chol., 527mg sod., 52g carb. (33g sugars, 1g fiber), 4g pro.

SKILLET CHOCOLATE DUMPLINGS

A la Mode, of Course!

The perfect finishing touch to a cast-iron dessert is vanilla ice cream—even better if it's homemade!

Vanilla Ice Cream Without an Ice Cream Maker

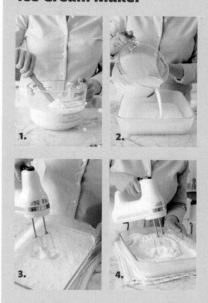

1. Combine

Freeze an empty freezer-safe dish. (Our Test Kitchen uses a 13x9-in. Pyrex dish.) In a bowl, stir all ingredients until sugar is completely disssolved.

2. Freeze

Transfer to the cold pan; cover and freeze until edges begin to set, 20-30 minutes.

3. Beat

With a hand mixer, beat the mixture until smooth, then return the dish to the freezer. (This helps make it smooth and creamy. You cannot beat the mixture too much.)

4. Freeze and Beat Again

Freeze, covered, until firm, 3 hours total, beating every 30 minutes. If it gets too firm too soon, move it to the fridge until it is soft enough to beat.

5i

HOMEMADE VANILLA ICE CREAM

We think this is the best ice cream recipe ever. With only four ingredients, it just might be the easiest, too. No ice cream maker? No problem—use the alternate method at right.
—Taste of Home *Test Kitchen*

Prep: 5 min.
Process: 20 min. + freezing
Makes: 1¼ qt.

2 cups heavy whipping cream
2 cups half-and-half cream
1 cup sugar
2 tsp. vanilla extract

Combine all ingredients, stirring to dissolve sugar completely. Fill cylinder of ice cream maker no more than two-thirds full; freeze according to manufacturer's directions. (Refrigerate any remaining mixture until ready to freeze.) Serve immediately, or store in covered containers in freezer.
½ cup: 308 cal., 22g fat (14g sat. fat), 78mg chol., 37mg sod., 23g carb. (23g sugars, 0 fiber), 3g pro.

General Recipe Index

This handy index lists every recipe by food category, major ingredients and cooking method, so you can easily locate the recipes that suit your needs.

||||||||||||||||||||||||||||||||||||||||||||||||||||||||||||||||||||||||||||||||||||||||||||||||

VANILLA CITRUS
CIDER, 12

**LOADED HUEVOS
RANCHEROS WITH ROASTED
POBLANO PEPPERS, 182**

SLOW-COOKED ROPA VIEJA, 208

ARRABBIATA SAUCE WITH
ZUCCHINI NOODLES, 144

Alphabetical Recipe Index

This index lists every recipe in alphabetical order so you can easily find all your favorites.

||||||||||||||||||||||||||||||||||||||||||||||||||||||||||||||||||||||||||||||||||||||||||||||||||||

STRAWBERRY
CHEESECAKE, 302